THE MILLION DOLLAR MERMAID

Esther Williams

WITH DIGBY DIEHL

SIMON & SCHUSTER

SIMON & SCHUSTER
Rockefeller Center
1230 Avenue of the Americas
New York, NY 10020

Simon & Schuster and colophon are registered trademarks
of Simon & Schuster, Inc.

Designed by Maura Rosenthal
Manufactured in the United States of America

3   5   7   9   10   8   6   4   2

Library of Congress Cataloging-in-Publication Data
Williams, Esther, date.
The million dollar mermaid / Esther Williams with Digby Diehl.
p. cm.
1. Williams, Esther, date.   2. Motion picture
actors and actresses—United States Biography.
I. Diehl, Digby.   II. Title.
PN2287.W472A3   1999
791.43'028'092—dc21
[B]   99-35872   CIP
ISBN 0-684-85284-5

ACKNOWLEDGMENTS

Thank you, Digby Diehl, for having organized my free associations into a manageable manuscript of remembrances so that the reader can place one foot in front of the other without tumbling down the rabbit hole of memory.

George Feltenstein and Roger Mayer, thank you for the generosity of your library and your encouragement.

Dear Chuck Adams, you believed there was a book in me.

Claire Gerus, my intrepid friend, whose skills as a diplomat and an agent kept the project running smoothly—sometimes.

Kay Diehl, for your support. Nan Breckenridge, who listened to and transcribed the many hours of tape. Michael Brarson, who shared his library and his knowledge of motion-picture history.

My dear friends at Turner Classic Movies, Bob Osborne, Tom Karsch, Jim Weiss, and Justin Pettigrew, for keeping all of us eternally young.

Alvin Ramrus and Alleen Morris Ramrus, for your minds, your hearts, your endearing and enduring friendship.

Thanks to the staffs of the Pasadena Public Library and of the Margaret Herrick library of the Academy of Motion Picture Arts and Sciences for keeping so many pictures I forgot I took.

And to you, Edward, this is all because of you. I love you.

*To my children, who have endured
the pain and the pleasure of my stardom*

CHAPTER 1

ESTHER WILLIAMS, CARY GRANT, AND LSD

*W*hich Esther Williams do you want to hear about? As I look back through the filing cabinet of my life while writing this book, I realize that there are many of us. I love that sweet little child who grew up in the depression and, being the fifth child, felt the need to try so hard to please her family. I'm still rooting for that determined teenage swimmer who kicked and stroked her way through hundreds of miles of training in the water to a national championship. I'm awed by the kid with no theatrical training who walked onto the stage of Billy Rose's Aquacade at the San Francisco Exposition and became a media darling overnight. Of course, I have to chuckle as that same kid walks through the gates of MGM a year later and swims her way to movie stardom. That long-legged GI pinup was me!

Sometimes I think that there must have been three different women who became Mrs. Leonard Kovner, Mrs. Ben Gage, and Mrs. Fernando Lamas. Sitting here today as the happy Mrs. Edward Bell, my heart goes out to all of them for the naive expectations, the misplaced trust, the passionate love, and the need for a safe haven. The world remembers me as a movie star, but most of my life I have thought about myself in various family roles—as daughter, sister, wife, and, above all, mother. The press portrayed me as a kind of post–World War II version of Martha Stewart—"the Mermaid Tycoon," as I was dubbed on the cover of *Life;* the perfect homemaker; the Hollywood glamour queen; and a sex symbol in a bathing suit—all rolled into one. Meanwhile, for most of that time I was working twelve-hour days in that huge pool at MGM, creating movie fantasies, and then coming home each night to a personal life that seemed to repeatedly unravel.

Never was I more "unraveled" than in 1959, when being Esther Williams became an exercise in schizophrenia. On the surface, everything looked rosy. The gossip columnists couldn't stop buzzing about my supposedly fabulous love life since I had divorced Ben Gage. My last movie, *Raw Wind in Eden,* had come out the previous year. During the location shoot in Italy, I'd begun a relationship, with my costar Jeff Chandler, which was still continuing. I was also considering the possibility of jumping into television. NBC was courting me to shoot a special called *Esther Williams at Cypress Gardens*. But it was all a Hollywood PR fantasy. Behind that public facade was a woman in deep emotional pain.

I remember, in late August of that year, boarding an American Airlines flight from New York and being in a state of exhaustion. It was one of those hot, humid times in New York, when brownout was a constant fear, air conditioners labored to no effect, and the air felt too thick to draw into your lungs. I prayed that my seatmate on the plane would not want to talk, which mercifully was the case. As we rose through the clouds, I stared out of the airplane window and indulged in the fantasy that this white and blue landscape was a vast undersea world in which I could float and swim effortlessly. In my mind, I drifted out the window, trying to escape the realities of my life. But tears soon welled up in my eyes. My chest tightened as I tried to breathe naturally. I was surprised by my own reaction. Ordinarily I loved flying, and I loved the idea that the blue sky reminded me of the blue water that was my second home. Now, however, I was fighting off panic—the same kind of panic you feel underwater when you're out of air. My terror was only beaten back when the stewardess handed me a vodka on the rocks, which I gulped gratefully and sat back.

That episode was a shot across the bow, a warning that I was in trouble on all levels of my being. During the years when I was making movies one after the other in rapid succession, so much was happening at such a pace that there was no time to think clearly about my life. But in that summer of 1959, I had a sense of gathering crisis. My divorce from Ben Gage had become final that spring, but I was just beginning to be hit with the fallout from that marriage. Ben had made my personal life a constant turmoil for years with his out-of-control, erratic, alcoholic behavior. I had three young children I loved and worried about constantly. Between Ben's drinking and the demands of a movie career, I saw them as fragile victims who needed a lot more of my help. Over the years I'd always shielded the children from seeing Ben at his worst—passed out drunk in the car in the driveway, or staggering around the house. As a result, they never fully understood how hard he was to live with, or why I'd finally left him. Now there was a new man, Jeff Chandler, in my life, which brought a new set of emotional baggage to three kids who already felt as if they didn't get enough of my attention.

And then I found out I was broke. Ben had literally thrown away money as fast as I could make it—no—in fact, faster than I could make it. In a series of disastrous investments, he managed to lose nearly $10 million. And what he didn't lose that way, he gambled away at the track.

Worse yet, he had hidden all of this from me and from the Internal Revenue Service. After the divorce I was left with three wonderful children and memories of happier times. But the IRS wanted cash. By their estimate, I owed three quarters of a million dollars in unpaid back taxes. Suddenly, I was without resources. To make matters worse, all of Hollywood was reeling from the rapid onslaught of television. My beloved MGM had all but crumbled after the departure of studio chief L. B. Mayer and the ensuing damage inflicted by Dore Schary. Nobody was going to make multimillion-dollar aquamusicals ever again. I was thirty-seven years old. I was still working, but I knew that there was not much mileage left in my movie career.

I had tried to ignore all of that while I was in Italy filming *Raw Wind in Eden*. I knew that my marriage to Ben was over and that my life was collapsing, so I plunged into la dolce vita. My affections ric-

ocheted between a charming Italian businessman with a fast Lancia
and my ruggedly handsome costar Jeff Chandler, whose own marriage was disintegrating. Once I was back in the United States, however, the bleak realities were impossible to avoid, and I was forced
to spend months focused on dealing with the wreckage of my finances and the needs of my children. Jeff kept asking me to marry
him, but somehow it didn't seem right.

At that point, I really didn't know who I was. Was I that glamorous femme fatale tearing up Tuscany? Was I just another broken-
down divorcée whose husband left her with all the bills and three
kids? Had I spent so many years reading the fantasy press releases
that Howard Strickling and his publicity team at MGM pumped out
that I actually had come to believe them? Had I lost touch with that
fearless young swimmer or that devoted mother I once had been?

Listlessly, I picked up a magazine. It was the September 1959
issue of *Look*, with Cary Grant's startling confession that he had
taken a drug called LSD under a doctor's supervision and that it had
changed his life. It seems he hadn't known who he was either! The
drug had made possible an incredible recovery from psychological
problems he was having, and he wanted to share his discovery with
others. Hungrily, I read Cary's words over and over: "I am through
with sadness. At last, I am close to happiness. After all those years,
I'm rid of guilt complexes and fears."

This sounded too good to be true, yet there he was, declaring
himself a new man: "I've asked myself what do I want out of Life?
Beautiful women? Fantastic houses? No, I'm finding courage to live
in the truth, as I want to live, not to impress other people. Posses-
sions don't make you happy. I take my sunny and foggy days with
me. . . . All my life I've been searching for peace of mind. I'd explored
yoga and hypnotism and made attempts at mysticism. Nothing really seemed to give me what I wanted until this LSD treatment."

In the article, Cary's therapist, Dr. Mortimer Hartman, described
LSD as ". . . a psychic energizer which empties the subconscious
and intensifies emotion and memory a hundred times."

Cary added, "I know that, all my life, I've been going around in a
fog. You're just a bunch of molecules until you know who you are.
You spend your time getting to be a big Hollywood actor. But then

what? You've reached a comfortable plateau, and you want to stay on it; you resist change. One day, after many weeks of LSD, my last defense crumbled. To my delight, I found I had a tough inner core of strength. In my youth, I was very dependent upon older men and women. Now people come to me for help!"

That day, I resolved that I would be one of those people.

Cary and I had known each other for years, having spent time together at many parties and public events, although we never had been close friends. But movie stars all belong to a sort of secret society; we share a special understanding of the burdens and comforts of celebrity. There is a shorthand we can use when we meet, and we empathize in ways other people cannot comprehend if they haven't stood in the spotlight. He came to the telephone immediately when I gave my name to his secretary. When I said, "Cary, I've got to see you right away about something," he invited me to come to his office at Universal the next morning.

"Cary, I'm at the end of my rope," I told him the following day. "I'm deeply troubled about my life, and when I read what you said about how LSD had changed your life, I wondered if it might help me."

"Esther, it takes a lot of courage to take this drug," he warned me. "You may not want to do it when I tell you what it's like, because it's a tremendous jolt to your mind, to your ego. Some people don't react well to it at all."

"But it was so successful with you."

"Yes it was," he admitted, with a flash of his glittering "Cary Grant" smile. "But it's only being used on an experimental basis. You'd have to be as desperate as I was to try it."

I smiled back my own "Esther Williams" smile. "But I *am* as desperate, Cary," I said as calmly as I could. "I need to find some answers, fast. Would you call your doctor and make an appointment for me?"

This conversation took place long before LSD became the recreational drug of the 1960s that Tom Wolfe wrote about in *The Electric Kool-Aid Acid Test* and the Beatles sang about in "Lucy in the Sky with Diamonds." The newspaper articles were always about the young people who misused it, and that is what most people remember today about LSD. We seldom heard about the benefits that people such as Cary and I experienced. All I knew was that my life was falling apart and I needed some answers. If LSD was the key, then I wanted it.

The Psychiatric Institute of Beverly Hills was tucked away on one of those quiet back streets where no one noticed comings and goings. Dr. Hartman, a radiologist and internist who had undergone five years of classical Freudian analysis in New York, and his partner, Dr. Arthur Chandler, were the directors of the institute. They had been conducting psychotherapy experiments with the hallucinogenic drug lysergic acid diethylamide (LSD-25), which was virtually unknown in the United States. After a cursory interview and explaining the procedure to me, Dr. Hartman asked, "Are you ready?" I answered with a fervent "Yes!"

He led me to a small room in the back. It was darkened with blackout drapes and had a traditional psychiatrist's couch in one corner. He gave me five little blue pills with a glass of water and told me to lie down and close my eyes. "Now I'm leaving you alone for two hours. Let it take you wherever you want it to take you. Don't be afraid." Then he closed the door behind him. I was about to take the most amazing journey of my life.

LSD seemed like instant psychoanalysis. With my eyes closed, I felt my tension and resistance ease away as the hallucinogen swept through me. Then, without warning, I went right to the place where the pain lay in my psyche. The first thing I saw was my father's face the day my brother Stanton died. My brother had been just sixteen when it happened; I was only eight. I saw my father's face as a ceramic plate. Almost instantly it splintered into a million tiny pieces, like a windshield when a rock goes through it. The shards fell to the floor. He was left faceless. Then I looked at my mother. All the emotion had drained out of her, and her soft, kindly features had hardened.

I began to relive the devastation to my two parents over the death of this wonderful, handsome boy. Stanton was their oldest son, and his good looks and acting talent had brought the Williams family to California, the place my parents had dreamed of when they left Dodge City, Kansas. My brother was going to be a star—everyone said that. They had pinned so much hope and expectation on him that his sudden death left them without a reason to live.

I lay there in the darkened room, spinning back in time, swirling through a host of unanswered questions. Why did my mother take me, the youngest, with her on the night of the viewing at the mortuary? Why did she take eight-year-old Esther, instead of sisters Maurine or June, or my brother David? Why did she take me to watch her absolute nervous collapse as she threw herself across Stanton's coffin, sobbing, "Why did you leave me? Let me go with you"?

I stood back in the shadows in that place of death, watching my parents fall apart. And I was a woman again, observing it from a distance as if I were acting in or watching a movie. Suddenly, with that double vision, a revelation hit me, and I knew what my life was all about. Everything that happened to me after Stanton's death came to me with a new maturity that had not been mine prior to his loss. I remembered that after returning home from that harrowing trip to the mortuary, I had, at the age of eight, come to the realization and a decision: Stanton had been our pride, our hope, our golden prince. His talent, his good looks, his ambition had been our only chance to break out of poverty; he had given us courage and kept us all together. Now that he was gone, somebody had to take his place or we would all be lost. My brother David was frail and asthmatic. My sister Maurine suffered from emotional problems that I couldn't understand at my age, but which made her sadly overweight from compulsive eating; my other sister, June, was a malcontent. My mother took refuge in her spirituality while my poor father was barely able to bring home enough money to keep food on the table (this was during the depression). So I looked about me and realized that if none of them could replace Stanton as the rock on which the family stood, then I would have to be that rock myself. My mission in life was as clear and simple as that.

I made that decision at the age of eight, and I made it without feelings of doubt, fear, or nobility. If my shoulders weren't strong enough as yet, then I would make them strong. I would become my family's hope; I would be the one to take care of them. Once I made that decision, I no longer felt eight years old. I said farewell to childhood, and virtually overnight I felt as though I was at least sixteen, Stanton's age. Suddenly this little girl was in a race against time to be an adult.

At the end of the session, Dr. Hartman gave me another drug to bring me gradually out from under the LSD. He warned, however, that some afterglow would stay with me, and that it wouldn't be until the next day that the drug would be out of my system.

This LSD trip, which explained so much about my life's script, and which was such a breakthrough for me, had a bizarre epilogue. I returned from the doctor's office to my home on Mandeville Canyon to have dinner there with my parents, something I did about once a month. In a way, true to my mission, I had taken care of them since Stanton's death, first struggling to fill the emotional void, then, after becoming a movie star, making sure they lived comfortably. I put them on a payroll so they had no financial worries, and eventually they could collect decent Social Security. I paid for their trips to Europe, and—the biggest treat of all for them—I got them invitations to glittering movie premieres, especially to mine, where they could watch their youngest daughter on a screen forty feet high.

At last, the LSD experience gave me insight into why I had taken on the role of the firstborn son. As I sat and looked at my parents at the dining room table, I saw into their souls. I saw my mother's angry, self-involved countenance that had sealed out all expression of feelings after my brother died. I looked at my father's sad, empty expression, the facade that was left after his real face shattered like a glass plate. I understood them that night in a profound way, and while I sympathized, I was also sickened by their weakness and their resignation. I saw that they both simply had given up, which, no matter what life had in store for me, was something I could never and would never do. At least, so I thought, so I hoped.

After dinner, I gently ushered my parents into the guest house for the night. Then I rushed back to my bedroom and locked the door. I needed to be alone. I went into the bathroom and looked at my face in the mirror. I couldn't see myself clearly. I scrubbed away all of my makeup. I splashed water on my hair and slicked it back because I couldn't stand to have anything soft around my face. I stripped off my clothes. When I looked in the mirror again, I was startled by a split image: One half of my face, the right half, was me; the other half was the face of a sixteen-year-old boy. The left side of my upper body was flat and muscular, like the chest of a boy. I reached up with my boy's large, clumsy hand to touch my right breast and felt my penis stirring. It was a hermaphroditic phantasm that held me entranced as I discovered my divided body. I don't know how long I stood there touching and exploring, but I was not afraid. Finally, I understood perfectly: when Stanton had died, I had taken him into my life so completely that he became a part of me.

CHAPTER 2

THE FIFTH CHILD
1922–1936

GARSON STUDIOS, INC.
HOLLYWOOD, CALIFORNIA

We are pleased to say that we consider little Stanton Williams one
of the finest juveniles it has ever been our pleasure to work with. He
is a real actor and is brilliant way beyond his years. His histrionic
ability is, in our opinion, a natural talent and with his charming
personality and winsome manner, there is no doubt a very exalted
niche for him in this world.

Harry Garson, President

*S*ix years old and an actor both on the legitimate stage and in
motion pictures—my brother had it all! He had made a decided hit
in *The Little Princess* in which he appeared with Mary McAllister,
another child actor. They called Stanton "... a wee bit of a youngster who hails from the state of Utah and now making his first traveling tour ... a bright future for this little fellow."

Stanton had a charisma, a personal magic that from his earliest years charmed everyone from stage luminaries to Hollywood producers. The beginning of his career was classic, the stuff legends are made of.

In the summer of 1919, noted Broadway actress Marjorie Rambeau came to the Wilkes Theater in Salt Lake City with a touring company of the *Eyes of Youth,* the story of a young "dunce boy" who meets his fairy princess and is carried away on an iron steed to a fabled land of turreted castles, glittering tinsel, and bright lights. My father, Lou Williams, a sign painter, had a small studio adjacent to the theater where he painted theater lobby cards. My brother Stanton, fascinated by the theater, would sneak through the stage door, hide in the wings, or curl behind the plush velvet seats to watch rehearsals.

One afternoon Marjorie Rambeau and the young actor cast as the "dunce boy" were rehearsing a scene in which she tells the tragic story of the lost fairy princess. Tears were to stream down the boy's face, but there was a problem—he wasn't crying.

In desperation, Rambeau called to the director, "I can't work with this child, I'm sorry. I'm playing this scene over and over, crying my eyes out and his eyes are glazed over. Nothing's happening! I need somebody to give me a little emotion."

Then she caught Stanton's eye as he cowered behind the seats. Pointing a finger at him she turned to the director, "I'll bet even he can give me more than the kid you cast."

Rambeau obviously had intended to vent her anger and humiliate the director, but the poor guy, in desperation, asked Stanton to come on the stage and let Rambeau tell him the story of the lost fairy princess. Stanton's big, beautiful eyes—he was a glorious angelic child—opened wide, the tears came streaming down, and soon he was sobbing and Rambeau was sobbing. She turned to the director and said through her tears, "Oh my god, this child is so wonderful; I have to have him."

The director, intimidated by the power of the star, called my father from the lobby and quickly made a deal. For the rest of the play's run, Stanton cried every night and at every matinee.

Marjorie Rambeau adored Stanton. She pleaded with his parents

Lou and Bula to let young Stanton join the Wilkes Theater stock company, and they agreed. Accompanied by Bula, he toured the circuit, including the Denham Theater in Denver, the Wilkes in Seattle, the Curran in San Francisco, and finally the Majestic in Los Angeles. Rambeau had more lines written for his part and insisted that he be cast in the movie version of the play. *The Los Angeles Examiner* wrote: "On the stage he's a dunce, but in real life, he's Stanton Williams, and far from being a dunce, he's negotiated a fine contract with Harry Garson, production manager of all the Equity pictures. Hollywood has a new star." Stanton played the role in the silent movie version of the play, but luckless Marjorie Rambeau was replaced by Clara Kimball Young.

Los Angeles was booming, and Stanton was put under contract to Garson Studios. My father found a tract development in the southwest area of town, where for one hundred dollars he purchased a small piece of land surrounded by truck farms. For another hundred dollars, he had the shell of a small house constructed on the tract. On August 8, 1922, I was born in the living room of that small house, where all of us slept until Daddy was able to add on bedrooms.

I'm an all-American girl whose grandmother and grandfather traveled west in Conestoga wagons. My mother never knew her first three siblings because she was the ninth child in the family, and they died before she was born. Being such a late child in that big family made it possible for grandmother to be in those wagons after the Civil War. She was a sixteen-year-old girl who had married a thirty-year-old Civil War hero. Pretty much anyone who came out of that war alive was a hero for just surviving. Samuel Gilpin, a Yankee, fought with the North, and shortly after he met beautiful Esther Ann Yarrington they were married and headed out for the prairies. Although I never met her, Esther Ann Gilpin seemed more like a great-grandmother to me. Because I was raised by my oldest sister Maurine, my own mother seemed like my grandmother. With all that propagation, our family seemed to skip a generation.

My mother, Bula Myrtle Gilpin, was born on her father's fiftieth birthday, October 8, 1885. She was the ninth of twelve children and had nieces who were older than she was. While she was still a child, her father suffered inflammatory rheumatism as a result of a Civil

War injury, and the family moved into the Soldier's Home in Fort Dodge, Kansas. Bula's brothers had to leave the home to make their own livings at twelve; the girls were asked to leave at fourteen. My mother told me how she was fortunate enough to go to what she called "normal" school and to obtain her certificate to teach school. At seventeen, she was hired to teach in a one-room schoolhouse in Dodge City, where she taught all the grades from kindergarten to high school. Because this was farming country, children only came to school when they were not needed to do chores. Small children came during the good weather months and twenty-year-old boys came in the winter months when the snow on the ground made it impossible for them to farm the land. My mother's nurturing skills occasionally took a back seat to her need to fend off those big boys, who wanted the Dodge City school marm for more than educational purposes. She had to become a strong and determined and independent young woman at just seventeen.

Actually, those boys were wasting their time. Bula was already spoken for. Louis Stanton Williams, a boy from a neighboring farm, had met her while she was still living at the Soldier's Home, when they were both thirteen. He knew immediately that he wanted to marry her, and despite their parents' objections, they carried on a faithful courtship for nine years, until they were both twenty-two. My father's parents still wanted him to stay and run the farm, and my grandmother, Esther Ann Gilpin, declared that she would rather die than see her daughter marry another farmer. Nonetheless, they eloped on June 1, 1908, and set out for California, but ran out of money in Salt Lake City, Utah. It was there that they settled until Stanton's sudden success as a child actor transformed the fortunes of my family.

This chubby, round-faced boy who made such a hit at the Wilkes Theater with Marjorie Rambeau and who caught the eye of Hollywood led the family to Los Angeles. The following season, as six-year-old Stanton became a fixture in the Hollywood movie studios, my mother traveled with him to California carrying new baby David. My father and Stanton's two sisters, June and Maurine, were soon to follow. Stanton's rise to stardom in the "picture business" was the family ticket to California.

By the time I was born, my mother had had enough of childbirth. She just wasn't ready for me, the fifth child. She handed me over to my sister Maurine, who was fourteen years old at the time, and said, "You raise this one. I want to get out and get in the world and see what's happening. I don't want to stay home and raise babies anymore." I thought, "Yeah. Four would have been enough for me, too."

She confessed that she tried to get rid of me. She took hot mustard baths; she went horseback riding; she jumped off a chest of drawers. Despite her efforts, I arrived, strong and healthy. "This one's for laughs," she said and shrugged. Like Stanton, I figured I better make my mother laugh because that's what my pass was; that's how I got born.

Bula took on a kind of grandmother role in my life, and Maurine played my mother. She made all my clothes, taught me how to walk and later to swim. Her boyfriends were all crazy about me. If you've been told that your mother tried to get rid of you when she was pregnant, you really tend to be very nice as a child. You've got to win popularity contests so that they won't say, "Throw her back. This one we don't want."

Stanton died suddenly and unexpectedly at the age of sixteen. From the chubby and cherubic youngster he grew into a frail and sensitive young man. He spent a great deal of time talking and reading to me and sharing his plans for the future. He loved me. I worshiped him. The day he died, I was outside playing kick-the-can noisily, which is what you do when you are an eight-year-old with no money for a bicycle. My mother came out of the house and said, "Be quiet. Stanton is very ill." We'd all had a late Sunday lunch and had eaten heartily, but he had complained of feeling funny. Mother suggested that he take a warm bath and get into bed. Later that evening, he told us that his stomach was numb. My father called the doctor. Bula called the Christian Science practitioner. In the process of normal digestion his intestine had developed a kink, and his colon had burst. The doctor never arrived; he got lost in a Los Angeles fog; the practitioner was out of town; and even the fire department couldn't find our house. By 9:30 that night, Stanton, alive and happy only hours before, was dead.

My mother and father would never be the same after Stanton

died. And neither would I. The little girl, who already had learned that to find her place in the sun she would have to please, would have to compete for attention and would, if possible, have to give what was wanted from her. That little girl now also had to take Stanton's place and become *strong*.

Personally and professionally, those two competing strains in my character—strength and giving—were to shape my life.

The depression of the 1930s was hard on us, especially now, without the money Stanton had been bringing in. But the family members remained devoted to each other, and life went on.

Bula, ever resourceful, heard that a city playground was being built just a few blocks away from our house on 88th and Orchard. She made an appointment with the heads of parks and recreation and convinced them that the playground needed one additional feature that the city had not planned to include. "I have three daughters," she said. "Girls don't play baseball. The neighborhood could really use a swimming pool," she said, "along with baseball diamonds—a big swimming pool, twenty-five yards long to be exact."

They asked which of her kids swam well enough to inaugurate the pool on opening day. "Someone really young and cute, so we can get some good publicity."

"Of course," my mom said. "My daughter Esther."

I wasn't particularly athletic—almost no girls were in those days; sports were considered sweaty and unfeminine—and I couldn't swim a lick. But that didn't worry Bula. She told my older sister, Maurine, "Take Esther to the beach and teach her how to swim."

Maurine and I rode the trolley, the Red Car, to Manhattan Beach. There, I stepped into the ocean, into real water, for the first time in my life. I had absolutely no fear, and though I couldn't swim yet, I could almost immediately ride the waves. Somehow, I sensed, the water was my natural element. This is where I belonged. It was only a matter of days before I learned to swim—not well, but well enough for the opening ceremonies of the pool.

On the great day, a couple hundred people, including my proud parents, gathered around the virgin water, with me crouched at the edge, and someone at a microphone announced, "And now, ladies

and gentlemen, to inaugurate our brand new pool, our first swimmer, Miss Esther Williams."

Hearing my name, I flung myself into the pool, hitting the water
in an ungraceful belly flop, and came up gasping and thrashing.
Boldy, I struck out for the nearest side, made it, turned, and swam
to the other side. By now, after swimming the width of the pool
twice, I was choking on water, my arms felt like lead, and I couldn't
do another stroke. I struggled out of the pool and heard something
absolutely delicious from the crowd—applause and cheers. And it
was all for me. I also got a little medal, my very first, which rests in a
box that I still have, labeled "Esther's Medals." Over the years, many
more medals joined that first one, but I treasure it as much as any of
the others.

But how could I have known that this awkward, thirty-yard swim
of eight-year-old Esther was just the beginning?

I took a job at the pool in order to earn the five cents a day it cost
to swim. I counted wet towels. As a bonus, I was allowed to swim
during lunchtime, when the four lifeguards took their daily workout. Maurine gave me my first lessons, but the terrific young men
swimming laps up and down the pool were the living, swimming ex-
amples of what beautiful swimming could be. They taught me
strokes and breathing and pacing. At first it was only one lap, but
then, before the summer ended, it was side by side, stroke for
stroke. They taught me strokes that at that time were for men only.
Years later, I broke records with one of those "men only" strokes: the
butterfly breaststroke.

I competed at the Metropolitan Meet, a swimming competition
for all of the children in Los Angeles, which was held at the 1932
Olympic Swim Stadium near the University of Southern California.
I won the fifty-meter freestyle race and caught the attention of
Aileen Allen, the swimming and diving coach of the Los Angeles
Athletic Club. I also won my first trophy.

Water was still dripping off me when Aileen came over and introduced herself. She didn't need to. She had been a former Olympic
diver and was now women's coach at the distinguished LA Athletic
Club. "I think you have a chance to become a championship swimmer. I'd like you to come to the Athletic Club pool and try out for

the team." Talk about getting out of the house! The Los Angeles Athletic Club was a venerable and very expensive health club. Never in a million years did I think I would wear that LAAC emblem on my hip. It was a prestigious organization. They recruited swimming champions for their team and exhibition swimming events. It was free to talented young swimmers, and I began swimming for the LAAC in 1937.

Almost every day, I trained in that wonderful LAAC pool on the seventh floor at 7th and Olive. Just a few years after my first public performance at the Manchester Playground Pool, belly flop and all, I was becoming, thanks to some of the best coaches, a rising young star in California swimming. Back in those days, competitive swimming for girls was nowhere nearly as popular as it is today, but I didn't care. I loved the competition. I loved the winning. I loved the feeling, day by day—and confirmed by a stopwatch—of increasing speed and strength.

Traveling to swimming meets took me beyond my small-town existence, gave me a hint of the exciting world outside of my own home. Everything about my teenage life was almost ideal. Except for one thing, and like an insidious disease it infected all the rest.

Buddy McClure, a sixteen-year-old neighborhood kid, had just lost his mother. With no father around, he was surviving alone in a shabby little apartment. One day he was chatting with my mother, who never seemed to stop grieving over the loss of Stanton. Buddy was very gentle, sympathetic, and understanding, and together they began to wonder if Buddy, with no parents of his own, could somehow take Stanton's place for her. Not completely, of course, but fill a small part of the void.

My mother, capable of extraordinary acts of generosity, and feeling overpowering sympathy for the orphaned boy, invited him to come live with us, under our roof.

Sixteen-year-old Buddy McClure was no ordinary boy. He was a superb student, captain of the high school football team, and student body president. He was popular, funny, and charming, and though he didn't *look* like Stanton—he was stocky and dark—he filled the emptiness in my parents' souls. He almost became Stanton for them. They eagerly waited for him to return home every day and their eyes gleamed when they looked at him. For them, laughter and life had reentered our house. My brother, sisters, and I also liked Buddy, and after a few weeks there was never any question of his not staying. He had become part of the family.

I was so happy for my parents that at first I tried to ignore ominous signs. One day when we were alone, Buddy told me, "You know, Esther, I fantasize about you. You've got a great body and I fantasize about it all the time." At thirteen, I wasn't sure what he meant, but I got the idea when he started to touch and grab me and follow me with his eyes, sometimes hiding behind a fence and waiting for me to pass. He even threatened a couple of boys I was friendly with, warning them to stay away.

With no sexual experience, I didn't understand erotic obsession or the danger looming over me, yet I sensed that something was wrong and tried to tell my mother. But I was so embarrassed I couldn't communicate exactly what was going on.

One night my parents took my brother and sisters to visit relatives in Alhambra, and I was home alone with Buddy. I retreated to my bedroom just to be away from him and had fallen asleep. I awoke in the dark when I heard the door open. It was Buddy. I was paralyzed with fear. He clamped a powerful hand over my mouth.

"Don't make any noise," he whispered.

I tried to struggle but he pinned me to the bed, ripping away my nightgown.

"Please. Don't," I pleaded.

"I love you," he said. "I don't want to hurt you. So don't make me. I just want to love you."

I felt him forcing himself between my legs, then ramming himself into me, tearing me inside, with searing pain. It seemed unreal. This couldn't be happening to me. A voice kept echoing in my head through the pain: "What have I done to deserve this?"

Finally he was finished. "This is our secret," he said. "If you tell anyone, they won't believe you. And *I'll* find out."

After he left, I cried long into the night, with a towel between my thighs to absorb the blood.

I didn't realize that I could prove what happened with physical evidence. But even if I could, something more powerful sealed my lips: embarrassment, shame, guilt. Rape is such a horrible word, and the stigma hangs over a victim until she dies. "She acted provocatively. She asked for it." In the 1930s, these were the prevailing sentiments. And I heard my mother's words echo in my head, words that she had said to all of us when something out of control happened: "What part of the problem are you?"

Maybe she was right, I thought. Was it something I did? Did I say something I shouldn't have? The thoughts swirled about my head. How could I bring myself to tell my mother, "I've been raped. I am being raped"? I was trapped, and the deeper I slid into that emotional quagmire, the more worthless I felt. I tried to scrub the scent from my body, Buddy's scent and the smell of my own shame, until my skin became blistered.

For months I didn't tell anyone, and the assaults continued. I was terrified. My mother was so blinded by her need to replace Stanton that she couldn't believe that Buddy would hurt me. My father pretended that he knew nothing. Only my younger brother David tried to come to my defense, and Buddy beat him mercilessly.

Finally, when I was fifteen, I couldn't take it anymore. The Esther who at eight had vowed to become strong and to be in control of her life, now felt hopeless and nearly destroyed. One night, desperate, I told my mother everything.

"But how could he?" she said, peering at me almost accusingly. "He's so sensitive, so dear."

The words hit me like hammer blows. After all this time, was it possible that she still didn't believe me, or didn't want to believe that this wonderful new son, the honor student, the hero athlete, was raping her daughter?

"Ask him," I demanded. "Tell him what I said."

Later that day, my parents confronted Buddy in the living room, not knowing that I was listening unseen in the nearby hallway. "Oh, Buddy," I heard my mother say, "how could you treat Esther that way?"

So they *did* believe me.

"I . . . I'm sorry," Buddy told them. "I just lost control. It won't happen again. I've learned my lesson . . . I love you all so much."

He was confessing. I expected my father to rise up and beat the hell out of him. I expected my mother to order him out of the house.

"We love you, too," my mother said. "But you betrayed our love."

"All I want is another chance," Buddy begged.

"How do we know, if we gave you another chance . . ."

My parents' voices weren't angry or furious. They were sad, almost sympathetic. I didn't fully understand it then, but they were trying to find a way to be both my parents and his parents. They couldn't help themselves. They couldn't bear to lose Buddy, who had taken Stanton's place in their hearts. They couldn't face another loss like that, and they fiercely wanted to believe that Buddy could stay and Esther would be safe.

Listening to their muffled voices through the wall, I felt abandoned, deserted. My parents—who were supposed to be my defenders, my protectors—were lost to me forever. I was alone, totally alone in the world.

Blinded by tears, I ran from the house. I wandered around for I don't know how long, and then without even realizing it, I must have taken the number seven Red Car, because I found myself in front of the LA Athletic Club. *Here*, at least, in the pool, knifing through the water, I could be in control, I would be safe—for the moment.

When the elevator door opened to the seventh floor, I stepped off and was hit by the familiar smell of chlorine. And there, all alone, Buddy stood, waiting for me. He knew me well. He knew that this is where I would run, that the pool was my private world, my haven.

"Esther, please. Listen to me," he said, his voice and face filled with pain. "I'm sorry."

I knew that he was sorry, but not for what he had done to me. I knew he was sorry that he had endangered his place in a comfortable home with doting new parents. Rage shot through me. I knew that I had to stand up to him now, this moment, or I would never be safe from him or from any man. If I was alone in the world, then I had only myself to fight my battles.

"You're never gonna touch me again, you son of a bitch," I snapped, clenching my fists.

"I know. I won't," he promised.

"And you're not living in that house any more."

"Your mom said . . ."

"I don't care what she said. 'Cause if you do come back, you'll try to rape me again."

"No. You'll see."

"Like hell. Only this time I'll fight. I'll kick and punch. I'll claw and scream."

I sensed his measuring me. I was fifteen, and the years of hard swimming had packed muscle on my frame and made me very strong. Not as strong as a football player, but strong enough to inflict heavy damage. He had to know that I was through being his trembling, passive victim. If there was going to be any more blood, it would be his as well as mine, something even my parents wouldn't be able to ignore much longer.

Our eyes locked and I refused to look away. Suddenly, his face crumbled and he sank to his knees, crying, pleading. "Don't do this to me. Please don't leave me, Esther. Please don't keep me out of my home."

"It's not your home anymore."

With that, I spun around, strode back into the elevator, and left him there, kneeling on the floor.

Two days later he joined the Coast Guard, and I never had to see him again.

So that's what bullies do when you stand up to them, I thought to myself. It was a lesson that would serve me well.

Still, that nearly two-year ordeal inflicted wounds that have never healed, that left scars that I carry to this day.

Now some sixty years later, I try to be philosophic about that chapter in my life. Like Stanton's death, it was a major, traumatic turning point. At the time, I didn't realize how many others loomed directly ahead of me.

CHAPTER 3

IN FULL BLOOM
1939

"Swimmers take your mark!"

*T*wo feet above the water on the starting block, I stare at what seems an endless expanse of water. My arms thrust back, knees bent, a slight pitch forward, my toes grab the edge of the block—a position as painful as that of a ballet dancer en pointe. I wait for the only sound I'll ever hear to send me hurtling forward toward the rest of my life. Seven lanes of swimmers stand next to me, their strong bodies crouched.

What goes through the mind of a seventeen-year-old swimmer as she stands on that block and hears the words, "Take your mark," followed by the pistol crack that sends her toward that finish line, 100 meters away? Will it be any different for the champion at Sydney, Australia, in the year 2000 than it was for me in that hot July of 1939 in Des Moines, Iowa, at the national championships? Will her brief life flash before her eyes as mine did in that second between the "mark" and the explosion?

My first event was the 100-meter freestyle, the top event of the meet, competing against the best in the nation, over a hundred swimmers. We would race in groups of eight. The three top finishers in each heat advanced and competed against the top finishers in the other heats, a grueling series of eliminations. I won my first race at 7 A.M., another at 8 A.M., still another at 10 A.M., each time at top speed, going all out, never letting down even though the water temperature had risen to bathtub level and beyond, sapping my energy, wiping me out. One bad turn, one split second of lost concentration, and I would've been eliminated. But I wasn't. In five races against the strongest girl swimmers in America, I won each time. I emerged a national champion.

Triumphant, I wasn't finished. The next day, I swam anchor on the 400-meter relay. Another gold medal.

That night, I was so exhausted that I feared I could never win another race without a long, long rest, but I had to compete in a final race in the morning. I retreated to a little cubbyhole dressing room, sat down on a bench and said to myself, "This is my prayer. Let me be the conduit for all of life's energy, all the strength that is in me, all the things that Stanton would be if he were going to swim this race tomorrow."

The next morning, I mounted the block as the starting swimmer in the 300-meter medley relay. Relying on strength alone I wasn't sure I could win. Not after the previous grueling days. I thought back to my prayer the night before and said to myself, "Dear Stanton, this is the first race that you are going to swim for me. I did the others. Now you take over."

The pistol shot echoed in my ears as I leaped from the block. "Aquaplane," I shouted to myself as I flew toward the water. I surged across the pool, keeping myself as high as I could in the resistant water. I was racing against girls who were using the conventional breaststroke, which kept their arms under the water at all times. But I thrust both my arms *out* of the water in every stroke in the much more difficult—and powerful—butterfly, which the lifeguards at the Manchester pool had taught me when I was only eight. In years to come, the butterfly would become a separate event, but at that time, so few swimmers, especially girls, could master it that it was allowed in breaststroke events. The last ten meters of the race I could see, in my mind, "The Little Man with the Hammer"—every world-class swimmer has seen him—banging on my legs, with my every stroke his hammer coming down harder, "You're not gonna make it. You can't fool me. You're tired, bushed, whipped. You can't make it to the end of that pool. Give up. Give up . . ."

But there was no "give up" in me.

A press photo caught me coming out of the water with a smile on my face that wouldn't quit. I had smashed the national, and probably world, record for my lap by nine seconds. I had given my team such a big lead that we won by almost the length of the entire pool.

Three events. Three gold medals. I was news, big news, in the sports world.

Before I had left for Des Moines to compete in the nationals, I sat down with my mother and said, "You know, this meet means a lot to me, and if I become a champion and break a record, and it goes into the record books, I'm not sure what to do."

She said, "When you're on the top of the mountain, you'll discover that the top is a cliff, and the edge of the cliff is covered with loose rocks. It's very easy to step on that gravel and slip and fall. So when you get to the peak, you take a good, firm stance because the top is fraught with danger.

"Those loose rocks represent a million different things—temptation, ego, flattery, a swelled head—all the things that can get in your way and trip you up when people make a fuss over you and you believe it. When you get to the top of that mountain, stand back, where you know your feet are firmly planted on solid ground; take a deep breath and look at your surroundings. If you win, remember who you are, and why you won. You won't win by accident; you will win because you have worked hard and you have trained. If you remember that, I think it's safe for you to go and win."

I was the happiest kid in the world when I came back from those nationals, because I was assured a spot on the U.S. Olympic team. I was going to need my mother's advice about watching out for those loose rocks, though. Shortly after I returned, my LAAC coach,

Aileen Allen, introduced me to a Hollywood lawyer named Roger Marchetti.

The newspapers loved pinup pictures of pretty young swimmers, and as a national champion, I got more than my share of space in the sports pages. Right after my victory at the nationals, *Life* magazine ran a page featuring me and three other girls that was clearly the precursor of the *Sports Illustrated* swimsuit issues. Through Coach Allen, my picture caught the eye of Roger Marchetti, a second-rate Hollywood talent scout and lawyer, who was always on the lookout for pretty girls for the movies. Deanna Durbin had been my classmate at Bret Harte Junior High School and had been "discovered" by Universal Studios. The aura of fame was not without its seductive charm. I had heard the applause.

Roger Marchetti and Coach Allen, who had become more than my swim coach, convinced me that they could guide me into a movie career. Before I knew what was happening, I had signed a contract with Marchetti as my manager/agent for 20 percent of my earnings, and he arranged a screen test at 20th Century-Fox studios.

I was totally unprepared.

But dutifully, I showed up at Fox Studios—no acting lessons, no advice, no understanding of what I was supposed to do. The drama coach at Fox, Tom Moore, came from a theatrical family and had worked his way up the ladder. Unfortunately, he reeked so badly of booze that it was difficult to stand at close range and have a conversation with him. The test was a scene with a handsome young actor, George Montgomery Letz, who later dropped his last name to become simply George Montgomery. George was under contract to Fox and went on to have a moderately successful career. A well-known man about town, he squired such stars as Ginger Rogers and Hedy Lamarr and later married Dinah Shore. George and I tried to rehearse the scene, but Moore kept falling asleep. He was worse than no help, not bothering to arrange for makeup or even something decent from the wardrobe department for me to wear; I wore a homemade dress that Maurine had sewn for me. I never saw that screen test, but I have no doubt that it was dreadful. Marchetti and I came in a week later to see Lew Schreiber, head of casting at Fox. I was on crutches because I had stepped on a sharp shell at the beach and cut my foot badly. He didn't mince words. "You're a swimmer, right? Well, get back in the pool."

"Are you telling me that I'm not any good at this?" I said, without much surprise.

"That's what I'm telling you. Rethink your future. It doesn't include movies."

I was glad to get out of there. I had an uneasy feeling about Coach Allen and this lawyer who signed me to a contract that I didn't understand. I felt I had been railroaded into something, and I didn't like the feeling. My instincts were right about both Aileen Allen and Roger Marchetti. She would soon betray me, and he would end up stealing money from me.

After the Fox fiasco I knew one thing for sure: I was not meant to be in the movies.

I continued to train hard because after winning the 1939 nationals, it was a given that I would be invited to the Pan American Games, which were being held in Buenos Aires in the spring of 1940. I was waiting anxiously for the invitation, which would say, "Dear Miss Williams, You have won the nationals and you are an American champion. You are cordially invited to Buenos Aires to the Pan American Games . . ."

The Pan Am Games were one of those things an athlete prays for. Here was the chance to fly to another country, to see other kinds of people, to compete internationally. I waited for the invitation to come. A telegram. A letter. Anything. Nothing came. I was bewildered. Maybe I'd get a phone call? Days and weeks passed. Still nothing.

I asked Coach Allen what was going on. Had she heard anything?

"No, nothing," she said. "Just be patient."

And then it was too late. I read in the paper that the games had begun. Had begun and ended without me.

I couldn't understand why, as a national champ, I hadn't been invited. Finally, I figured that with thousands of athletes under consideration, my name just got lost in the shuffle.

I forced myself back into training for the indoor nationals in Miami, where I was to defend my 100-meter freestyle title.

I joined up with the American team in Miami, which was just returning from the Pan Am Games. I was still smarting over what had happened. During a lunch date with Taylor Drysdale, a handsome young backstroker from Michigan, he asked me, "Why didn't you go to Buenos Aires?"

"I never got an invitation," I said. "They never sent me a wire."

"Sure they did," he said. "I know it for a fact. We were all waiting for you to arrive."

I sat there stunned. What was he talking about? I excused myself early and ran back to the hotel, crying all the way. Edie Motridge, with whom I shared a room and who was defending her title in the 100-meter backstroke, calmed me down enough for me to gather my thoughts and try to piece together this awful mystery. Finally, I thought I had the answer.

I rushed from the room and hunted down my coach, Aileen Allen, who was playing bridge with some other coaches in the hotel lobby. "Excuse me, Mrs. Allen. Could I have a word with you?" I said as I approached the table.

"I'm playing bridge, Esther," she said, without even looking up. "Don't interrupt my game."

"I'm sorry, but I will have to interrupt your game because this is the last time we're ever going to speak."

Now I had her attention, as well as the attention of half the lobby.

"Why is that?" she asked.

"Because *you* received a wire last year, inviting me to the Pan Am Games. Didn't you?" I was bluffing because I couldn't be completely sure, but it was the only explanation.

"Yes, I did," she said.

"But you never told me. Why?"

"Because you'd have had too good a time in Buenos Aires, all the time. You'd have met some boy; you'd have broken training, gotten out of shape, and never been in condition to defend your title here in Florida. I did it for your own good."

I couldn't believe what I heard.

"But, but . . . I won three medals in Des Moines. How could you say I do things like that?" I didn't know whether to cry or scream.

She just shook her head and went back to her card game. What she said was a lie. I never broke training. I was as strong as I had ever been. And dates are the furthest thing from an athlete's mind, particularly one in training. Maybe the failure at Fox had something to do with it. Perhaps she had planned to receive a percentage of my salary from Roger Marchetti and now that would never happen. So she finally got back at me. I was furious.

Now it was my turn. I stood tall, and with a clarity in my voice, I said, "Coach Allen. If I couldn't compete in the Pan Ams, I'm not competing here. Find somebody else on the team to swim in the 100 yards because I'm going home."

She whirled in her chair. "You can't do that," she said.

"Just watch me."

I strode from the lobby with Edie at my side, both of us in tears. Out of loyalty to me, *she* was quitting, too. We packed, taxied to the railraod station, and caught a train for the five-day trip to Los Angeles. All the way back, we talked about what we had done and what we would do with our lives. I treasured Edie's loyalty, and I would eventually find a way to repay her for it.

Looking back now, I realize that I had been extraordinarily brave for a young girl with no resources. I wanted to continue swimming, but without the backing of a wealthy club like the LAAC I'd have to do it as a freelancer. Somehow, I vowed, I would do it because I wanted to compete—I just *had* to compete—in the upcoming 1940 Summer Olympic Games. This would be the pinnacle of my swimming career. If I could win Olympic gold, I thought, it would be the greatest achievement in my life. Nothing could ever equal that.

But then Hitler invaded Poland, and World War II was underway, canceling the Olympics. My dreams were crushed, a minor thing in comparison to the horrors that soon engulfed the world, but to a teenage girl the world can seem very small. It would not be until 1948 that the Olympics would be held again. By then, I was among the top ten box office stars in the world. Stardom would be my consolation prize.

CHAPTER 4

THE BIRTH OF A PROFESSIONAL MERMAID
1940

The San Francisco World's Fair, which opened on Treasure Island in San Francisco Bay in the spring of 1939, was destined to change my life forever. Of course, I didn't know it at the time. This extravagant show was a colorful burst of optimism punctuating the end of a long, enervating depression. Treasure Island was an extraordinary feat of engineering, in which four hundred acres of reef that lay under the bay had been transformed into what was then the world's largest man-made island. This was Disneyland, Las Vegas, and Broadway wrapped up in one. Amidst the splendor of pseudo-Mayan architecture, the Triumphal Arch and the 400-foot Tower of the Sun, millions flocked to the rides on the Gayway, to see the 1,000-pound fruitcake, the new Boeing-314 flying boats in the Hall of Air Transportation, and to hear concerts by Bing Crosby and Benny Goodman.

Not enough millions attended for the concessionaires, however. Although tickets were only twenty-five cents, the crowds had dwindled by the end of the first year. The organizers of the Exposition needed a bigger attraction, and they knew what it was. Famous New York showman Billy Rose had invented a form of entertainment called the Aquacade. This show originated in Cleveland and later became the box office sensation of the New York World's Fair in 1939, where it attracted 5 million spectators. The idea was unique, and huge crowds flocked to see Olympic swimming champion Johnny Weissmuller and Olympic backstroke swimmer Eleanor Holm (who was also Mrs. Billy Rose) perform along with the best Olympic divers in the world.

When he was contacted by the backers of the Pan-Pacific Exposition, Billy Rose was happy to bring his Aquacade to their fair in the summer of 1940. He would move Weissmuller to San Francisco and keep Eleanor Holm in the New York show. But he needed someone to replace Eleanor as Weissmuller's partner.

Rose had read in the newspapers and in *Life* magazine about an attractive, up-and-coming seventeen-year-old swimmer named Esther Williams, who had won the 100-meter freestyle at the national championships. I had no idea at the time, but he planned to fly to Los Angeles to see me.

Neither Rose nor anyone else knew that with the cancellation of the 1940 Olympic Games and the cruel betrayal of Aileen Allen, I felt my life in the water was over. Even my hopes for getting a swimming scholarship at the University of Southern California were drowned when my high school teacher gave me a D in algebra at the end of my senior year. I argued with him about how seriously this grade would affect my life by preventing me from entering USC. His response was, "Esther, you've given me a very charming argument as to why I should give you a better grade. Unfortunately I'm not grading you on charm. I'm grading you on algebra." The D remained and I entered LA City College to take the course again.

Money was scarce. Champion swimming at this point in my life brought in no means of support, and in order to keep my amateur status, I couldn't even work as a lifeguard. I had seen a Hiring sign in the window of the posh I. Magnin department store on Wilshire Boulevard, where they were looking for a stock girl. In those days, there were no racks of clothes to browse through. Salesgirls presented clothing one item at a time to customers, and then stock girls went around the floor picking up the items that had been shown. The job opening was in sportswear, up on the fourth floor, and I reported to the buyer—Mrs. Clewell, a little, no-nonsense, snappy lady—for an interview. Since I might occasionally have to model, she first wanted to see me in a swimsuit. Obviously, that was no problem, because to me a swimsuit was like a uniform. I took the suit and went into one of the fitting rooms and put it on. Then I waited for Mrs. Clewell to return.

I waited and waited, until it was nearing closing time, six o'clock. At a quarter to six, I heard the sounds of people covering up the furniture and peeked around because I didn't want to stroll about in just a swimsuit. At six o'clock, the closing bell rang and the loudspeaker blared, "The store is now closing." Deciding finally to look for Mrs. Clewell, I went down a corridor of offices in the back and found her sitting at her desk. When I appeared at the door in my swimsuit, she jumped. She had completely forgotten I was there. "Oh yes—you are the young lady who wants the job. Who referred you to me?" Referrals were always an important part of getting a job.

I had seen a sign on a door in the corridor that read EDWARD JOSEPH, MANAGER. I hoped that Mr. Joseph had already left, and I said, "Mr. Joseph suggested I come in to see you."

"Hmm . . ." She looked at her watch. Mr. Joseph just left on a two-week vacation," she said. But then she looked at me approvingly. "Never mind. You got the job."

I figured that if Mr. Joseph didn't come back from his vacation for two weeks, I would have time to convince Mrs. Clewell that I was worth keeping, with or without the swimsuit. And that's exactly what happened. My seventy-six dollars a month salary seemed perfectly adequate. I thought I was the luckiest girl in the world.

The head salesgirl, Connie Conover, took a liking to me. I modeled clothes frequently and appeared in I. Magnin newspaper ads. They didn't pay me extra for it, but I didn't care. I was learning the department store business. Every day, I took the streetcar from my home to Vermont and Wilshire and dreamed of becoming an assistant buyer in the sportswear department. By this time, my swimming sessions had tapered off because I was too tired after a full day at the store to go down for the eight o'clock workouts.

About one month into my new job at I. Magnin, an intriguing telephone call reached me at the fourth floor. A voice on the other end of the line said that he was an assistant to Billy Rose, the producer of the Aquacade in New York. "Mr. Rose," he said, "is at the Ambassador Hotel pool holding auditions to find a replacement for Eleanor Holm to star in the San Francisco Aquacade. Would you be interested in auditioning for the show?"

I had heard about Billy Rose, and the Aquacade. I was curious about "swimming as entertainment" and the Ambassador Hotel pool was only a couple of blocks away. But I was working, so I said, "I can't come over right away. I have to wait for my lunch hour at twelve."

"Mr. Rose has a plane to catch."

"I understand, but I can't jeopardize my job. Can somebody else see how I swim and decide whether I qualify or not?"

He had a muffled conversation with somebody nearby while I waited on the line. He came back on and said, "Mr. Rose has seen your picture in the newspapers and he wants to see you himself. He will take a later plane and see you at noon."

Conover had overheard the conversation and offered to get a swimsuit for me, but I declined because I didn't have the money to pay for it. "I'll buy it for you," she insisted. "You've got to go audition for Billy Rose. This is too important for you to miss." She went to the swimsuit department and chose her pretty red suit. Handing it to me, she said, "Put this on and go get that job."

I walked the couple of blocks to the Ambassador Hotel wearing my new swimsuit under my sweater and skirt. There must have been fifty girls in swimsuits around the pool. A short little guy with slick, black hair smoking a big cigar approached me. It had to be Billy Rose. "You're Esther Williams. I've seen your picture in *Life* magazine."

I said, "Yes, I am, and yes, my picture was in *Life*."

He looked me over. "Your Olympics have been canceled, you know."

"Yes. I know."

"I suppose you're disappointed." Billy Rose always spoke in conclusions. He didn't ask questions.

"Yes, I am," I replied.

"Then you better find something good to do."

"I have. I've got a job in a beautiful department store."

He champed on his cigar and said, "Well, I might have something a lot better for you. Let's see how you swim."

I didn't know how he wanted me to swim, but I figured that if he wanted to see how strong I was, I should swim fast. The LA Athletic Club pool was 33 1/3 meters. Three laps to the hundred. This pool was twenty-five yards, so it would take four laps. No problem. I did a racing dive and swam the four laps as fast as I could. I jumped out and stood there all wet in my new red I. Magnin tank suit. I towered over him. It was the first of many meetings I would have with short men, and they tend to look more into your bosom than into your face, because that's where their eye level is.

"You swim very fast," he said.

"That's what I do, Mr. Rose. I'm a sprint swimmer. The U.S. 100-meter freestyle champion."

"I don't want fast; I want pretty."

"Mr. Rose, if you're not strong enough to swim fast, then you're probably not strong enough to swim 'pretty.' "

He puffed his cigar and thought about that. "You're probably right. I want you to swim with your head up and your shoulders out of the water."

"That would take a really good, strong kick," I told him, "and when you swim fast you have a really strong kick."

"Well, that's very informative. You know your stuff about swimming. Do you want the job?"

"Mr. Rose, I already have a job at I. Magnin, and if I take a job swimming professionally for you, I'll lose my amateur standing and any chance ever to be in the Olympics."

"Young lady, there's a war on and there aren't going to be any Olympic Games for a long time. What are you gonna do in the meantime, eat your medals? You might as well make some money with your talent." He handed me a business card and said, "Look, do you have an agent? Have him call me. I'll explain the deal to him."

Billy Rose flew back to New York and I walked back to I. Magnin.

My head was spinning with all the thoughts of what a change this would make in my life.

I phoned Roger Marchetti, the agent who had taken me to Fox Studios. Despite the lack of success we'd had, I still had a signed contract with him. He was thrilled, of course, that Billy Rose had hired me. This was a fine omen for my future. I was not to worry. He would handle all the necessary legal matters and negotiations with the Rose organization.

I couldn't wait to get back to the fourth floor sportswear department to tell Connie Conover what had happened. I was to move to San Francisco and star in the Aquacade.

But there were still a lot of unanswered questions. What was I going to tell my mother? Could I learn to swim pretty? Were they going to teach me how to dive? What would Johnny Weissmuller be like?

Connie was at the store waiting for me and I had to tell her everything. I worried about the suit being wet. She said, "Don't worry; you keep that. You'll need a bathing suit up there when you start rehearsals. It's my gift to you—it's a good luck present."

I hugged her and walked down that corridor over to Mrs. Clewell's office. She said, "Come in." It was a moment I dreaded.

I said, "Mrs. Clewell, you've been very kind to me and I've learned a lot working for you; but something has just happened that has changed all of my plans. I have to leave because I have just gotten a job swimming in the Aquacade at the San Francisco Fair."

She was not pleased at all, and she looked at me very sternly. I tried again. "I just auditioned for Billy Rose for his Aquacade."

She expressed disbelief. "Billy Rose—the New York producer? When did you do that?"

"On my lunch hour, Mrs. Clewell. I didn't go on store time."

"And he hired you?"

I assured her that he had offered me a job. She asked me what my salary would be, and I told her that I hadn't asked. I didn't want to insult her by saying that it had to be more than seventy-six dollars a month, but I'm sure she figured that out. "Well, young lady, you go ahead. You'll be back. But there is no guarantee your job will be available." And with that terse little remark, she dismissed me by sitting down and picking up the telephone.

The first thing Mother said to me was, "I have to go with you. You're not even eighteen years old yet."

I resisted. "No, I really have to go alone," I said, "because I'll be so busy and there's so much I have to learn. You won't understand, and I won't be able to teach you at the same time I'm learning. Besides, you have your parent education program, and Daddy needs you to take care of him. I'll be fine."

"But you don't have any clothes to wear."

"There was a sale at the store today, and before I left, Miss Conover helped me pick out a suit, just right for San Francisco, a black, lightweight wool suit that fit me perfectly. She opened a charge account for me. I'll be making money, so I'll be able to pay for it with my first paycheck."

My mother asked me how much the suit cost, and I was astonished to hear myself say, "Eighty-five dollars." I'd never owned anything that had cost that much before, and the price of the suit astonished my mother even more than the idea that her daughter was leaving home to swim in an Aquacade.

The next night, my father took me to Union Station in downtown Los Angeles and put me on the Lark, the night train from Los Angeles to San Francisco. I was shown to a private compartment that was reserved for me. When I was traveling with the LAAC, I had always slept in one of those uppers or lowers with the rest of the team. This time I was in my own compartment, with its own bathroom. I was wearing my new black wool suit, and I felt very sophisticated. I was traveling to the beautiful city of San Francisco—by myself.

As I went to sleep that night in that little roomette on the train, I thought about Stanton, because I knew that something wonderful was opening up for me. I didn't know how, but I knew that he would be there with me. At the end of my prayers I always made three wishes. That night one of the three wishes was, "Dear God, please help me learn to swim pretty—fast!"

I arrived in San Francisco the next morning. I was met at Union Station and taken to the Broadmoor Hotel, where the rest of the swimmers were staying. The room there was not much bigger than my train compartment, but it was clean. After I unpacked, I was told to report to the Crystal Plunge, where the Aquacade was rehearsing.

The choreographer of the show, John Murray Anderson, was working with the swimmers, and I was introduced to the concept of "swimming pretty." "If you're going to swim so that people can see you, you have to swim with your head and shoulders up out of the water," he said, repeating Rose's mantra. "This is just the opposite of how you want to swim for speed, with your body below the surface." I knew my deep, strong freestyle kick would enable me to get my head and upper body elevated.

A group of swimmers from the University of California, Berkeley hired for the show had been training there for several weeks and had already mastered the technique. I watched closely and learned what they did. The phrase "synchronized swimming" hadn't been invented yet. It was called "water ballet," swimming in rhythm to the music. We did swimming drills with two, then four, then six, and eight, and then a line of girls all the way across the pool. The show was to open in a month and our routines had to be ready.

As the star of the show, I was to open with a solo, followed by a complicated duet with Johnny Weissmuller that I had to learn quickly. Johnny hadn't arrived yet, so his stand-in would teach me the routines. I had to learn all kinds of new "pretty" strokes, and how to swim in unison with him. I practiced switching from the crawl to the backstroke with grace, then rehearsed the moves that were needed to make that routine work. Swimming pretty took enormous stamina. Unlike fast swimming, it was a series of isometric maneuvers high on the surface in order to maintain stability in the water. It was not a natural swimming position.

The Broadmoor was a dormitory for the girls in the Aquacade. Like me, the other swimmers were young athletes having the time of their lives being away from home and performing in a big show in San Francisco, the first of its kind. They came from a wide variety of backgrounds, having been recruited at swimming meets by Billy Rose's scouts because they were pretty and looked good in a bathing suit.

Just after I began rehearsals, I received a telephone call from James Colligan, Billy Rose's longtime assistant. He told me that Mr. Rose had arrived in San Francisco and wanted to see me. He was staying at the elegant St. Francis Hotel downtown and was sending a car to pick me up in an hour. I figured that this was a business meeting. Because he was the producer of this big wonderful show, he wanted to tell me what was expected of me and that we would talk about my salary.

Colligan was in the black sedan when it picked me up at the Broadmoor. I found out later that he was a type that was common enough in the entertainment industry—the loyal right hand who served as personal henchman and keeper of secrets. I was to learn that this practice was not limited to Billy Rose. Moguls like L. B. Mayer, Howard Hughes, and Mike Todd each had someone close to them who knew where all the bodies were buried. Colligan knew everything about his boss's business, and even more important he knew how to keep his mouth shut. I asked him many questions on that ride across town, but he just sat there with his Irish grin. "You'll find out all in good time, dear," was all he would say.

Colligan escorted me up to Billy Rose's suite, and to my surprise he turned on his heel at the door and said, "See you tomorrow." I assumed that "tomorrow" meant that I would be sent home in a cab later that evening. I asked him how much cab fare would be back to the hotel. He told me about five dollars, but not too worry, Mr. R. would take care of that.

Billy Rose came to the door, wearing trousers and a silk foulard robe with a matching silk cravat. Behind him I caught a glimpse of a table set for two, complete with candlelight and a champagne bucket.

It didn't take a college graduate to recognize the layout. This was no business meeting. This was a seduction scene, pure and simple—I saw that look in his eyes. The attire was supposed to make Billy Rose look very dashing. He was making me an offer I couldn't refuse, as if sex with him would be the best thing in the world. Couldn't he look in the mirror? He was already in his fifties, married, and five feet two inches. I was seventeen, not even the legal age for such antics.

He pulled a large wing chair away from the room service table and invited me to sit down. Instead of taking a seat opposite me, he sidled around behind my chair, reached down, and took hold of my shoulders. I knew that it was just a matter of time before those hands would be headed due south, so I stood up, allowing my full five feet eight inches to loom over his five feet two inches. Then I straight-armed his nose out of my cleavage and said, "Mr. Rose, I've already had dinner. Are we here to talk about my job?"

"No," he said, in a voice he thought was sexy. "I thought we should talk about . . . you and me."

"I've been learning so much working for you in this job, Mr. Rose," I said, smiling prettily. "In fact, I just learned something new tonight."

"What's that, Esther?" He started coming closer, a big, silly grin on his face. His eyes hooded over as if this would be the ultimate se-duction.

"I've learned that I should always have taxi fare in my purse," I said as I backed toward the door. "Can I borrow five dollars to get back to my hotel?"

He recoiled as if he had been slapped. "You mean you're leaving?"

"I'll pay you back out of my first paycheck."

Billy Rose looked sadly at the champagne in the ice bucket and then reached into his robe and pulled out the biggest roll of money I had ever seen. He peeled a five-dollar bill off the top of the wad and said, "Get out of here."

I left the St. Francis faster than I ever swam the pool at the LA Athletic Club. Fast and not pretty! He never tried that again. I could see the genesis of another bully. I said no and he backed off as I knew he would. Much to my surprise, I kept my job.

In 1996, Barney Gould, longtime columnist of the *San Francisco Examiner,* sent me a letter that Rose had written to him when he was a publicist for the Aquacade. In his own letter, Barney wrote to me, "Esther, you made quite an impression on Billy Rose." I guess he was right. In the letter, Rose was emphatic about the need to focus publicity for the Aquacade on me. He closed by noting, "You can quote me that . . . she is the most beautiful swimming cham-pion in the history of aquatics."

As opening day drew near, rehearsals moved to the Aquacade sta-dium at Treasure Island. The building looked like a huge airplane hangar, constructed of wood, with an impressive 200-foot-long, 60-foot-wide, 50,000-gallon pool across the front of the stage, and two tall diving towers on either side. Despite the size and grandeur of the stadium, I couldn't believe what they called a "star dressing room." I was given this crummy little cubicle furnished with a broken mirror, a cot, and a stool with one short leg that had to be propped up so I didn't fall off when I sat down. Billy Rose was not only an unattractive old lecher, he was also a cheap sonofabitch.

This was my second foray into show business, and I didn't think it was anymore glamorous than the first. With everybody dripping as they were coming and going from the stage, the floor was always covered with several inches of water. The whole place was wet, wet, wet. And dank. And cold.

Things heated up considerably in our last two weeks of rehearsal, when the cast from the New York show arrived to join us. Johnny Weissmuller and singer/host Morton Downey were the first to arrive, followed shortly by a number of male swimmers and divers. They were a handsome group of young athletes, with strong, beautiful bodies. As far as I was concerned, it was as if the troops had landed, because all of them were on the make from the minute they hit the water. They found willing partners in the California girls, who never seemed to run out of energy or endurance. During the show, the cots for resting up in the diving towers were never empty, and the sexual carnival lasted well into the night back at the Broadmoor.

Everyone seemed to be in heat. Interestingly enough, there was even a pecking order in the seduction department. It was the first time I had encountered this phenomenon, although through my years at MGM it certainly was not the last. The male swimmers, "Aquabeaux," as they were known, took an active interest in the "Aquabelles." The championship divers, on the other hand, were a category up—only showgirls, nonswimmers, or "Aquafemmes," were appropriate for them. As for the star, well, that was a category unto itself: Aquadonis!

Johnny Weissmuller didn't just play Tarzan. He thought he *was* Tarzan. He had this magnificent physique and he was very strong— six feet four inches, with muscles that rippled and flexed as he moved. Heaven knows, he was handsome. He had a classic profile and he loved to pose. He thought he was God's gift to women. The holder of many U.S. and world swimming records, he had been the gold medalist in the 100-meter freestyle, at the Paris Olympics in 1924, and again in Amsterdam in 1928. In 1932 he donned a loincloth for the first time as *Tarzan the Ape Man,* a role he repeated many times in his career on and off the screen.

Later on Weissmuller also played a character named Jungle Jim, who was really nothing more than Tarzan with his clothes on—not that he *wanted* to keep his clothes on. He had remarkable genitalia that he loved to exhibit and was constantly stripping his clothes to his swimsuit and beyond so that everyone could appreciate his extraordinary male attributes. It was his way of saying, "Look at me. I was made perfect. God gave me everything a man could dream of having."

In the show, I performed the solo number first, and then Johnny and I swam the duet. We looked good together, because we both had powerful kicks and could lift ourselves high in the water and swim in unison to the music. Weissmuller and I both had what swimmers call "balance in the water," the ability to hold your balance and be able to rise out of the water while swimming. I learned to swim in tandem with him, swimming backstroke while he was swimming crawl. I touched my toes on each side of his waist to be propelled forward (and to hold him back) as he swam toward me as if in a race. Johnny Weissmuller had the most powerful crawl stroke, and swimming with him was like traveling in the wake of an ocean liner. At the end of our duet, we had to exit by swimming under the stage to a set of stairs that came up out of the water backstage. Under the stage it was pitch black and when we made this exit, there was no one in the water except the two of us.

I wish someone had been able to time me with a stopwatch as I swam for those stairs, because I'm sure that I broke speed records during every show. From the second we slipped behind the banana leaves hanging into the water from the stage and out of the audience's sight he was after me. Under the stage, he'd whip off his trunks so I could see that he was beautifully equipped, and if he caught me, he'd try to get my suit off. If he grabbed me at the platform before the stairs, he would hold me and grope me and let me know that he had this lovely erection. I would swim for those steps as though I was swimming for my life. Chasing me totally in the nude, he would splash and grunt like a lion. I think maybe he took that jungle character a little too seriously. On-screen it may have been attractive to the ten-year-olds who filled the theaters. Underwater, it was a menace. There was no one else ever in that tunnel-like passageway under the stage. It was an Alfred Hitchcock erotic nightmare! He was always right behind me, that big smile on his face, those groping hands—three shows a day (four on Saturday and Sunday), six days a week.

The torment didn't end when I left the Aquacade stadium at the end of the day. I had moved out of the Broadmoor to get away from the all-night sex follies and had taken an apartment in the marina district. By now, Johnny was notorious in San Francisco for getting drunk and ripping up the town. He was a danger as well as a nuisance, but no one did anything about it because he was a star. He was Tarzan! Every night, he would drive to my apartment and honk the horn or stand under my bay windows and yell my name. I locked my doors and turned out the lights, but that didn't discourage him. He prowled around, banging on the door. The neighbors would yell, "Go away, Johnny!" but he would just laugh and give his Tarzan yell that echoed through the marina.

His wife, Beryl Scott, was a prominent socialite who also happened to be very pregnant that summer. She was wife number four. (Wife number three had been "Mexican Spitfire" Lupe Velez, and the fireworks that accompanied their tempestuous marriage had been a rich source of fodder for the tabloids in the 1930s.)

Beryl always wore big hats and fur coats and seemed to know exactly how Johnny operated. One evening early in the season, as the last show finished, she caught me at the stage door as I was leaving. I had seen her many times before waiting to drive Johnny back to the city across the recently opened Bay Bridge. We hardly ever spoke, usually exchanging just a nod to say good evening or good night. This time she came over to me.

"Would you like me to drive you to the ferry?" she asked.

Each night after the show, I would walk to the ferry dock on Treasure Island to catch the last boat to the Embarcadero. From there I would meet the waiting trolley cars in the marina to take me to my little apartment overlooking the bay, which I had rented for the duration of the show. San Francisco can be particularly chilly and foggy in the summer. My hair was wet and the car coat that my sister Maurine had given me before I left Los Angeles was woefully thin and didn't keep the damp from penetrating through to my skin.

"Thank you," I said. "I get so cold after the shows. And I never look forward to the walk to the ferry terminal."

I didn't expect Beryl or Johnny to offer me a ride home. They never had before. I didn't have a car and I wouldn't know how to drive even if I did have one.

I climbed into what seemed like the biggest car I'd ever seen, with a smart *JW* monogrammed on the passenger door. We drove silently to the terminal.

"Thank you again," I said as I turned to get out of the car.

"No, please don't get out yet. May I ask you a question?" she said, and then quickly continued. "Has Johnny ever made a pass at you?"

She didn't wait for an answer.

"You can tell me. Because he does it all the time. I wouldn't be surprised if you say yes. You look so beautiful together."

In the half-light of the car, I could see that her eyes had glazed over.

I said nothing.

"I love the way you both swim." Her voice trailed off.

I hesitated a moment. I knew that if I told her that nothing had happened, she wouldn't believe me. She had asked these questions before. She knew what to expect. I also knew that in a strange way she was right. Despite my fears, I was wildly attracted to Johnny. My experiences with Buddy McClure had repelled and attracted me. Johnny was not unlike Buddy with his grabbing hands and his efforts to overwhelm me. If it continued, I was afraid I wouldn't be able to say no, that it was only a matter of time before I would open the door to my apartment.

I got out of the car and mumbled my gratitude for the ride. She got out to walk with me, and quietly slipped her arm through mine as we headed toward the waiting boat. Later, as the boat pulled away, I could see Beryl through the misty haze, standing on the dock, her fur coat billowing out with Johnny's and her child.

I was alone. I knew I had to protect myself, not only from Johnny, but also from my own wounded psyche.

Johnny chased after me all summer long. Fortunately, it did not affect the show, which was a huge success. We got great reviews. Louella Parsons wrote that "Johnny Weissmuller, Esther Williams, and Morton Downey are the biggest forty cents worth of entertainment I ever saw." And Hollywood stars were frequently coming backstage for photo opportunities. Lana Turner even asked me for my autograph—such an inauspicious beginning for two lives that would soon intertwine in so many different and disparate ways.

Johnny's antics did make me wonder about what he put poor little Maureen O'Sullivan through in those "Me, Tarzan, you Jane" films. He was totally amoral. Years later, I met Maureen at a Hollywood fund-raiser and asked her how she handled the problem of the little leather flap he wore in the Tarzan films.

I said, "Didn't he always want to take it off and show it to you?"

"Yes," she said.

"What did you do?" I asked.

"Simple. I let him."

Billy Rose had sold a 49 percent partnership in the Aquacade to Chesterfield cigarettes, and although the fire marshals were not exactly pleased to find thousands of people inside a large wooden building being invited to "Light up a Chesterfield," somehow he managed to placate them. Rose always was clever enough to make a deal with the promoters of Treasure Island so that the box offices for competing shows had to be closed for an hour before each of our performances. Essentially, the Folies-Bergère, America! Cavalcade of a Nation, and Sally Rand's Nude Ranch (which wasn't really nude) had to wait until we had a full house before they could begin their shows.

In addition to swimming out of Johnny's clutches after every show, I had to listen to Morton Downey as I walked out onstage for each entrance. Morton had brought in Coca-Cola as an Aquacade sponsor, and thereby acquired a piece of the profits for himself. He was also Master of Ceremonies. He had a beautiful Irish tenor voice, and could be rather charming onstage, but around me he turned into another liquored-up old man who couldn't keep his hands to himself.

Each time we took that long walk across the stage, we both smiled and acknowledged the applause of the audience. But in sotto voce, heard only by me, Morton spewed four-letter words, regaling me with graphic descriptions of what he would like to do on and to my body.

Of course, it was useless to complain to Billy Rose about either Johnny or Morton Downey. Together they made a trio from hell, although Billy kept his distance after our initial sparring match at the St. Francis. He also kept his wallet closed where I was concerned. For the entire run of the Aquacade, he provided his star with only one bathing suit. I had to hang it up next to an electric light so that it would dry off a bit between shows. Not only was the suit permanently damp, it kept shrinking—this was before latex was invented. For a cover-up, I got Eleanor Holm's hand-me-down from the New York show. It was made out of heavy, shimmering metal, like chain mail, and on Eleanor it had been a stylish, ankle-length evening coat. But Eleanor was a petite woman, and on me it reached somewhere in the middle of my thighs and was too snug to fasten in front.

So I made my "glamorous entrance" to the audience at the Aquacade, wearing this too-short, too-tight jacket, with this lecher babbling filth as we both smiled to the crowd. When we finally reached the pool, Morton helped me remove the jacket. And, of course, he had a lot more to say when it came off. I could hardly wait to dive into the water so I didn't have to listen to his crass remarks anymore until, of course, the next show. When I surfaced, I swam to old music with new lyrics, *Tales from the Vienna Woods*, written by Johann Strauss Jr. and lyrics by Billy Rose—Billy certainly wasn't going to pay royalties for original music.

Downey's behavior would have been called sexual harassment (as would Weissmuller's and Rose's, for that matter), if we had thought of it back then. I was a seventeen-year-old girl and Morton Downey was a powerful man. It never crossed my mind to complain; I figured his mouth just went along with the deal. His babbling at me went in one ear and out the other. "At least," I thought, "I can dive in the water and be rid of him."

Downey eventually realized that he wasn't going to get a rise out of me with his filthy patter, so he decided to say something that *would* get a reaction. As we strolled out from behind the curtain one afternoon, he said, "Do you know how dumb you are? Do you know that your agent, Roger Marchetti, made a deal for you to get peanuts for swimming in this show while Eleanor Holm got two thousand dollars a week? I'm part owner of this show and I see the books." I had heard rumors about Holm's salary; but I wasn't upset because I was just a kid and Holm was already an established star. Besides, she was Billy Rose's wife. So I ignored Downey until he hit me with, "You think you're so smart, huh? Listen to this: Billy Rose is paying Roger Marchetti five hundred dollars a week for you, but I happen to know that you're getting a check for only one hundred twenty-five dollars."

For the first time, I stopped dead in the middle of the stage and turned to him, dumbfounded at what I heard. Compared to seventy-six dollars a month from I. Magnin, $125 a week was a fortune, but not if someone else was getting the other $375 that was rightfully mine.

"That's right, kid. See how dumb you are? You didn't even know."

I was in shock, and he kept tormenting me until we reached the pool. As he helped me take the jacket off, I turned to him and said, "Thank you, Morton, for that information. That's the most exciting thing you've ever said to me." I blew him a kiss and dove into the pool.

Although I had no proof of Marchetti's larceny until then, part of me had never trusted him. Roger had a brother who was a judge with a sterling reputation. I naively thought maybe that was a sign that honesty ran in the family. With the truth about his nasty little skimming operation burning in my ears more painfully than anything else Morton had ever said to me, I ran to a telephone right after the show. Dripping wet, I called Marchetti in Los Angeles. "How much money do you owe me, Roger? Morton Downey told me how much you've been getting and how much I've been paid."

"What money?" he said. Marchetti denied everything, and I realized that if I confronted Billy Rose and Morton Downey, they would deny it, too. I cried that night about being cheated and not being able to do anything about it. I was being exploited and laughed at by men in powerful positions, who used women for their own sleazy purposes. I knew there was nothing I could do at this point, so I went on saving my $125 a week and fleeing from Johnny after every show. While I had no immediate solution, I vowed this would never happen again, not on my watch. Brave words, indeed!

While I had been at Los Angeles City College, struggling through my algebra class, I had met Leonard Kovner, a young premed student who was headed for USC. I crammed with him when he had tests and read *Gray's Anatomy* with him. He was smart, handsome, dependable . . . and dull. I respected his intelligence, and his dedication to a future career in medicine. He loved me, or so he said, and even asked me to marry him. He was like some of the boys I had dated in high school after I was freed from the nightmare relationship with Buddy McClure. They were just Friday night rides to the swim meets. They even understood when I fell asleep on the way home.

Leonard and I wrote to each other while I was in San Francisco. Although we spoke on the telephone, I missed his warmth and tenderness. At the pool I couldn't help overhearing the swimmers as they came down from the cots in the diving tower after a romp with the Aquabelles. It was sexual promiscuity all right, but at least they were having more fun than I was. I had been so deeply scarred by Buddy that I was not about to allow myself to be "a girl on a cot in the diving tower." I was lonely. I needed more. I would marry the young med student who I liked well enough and who loved me so very much. I would be a good wife. This marriage to the doctor would protect me from those busy men with grasping hands—and in a way, from myself. I would be safe now from the advances of Johnny or Morton— or so I thought. As if that band of gold would be some kind of protection. It is amazing how naive a sweet seventeen-year-old's faith in the sanctity of marriage can be! I was looking forward to the end of the Aquacade in September and returning to Los Angeles as Mrs. Leonard Kovner, the wife of a doctor-to-be—and if Mrs. Clewell would have me back again, just maybe, as a future assistant buyer at I. Magnin.

Leonard came to see the show in June and we were married in the San Francisco suburb of Los Altos, on June 27, 1940, just before my eighteenth birthday. The cast of the Aquacade gave me a bridal shower, and we literally eloped between the shows. The Rose publicity unit thought it was a great promotional opportunity and our marriage made headlines in the San Francisco newspapers. Leonard had to return to school almost immediately, and I had to continue in the show; so we had a weekend honeymoon. I remember the beauty of going to bed on our wedding night, the relief of not having to fight for my life, the joy of welcoming a man's touch. I was so glad that I wasn't destroyed because of having been forced into sex. I thanked God for my normalcy and my welcoming of being loved, the right way.

However, I never shared with Leonard what I was going through with Billy, Johnny, or Roger Marchetti. I believed once more that my problems and their solution were mine alone.

CHAPTER 5

L. B. MAYER MEETS HIS MATCH
1940–41

*T*he San Francisco World's Fair—and the Aquacade along with it—ended on September 29, 1940, and I was happy to be finished with it. As everything was closing down, many of the swimmers and divers were clustered in corners, crying as they prepared to go back to school at Berkeley. The Aquacade had been a once-in-a-lifetime experience for them. I was dry-eyed. I just wanted to go home.

I had weathered some bitter moments; however, I could not allow those disappointments to diminish me. On the positive side, I had mastered a different style of swimming and had come to appreciate that swimming with grace and beauty could be as satisfying as swimming fast. I enjoyed developing the innovations that became known as "synchronized swimming." There was an exhilaration in performing. But that emotional lift was not sufficient to make me listen to the Hollywood executives who had come backstage during the run of the show, saying they were going to make me a movie star. I really didn't care. Besides, if my experience at the Aquacade with the dingy dressing room and the grabby hands was any indication, they could keep their "stardom." All things considered, I thought show business was no business for me.

"I don't think so," I would tell them.

They said, "But it's MGM!" as if this would make a big difference to me.

It didn't. I had a husband, a career at I. Magnin to look forward to, a whole new life. That would be enough for me.

This was the fall of 1940; Europe was already at war. France fell to the Nazis that June, and the Battle of Britain was raging. The United States was still technically neutral, but it was clear whose side we were on. Roosevelt was doing everything he could short of committing troops to help Churchill and the British. For Hollywood, however, the war had already begun, and movies such as *Flight Command, The Mortal Storm,* and *A Yank in the RAF* were already either in the theaters or in production. The Hollywood executives who came to see me had visions of featuring me in an escapist fantasy. "We're going to make a Technicolor swimming musical; you'll be an MGM star!" they promised. I didn't care. I knew what show business promises were worth. It was so easy to say no.

Now Jack Cummings, an MGM musical producer who had produced *Broadway Melody of 1937,* came to see me as an emissary from his uncle, L. B. Mayer, head of Metro-Goldwyn-Mayer. Unbeknownst to me, Mayer was determined to find a female athlete and turn her into big box office, much as 20th Century-Fox had done with Sonja Henie, three-time Olympic gold medalist in figure skating.

Sonja Henie had gone from the Olympics to the movies and become a star. Audiences flocked to her films, and she was a major revenue generator for 20th Century-Fox. She was also a true entrepreneur. After retiring from the movies, Henie continued to star in her own highly profitable traveling ice extravaganza, the Hollywood Ice Revue. It was said that she could make one turn of the rink and count the house.

In 1940, the pressure was on at MGM to come up with an answer to the ice skating musicals. Studios were known more for building on somebody else's ideas rather than originality . . . as long as it was profitable. "Melt the ice, get a swimmer, make it pretty!" cried Louis B. Mayer. I was the young female star of the San Francisco Aquacade who fit the bill.

"Do you know where MGM is?" Cummings asked me.

"Yes, of course. I grew up in South Los Angeles."

"Have you actually seen the studio?"

"Yes, when I passed by on the streetcar on my way to the beach."

MGM was on the red streetcar line from downtown Los Angeles to Venice Beach, where I swam and rode waves in the warm Los Angeles summers. I told Cummings that there was not enough money in all Hollywood to entice me to spend years of my life getting my sinuses filled with water and being pushed around by little guys with big libidos.

Cummings asked me how much I was paid by Billy Rose. I mumbled something incoherent. I didn't tell him about Marchetti. It was too embarrassing. Besides, I hadn't settled the score with Roger. Not yet.

He said, "Whatever it is, MGM will pay you better."

"No," I said firmly. "You'll have to find somebody else to make these movies. Besides, you'll probably make one swimming musical and never make another." It seemed foolish for me to throw away a potential career in retailing for such an unlikely shot as a swimming actress, which I didn't even want. In the back of my mind, of course, was the memory of my disastrous screen test at 20th Century-Fox, where I had been told that I had absolutely no talent, no future, nothing.

When I came back to Los Angeles, word of my ongoing refusal spread through Hollywood (which is really just like a small town when the gossip mill gets going). Harrison Carroll among other columnists in Los Angeles thought my refusal was amusing, if not naive, and he played it up. However, when I said no to Jack Cummings, it was like a declaration of war—nobody ever said no to MGM. It made its executives more tenacious than ever; the one who said no was the one they were determined to have.

I still found it easy to resist. I knew that making a star of a pretty swimmer was not their primary motivation for seeking me out. They were keenly aware of the box office receipts Fox had taken in with Sonja Henie. And as far as I was concerned, I was just a commodity, a girl in the right place at the right time, with the right equipment. They had tested Eleanor Holm. Despite the fact that she had been the star of the New York Aquacade and was Mrs. Billy Rose, this pert little champion from Queens talked out of the side of her mouth with an accent that rivaled Humphrey Bogart. Eleanor wasn't quite the Aphrodite image they sought. They wanted a tall, wholesome, all-American girl.

"All-American" was the operative word for Louis B. Mayer. He was an immigrant, an Eastern European Jew, whose "American ideal" was a "blond, blue-eyed shiksa." I was close enough—tall, tan, and with a nose that turned up at just the right angle. He was not alone. Harry Cohen, head of Columbia Pictures, once told Broadway star Judy Holliday, who wanted to re-create her stage role in *Born Yesterday* for the movies: "Jews make movies and write movies for Jews. They don't *star* in them." Mayer went so far as to claim that he didn't know his actual birthdate and decreed that he was born on the Fourth of July.

What Louis B. Mayer wanted, however, had absolutely nothing to do with what I wanted. Now that I was back in Los Angeles with a husband to take care of and children to look forward to, I wasn't going to subject myself to studio bosses, whatever they promised. I was going to be the good doctor's wife.

Leonard hadn't yet finished med school, and unfortunately his parents had run out of money. It was imperative that I have a job, not the promise of a career. I went back to Mrs. Clewell at I. Magnin. Of course, she had to do a few "I told you so's," but she gave me back my position on the fourth floor. I picked up where I left off, as a stock girl with plans of becoming assistant buyer of women's sports clothes. I fell back into the routine of the store, returning the dresses to the stock rooms and periodically modeling.

I. Magnin was the classiest store for women's clothing in Los Angeles and attracted its share of Hollywood stars. That, of course, was no guarantee they were big spenders. The Andrews Sisters used to come whenever there was a sale and would buy one of everything that was marked down below 50 percent. When those three ladies and their crazy stage mother swept into the store, it was like an invasion. I would rush around helping the salesgirls serve them, exhausted at having to restock the numerous items that had been strewn throughout three dressing rooms. They virtually took over the store.

Hidden behind dark glasses and scarves, Greta Garbo would

come in almost daily, paw through the entire inventory of the sweater department, and never buy a thing. She always felt she "deserved" an item gratis by virtue of the fact that she was Garbo. And we'd all have to pretend that she was just another shopper. Strict orders were given that no one was to address her in any manner that would reveal who she was.

However, the day Marlene Dietrich came in was the most memorable. She went straight to the designer floor and demanded a private showing. Because I was as tall as she, I was asked to model the dresses that she selected. I put on the first selection and knocked on her dressing room door. This deep voice said, "Come in, dahlingh." As I opened the door, I saw Dietrich, the world's most celebrated sex symbol, lounging on a chaise longue, totally nude. The rumors that Dietrich was an exhibitionist were obviously true—she loved the look of shock on my face and coolly proceeded to instruct me as to how I should model the dress. I was so taken aback by her apparent immodesty that I couldn't find my way out of the room. I kept walking into the multimirrored reflection of the door as she sat laughing seductively at my confusion.

One early summer day, almost a year after I had returned to the store, I was asked to model at the grand opening of the Arrowhead Springs Hotel, a posh mountain resort with an elaborate scalloped swimming pool. The store's top brass had come from San Francisco for the opening. Connie Conover and Julie Tressell, who were training me to become a buyer, insisted that as part of my training, I would need the experience of location modeling.

All of the executives were sitting poolside as we showed off the clothes. Grover Magnin, the family's elderly and distinguished patriarch and chairman of the board of the I. Magnin Company, came along with his staff. I was asked to model a cotton swim dress with a strawberry print, which had been very popular that summer, an $8.95 special. Conover also gave me a basket of strawberries as a prop to carry with my outfit. When I got to Grover Magnin, I asked, "Are you Mr. Magnin?" He nodded and answered: "Are you Esther Williams who swam at the San Francisco Aquacade last summer?" I was dumbfounded that he knew who I was. I didn't know what to say or do, so I took a strawberry and popped it right into his mouth. Grover Magnin sat sternly deciding whether this attempt at audacity should be reprimanded or applauded. The ensemble group of executives all dressed in their business suits stood up and applauded. Grover Magnin had no choice.

I was happy. It felt good that I had said no to MGM. I was living a normal life, married, working in a good stable business, where my bosses thought I was doing a good job. After my modeling session at Arrowhead, Mrs. Clewell told me that the store was going to make me an assistant buyer and give me a raise.

During all that time, Johnny Hyde, one of the top agents with the William Morris Agency, continued to call me at the store, begging me to at least visit MGM. Since I had rejected the offers from the studio directly, Jack Cummings had assigned Johnny Hyde the job of reeling me in. At that time, the talent agencies were virtually pressure arms of the studios. Every week Johnny Hyde would ask me, "Have you changed your mind?" And every week I would tell him not to call me at work.

One hot August day, the Santa Ana winds were kicking up and nobody was in the store. The place was empty. Conover came to find me and said, "Esther, look out the window. There's somebody in a limousine under the porte cochere. He says he's waiting for you."

I looked out at the limousine. It was Johnny Hyde, who was so small he could have been a jockey. He reportedly had had a sizzling love affair with Jean Harlow, and later he was responsible for bringing Marilyn Monroe—then Norma Jean Baker—to the studios. He also had a torrid romance with Marilyn. In many cases, that was how the agent-actress business worked.

Johnny sent up a note, because he knew I wouldn't talk to him if he came into the store. The note read, "Mr. L. B. Mayer is waiting to see you. You have an appointment today at 4:00. Can you get off work? You don't have to do anything about it, but at least you can tell your grandchildren that you met L. B. Mayer." It was signed, "Johnny Hyde."

All the salesgirls were my friends. With no customers in the store, they had nothing to do anyway and they told me that I absolutely *had* to go. "But I have nothing to wear!" I protested. Miss Conover looked at me and smiled. Hadn't she given me the red swimming suit when I met with Billy Rose?

Tressell led the chorus. "Don't worry. We'll take care of it. Just promise to tell us everything." They scoured the store for the right outfit and finally brought me a Chanel suit, with matching shoes and jewelry. Then they did my hair, helped me get dressed, and pushed me out the door.

As I was leaving I asked, "When do I have to get this back?" They told me the store closed at six, and everything had to be returned and hanging in its proper place when Magnin opened the next morning. I felt just like Cinderella.

I climbed into the back of the limo and said, "Hello, Mr. Hyde."

"Please call me Johnny." With that, the driver slammed the door and off we glided to Culver City.

When we arrived at MGM, the limo pulled up in front of the Irving Thalberg Building, the administrative headquarters of the most powerful movie studio in the world. I said to Johnny, "This isn't going to work if we walk in together. Alongside you, I'll look like a giraffe. You go ahead of me and be sitting down when I come in. I'll get the driver to escort me to the office." Somehow it felt natural for me, at nineteen, to give him orders, probably because he had been pleading with me to make this trip and because he was such a diminutive man.

He started to object, then thought better of it and said, "Okay, okay." He didn't want to have to explain to Mayer that he got me as far as the front door, only to have me leave before I got upstairs.

Mayer's office on the third floor was a masterpiece of Hollywood ingenuity. It was designed to intimidate, from the grandeur of the anterooms, where his secretaries sat, to the mammoth walnut doors that opened to his office. Once inside the office, a sixty-foot-long plush white carpet led to a white leather crescent-shaped desk, behind which sat Louis B. Mayer, the MGM potentate. I looked at all of these expensive surroundings and thought, "This is what Jack Cummings tried to sell me a year ago when I complained about the lousy quarters Billy Rose had provided."

As I walked that sixty-foot-long walk on this white carpet, Mayer scrutinized me through his thick glasses as if I were a piece of merchandise up for sale. It didn't bother me in the slightest. I. Magnin had trained me well. As far as I was concerned, Mayer was just another Grover Magnin sitting at the end of the runway. If I'd had a strawberry, I would have popped it in his mouth.

Sitting in back of him was a phalanx of executives—L. K. Sidney, Sam Katz, Eddie Mannix, and Benny Thau—all the top management who came to see "that swimmer who keeps saying no." Although I didn't know it then, they were the men who ran MGM. Like Mayer, they were all short. In this company, Johnny Hyde looked perfectly normal. I felt like Snow White with the dwarfs. When I reached the desk, I put out my hand and said, "Hello, Mr. Mayer." No one stood up.

"It's good to see you," Mr. Mayer mumbled weakly, taking my outstretched hand. Not, "It's good to see you *at last,* Miss Williams" . . . Not, "Thank you for coming to our studio, Miss Williams." . . . "It's good to see you" was the best I could expect.

"May I sit down?" I asked, quickly realizing we would then all be on the same level.

Mayer pointed to a chair opposite him. On the desk sat a large pitcher of orange juice and a glass. Mayer proceeded to pour himself a glass of juice and then drank it noisily.

"Could I please have one, too, Mr. Mayer?"

He seemed stunned by the request. "One what?"

"Orange juice. It's good for everybody," I said. He pushed his own glass toward me. "You don't have a clean glass?" I asked.

He looked at me, "You're a very forward young lady."

"Yes, I suppose I am," I said. "But I would still like a glass of orange juice . . . a *fresh* glass of orange juice." He shook his head and summoned his secretary, who poured me the juice. She didn't offer any to the others, however.

Mayer studied me as I drank the orange juice and said, "You're very tall."

At this point, I shot an I-told-you-so look at Johnny Hyde.

"I told Johnny," I said to Mayer. "I told him I was too tall." I put my orange juice back on the desk. And then I stood up, rising to my full five feet eight inches, plus the three-inch heels that Julie Tressell had chosen for me. I turned my best model turn and began that long trip back across the room to the door.

"Wait a minute! Come back!" Mayer called out, "You're not *that* tall. Ingrid Bergman is *very* tall."

He looked at the group of obedient executives, and as if on cue they nodded briskly in agreement. "When she works with Charles

Boyer, he stands on a box. Alan Ladd is very short and he works with Loretta Young, who is tall." He warmed to the job: "When he's on a horse and he's shorter than she is, they dig a hole for her horse." Then, abruptly, he got to the point: "Would you like to be part of this studio?"

"I'm not sure," I said honestly. "I'd like to see a dressing room. When Billy Rose said he would make me a star, he gave me a cubicle with a cracked mirror and a broken cot."

Mayer tried to look exasperated, but he was beaming with pleasure. "Somebody take Miss Williams to see one of the star dressing rooms."

Benny Thau gave me the tour. He showed me where I would be trained, where I would learn to sing and dance, and where I would learn how to walk into a room like an MGM lady. But it was the star dressing rooms that really got me. The men's dressing rooms were on one side of the studio; the women's were on the other, near the makeup department.

The MGM star dressing rooms would have impressed anyone. I was awed by the names on the doors. "Lana Turner" was on A, "Greer Garson" on B, "Judy Garland" on C, "Joan Crawford" on D, and "Katharine Hepburn" on E. Benny Thau, talking like a real estate agent, took me into Greer Garson's dressing room. It was beautiful, a small tastefully decorated apartment, complete with living room, kitchen, and bathroom, larger than the apartment I shared with Leonard.

I looked at Benny and said, "How am I supposed to get one?" I figured that maybe somebody had to die, or get fired, or be in a box office disaster. Thau explained that eventually one would be mine, if I earned it. I thought, "I'd like to be in this room, I'd like this to be mine." The dressing room sold me, just as Mayer knew it would.

Benny asked softly, "Now, would you like to talk about a contract?"

"Please give me some time to think about it," I said. I truly didn't know what to answer, because in addition to having my own doubts about working in show business again, I knew I'd have to contend with the objections of my husband. Leonard had not liked the idea of me being in show business from the moment we married. He made me promise that when the Aquacade was over I would "settle down" and be a respectable doctor's wife. He had his own struggles. As a medical student, he had decided to specialize in osteopathic surgery, which was then a pioneering field of medicine. After Leonard's family had run out of money, I was picking up the cost of his tuition, as well as paying the rent—all on my I. Magnin salary. Leonard felt the studios were all run by thieves.

After my meeting with Mayer, Johnny Hyde had his driver take me back to I. Magnin. I thought about all that had happened that afternoon, how different my life would be if I were to believe the men I had just met. They sounded so convincing. Could it all be possible? Maybe the Aquacade was just a rotten example. Maybe I had been too young. It was now a year later, and I was a married woman.

It was a little before 6:00 P.M. when the limousine dropped me off at I. Magnin. Unlike Cinderella, I made it back in time. I returned the Chanel suit and the shoes and the jewelry to their proper places in the store, and then answered all the girls' questions. "Yes, I was offered a contract." "No, I hadn't seen Clark Gable." I laughed about the possibility of having it all. I helped close the store that night and caught the bus home.

Leonard and I lived on Parkman Place in a blue-collar district of Los Angeles known as Silver Lake. We had a small apartment in a set of units that were like little cottages. The rents were cheap and there was a nearby bus stop so I could get to and from I. Magnin. Leonard was home early that evening. As I came through the door, I blurted out a sentence as if there were no spaces between the words, "LouisBMayersentalimousineformethisafternoonandofferedmean-opportunitytobeinthemovies."

Leonard looked at me quizzically as if he understood nothing. I took a deep breath and slowed to what seemed like a snail's pace. "I've been offered a contract at MGM, and they say they really want me to make a swimming movie. This is an opportunity that will bring in a lot of tuition money." I tried to sell the idea as something that would make it easier for him to finish med school, but as I knew, he was totally against the idea of my signing a contract with any studio. I begged him not to argue and asked him to take me to see MGM's *Ziegfeld Girl* at Grauman's Chinese Theater, in Holly-wood. Perhaps the reality of the movies would alter his opinion.

Not a chance. As we sat there in the dark theater, Leonard was in a terrible mood, but I was entranced. It was a wonderful fantasy extravaganza about three girls—Lana Turner, Judy Garland, and Hedy Lamarr—who are discovered by Ziegfeld and become stars in his Follies. The audience ooohed and aaaahed over the intricate Busby Berkeley musical numbers with a hundred showgirls dressed in the elaborate costumes.

As Tony Martin sang "You Stepped Out of a Dream," I was swept up in the glamour of it all. I thought back to what Benny Thau had said that afternoon, "This could be yours." I thought about that huge office and everybody I had met, the sets, the buildings, and most of all, the star dressing rooms. I watched Judy Garland singing "I'm Always Chasing Rainbows," and I gaped at how beautifully dressed all the stars were. I thought about standing in the MGM wardrobe department and being fitted for clothes like that. I had this strong, long-legged, long-waisted swimmer's body, and I knew I could carry those clothes with my height. I knew I could learn to walk down those stairs like Lana Turner had in the movie.

Ziegfeld Girl was the most lavish and exciting musical film I'd ever seen, and now I was being offered a chance to be a part of that world. Suddenly, after saying no for all this time, I was starstruck. I was hooked on the possibility that all those dreams could actually come true.

Later, back home, however, Leonard remained unimpressed and rigid about my not accepting the offer. Show business was to be avoided. "You've already been burned," he insisted. I said nothing. What he said was true, yet why was he so threatened by the possibility of a career for me in the movies? Why was he so sure that I wouldn't be able to handle it? Didn't he feel he could trust me? Despite the fact that I had felt unfulfilled by the San Francisco experience, it had still been a critical success. And I had saved enough money to help pay his way through his studies. Or did he just want to keep me home? I could see our marriage was already in trouble. Trying to understand him, my mind flashed back to Leonard's background.

His parents were hard-working people who ran a mom and pop grocery store not far from where we lived in Silver Lake. They had come from Russia, and instead of settling in New York City's Hester Street, they had traveled to California where they believed that there were more opportunities for living well. They had four children, twin girls and two boys. Leonard was the youngest. His brother, Victor, was already an osteopathic surgeon.

His parents had sacrificed to try to make a good life for their children, but Leonard never appreciated them. He was condescending and demeaning. I remember a terrible scene where he said, "They're Jewish, but I'm not."

I couldn't understand. "How can you say that your parents are something that you're not?" I asked.

"I am *not* Jewish," he snapped. "I am going to change my name from Kovner to Connor."

"Connor is an Irish name. What are you talking about?"

"I'm going to separate myself from my parents."

If I had been astonished before, now I was horrified. "Do you know what a sacrifice they made for you?" I asked him. "Don't you know how good they are? Don't you appreciate them? What does being Jewish have to do with anything? And what happens when we have children?" Children were very important to me. I wanted a big family.

Leonard contorted his face and poked his finger into my chest. "I don't want to have children—and I especially don't want to bring another Williams kid into this world!"

I was stunned. It was as if he'd slapped me in the face. "Why do you say that?"

"Because I don't like your mother," he answered matter-of-factly.

"You don't like my mother, so you don't want my child? That's the dumbest thing I've ever heard." I realized suddenly I was married to someone I didn't know. This was all too crazy!

The truth, of course, was that I hadn't known Leonard at all. I had married him first because he was Tyrone Power handsome, and second because I was repelled by all the rampant promiscuity that I saw at the Aquacade, which I instinctively knew was the wrong reason to marry anyone. He seemed so threatened by the men who apparently lusted after me that I, too, had vowed never to be in show business again. I talked myself into believing that a wedding ring would shield me, and I had convinced myself that love would come in time. However, this dark side of Leonard Kovner gave me pause.

As I watched the final credits roll on *Ziegfeld Girl*, my mind was made up. I worked up my courage and told Leonard, "I want that. For me."

By the time we got home, we weren't speaking. Leonard was so angry that when we went to bed, he just turned over and went to sleep. I lay wide awake, measuring the decisions I would now make. I was keenly aware of the financial realities. It would take me years to learn how to be a buyer at I. Magnin at seventy-six dollars a month, and MGM wanted to pay me $350 a week while I learned how to be a movie star. This was 1941. The sum was staggering!

And finally I thought, "I *want* to be at MGM." My family had not been able to afford to send me to USC. MGM would be my finishing school.

It was still dark when I got up early that morning. Leonard stayed in bed crunched into a fetal position murmuring, "Please don't do it, please don't do it, please don't do it." He was chanting the words like a mantra—I think he knew I had made my decision, but he couldn't (or wouldn't) stop.

I went to the kitchen and called my mother. I felt so alone. "Mom, I think I'm going to sign a contract at MGM."

While I was talking, Leonard came into the kitchen and snatched the phone out of my hand. I felt myself falling back against the wall. He just kept muttering, "Please, please don't do it, don't do it, don't go to that meeting."

Up until then, I didn't even think he was capable of that kind of anger. He just kept mumbling the same thing over and over. I thought he had gone mad. I had to get out of there.

I backed away slowly and burst out the door. I ran through the streets of Silver Lake in my nightgown with Leonard yelling at me in crazed pursuit. I doubled back to the rear of the apartments and ducked into the landlady's cottage. Seeing how distraught I was, she quickly understood that I was being chased and locked the door behind me. Leonard was upon the apartment almost immediately. He banged on the door shouting the same words. I hid in the bedroom until the banging stopped.

I sat and told this dear lady, who had been so sweet to me, the whole story of my marriage and of my opportunity at MGM. We laughed and cried together. She made tea and we talked all day. Most important, she said, "Do it! Do it! This is a wonderful thing, to have this opportunity. Your life will open up. You are so beautiful and you can do so many things, and there is so much you have to learn." She was a maternal arm around the shoulder when I needed one, and she said just what I needed to hear at that moment.

"Would you like to stay here tonight?" She was offering me the safety of her home.

"I can't go back there," I admitted. I slept at her house and her husband double-checked all the doors and windows.

The next morning, when Leonard took his bus to medical school, I packed my things and took refuge in my mother's house. I cried bitterly as I told her what had happened the night before and how frightened I was to be with Leonard. I knew a divorce was inevitable. Despite my fear of Leonard, the idea of divorce was as difficult a decision as any I'd ever have to make. This would be the first divorce in the Williams family. But Bula gave me strength. Don't fear life's experience, but embrace it, she said. Divorce was a social dissolution of an unworkable contract, not a sin from above. She would later testify for me in the divorce proceedings.

Leonard moved from Silver Lake to take residency in the hospital. I later learned he was having an affair with a nurse all the time I was working and paying his bills.

I called Mr. Mayer's office right away and told them I would accept his offer. Johnny Hyde was assigned to handle the contract details. Before I could sign anything, I had a problem to solve. I told Johnny, "There's somebody I've got to see."

Johnny took me in the limo to Roger Marchetti's office in the elegant Hancock Park area of Los Angeles. Marchetti had foreclosed on some poor client who had lived in this house and was using it as an office. As far as I knew, my contract with Marchetti as my agent/manager was still in force. He owned 20 percent of me—for my lifetime. I hadn't exactly told Johnny the situation, but he must have sensed something because he said, "Esther, let me help you deal with this guy."

That was the last thing I wanted. "Help me? Johnny, you're a famous agent. If you ever show your face, Marchetti will know something is happening. He's no fool. The only way to help me is to stay away." That was all I needed to say. Johnny had the driver park down the street, and I walked the rest of the way to Marchetti's office, my heart thudding all the way. I was entering a pool with a hammerhead shark.

Roger Marchetti was seated behind his desk, a small, stocky man, with an oily complexion.

"What can I do for you, Esther?"

I came right to the point. "Mr. Marchetti, I was being paid $500 a week for my work in the Aquacade, and I received only $125 a week. You pocketed the rest, and don't tell me you don't know what I'm talking about."

He leaned forward in his chair, interrupting me. "I hear MGM has been having meetings with you."

This took me by surprise because Johnny assured me that nothing appeared in the columns about my discussions with MGM. Marchetti had been keeping his ear to the ground.

"I want to make this clear. I am no longer your client," I continued.

"Oh? Really?" He had already taken the contract out of his filing cabinet and put it into a desk drawer while we were talking. He knew I had scant proof of his thievery.

"I'll never sign a movie contract. I've hated show business from the beginning. I never liked the Aquacade with all its slimy characters." This confrontation was fast becoming my first really important acting job. I had to get Marchetti to tear up that contract.

My voice softened. "There's no point in holding me. Leonard and I are going to New York where I'm going to pursue a career in fashion merchandising. I'm going to learn to be a buyer."

"What do you want me to do?" he asked with that manufactured smile.

"Please tear up my contract. It's not worth anything to you." I think I squeezed a tear from my eye.

He reached into the drawer and placed the contract on the desk.

"I tell you what, Esther. You and Leonard go to New York, and let's see how long you stay when some studio waves serious money in your face. Meanwhile, I'll hang on to our contract."

He swiveled in his chair and picked up the phone as if to make a call. It was a gesture of dismissal.

That did it. I stood up and moved back from his desk. I was no longer acting. "You're a crook," I shouted. "You stole my money. I'm going to call your brother. I know how close the two of you are. I'll tell him what you're doing. He's got to know that you've done this before. And I have the proof. It'll be in all the newspapers."

My threat seemed to have hit home. Marchetti knew that I had access to the press. The last thing he needed was to deal with his "distinguished" brother; besides, he figured he'd got his money from me. And maybe he did believe I would never sign a contract with MGM. His cool demeanor quickly evaporated. He slammed the phone down and looked up at me. "I don't have to put up with any more of this crap!" He tore the contract into shreds, threw the pieces in the wastebasket and set them on fire with a match. I watched the flames crackle, the smoke rise. "Now, get out!"

"Good-bye, Mr. Marchetti," I said. "Thank you very much." I turned, straightened my shoulders, and walked out the door.

Back on the street, I waited for Johnny Hyde to pull up in the gleaming, black limo. Marchetti was peering through the window curtains. I looked up at him and waved.

I got in the limo, turned to Johnny, and said, "Let's go sign a con-tract."

CHAPTER 6

MGM UNIVERSITY
1941

After I signed my contract, I was escorted to a dressing room in one of those wooden buildings that must have dated back to World War I, when Louis B. Mayer started making pictures in California. The dressing room wasn't grand. It certainly wasn't the dressing room Benny Thau had shown me. But I was just a contract player, and this was the dressing compound to which all new contractees and featured players were assigned. At least it was dry. From my window, I could look down on the star dressing rooms, knowing that the pot of gold at the end of the rainbow was just downstairs to the east, with a star on the door.

I was welcomed at MGM with open arms. They had tried for one year to get me to the studio and I had said no. And now I was here. They were all congratulating each other because this difficult girl had signed at last.

Timing *was* everything and I knew it. Although my instincts told me I wasn't ready for the camera, I knew that the Aquacade and the Sonja Henie ice skating extravaganzas were big box office successes, and that the kind of films they were talking about for me just might work. I had two clauses put in my contract that would serve me well. One entitled me to a guest pass at the Beverly Hills Hotel swimming pool where I could swim on a daily basis; the other stipulated that I would require a nine-month "gestation" period before they could use me in front of the camera. If it took nine months for a baby to be born, I figured my "birth" from Esther Williams the swimmer to Esther Williams the movie actress would not be much different.

The studio executives thought the nine-month clause was the funniest thing they'd ever heard. They all laughed and winked at each other and said, "Isn't she cute, and naive, and insecure!" But you don't call it insecurity when you're trained to be a champion— you call it reality. I knew that if I didn't show promise from the beginning, the studio would close me down in six months. I would hedge my bet, give myself enough room to breathe (or enough rope to hang myself), and grab a nine-month shot at success before returning, once more, hat in hand to I. Magnin.

When I signed with MGM that October of 1941, my contract read $350 a week. It was a fortune compared to the $76 a month I earned as a stock clerk. I had neither the courage nor the experience to ask for more, at least not at the beginning. Johnny Hyde, who was now my agent, recommended that I take what was offered. He told me that when the studio picked up my option, the salary would increase. I always had the impression that the agents were working hand in hand with the studios, and I wasn't wrong. There was always a payoff for bringing the horses to the stall. I learned later from Sam Katz that Johnny Hyde had received a sizable bonus plus his contractual 10 percent for having delivered me to the MGM stable.

MGM University—that's what I called my apprenticeship on the studio lot, the college education my family couldn't pay for. The studios groomed their discoveries for stardom. They took young people who had a certain "something"—a look, a voice, a sparkle, or a smolder—and turned them into professionals. The publicity department generated images and notoriety, but only a handful of these hopefuls were singled out for stardom by the executives. The rest were left to struggle for supporting roles. And then there were those who never got in front of a camera at all.

I was immersed in acting lessons, singing lessons, dance lessons, diction lessons. There were also never-ending photo sessions and interviews with fan magazines. These were the MGM stepping stones to "stardom." In one summer, I appeared on the covers of twenty-seven fan magazines simultaneously.

Bags of fan mail enabled the studio to gauge an actor's popularity, which was more a measure of how successful a job the publicity department had done. The publicity department was ordered to conceal the quantity and the contents of the fan mail.

Every day that I reported to the studio, I would fight off a nagging suspicion that I really didn't belong there. I kept worrying that it would just be a matter of time before Sam Katz or Louis B. Mayer realized that all these lessons weren't going to be enough to transform a swimmer into a viable film property. But I knew that no matter what happened, this experience would turn out to be worthwhile. It was to be my "finishing school." The studio was going to teach me how to look and sound like a lady—an MGM lady. If the studio changed its mind and decided not to make that swimming movie, I'd still have my diploma.

Although Mayer liked the way I looked, he was dissatisfied with the sound of my voice, that flat, midwestern *a* that I had inherited from my Kansas-born parents. Any regional accent for his "American" leading lady was a problem to be dealt with immediately. Mayer sent me to Gertrude Fogler, a well-respected Beverly Hills voice and diction coach. Mayer was so satisfied with my "vocal transformation" that he brought Fogler to the studio, where she was to homogenize everyone's speech, eliminating everything from southern drawls and Texas twangs to unintelligible German gutturals. She could have made Maurice Chevalier speak English like Laurence Olivier, but then who would have wanted that? With actors like Chevalier, Ricardo Montalban, and Louis Jourdan, she knew enough to leave just a charming touch of their native accent. We always referred to our teachers as "Miss"—*Miss* Fogler, *Miss* Burns, *Miss* Bates. And we in turn were to be addressed as *Miss* Williams, *Miss* Allyson, or *Miss* Turner. I was told that when John Gilbert first met Greta Garbo on the set, he said, "Hello, Greta, nice to meet you," and she responded, "I am *Miss* Garbo."

We were sent to Jeanette Bates for dance and movement. MGM

girls had to learn to walk down stairs, in heels, without ever looking at their feet. Posture was a serious matter to Jeanette—or rather, *Miss* Bates. We studied simple movements, such as getting up out of a chair, keeping your knees together, making exits and entrances, and how to tuck your bottom in when you walked. "An actress has to have a look of authority when she enters a room," Miss Bates would intone. Years later, following a hip replacement operation, my doctors told me I would never walk in heels again. Six weeks after my surgery, I was walking down a Macy's runway in three-inch heels, flanked by twelve swimsuit models. Those endless repetitions of Jeanette Bates's exercises during those early years prepared me for a lifetime of good posture.

I learned basic ballet moves, which I later used to choreograph my "water ballets" in the pool. Miss Bates talked about the importance of body language, the language of athletes. She seemed to have an appreciation for my height. I watched her graceful moves from one exercise to another. I learned to carry my height with pride, something I was definitely going to need in and out of the water.

My singing teacher, Harriet Lee, was what one might call a realist. She took whatever voice I had and taught me how to use it. She didn't attempt to teach me how to read music. She taught just enough vocal technique to handle a song. "Simple basics, Miss Williams. Just stay on key," she said. Eventually a song I would perform with Ricardo Montalban, "Baby, It's Cold Outside," would win an Academy Award. Simple and on key.

I didn't really like singing. I felt I didn't have much of a voice. Harriet said, "No one expects you to be another Judy Garland. Just feel comfortable with your song, whatever the lyrics may convey. Think of it as an acting scene with dialogue."

When I was asked to sing *"Acércate Más"* ("Come Closer to Me") in Spanish to Van Johnson in *Easy to Wed*, I went to Harriet with misgivings not only about singing, but about "an acting scene with dialogue" and not even in a language that I understood. "How am I supposed to sing *this* song? It's in Spanish!"

Harriet's answer was simple and sensible, MGM sensible: "If they want you to sing in Spanish, you sing in Spanish."

Lillian Burns was the drama coach, and she clearly made her mark on the leading ladies of MGM. Burns was a proponent of the one-size-fits-all school of acting. She was oblivious to the fact that one might be taller, fatter, thinner, older, younger than she. When she left a room, she left in a huff. Up went her shoulders, up went her chin. Then she snapped her head back—you could almost hear it—and sailed out the door. We all learned the same mannered technique. Ava Gardner snapped her neck; so did Lana Turner and Janet Leigh. Even little Margaret O'Brien left a room that way. It's a wonder we all didn't end up at the chiropractor's.

Even though Lana Turner, Donna Reed, Debbie Reynolds, and Janet Leigh all swore by her, Lillian Burns and I were a mismatch. I knew instinctively that a five-foot-eight-inch girl could not behave like a feisty, indignant little poodle with quick, jerky movements. Lillian's teaching method consisted of reading chunks of dialogue in her style, which we were then expected to imitate, but her melodramatic incantations didn't work for me. I thought I had avoided picking up most of her mannerisms, but seven years of classes were bound to leave their mark. I remember watching *Neptune's Daughter* and when I saw my nostrils flare and my eyes pop out of my head, I thought, "Oh Lillian, you sneaked those into my subconscious!"

It was mandatory at MGM to work with Lillian Burns. She was married to George Sidney, whose father, L. K. Sidney, was a powerful marketing executive at the studio. Early on, George Sidney was a screen test director. Although screen tests were common for newcomers, stars also tested, but for different purposes. Stars were generally assigned scripts by the executive office. Established stars would frequently "test" for a movie despite their current standing, in order to satisfy film producers. Other times stars might ask to be tested for films that they thought would best suit them, even demand to be tested for roles they coveted, sometimes even threatening to quit or tear up their contract, if they weren't allowed to test. Paulette Goddard, Katharine Hepburn, and Tallulah Bankhead all tested for David O. Selznick for *Gone With the Wind* before Vivien Leigh was chosen.

Three weeks after I signed my contract, George Sidney directed my initial test, primarily to establish my "likeability" quotient on camera for the executive parade on "the third floor." (MGM executives were referred to as "the third floor," since they all had their offices on the third floor of the administration building adjacent to the studio soundstages.) It seemed to me that "the third floor" should have put the horse before the cart and tested me before I signed my contract; but they were intent on creating at least one swimming movie, and my Billy Rose Aquacade performance in San Francisco had clinched the deal.

George was clever enough to test me without dialogue, just in case Gertrude Fogler had not succeeded in entirely eradicating my Kansas twang. Instead of giving me scripted dialogue, he had me perform a one-woman fashion show. I wore four different outfits—an evening gown, a suit, a cocktail dress, and a bathing suit. First I put on the evening gown and George directed me to twirl. Then he shouted, "Cut!" and I changed into the suit. Another twirl. "Cut!" Third, the cocktail dress. "Twirl! Cut! Change!" And last, and most important, a white two-piece swimsuit. Through the magic of the editing room and dissolves each spin blended the series of costume changes, which finished, of course, in the swimsuit. George talked me through each turn throughout the test, distracting me from my fear of the camera. "Hold that!" he would say. "Do you always use a nose clip when you swim?" "Has any man ever tried to get your swimsuit off?" I thought of Johnny Weissmuller immediately, and my animated reactions compensated for any lack of dialogue. George wanted to show "an Esther whose personality would take her wherever she wanted to go," and in beautiful Technicolor, which at the time was still fairly new. What he captured was a pure, unadulterated teenage girl who felt confident in a swimsuit. It looked fresh. I knew it could have gone either way, but the studio bought the vision, congratulating themselves once more on how right they had been in signing me.

The MGM commissary was a remarkable experience. It was not only the local watering hole, but a respite from whatever was going on in those soundstages. It was on a little side street just past the East Gate, across from the barbershop. Although the tabletops in the commissary were Formica, the clientele was pure platinum. What an amazing sight! I saw the faces of people I had only seen on my neighborhood movie theater screen.

Louis B. Mayer had clearly put his stamp on the commissary, if not his own chef. The chicken soup was prepared according to his mother's recipe. With a matzo ball! For a local girl from Kansas-bred parents, the food seemed nothing short of exotic. Bagels, lox, and pastrami were not the staples of my mother's kitchen.

The studio commissary was perhaps the only area where executives and stars, starlets and crew mingled. This was as democratic as it was to get. As I stood in line waiting for a place at a table, I found it hard not to gawk while the Hollywood greats table-hopped. Perhaps I was staring, but if so, no one paid any attention to me. In one corner, I saw Spencer Tracy having lunch with Katharine Hepburn. They were eating and talking, just like ordinary people. It seemed odd that stars in the Hollywood stratosphere would be doing something so . . . normal. But I was there, too. I knew I'd come a long way from Southwest Los Angeles.

I remember seeing Lana Turner and Robert Taylor having sandwiches. She had just finished *Johnny Eager* and was in all her blond gorgeousness. Robert Taylor, who had done *Camille* with Greta Garbo, was even prettier than she was, and she was the prettiest woman in the world, or so I thought. I remembered having met Lana Turner when she visited backstage at the Aquacade, but I was sure she wouldn't remember me. I just sat and looked. I was on the inside now, not outside on the curb wishing someone would give me an autograph. I was in this rarefied air with the makers of those beautiful movies. I looked at Lana Turner there across the room and I thought, "That is glamour!"

The stars had all learned from the experts, and through these studio Svengalis they had become the personification of glamour. They smelled good and they looked good; and they had lovely, gracious manners. They weren't yelling from diving platforms. I knew all the mythology about how Lana had been "discovered" at the counter at Schwab's drugstore on Sunset Boulevard. I also knew she had been just plain Julia Jean Mildred Frances Turner, a buxom brunette from Hollywood High, before the MGM star factory transformed her into Lana, the perfectly coiffed, perfectly dressed blond movie star I saw sitting across the room. She had taken Fogler's elocution classes, Lillian Burns's acting classes, and all the other lessons that I was now going through, and she had emerged a star. For me, that was proof positive that the system worked. She was the perfect product of the factory. Whatever else people thought of her, Lana Turner was a bona fide graduate of MGM U, if not its valedictorian. As I looked at her, I thought that somehow I was going to do that, too.

One thing I learned for sure is that everybody looked at everybody else in that studio, and you had better look your best when they see you. I knew that from now on, whenever I came through that commissary door I was going to have my makeup on straight and every hair in place.

Meanwhile, I kept swimming, taking advantage of the guest card MGM provided for me at the Beverly Hills Hotel, known locally as the Pink Palace. It became almost a Hollywood cliché to have yourself paged as you lounged by the pool of the Beverly Hills Hotel—I must have been one of the few people who actually wanted to swim in it.

Every morning I'd go to the pool and swim my laps, then go to my studio appointments. One day as I was doing laps, Eddie, one of the pool boys who handed out the towels, ran alongside the pool and said to me, "Esther, you're wanted on the phone."

Eddie and I had become friends. He was closer to my age than anyone else at the pool, and I was only a few years beyond handing out towels at the city playground pool myself. I hated to interrupt my workout, not only because it broke the rhythm of my exercise, but also because it broke my mental concentration. I used my laps to review what people had said to me at meetings and in my classes, and to sort out important decisions.

"Who is it, Eddie?" I yelled.

"It's Ida Koverman."

"Oh."

You didn't say no to Ida Koverman's call. She was Louis B. Mayer's assistant, and a power behind the throne. She was accustomed to being in the corridors of power—before she began working at MGM, she'd been the secretary to Herbert Hoover. Now she had her own secretary and two assistants. L.B. relied on her judgment. I had been told by Harriet Lee that it was Ida who had encouraged Mayer to feature classical artists in the movies, a decision that had paid off hand-somely for the studio. She was instrumental in bringing opera stars Ezio Pinza, Helen Traubel, and Lauritz Melchior to MGM. In 1935, Ida Koverman brought a teenager to Mayer's attention, a "little girl with a great big voice" named Frances Gumm, who was soon rechris-tened Judy Garland. Harriet had also advised me that Ida could be a wonderful person to talk to. She was an understanding supporter of the younger people at the studio. "If she's your friend," said Harriet, "she'll look after you. You're all set."

I dried my hand and picked up the receiver. "L.B. wants to see you this morning, Esther," Ida said.

"Mrs. Koverman, you can't imagine what I look like right now. I'm a sight. I'm dripping wet. I have no makeup, a wet head, a pair of old sloppy slacks and a baggy old sweater. Couldn't we do this to-morrow?" My appearance was light years removed from Lana Turner's glamour in the commissary, and definitely not fit for a visit with L. B. Mayer.

"Esther, when Mr. Mayer says 'Come,' you come right now," she commanded crisply.

So I jumped in my little Dodge Coupe, which Johnny Hyde in-sisted I buy ("You can't take the bus, Esther. You've got an image to maintain now"), and sped for Culver City. As I drove, I tried to figure out the reason behind the command appearance before Mr. Mayer. I'd signed my contract. I was taking my classes. They liked my test. I couldn't think of anything I had done to upset anyone. After all, I'd only been there about three weeks. If Ida knew why I'd been sum-moned, she didn't let on.

I ran up to the third floor executive offices looking like a dish rag and walked into Ida Koverman's office. Her face fell. "My God, you look like a drowned rat! You can't go in to see Mr. Mayer like that. Fix yourself up. Fast!"

"I told you," I said.

She opened her desk drawer and handed me a lipstick and a comb. "Pull yourself together and make it speedy. He's waiting!" I was quick about it, since I was certain that Louis B. Mayer was im-patiently tapping his toe, waiting for me behind that white desk.

As I went through his office door, I took off my glasses. I'm terribly nearsighted, but vanity demanded that I get rid of my glasses before I began that long walk across the thick carpeting. However, without them I could make out just a blur of someone in addition to Mayer in the room. As I got closer, I could tell from the back of his head that it was a man with large ears. As I approached the desk, I thought I realized who that "somebody" was: Clark Gable.

He stood up to greet me, looking every inch the handsome, dashing matinee idol that he was. Those dimples! His wicked smile and his flirting eyes were even more magnetic in person than they were on-screen. As Mayer said, "Miss Williams, I would like you to meet Mr. Clark Gable," he put out a big paw for me to shake.

When I shook his hand, it was like making contact with a live wire. It was electricity. I couldn't let go. Gable was like a force of nature. I'd had an adolescent crush on him ever since *Gone With the Wind*, when I'd seen his face about forty feet high at the Balboa Theater in southwest Los Angeles. He *was* Rhett Butler. As we shook hands, I felt like I was going to dissolve into my shoes. My knees began to shake, and I uttered the world's dumbest thing, "Mr. Gable, I've heard so much about you."

He flashed me that 1,000-megawatt Rhett Butler smile. He looked over at Mr. Mayer. "I've heard a lot about you, too, Miss Williams."

When Mayer said, "Sit down, Esther," it was not a moment too soon. My trembling knees had turned to jelly, and it would have been only a few more moments before I collapsed anyway. Mayer was talking, but I was in such a state of shock I could hardly comprehend what he was saying. He mentioned something about Gable and Lana Turner making a film called *Honky Tonk*, and that they were supposed to star together in *Somewhere I'll Find You*. I couldn't take my eyes off Gable's face. Mayer was whining about Lana marrying Artie Shaw, "That damn Lana went off. Never even asked me . . ."

Mayer was practically talking to himself, getting all worked up about Lana's insubordination. He mentioned that the picture with Gable was to begin next week. "Who cares?" I thought. "Here's Gable right in front of me. What did all this stuff about Lana Turner have to do with me?"

I was still sitting there, dreamily drinking in Gable, when Mayer finally got to the point. "As a result of Miss Turner's total neglect of her obligations under the terms of her contract with this studio, I am going to replace her on this film with an unknown girl." Now he had my attention. "Miss Williams, please report to Lillian Burns and begin rehearsing immediately. Mr. Gable will screen test with you in three days."

I could hardly move when I stood up. Gable sensed my problem. He put his arm around me and walked me to the door. I felt even dizzier with that strong arm around me. "It was wonderful to meet you, Mr. Gable," I said. "I guess I have to go to work now."

"I'll see you in three days," he said with a smile. My head was throbbing, as if somebody had set off an explosion.

Ida Koverman was waiting for me. "How'd it go?"

"Mr. Mayer wants me to make a screen test with Clark Gable," I said.

"I know," she replied.

I thought, "Ida Koverman, you knew what was waiting for me. Did you really think a lipstick and a comb would be enough?" As it turned out, that's all I needed.

When I reported to Lillian Burns, she had already looked over the four onionskin pages of dialogue and sniffed that it was highly unlikely that Clark Gable would actually do *my* screen test, but I really didn't mind. Sitting there was Dan Dailey, a featured player who'd just finished *Ziegfeld Girl*, waiting to do the rehearsals with me. To a kid who had been on the lot for less than a month, Dan Dailey was a star. We went right to work reading the scene. As Dan and I began reading the dialogue, Lillian drifted over to the window, totally ignoring the scene, and yelled to a passing producer about casting one of her favorites in an upcoming film. It was clear that Lillian and I were not a match made in MGM heaven. I was accustomed to her routine by now. Dan and I continued as if she weren't there.

George Sidney called over and told me, "You and Dailey report to Stage 28 tomorrow morning at 9 A.M., camera ready. They're waiting for you in wardrobe." Lillian was right. Why would Clark Gable test with a contract player?

Wardrobe was a major garment factory. They designed, patterned, and fit clothes with the finest fabrics from around the world. On staff they had skilled seamstresses, pattern-makers, and fitters. I was ushered into one of the dozens of private dressing rooms, small cubicles reserved for starlets. The large, beautifully decorated fitting rooms were reserved for the stars. They brought me a suit that smelled of cleaning fluid. The jacket didn't quite fit, so I looked inside to check the size. The label read "Ingrid Bergman." The fitters realtered the jacket to fit and sewed on a label that read "Esther Williams."

The next day, the day of the screen test for *Somewhere I'll Find You*, they dressed me in the blue and gray "Ingrid Bergman" suit, then sent me to hair and makeup. The studio used very little makeup for tests, just a bit of lipstick and blusher, except that we still called it "rouge." I was impressed when they told me that Sydney Guilaroff, "hairdresser to the stars," was to do my hair. He was as famous as anyone on the lot, having created the looks of Crawford, Colbert, and Dietrich.

Nobody ever thought of anyone as gay back then or at least it wasn't mentioned. It was something you just didn't speculate about, even to yourself. We just thought of Sydney as, well, *grand*. "You have nice hair," he said as he began combing me, "but it should be shorter." As he trimmed my shoulder-length hair and set it in a wave, he felt compelled to say to me: "You're a nice girl, Esther, and they'll ruin you. You don't belong in this business. Go home, Esther. Take your new chic haircut, get in your car, and go home. Save yourself a lot of grief."

He certainly sounded as though he knew what he was talking about. But I said, "Mr. Guilaroff, I don't think so. I want to do this screen test with Clark Gable."

"He'll never show up," snorted Guilaroff. "Who did you rehearse with?"

"Dan Dailey."

"That's who you'll do the scene with. You'll see." He and Lillian Burns were clearly of one mind. They had seen this before.

George Sidney escorted me out of hair and makeup and propelled me toward Stage 28. The scene was to take place on a restaurant banquette, which they'd put up in a corner of the soundstage.

The stage was cavernous and drafty. Moreover, except for this little set it was completely empty, so that your words echoed all over. The effect was rather surreal, a bit like a sofa and table plunked down in the corner of an airplane hangar.

Dan Dailey was already there. Hiding my devastating disappointment, I slid in beside him while they lit me for the scene. "I'm nervous," I said. Gable wouldn't show up. Guilaroff and Burns were right.

"Esther, I'm right here for you," Dan said, giving me a reassuring pat. "We all love you. Believe me, we won't let you down. Just be yourself."

The truth was that was all I could be. I was not a graduate of the New York stage; I knew nothing about Stanislavsky or Stella Adler. I had no pretensions that I was an actress. I was suddenly catapulted back to my test at 20th Century-Fox. "Get back in the pool, Esther," was the message on the tape that replayed itself in my head.

The scene involved two lovers, war correspondents who worked for rival newspapers. (If anyone had reservations about the credibility of a nineteen-year-old girl as a combat journalist, it was never mentioned.) In the story, both of us had been assigned to Indochina by our papers to cover the fighting, but I'd decided not to go. I was afraid that my romance with him was going to interfere with my work as a reporter, because I was madly in love and didn't want to compete with him on the job. The purpose of the screen test was to see if I could portray this conflict between love and career. At the end of our scene, he was to give me a little punch on the shoulder and leave. At that point, I was supposed to cry, but I had no idea whether or not I could cry on camera. By nature I'm not a particularly tearful person, and somehow Lillian Burns hadn't quite gotten to that part of the rehearsal.

Just as I was beginning to obsess over whether I'd be able to cry or not, there was this sudden commotion at the door. Somebody had done that thing that should never be done when you're shooting a scene—opened the soundstage door while the red warning light was blinking outside. Everyone on the set turned in unison toward the door to see who had committed this violation. Then I heard this gasp, but of course I was the last person to know who had arrived, since I didn't have my glasses on.

Suddenly I heard George whisper, "Oh my God! It's Gable, and he's got Carole Lombard with him." When they got closer, I saw Clark Gable, accompanied by this vision of blond hair, decked out in black velvet and black fox. As he elegantly seated her in the canvas sling chair that was right under the camera, George said, "Clark, I think that's my spot."

"Carole is sitting here, George," Gable said smoothly. "You take the other side." George Sidney was a test director, and Clark Gable was the biggest star in the world. If he wanted Carole Lombard in that chair, there would be no further discussion. George would have to do without a lens finder, which was attached to the camera on the side where Lombard was now sitting. Dan Dailey had been around long enough to know that he wasn't going to like what happened next. Clark Gable approached the banquette, tapped him on the shoulder, and said, "Thanks a lot, kid. I'll take over from here."

Dan shot George a withering look, and said, "Thanks a lot, George," as he stood up. To me he said, "Good luck, Esther."

George said, "Clark, are you ready?"

He answered, "Yes, I am. Is Miss Williams ready?"

"Yes, she is," George said. "She's been rehearsing. Clark, do you want to leave the pages of the script on the table? I think they're going to show on camera."

"I'd rather keep them here, George. I don't know them all that well."

George and I looked at each other. Even I realized that it wasn't that Clark Gable didn't know the script "all that well"; he didn't know the script at all. No one, however, was going to argue with the King.

As this little melodrama played itself out, I kept stealing glances at Carole Lombard. I couldn't make out her features clearly, but I could see the radiance of her blond hair and the wonderful tilt of her beret. I knew she was wearing diamonds, because every so often I caught a bit of sparkling out of the corner of my eye. "I'd better look away," I told myself, "because she could really rattle me." For the first time since my arrival at MGM, I blessed my nearsighted-ness. It made it easier to fool myself and put her out of my mind. If I couldn't really see her, maybe she wasn't really there.

All of a sudden George said, "Roll 'em." No rehearsal. No nothing.

I said my first line, which was, "As you can see, my mind is made up." Within the context of the plot, that meant that I was sending my love off to Indochina without me. As I said my line, I tilted my chin the way George had told me to and waited expectantly for Clark to say his first bit of dialogue. But of course he didn't know the script. As it turned out, he didn't have to.

Instead of saying his line, he brought his face close to mine. There was a moment as he came nearer when I realized what was about to happen and I became a little lightheaded. Then he planted a terrific Gable kiss on my mouth. It was a really good, strong kiss. When he pulled away, I gulped so noticeably that I was sure the sound boom picked it up. This was all really heady stuff for the kid from Inglewood. He was supposed to say something, but instead he whispered, "Go ahead, honey. What's your next line?"

"Aaah, aah, umm . . ." I struggled to find the words, but I felt as though I was floating. "Aaah, uh, so . . . so however you feel about it, aaah, I'm not going to change my mind. I'm really not going because everybody will know that there is something wrong with our being there together."

He had another line to deliver, but whatever it was, he had no intention of saying it. He leaned over and kissed me again. By this time I had no idea what was going on, except that no one had said "Cut!" While we were rolling, I knew that I wasn't supposed to look at the camera, or at George Sidney, and I certainly wasn't going to look at Carole Lombard, aka Mrs. Clark Gable, who was still out there just beyond my myopic haze.

That left only one person for me to look at. As I turned to Clark Gable with a very quizzical expression, he began ad-libbing dialogue. "Tell you what, baby," he began. "Go ahead and do what you want to do, because after all, you know everything, even though you're very inexperienced."

I didn't even know what he was saying, because I could tell that another kiss was on its way. Then he kissed me *again*. This was a *long* kiss. Interminable! His lips finally left my mouth. I felt as though I were going to faint. He looked at me with his roguish smile. He had done this before. "And with that," he said, "I bid you adieu, my dear."

There was total silence on the soundstage. We had a cameraman, an assistant director, a wardrobe lady, a hairdresser, a makeup man, and George Sidney. No one said anything. Everyone was just stunned. Gable walked away from the set, helped Lombard to her feet, nonchalantly took her arm, and they walked toward the door. Their footsteps echoed loudly in the empty soundstage. They left arm in arm, laughing merrily, the world's most glamorous couple, thoroughly enjoying themselves. Just as they got to the soundstage door I heard him say to her, "Well, baby, I told you I was gonna kiss me a mermaid today." Then they went through that big heavy door and it clanged shut behind them.

"Cut," George whispered.

George, God bless him, came right over to comfort me as soon as they left. I was a basket case. Real life emotion had taken over where on-screen drama had left off. My lip was quivering, and my eyes had started welling with all-too-genuine tears. Seeing my condition, George ran behind the camera. "Roll 'em," he said, and spoke the lines to me that Gable was supposed to say, "You go your way, and I'll go mine. If this is what you want . . . if your career is more important than the two of us. . . ."

I was still trying to comprehend what had happened. Were they laughing at me? Was I a joke? As George was saying the dialogue, all those thoughts started racing through my head and the tears began running down my face. Nevertheless, I was able to give my lines back to him. "Just say good-bye. Don't say anything more."

"Cut! Makeup!!" They came and patted away my tears and reapplied the lipstick that Gable had entirely kissed away. George asked Harry Stradling, who was the cameraman on the test, to shoot a big close-up of me, and that was the end of the session.

I never saw Clark Gable again. In all the time I was at MGM, our paths never crossed. I didn't know until years later that he and Lombard were notorious for playing loving pranks on each other. Word about the screen test got around the studio fast. So did Gable's name for me—"the mermaid"—and from then on, that's what I was called—The Mermaid.

CHAPTER 7

THE ANDY HARDY TEST
1942

*T*he next time Ida Koverman called to tell me that Mr. Mayer wanted to see me, I was careful to make myself look a great deal more presentable than I had the last time. As I walked into his office, he was smiling, and as soon as I sat down he said, "Well, Miss Williams, you are going to costar with Clark Gable in *Somewhere I'll Find You.*"

I was flabbergasted. I would have said "No shit" if those words had been part of my vocabulary at that time, but since they were not, I just said, "You're joking."

Inside, I was reeling from Mayer's announcement. My heart was pounding. My hands began to sweat. What nineteen-year-old girl in America wouldn't want to star in a movie with Rhett Butler? Mayer was offering me the fantasy of a lifetime.

At this crucial moment, however, there was another part of my mind operating with an analytical maturity unusual for a girl my age. (Maybe it was the sensible voice of my mother.) I had seen the edited screen test and understood the screen magic George Sidney had conjured. As he had with my first on-camera fashion show, George found a way to minimize my inexperience and maximize my all-American wholesomeness. He had put a scene together using the long shot of Clark slipping into the banquette and sitting beside me, my first line, one kiss, the tearful reading of my last line to him after Gable had already left, and that big close-up at the end. The rest of the session he'd left on the cutting room floor. I couldn't get over how beautiful the close-up was. Harry Stradling had filmed a shot of me that looked like a George Hurrell portrait. If you hadn't been there for the actual filming, you could have been fooled into believing that I really knew what I was doing.

I, of course, was under no such illusion. I knew that my screen test was mostly a display of George's talents, and Stradling's artistry. I may have been a relatively unsophisticated young woman, but I understood clearly that I had a lot to learn. Having seen the screen test, it was more obvious than ever to me that I really needed my time at MGM U. From the beginning, I had felt that the worst thing that could happen to me was to land a part in a film before I was ready. That was why I had made sure that my contract gave me time to prepare myself.

Louis B. Mayer was ecstatic when he saw my screen test with Clark Gable. It was a twofold victory for him. First of all, he thought the test vindicated his confidence in me, and he liked nothing so much as to be proven right. Second, it gave him a powerful weapon to use in bringing Lana Turner back into line.

In that rational core that has protected me at important moments throughout my life, I calculated with remarkable clarity just how Mayer's enthusiasm of the moment might play out. George had proven that I was obviously photogenic, but Hollywood was full of photogenic young women who were lousy in their first picture and never got a second chance. I was afraid that if I were cast in a film before I was really prepared for it, I'd be a dismal failure. It seemed the easiest way to short-circuit a career in the movies. Worse yet, I could easily imagine a contrite Lana cooing her way back into Mayer's good graces and replacing me, with all the flourishes of ignominy, in the early weeks of filming. As much as I wanted this "once-in-a-lifetime" opportunity, I feared that it would come to disaster. I couldn't accept the role.

Breaking this news to the beaming Louis B. Mayer in front of me was another matter. Taking a deep breath and screwing up my courage, I said, "Mr. Mayer, I may have been able to do one scene with the coaching of a sweet man and a big, beautiful close-up. But I can't do a whole movie with Clark Gable, not yet anyway. I'll be a fish out of water."

His face was beginning to turn red. He peered at me and blinked in disbelief. People didn't say no to Mayer very often, even if they said it nicely. "Miss Williams," he intoned sternly, "I am the last word here, and I know you can do it . . . you *will* do it."

I was intimidated, but I forged ahead: "Mr. Mayer, you'd better call the legal department. You have to read my contract. I know you're ready to start shooting this movie immediately, but my contract says I am not to appear in a film for nine months, and I've only been here for three weeks."

I had heard tales about the legendary Mayer temper; but this was the first time I had ever witnessed it, and here it was, aimed at me. His face turned almost purple, and he began pounding the desk and screaming at the top of his voice, spewing spittle. "How dare you question my authority!" His fist hit the desk with a bang, and everything on the surface jumped. "I'm the head of the greatest motion picture studio in the world, [bang!] and you . . . [bang!] work . . . [bang!] for me!!" He continued to lecture me, using his fist as punctuation. I was sure his hand must hurt like hell.

Ida Koverman had very acute hearing, and as soon as she'd heard me say the word "legal," she pulled out a copy of my contract. Mayer was still ranting at me when she placed it on his desk, right under his fist. "Mr. Mayer," she said. "Esther is correct." Her remark at least deflected his ire toward another target. He was still yelling at Ida when I left. I had a terrible suspicion that those young lawyers in the legal department would be next.

Feeling a bit jittery despite my "victory," I headed straight for the commissary and proceeded to comfort myself with a cheeseburger. I was not accustomed to people yelling at me, and I really had no desire to get used to it. On all sides, the stars were there having lunch, but as I looked around this time, I did so with new eyes. Unfortunately they were no less myopic than the old ones, but for the first time I didn't feel like a starstruck outsider who wandered into a fan magazine photo that has suddenly come to life. With a great deal of help from George Sidney, I'd passed a critical test, and the knowledge that I might really be able to work in front of the camera gave me a new strength and confidence that I hadn't had before. I was a long way from having the self-assured presence of stars like Ginger Rogers and Myrna Loy, but for the first time I began to believe that I really could get there from here.

Meanwhile, though I didn't know it, my reputation on the lot was growing. I had held the studio at arm's length for almost a year by refusing to sign a contract and became known as "the swimmer who keeps saying no." Now I had signed the contract, but still I had the audacity to tell Louis B. Mayer that I was not going to do the picture he wanted to put me in—and I had made it stick. People at MGM were looking at me with new eyes, too.

Two of the most lustful of these eyes belonged to Sam Katz, the studio's head of musical productions. He repeatedly made appointments with me to have lunch, always to be served in his office. After my experience at the St. Francis with Billy Rose, it didn't take much to figure out that *I* was supposed to be dessert. He set up these dates, but somehow I never showed up for any of them. It was nothing I did on purpose, at least not consciously, but I kept standing him up. There I'd be, swimming laps or in the middle of my tennis lesson, when I'd remember that I'd missed my appointment for a seduction session with Sam Katz.

His secretary was a sweet soul named Mary, and she'd obviously been through this drill many times before. After I didn't show up for a number of these dates, she called me and said, "You did it again, Esther. This is the fourth time. He's fit to be tied, but I think it just intrigues him more."

I didn't want Sam Katz to be intrigued. I wanted him to put the make on someone else. "Look, Mary, I know what he wants, and it's never going to happen. I guess I'd better come in and tell him so."

"I think so."

When I arrived in his office, it was obvious that he was still angry, and I suppose that was understandable. I'd offended his masculine vanity, which, despite his rather nothing appearance, was substantial.

"Are you doing this to humiliate me, Esther?"

I wanted to tell him that he was far from the first thing on my mind in the morning, that he was much too short and much too old for me, but I didn't think that tactic was wise, considering what I'd done to him already, so I decided to try another approach. "Mr. Katz, . . ."

"Please call me Sam."

"Sam . . . you want me to learn rapidly, and right now that's all that I'm thinking about. I very much want to do what is expected of me, but I've never sung in public before. I've never danced. I'm putting as much energy into my studies as I did into becoming a championship swimmer. Right now everything in me is aimed at being what you hired me for."

"Of course. I understand."

"But having lunch with you is not what I was hired to do."

He looked at me almost apologetically for trying to take me away from my work. Then he brightened. "Esther, we don't have to have lunch. Why don't we have dinner together when your work day is over?"

I knew how to deal with this one. "Sam, aren't you married?"

"Yes, I am. I have two beautiful daughters."

"And so am I," I said. "Don't you think that it would be embarrassing if you and I were seen in public having dinner together?"

"Well . . . I have little places."

"I'll bet you do."

Sam Katz would make you think that "dinner with Sam" was an essential ingredient in the "making of the star" mix. The truth was that Katz's philandering was common knowledge, so I decided to deal with this head-on. "You've done this before, Sam. Did the other girls become big stars?"

Astonishingly enough, he actually tried to answer the question. He began ticking off his other conquests. "Well, let me see. Kate Groom? No. Ilona Massey? Not really . . ."

I stopped him before he got in too deep. I didn't want to be another 8 x 10 glossy on his wall of conquests, and I didn't want to know the names of the rest of them; but it was clear that sleeping with Sam Katz was not a way to sleep your way to the top, or even to the middle.

"Esther, they're just actresses. You're going to be in a swimming musical!"

"Great. Then why don't we leave it at that and stop talking about intimate lunches and dinners?"

He looked serious again. "You don't want to get involved with me, do you, Esther?"

"No, Sam, I don't."

"Don't you care about me?"

"Not in the way you want me to. I think of you as my father." I knew that was a low blow, but it seemed that the moment called for it.

He decided to try another approach. "How would you like to go into Laykin et Cie and pick out a diamond bracelet for yourself?"

I knew Laykin et Cie well, but not as a customer. It was the very exclusive jeweler within I. Magnin, where I used to work. Sam believed that everyone had a price. This was his effort to find out mine.

"Sam, I don't need a bracelet, but if you want to give me an expensive gift, I've got a better idea. My mother and sister are psychologists, and they're starting a nonprofit family counseling center. I'm not making enough money yet to help support it myself, but if we can figure out what that diamond bracelet might be worth, maybe you could donate that amount of money to fund their clinic."

He stared at me in disbelief. "You'd really like that, wouldn't you?" he said.

"Yes, I would like that very much," I said.

"You'd really like that," he mumbled. "Okay, okay, I'll back your mother's charity."

The meeting ended on a high note. Sam Katz felt like he'd scored (almost). I thought that my first attempt at charity fund-raising for the Southwest Counseling Center, though it came from an unexpected source, was a howling success.

Meanwhile I knew I had to reconcile with Mayer. A couple of months after my run-in with him, I saw him waddling down one of the little streets on the lot. As usual, he was trailing an entourage of sycophants and yes-men behind him. He saw me first. "I want to talk to you!" It was an order, not a request.

"Hello, Mr. Mayer."

He was still miffed at me. "You think you're so smart, Miss Williams. I'll have you know that Lana Turner is back from New York. She's divorcing Artie Shaw, and she's shooting *Somewhere I'll Find You.* That could have been your picture."

What he was telling me wasn't news. The studio gossip mill already revealed that Lana had returned to MGM, as I predicted she would. She sat on Mayer's lap, called him "Daddy" like she always did, and begged for forgiveness. Because she had been sufficiently penitent, he'd given her back her role alongside Clark Gable in *Somewhere I'll Find You.* As far as I was concerned, that was as it should be. She belonged in that part opposite Gable. The character had been written for a sassy blonde, and he'd already told me that one of the reasons for my screen test was to rein in the errant Turner. "I think that's wonderful. Would you believe that I knew that would happen, Mr. Mayer?"

"No, Miss Williams, indeed I would not." He was still curt with me, but maybe, just maybe, I saw the flicker of respect in his eyes. Louis B. Mayer had an enormous ego, but underneath all that was the smart little Russian Jewish immigrant with a lot of chutzpah who had built his reputation by knowing when to say yes and when to say no. I sensed that he was willing, however grudgingly, to give me credit for having the same qualities he possessed.

Now I resolved to throw myself into my lessons with more dedication than ever, but I realized that I had an almost terminal personality conflict with Lillian Burns. She had an obsession with her legs; she was always stroking and touching them. It was disconcerting, to say the least. I couldn't imagine how George Sidney stayed married to her.

I went to see Ida Koverman, who now had taken me under her wing. "I'm having trouble with Lillian," I confessed to her. "I think she's encouraging me to develop habits that don't go with my image." There was never any doubt that I was pegged as the wholesome all-American girl. "I'd like to see what I can learn from other actresses," I continued. "What I want to do is to watch a movie every day at noon. I'll just bring a bag lunch into the projection room. I'd like to learn why Myrna Loy has such a delicious sense of humor, and how Ingrid Bergman projects such power and vulnerability—at the same time. How is it that Irene Dunne always seems to have a grasp on reality, and why does Claudette Colbert give off this sense of elegance that transcends any scene?"

I could tell Ida was pleased. She would pass my comments on to Mayer. "You've chosen four great role models," she said. "I'll set it up for you."

As I neared the end of my nine-month gestation period, I knew that soon I had to get in front of a camera for real, and I also knew that I wouldn't have George Sidney to protect me. I'd been taking my lessons, but I was still ignorant of the technical aspects of moviemaking. I envisioned myself tripping over cables or ruining a day's filming out of sheer inexperience. I went to Sam Katz and asked him if there were some little part on a film that would enable me to get my feet wet (as it were).

Mr. Katz and I were on a business basis once again. I never had to formulate a battle plan to fend off his advances, because he never came through with the check for my mother's counseling center. That made it easy. Even Sam Katz knew that you didn't get the merchandise until you'd bought and paid for it. Consequently, he'd finally given up trying to get me in the sack. "Well, Esther, there is a picture where I think we could use you. It's called *A Guy Named Joe*, starring Spencer Tracy and Irene Dunne. We halted production while Van Johnson recuperated—he was in a terrible automobile accident—but we're filming again and there's an ingenue role in the film that I think would suit you."

I was cast as Ellen Bright, a girl who worked at the USO on Cahuenga Boulevard, entertaining American servicemen when they came to Hollywood. It was the first time I met Van, who was still sporting a large scar as a result of his mishap. He had a unique quality, part strong man, part eager boy.

"That must have been some accident," I said when we were introduced.

"I'll say," he replied, tapping the side of his head with a grin. "I've got service for twelve in here. And it's sterling, not silver plate. Only the best for MGM." That encounter was the beginning of a friendship and an on-screen relationship that spanned six films and many decades.

I had a tiny part. All I did was dance with Van, say a few lines, and cry, for which I got much bigger billing than I deserved. My credit appeared above Lionel Barrymore's, and he played God! It was all Sam Katz's doing. He couldn't give me a diamond bracelet, so he gave me billing instead. Frankly, I needed the billing much more than I needed the bracelet.

My nine-month incubation period ended just as the studio was looking for a girl to play in a new Andy Hardy movie. Andy Hardy was the main character in a very profitable MGM series that starred Mickey Rooney as a typical teenage boy. The studio had been making Andy Hardy films since 1937; eventually they cranked out fifteen of them. In many ways it was America's first family sitcom, the ancestor of TV shows such as *Leave It to Beaver, Father Knows Best,* and *Family Ties.* Fay Holden portrayed Andy's mother, and Cecilia Parker played his older sister, Marian. Veteran actor Lewis Stone played his father, Judge James Hardy, even though it seemed to me that he was old enough to play Mickey's grandfather.

In *Andy Hardy's Double Life,* I played Sheila Brooks, a college girl who is a friend of Mickey's ever-faithful sweetheart, Polly Benedict, played throughout the series by Ann Rutherford. MGM used the Andy Hardy series as a popularity meter to gauge public reaction to its more promising young actresses, and it was considered a plum to be cast in one. If audiences liked you, you went on to bigger and better films. Lana Turner and Judy Garland had started that way. So did Kathryn Grayson and Donna Reed. The idea was that Andy would become smitten with the young starlet appearing in the film, but always return by the end of the movie to the long-suffering Polly.

Working with Mickey was a challenge. He felt justifiably self-important because of the success of those dazzling musicals he made with Judy Garland, which brought millions to the studio. Just as Shirley Temple had saved 20th Century-Fox from bankruptcy, Mickey and Judy had been the mainstays of MGM's continued prosperity. The ever-so-paternal Louis B. Mayer had a special affinity for child stars, and Mickey had literally grown up in the studio system. In the 1930s, he attended the Little Red Schoolhouse on the lot with Judy Garland (Elizabeth Taylor and Roddy McDowall were to follow later, when they were making *Lassie Come Home* and *White Cliffs of Dover*).

There was, of course, the problem that Mickey was much shorter than me, he being just five feet and change. Despite the fact that he was obviously the key ingredient in this very profitable series, he always had the need to make himself seem "bigger." He had a feisty way of going through life with his elbows out, expecting everyone else to get out of the way. And by and large, they did. After all, Mickey Rooney had been a star since he was a small boy, having made his film debut at the age of six, before the movies had learned to talk.

(Years later, after I had earned my own place at MGM, I ran into Mickey at the Beverly Hills Hotel. He came bounding up with that endless energy of his and got on tiptoe to give me a kiss. Jokingly, I said to him, "Mickey look at the two of us—almost a foot apart. How did we ever play love scenes together?" The Mick wisecracked back, "What's the matter, Esther? You got a problem with your height?" And he turned on his heels. Mickey never changed.)

In a way, he never grew up. Now in his early twenties in *Andy Hardy's Double Life*, he was still a self-absorbed kid. I didn't find him very likable at that time, but I didn't expect to. People who worked as hard as he did probably had earned the right to be imperious. I thought to myself, "I guess that's the way it is. When you are a star, you can do just about anything you want to do." Mickey took advantage of his stardom. Everyone in the studio gave him free rein. He had a bookie waiting for his calls every day, always playing the horses. We all knew that "Mickey's on the phone" meant that filming could not resume until he'd concluded his "business."

On the other hand, because he was such a veteran, the shooting went much more smoothly. He had a photographic memory—he could pick up a script, read it once, and know it cold. That also meant that he wasn't very tolerant when I flubbed a line. But we were always on schedule.

The Andy Hardy series was a proven formula. The actors were a tight-knit group, a family on and off screen. If I had feelings of insecurity about joining this successful family, I tried not to show it, even though I towered over Mickey in our romantic scenes. George Seitz, the director, took me aside at the beginning of the film and advised me: "When Mickey stands, you sit. If you have to stand, bend your knees, lean down. Be short!" Naturally, this advice was never to be mentioned in front of Mickey.

"Mr. Seitz," I said, "this is my first role. I think I need some additional direction." He looked at me as though I had just made one of the dumbest comments in the history of show business.

He sighed and answered, "Do what Spencer Tracy says to do: Learn your lines and don't bump into the other actors." Some direction! It was not until I got into the pool that I could relax in that movie.

In my first scene, Mickey was at a swimming pool, lying on the diving board asleep in the sun. The noise of someone approaching wakes him, but he can't see who it is. "Polly?" he asks.

"It's not Polly," I answer, and at that point he turns around. For the next shot, the camera panned all the way from my toes up to the top of my head. I was wearing a two-piece blush pink swimsuit similar to the one I wore in my first screen test. In deference to the Hays Office, it had a little skirt across the panty and my navel was nowhere to be seen. To be sure that no cleavage was revealed, there was a tie on the bra to cover any possible exposure.

Dizzy from seeing me, Mickey falls into the pool and I dive in after him. The pool we used was out on Lot 2. It was the same one where my old nemesis Johnny Weissmuller had wrestled with all those rubber crocodiles. However, for the underwater shots, Mickey and I filmed in the "saucer tank"—a deep, large, round elevated outdoor pool that had an underwater window. The camera crew would film through the window, which required us to remain at a prescribed depth in order to keep within the camera frame. It wasn't until later that MGM built an underwater tracking system for the camera and crew to follow me underwater.

When Mickey and I got into the tank, I did something that nobody had told me to do. I began lolling underwater, rolling over and over very languidly in that pretty little suit. They had left my hair long and it flowed around me in a way that was almost dreamlike. I wasn't thrashing or gasping for air like most people do underwater. It looked like I'd never have to come up. It was as if I were at home. And of course I was—I genuinely loved swimming and being underwater. It was a fabulous shot because it had no frame. It appeared as if I had invited the audience into the water with me, and it conveyed the sensation that being in there was absolutely delicious.

At one point Mickey was right in front of that underwater window, looking at the camera with that adorable elfin face of his. I circled him, then gave him a big kiss. I'd shown him how to hold his palate at the top of his throat, so he could open his mouth down there without going "blub blub." After I kissed him, he mouthed the word "Woo!" right in front of the camera.

When *Andy Hardy's Double Life* was released, the studio carefully monitored the mail it received. They had people who did nothing but open letters and read what fans were saying about you. I learned that everyone had gone crazy over that underwater scene between Mickey and me. It was an Andy Hardy movie, all right, but the audience loved the girl in the two-piece swimsuit. MGM now put the big publicity guns into motion. I was known as the "Woo-Woo Girl, The Girl Who Had It All." The word "Woo-Woo" was an approximation of how you spelled the whistling sound that every red-blooded male was supposed to make upon seeing a pretty girl— at least, as far as the MGM publicity department was concerned.

Coca-Cola used drawings of me on billboards and signs around the country. There were no endorsement payments—certainly not to me. "Under contract" at MGM meant exactly that. The studio determined under what circumstances your image was used and how you would be paid. The studio never shared any further remuneration it received on your behalf. That summer, the two-piece swimsuit became the fashion statement at beaches, country clubs, and swimming pools.

Almost every aspect of my personal life appeared in the press. MGM did not have to concoct any stories. They simply took what was available and redefined it. My small house in Silver Lake turned into the "cozy cottage." My absent husband became the "hardworking medical student." And my twelve- to fourteen-hour work days at the studio were simply a "busy schedule."

That "busy schedule" became even busier as the publicity machinery roared onward. There were photo sessions daily from 6:00 A.M. to dusk—at the studio, at home, on locations, wherever they could put a camera. I was photographed standing, sitting, jumping, walking, cooking, sewing, shopping—and always smiling. Of course, I was photographed in a swimsuit in as many ways as could be imagined. I wasn't put off by any of it. I knew what the studio was doing. I was being presented to the American moviegoing public as the next star.

The studio had a policy that kept an actor from knowing what the public response might be to a particular public relations campaign, especially if it was successful. I had seen the brochures with my pictures that were sent to the distributors, and the fan magazines with my photographs on the covers. But I never knew the amount of fan mail I received in return. Had I known, I might have asked for a raise in salary. This arcane custom continued through my years at MGM. They were keenly aware that if I knew of the bags and bags of mail that I received, I would have had a financial bargaining tool at the beginning of each new contract period. Meanwhile my father kept scrapbooks with clippings and photos of my career, from my swimming championships through my years at MGM. As I look back through the books, I can see how far-reaching and thorough the studio publicity department was. Every major newspaper and magazine in the country heralded me as "The Hollywood Mermaid."

Andy Hardy's Double Life was a success. MGM saw to that. And I was about to enter that mythical world of stardom. MGM moved into action on that big swimming musical they had always envisioned for me.

CHAPTER 8

BATHING BEAUTY
1943–1944

*N*ow that I was being given the full promotional treatment, the studio wanted to send me out on public appearances. They had to prove that this new "find" was the real thing. Les Peterson, who was the assistant to MGM publicity chief Howard Strickling, asked me if I would do a military hospital tour. Anything the studio could do to uphold its patriotic image was considered a prime assignment now that America had entered World War II.

I had already made a black-and-white short film entitled *Inflation* to contribute to the war effort. In this piece, I play a young wife married to Stephen McNally. (He was signed at MGM the same year I was and bore an unnerving resemblance to Buddy McClure.) I am tempted to spend money foolishly by the devil, played by Edward Arnold. The point of this little morality play was that good Americans should resist temptation, be frugal, and put their money into war bonds. I made this just before *Andy Hardy's Double Life* as sort of the next step after a screen test.

Les Peterson was asking for a much larger commitment: "Esther, the hospitals all along the East Coast are full of wounded boys who are being sent home from the front. What they need is a beautiful young girl walking through the wards and cheering them up like Betty Grable."

"But Les," I said. "They don't know who I am. They haven't seen *Andy Hardy's Double Life,* or *A Guy Named Joe.* They've seen Betty Grable."

The truth is, other than swim meets in Des Moines and Miami Beach, I'd never traveled far from Los Angeles, much less appeared before thousands of wounded soldiers just back from the war. I was proud to be an American, but my war efforts took me no further than a victory garden at my parents home, where we grew vegetables.

"There's only one Betty Grable, Esther, and she really needs some help out there. Besides," he added wistfully, "Betty is on a bond tour."

A bond tour was always reserved for the top stars, and the tour would usually end at the White House, where there would be a photo session with President Roosevelt. Judy Garland did bond tours, as did Shirley Temple and Humphrey Bogart. I wasn't sure whether Les was asking me or ordering me on this hospital tour, but the way in which he presented it didn't leave much room for no.

It was all happening very quickly. MGM did not waste time capitalizing on what they considered to be a viable property. Because of the MGM publicity rush, I was now a genuine "pinup girl." The studio had issued a picture of me standing on my toes and showing off my figure, just like Betty Grable and Rita Hayworth. (I still thought of myself as a swimmer.) I was told that the soldiers had my picture hanging in their locker chests.

Les told me that doing a hospital tour was like doing a movie. "Three months, including all wardrobe. All you have to do is smile, look pretty, and sign eight-by-ten glossies." Even then, I knew that a performer had to put on some kind of show. I told him that Bing Crosby sang and Bob Hope told jokes, but I would feel ridiculous to just stand there and let GIs ogle me. I asked for help. Shouldn't I have a writer? I needed someone from the publicity department. I had no idea what to do with that "someone," but I knew that such a person was supposed to be assigned to me as a requirement of my contract. Every contract player was assigned a publicity assistant, as needed.

"Man or woman?" Les asked.

I decided that I would prefer the companionship of a woman. She probably wouldn't mind helping me hang up the wet suits. So Les phoned the publicity department and said, "We need someone for Esther Williams. She's going on tour. Who have you got available?" They sent me a young woman with even less experience in the film industry than I had. Her improbable name was Melvina Pumphrey. We turned out to be a good pairing, though—Melvina was with me for my entire career at MGM.

So Melvina Pumphrey and I—and a stack of 8 x 10 glossy pinups—went off on a hospital tour. As the train carried us to the East Coast, we listened attentively to the Bob Hope and Jack Benny radio programs so that I could at least have a few jokes to offer when I went out on a stage to face a thousand GIs. If we laughed at what we heard, we wrote it down. In addition, Melvina and I hit upon an idea that seemed like good entertainment.

We borrowed a collection of Big Band records from the studio library and figured out the logistics of a jitterbug contest. One by one, I was to invite the GIs to come up and dance with me while everybody would sing along to something like Glenn Miller's "Little Brown Jug." The wardrobe department came up with a collection of thin sweaters and flippy little skirts in bright colors just for the tour, and I wore very high heels to dance in. The skirts weren't all that short, but when I would twirl, the boys would get a good look at my legs. Every time my skirt went up, we knew they would hoot and holler.

The dance contests were a great success. The boys never got enough, and they didn't want to let me off the stage. For a closing bit, we conducted a mock screen test. Melvina and I made up some questions, and put each one on an index card. Then she handed them out as the guys came into that little auditorium every military hospital seemed to have. Melvina always made certain that the last question was given to the cutest and smallest soldier in the place.

I announced that I needed a bodyguard, and I chose a GI from the audience and asked, "Would you come up here with me, please?" Then I deepened my voice and cooed into the microphone, "I'd like to see who wants to guard this body." And of course the others yelled in appreciation and my poor "victim" turned beet red. After he made his way to the front, I told him how I'd been sent from Hollywood to give him a little screen test right there onstage, and that if he passed he'd get to come to California and have another test at MGM. "All you have to do," I told him in a serious tone, "is say your lines. No matter what I say to you, no matter what I ask for or tell you to do, you must answer, 'No.' "

I had the lights lowered, and I set the scene. "You've been away at war a long time. You're my boyfriend that I've loved so much. We never consummated our love." (Words like "consummated" brought the auditorium to a frenzy.) "And now at last we're going to be together. I've arranged for everyone to be gone tonight and I've put the lights down low. You come through the door and I run to you and put my arms around you . . ." As I said this, I began to act out the scene. I hugged him boa constrictor tight and said, "Oh, darling, I've missed you so much! Have you missed me?" Now we were chest to chest, and he was up against that little thin sweater; but of course he had to choke out "no" in front of all his pals.

Then I said, "But sweetheart, I've dreamed about you every night. Please kiss me."

"No," he forced himself to answer.

"Please?"

"No."

That last "no" was always extremely difficult for the poor young man to say, and it only got worse for him from there. Those sweaters and skirts were actually breakaway costumes. All I had to do was reach behind and tug at the snaps. The sweater and skirt fell away and I was left standing there in a gold lamé swimsuit.

"Please. I'm begging you. Please kiss me," I implored, standing there in my swimsuit.

By then, it was pandemonium in the auditorium, and of course at that point the scripted dialogue went out the window. When the young man finally kissed me, the show was over and the curtain came down. Sometimes it was an effort to convince the fellow to let me go.

I came to genuinely enjoy those nights with the soldiers because they were all in the act, singing and dancing with me and dancing with each other. We often danced late into the night. Sometimes, it was as if they were not aware of what had happened to them. They seemed to forget the devastation done to their faces or their bodies. The music and the fun carried them away. I knew that the scars and the wounds would never really heal, but for that moment, they didn't seem to care. They were home. And they were alive.

If the hospital had a pool, I would often stay overnight and have a swim meet with the boys the following morning. Melvina would arrive early and recruit the best swimmers. They would all turn out. My new friends who danced their hearts out with me the night before would swim with me in the morning.

At Forest Glen, just outside of Washington, D.C., it was different. It seemed more subdued. We danced that night as we had elsewhere. The next morning, I got to the pool early, swam a few laps and waited for my new teammates to arrive. As I sat on the steps of the pool, I saw the same boys who danced with me the night before being wheeled to the edge of the pool where we were to begin our race. Some had no legs, others had one arm. Others had just stumps.

My heart broke. No one had told me that this was a hospital for amputees. The night before they had danced on artificial limbs. Tears welled up in my eyes. The last thing I wanted to do was to embarrass them or hurt their self-esteem. They'd get quite enough of that without me. I asked the commanding officer, "Are they up to this?" I looked into his face, which was not much older than mine.

"Are *you*, Miss Williams?" he shot back. "These men don't need your pity. They signed up because they wanted to swim with you. They were all top swimmers on their high school or college teams before they were wounded, and they've been training ever since they heard you were coming. Frankly, a lot of them think they can beat you."

I swallowed hard and lined up to the familiar refrain of "Swimmers, take your mark." Some of the men were lowered into the water. Others could stand, some balanced on one leg, and took their places in lanes next to mine. The gun went off, and I dove into the pool. Some of them swam amazingly fast, and I let a whole bunch of them touch the end of the pool before I did. The win belonged to them. They deserved the taste of victory. Shouts rose from the makeshift stands that were set up along the side. I hugged all the swimmers and laughed with them. It was such good medicine, not just for them, but for me, too.

It was much more difficult for me to visit the psychiatric wards, where young soldiers who had seen too much death were trying to recover from battle fatigue. Some of them mumbled to themselves or screamed out loud, but many of them just stared off into space. I was more than a little afraid at the first ward I visited, especially when I saw that the doors were locked from the outside. Because I didn't really know what to expect, I asked one of the psychiatrists to come with me.

"It's better if I don't," he said. "You're only going to be with each patient for a few minutes. You'll talk to them briefly, sign a picture, and move on. These boys will be so delighted that you're there to see them that they'll be on their best behavior."

When I got back to California, I got a letter from that psychiatrist, who told me I had made a difference. Some of his patients had asked whether they were getting better, and he was able to say, "You were great when Esther Williams was here, and that proves you're beginning to recover." Knowing that they could behave normally, even for a short period of time, helped his fragile patients believe they'd be able to become sane again.

Walking through the surgical wards, I got the feeling that some maniac had shot up a high school graduation. Many of the patients were younger than I was, and I was just twenty. These young men had the sweetest faces. Despite all that had happened to them, they were overjoyed to be home, back in the States. Some were so recently wounded that the seriousness of their injuries hadn't yet sunk in, but I learned to read the signs of impending heartbreak in the markings on their casts. The worst were those dashed lines on the fresh plaster of Paris, which meant that an arm or a leg was to be removed.

Three months later, when I returned to MGM, I saw Les Peterson as he was coming through the studio gate. He shouted from his car that he was glad I was back and asked how the tour went. I smiled and told him it had gone well, and I thanked him graciously for having given me the opportunity to go. He looked puzzled. He could not have understood how much I grew up in those three months. I was no longer an innocent. I was sent out on tour as a pinup, a sex symbol, but as I looked into the faces of those boys in the hospitals, I had seen another world, one of suffering, sacrifice, and survival. Whatever was left of Esther the teenager evaporated. I was a mature young woman when I returned.

I was relieved to be back at MGM, safe behind the studio gates. MGM was in the process of planning *Mr. Coed*, the film starring comedian Red Skelton, a young comic who was being groomed by MGM to be a leading man, a la Bob Hope. The first time I had met Red, he was being introduced to the studio at Talent Lunch, and he was very funny and charming. I expected Red to have a sense of humor when I worked with him, but he didn't. At that time, I assumed that comics were inherently funny people. Onstage, Red could be hilarious; but off stage he was pleasantly businesslike.

I portrayed Caroline Brooks, a swimming instructor at an eastern girls' college. Red was Broadway songwriter Steve Elliott, who enrolls as the only male student in the school in order to romance me. The original script had been "dry." The swimming was added pretty much as an afterthought, but I was delighted. Best of all, it was to be directed by George Sidney, who had finally been promoted from test director to feature director. George had brought Harry Stradling, the man who'd shot that fabulous close-up, as his cameraman.

On our first day of shooting, I was all set to make my entrance when I heard the beginning of an argument between Red and George. "George, I won't do it, and that's final." Red was in a pair of trunks, seated by the pool with a look of grim determination on his face and his arms folded defiantly across his chest. An ex-vaudevillian, he had been a star for years, but unlike Clark Gable he was not such a big shot that he could win an argument with his director hands down.

"Red, you have to," said George.

"Why?"

"It just looks neater. Otherwise, the camera will read it as a shadow or some dirt, as if someone sprinkled you with reddish brown dust."

I still had no idea what they were arguing about. Then Red uncrossed his arms and fluffed up the auburn curls that adorned his chest. "I've always loved these, and I'm not shaving my chest."

George tried coaxing. "What can I say to convince you to do it? How about we give Edna a call?"

Although he was in his mid-thirties, Red was very much an over-grown kid. Edna was Skelton's wife, and in a way she was also his agent and his personal manager. She made all of his decisions for him. When Skelton got her on the phone, he was actually in tears. We could only hear half the conversation, but that was sufficient. "Mamma, they want me to shave my chest. Do I have to? . . . What? . . . $200 . . . cash?"

He hung up the phone and told Sidney, "Edna says that for two hundred dollars you can shave my chest, but it has to be cash . . . and I want to save the curls. Who knows whether I'll ever be able to grow any more."

Quickly, someone appeared poolside with a bundle of twenty-dollar bills, a can of Burma Shave, a safety razor, and a small cellophane bag. After Red's chest had been shaved, and the curls safely tucked in the little bag, we were finally ready for the first swim number. They called for my stand-in and asked her to get into the pool. Then they handed her the "lily," a heavy and unwieldy contraption made of metal and glass, whose purpose was to check the color balance of the film. Color photography was still quite new, and getting a perfect color match was tricky. The young woman trying to hold up the lily while treading water sank to the bottom like a brick and had to be fished out, sputtering all the way. She looked understandably miserable—not only had she nearly drowned, but she knew she was fired, too. George Sidney looked almost as dejected as she did—he now had a production delay.

It was starting to dawn on me how movies get behind schedule and over budget. "George, I know I can solve this problem. My stand-in has to be a swimmer, not an actress. Let me find Edie Motridge," I said. That's how I reconnected with Edie, the swimmer who quit the team with me when I confronted Aileen Allen about hiding my invitation to the Pan American Games. After that first day on *Mr. Coed,* Edie was with me on every picture.

Finally we were ready to begin shooting. George wanted a more affluent look than the saucer tank we used for the Andy Hardy swimming sequences. The Lakeside Country Club in San Fernando Valley had that classic American style: beautiful pool, manicured grounds, and an exclusive-looking clubhouse. George moved cast and crew across the city, and we were "on location." At that time, studios preferred "locations" to be in their own backyard. It was a question of expense and expediency. If anything were to go wrong, we were only half an hour from home base. It wasn't until later that MGM would send me off to Mexico, Hawaii, and Florida for location sights, and not without considerable problems. Notwithstanding the close proximity to the studio, Lakeside Country Club had its own unique set of difficulties. The scene was set in the summer, around the pool, with the soft rolling valley hills as a background. However, we were filming in January, and all of the club's lawns had turned brown. Poor George was beside himself. Filming came to a halt. We were about to pack when I went to him and asked if they could spray the lawns green. George smiled, looked at me slyly, and said, "You're catching on fast, kid! You'll be around for a while." The lawns were sprayed with green paint as if summer had blossomed instantly, and it lasted for the week of shooting. We left the Lakeside Country Club a prettier sight than when we arrived. However, no one told the club that the paint destroyed their lawns for the rest of the year. The studio had to send a crew to reseed acres of painted lawns.

My Technicolor debut was in a shocking pink satin, one-piece swimsuit with a colorful "capote," or matador's cape, about my shoulders. The addition of this capote as a swimsuit cover-up served more as a segue to the Colombian-born baritone Carlos Ramirez, who sang "Te Quiero Juste," than as a costume design. "Te Quiero Juste" was translated as "Magic Is the Moonlight," and this became the first of my "signature" songs as I swam to its romantic melody. Later, when I would enter nightclubs like Mocambo's or Ciro's, or The Stork Club in New York, the orchestra would stop what they were playing and begin the strains of "Magic Is the Moonlight."

As I climbed the diving board, the song rose in scale until I reached the top of the ladder to a finishing fanfare. I dove into the pool and swam to Carlos's beautiful voice accompanied by Xavier Cugat's orchestra.

In those years Hollywood had a love affair with anything Latin. *Down Argentine Way* starring Betty Grable was a major hit for 20th Century-Fox. The sounds of Xavier Cugat and Carmen Miranda were all the rage. Cugat, who was born in Spain and later emigrated to Cuba, starred poolside with me in three films, including this one. Brazilian musical star Carmen Miranda later taught me to sing in Portuguese for *Easy to Wed*.

Before we began the scene, I asked George what he wanted me to do in the pool. George said he knew nothing about swimming. (He would learn to get wet in subsequent films.) "Just do what you do, Esther," he said.

My first major film and I was completely on my own! The Aquacade had been carefully rehearsed and choreographed with swimmers and divers, and Johnny Weissmuller to lead the way. This was to be total improvisation. My mind raced back to the exhibitions I had seen at the Los Angeles Athletic Club where divers dressed as clowns cavorted about the pool. They would splash around the pool using what was called the "Garbo Freestyle," splashing feet as if they were paddles; (Greta Garbo was known for having feet as large as paddles). Their hands would flip through the water in a stroke called the "East River Crawl," which they said was the way New Yorkers swam, flipping the garbage away from their faces while swimming up the East River. The Lakeside Country Club was far from being New York City's East River, and my "flippy" hand strokes and paddling feet played beautifully on camera. Everyone loved it. "Only champion-turned-star Esther Williams could swim that way," the reviews said.

The rest of the filming went smoothly, and before I knew it, it was time to shoot the final number. They told me to report to Sound Stage 30, and when I got there, my mouth dropped open. What had been a dry stage was now a ninety-by-ninety-foot pool, twenty-five feet deep. It had all kinds of special effects equipment for underwater fountains and geysers and fireworks, not to mention a central pedestal on a hydraulic lift. They could raise me fifty feet up out of the water like Venus on the half shell. I was still in shock when someone handed me the phone.

"How do you like it, Esther?" It was Sam Katz.

"There must be enough pipes down there for the entire city of Los Angeles!" I told him. "I think it's the most fantastic plumbing job I've ever seen."

"It should be. You're looking at $250,000 worth of plumbing! Do you know that it's just for you?"

"Well, it's $250,000 worth of magic," I gushed.

As I looked around, I realized that it was yet another demonstration of my mother's wisdom. "If a man wants to give you something and you don't accept it," she used to tell me, "he'll find a way to give it to you, one way or another." I didn't want the bracelet Sam wanted to buy for me from Laykin et Cie, and he hadn't made the donation to the counseling center; so he'd given me a quarter of a million-dollar swimming pool instead.

There was no question that the final musical number in *Mr. Coed* defied credulity from a commonsense, stick-to-the-script point of view. Here at what was supposed to be a small women's college, Harry James and his orchestra were stationed at one end of the pool, and Xavier Cugat and his band were ensconced at the other. Meanwhile, there were 150 girls in or around the pool, ready to swim to the music. Coordinating all this was John Murray Anderson, the testy English gentleman who had choreographed the Aquacade for Billy Rose. I'd worked with him in San Francisco, and now he was really ready for retirement. George, however, was determined to get one more show out of him, and the old curmudgeon really rose to the occasion.

We didn't know it, but we were about to invent synchronized swimming as it had never been seen before on film; and this finale set an amazing standard for the aqua musicals to follow. We gave the razzle-dazzle special effects equipment in the new pool a workout, and George Sidney showcased John Murray Anderson's last hurrah with great ingenuity. The swimming sequences were rehearsed for ten weeks before the number was shot, and many of the moves in the finale are the basis for what we see today in state-of-the-art synchronized swimming at the Olympics and elsewhere.

The opening shot pulls back from the bell of Harry James's trumpet to reveal that huge stage full of dancers between the two orchestras. After a dance sequence—a swirling fantasy in pink—the swimmers come down to poolside and open their coats as they line up for what we called "the tiller." They dive into the pool one after another with perfect timing, creating a ripple effect that resembles the tilling disk on a plow. The girls surface and begin swimming across the pool together, moving their arms in unison to the music. When it proved too difficult to get all those arms to hit the water at precisely the same time, George ordered pillars installed at regular intervals along the side of the pool. This gave the swimmer a series of marks to hit, and as the camera panned, it didn't matter if one of the girls was a little off, because a pillar interrupted the visual sequence and it could be corrected in the editing room.

The shot widens to show the swimmers in the water and the dancers onstage, revealing the immensity of Stage 30. As the swimmers dance in the water to the strains of "One O'Clock Jump," treading water with their legs and just moving their elbows to the beat, they dive under in unison in what is called a "porpoise dive."

My entrance is made on the hydraulic lift that comes up out of the water. (I love those pink seahorses in the background of the lift.) I remove my white chiffon Roman toga with the help of two of the showgirls dressed in black, each over six feet tall, and both of whom are decked out in huge hats. Then I come down the stairs to dive into the pool. My suit was actually sewn together with panels of small mirrors, so that the camera would catch the sparkle as I moved underwater.

Johnny Green, the musical director, chose the waltz from the operetta *Die Fledermaus* for the studio orchestra to play. It was an unusual choice because it demanded more invention than the casual crawl stroke, which is what I had been used to. As I come toward the camera, I do a combination of one front stroke and one backstroke that we called "the spiral." When I do a "back dolphin" into the center of the swimmers, you can see that I'm a little off-center. Frankly, it is a miracle that I could swim at all. After the shooting schedule for the finale had been set, I came down with pneumonia. When I arrived on the set that afternoon with a 102-degree temperature, my head throbbing, my chest wheezing, I was there only because George Sidney begged me and told me they would have to dump the whole finale if I didn't come to shoot it on that day. Ironically, that day was Christmas Eve.

Watching videos of that scene now, I can't believe that big smile I manage underwater as I swim in and out of the swimmers doing pinwheels. The overhead shots of the swimmers moving like a wheel are very much the Busby Berkeley style from the Warner Bros. musicals of the 1930s.

Sam Katz had to get his money's worth out of the quarter million-dollar pool job, so toward the end of the number we began to make use of all the new special effects. When I give one signal with a flip of my backstroke, fountains spouting colored water rush up. With another hand signal, the fireworks go off. Another and a curtain of water six stories high rises from a row of needle jets at the edge of the pool. The engineering department adored me because they got to play with all this innovative equipment. Never had plumbing been put to a more glamorous use. This was the first Technicolor swimming musical production spectacular, and it ends with a flourish. With flames shooting up all over the pool, fountains blasting like a hundred fire hoses, the swimmers treading in unison, I rise up out of the water on the hydraulic pedestal, an Aphrodite-like Venus, rising from the sea—weak from pneumonia.

While my film career was beginning, a segment of my personal life was ending. I found, much to my relief, that all I needed for my emotional and personal security was my own resolve and determination. I didn't need a marriage and a ring. I had come to realize all too quickly that Leonard Kovner was not a man I could ever really love.

We had agreed earlier to go our separate ways, but not without a little extortion on his part. "I need money to open an office," he had told me when we separated. "You've got fifteen hundred dollars in the bank, and I want it." That was every penny I'd saved from the Aquacade, but there was an unspoken "or else" at the end of his demand—or else he wouldn't go along with the divorce.

I was disgusted by his attitude, but Leonard seemed perfectly capable of carrying out his threat. I went to see Sam Katz about the problem. Having just spent $250,000 on my swimming pool, he had a perspective on the relative importance of $1,500. "Give it to him," he said. "You're going to make so much money that you'll never miss it. You're going to be a gold mine. Give him the fifteen hundred dollars, but be sure to get a letter from him that says this is the complete and final settlement. Not a penny more."

After the filming of *Mr. Coed* ended, I had a date in divorce court. Leonard had taken the Aquacade money that he'd squeezed out of me, but at least he had signed the financial agreement. In those days you had to give a reason for divorce, and it was far from automatic. I told the judge that Leonard refused to have children with me. My mother corroborated my testimony. The judge stopped me before I could finish my sentence.

"You don't have to say anything more, Mrs. Kovner." I must have looked at the judge in surprise, since it was a bit of a jolt to be called "Mrs. Kovner" again—at MGM I was "Miss Williams" fourteen hours a day. He smiled benignly at me from the bench. I didn't know it then, but he was a Catholic, and what I'd told him made it very easy for him to make a decision. "The fact that he refuses to have children with you is sufficient. Your divorce is granted." When the gavel banged down, I was single again.

I knew that I would have promotional obligations once *Mr. Coed* had been released, but before that I had one public appearance commitment to fulfill that had nothing to do with the film, at least not directly. It was a fund-raiser for the Jewish Home for the Aged. There always has been a great deal of nepotism in Hollywood. Jack Cummings, the man who produced *Mr. Coed*, was the son of Ida Mayer Cummings, Louis B. Mayer's sister. This was her pet charity, and she was always able to cajole her brother into loaning some MGM star power to the fund-raising effort. "No" was not an option: An invitation from Ida Mayer Cummings was tantamount to an order.

I still had no real wardrobe of my own, so on this particular evening I was decked out in a gown from the movie, an off-white number that Irene had designed for me, with rows of emerald green and shocking pink sequins. As I was working my way around the room soliciting donations, a handsome blond sergeant asked me to dance. I was in high heels, and to my delight, I found myself looking up at him.

"My name is Ben Gage, and I'm six feet six," he said by way of introducing himself.

Ben was in the air force. He had been Bob Hope's radio announcer, and before that he was a band singer with Anson Weeks.

As we danced, this breezy singing sergeant swept me around the room, laughing all the way. Ben was into fun. He was boyish, almost puppylike, and that was exactly what I needed after all of Leonard's darkness. When we parted that evening, we agreed to see each other again—soon.

After the editing was completed, *Mr. Coed* went into previews. MGM had a network of small cities just outside of Los Angeles—Anaheim, Riverside, San Bernardino, Long Beach—where it screened the film for the movie public and asked them to fill out a survey voicing their opinions of the movie. The executives from the studio rode to the previews in their limousines. A preview in Pomona was my first "date" with Sergeant Ben Gage.

The comment cards filled out by the audiences all over southern California were not just positive, they were glowing. There was every indication that MGM had a big hit on their hands. What the moviegoers liked best, of course, was the improbable stuff that had little to do with the script. They were wild about the swimming numbers, especially the water carnival musical extravaganza at the finale, and they were enthusiastic about me, too. As a result, a decision was made on the third floor. When the picture was released, it was no longer *Mr. Coed*. The new title was *Bathing Beauty*, and I got to share top billing with Red Skelton. I could just imagine his wife, Edna, fuming. My only hope was that his chest hair had started to grow back.

CHAPTER 9

HITTING MY STRIDE
1944–1945

*W*ith a brand new name for the movie and those very encouraging preview comments (we wouldn't have called it "buzz" then, but that's what it was), the big MGM publicity machine thundered into action to promote *Bathing Beauty*. The movie premiered at the Astor Theater in New York, and for the event they put up a six-story-tall billboard of me diving into Times Square with a large sign that said, COME ON IN! THE WATER'S FINE!

Bathing Beauty opened in July of 1944 to splendid reviews. Even curmudgeonly Bosley Crowther of *The New York Times* approved. I think the reason why the movie did so well was that it was exactly the right kind of breezy summer entertainment for a war-weary public. It premiered just a month after the Allied invasion of Normandy. We were turning the tide on Germany, but the fighting was by no means over. *Bathing Beauty* offered pure escapism, with good old-fashioned romance, music, dancing, and a water extravaganza—all in lush new Technicolor. The film brought people into the theaters in droves, not just in the United States but overseas as well. It was called *Escuela de Sirenas* in Spanish and *Bellezza di Bagno* in Italian. MGM made a monster profit, more than making up for the $250,000 they'd sunk into "my" pool. (I was quite sure that Sam Katz was most relieved about that.) Movie grosses were not public knowledge back then the way they are now, but in its era *Bathing Beauty* earned more money internationally than any other picture except *Gone With the Wind*.

This was a heady time for me, but I hardly had a moment to enjoy my first taste of stardom. I was working nonstop, either on the set of my next picture, or in publicity sessions. I was aware that Mayer and Katz had given me an extraordinary opportunity, and that the public was responding favorably to the MGM publicity machinery, but I had to stay focused on my schedule at the studio, which kept me occupied from early morning calls at the set through late nights studying my lines. I was too busy working on the production line in the dream factory to think much about how my life had changed or where I was going.

When the MGM executives saw that *Bathing Beauty* was headed for box-office victory, they immediately thrust me into a new project entitled *Thrill of a Romance*. Sam Katz called to say that as a result of the success of *Bathing Beauty*, I was to be given a star dressing room. He'd been right about one thing, at least. I had a lot more earning power ahead of me, and it was already worth my $1,500 from the Aquacade to be rid of Leonard.

The star dressing room was a huge step up in the studio hierarchy, because there was indeed a rigid pecking order within MGM. There were the stars—the chosen few—who had dressing rooms in what was known as the Stars' Building. Lesser lights made do in what was called Featured Players Hall, but everyone there, of course, dreamed of moving up. Lana Turner once said that getting a dressing room in the Stars' Building was like entering a new kingdom in which you were the queen. She was right. When Sam Katz gave me the news, I realized, wistfully, that Mrs. Clewell at I. Magnin would have to wait for me to come back, probably for a very long time.

My room was to be Dressing Room B, the very same one I had been shown four years earlier when I had my first interview with L. B. Mayer. It had been vacated by Greer Garson, who had returned to England, with her Oscar for *Mrs. Miniver* firmly in her grasp. The silks and satins on the walls and windows were very like the actress herself—classy and refined—but just a wee bit, well, matronly for me. One of the perks of a star dressing room, however, was that you got to choose your own decor. The set designers gutted the room, removing Miss Garson's froufrou and installing my selections. When they asked me what color scheme I wanted, I told them red, white, and blue. I chose a pretty marine blue chintz with little red and white flowers for the walls. Then they sprayed all the furniture a lovely cobalt blue. When it was finished, it did indeed look like the home of the all-American girl.

They hung my terry cloth robes in the closet, and when I moved in, I felt if not like a queen, certainly like a princess. I made sure everything in the dressing room was washable, because I knew what it took to get me ready for a day of shooting—and mostly what it took was grease.

The swimming musical presented new challenges in hair, makeup, and costuming. Techniques that worked on dry land didn't work in the pool, and we had to feel our way as we went along. We all experimented together. Like the engineering department rigging my fabulous pool, the hairdressers and the makeup artists loved working on these movies because it gave them a chance to play with a new set of toys. They had to invent a way of making me up so that it lasted through a day in the water. Pancake makeup, which was ordinarily quite durable, just washed off, leaving a cloud of pale beige floating on the surface of the pool. They found a cream makeup with a very thick base. The makeup woman slathered it all over me from head to foot—I think she got to know my body better than she knew her own. Then she powdered me and ordered me into the shower, so it could set for the day.

The hairdressers poured warm baby oil and Vaseline into a bowl, patted the mixture onto their hands, and said, "Come here, Esther." I always thought there was a little too much glee on their faces when I arrived for my morning session. They smeared this gooey mess that looked suitable for lubricating cars into my shoulder-length hair, and then made tiny braids all over my head. After that they affixed artificial braids to the natural braids, using two giant interlocking hairpins that looked like crowbars—and felt like them, too. The pins created massive welts in my scalp, but even when I dove off a high platform, those braids stayed put. They became my trademark underwater "do," and I still have an indentation down the middle of my head as a souvenir.

By the time I came out of hair and makeup, I was as waterproof as a mallard. Every so often, however, I arrived at Stage 30 only to discover that I'd done it all for nothing. Once the assistant director told me, "Esther, go back and get all that stuff out of your hair. Then report to Stage 28. We're going to be dry today." The change came about that day because a new set decorator had come up with a great idea for how to get precisely the right shade of aqua for the pool, but he had used the wrong kind of paint. When they added chlorine to the water, it had simply dissolved. The entire pool had the consistency of homogenized milk—all 15,000 gallons of it. There was nothing to do but drain it and start over.

When I returned to makeup, the errors were compounded. Someone put a rubberized liquid on my hair in an effort to get the grease out in a hurry, but it proved to be a big mistake. Instead, it was starting to harden—my hair was turning into a helmet. Everyone was trying very hard not to look panicked, but even my nearsighted eyes could see huddled urgent consultations in the corner of the salon. Finally someone remembered that acetone would remove just about anything. To get rid of the rubber, they soaked my hair in what was basically nail polish remover, which of course made those big welts on top of my head sting. The rubber came out, as did the grease, but I considered it a miracle that my hair was still shoulder-length. With what they were doing to me, I should have been bald as a billiard ball.

Joe Pasternak was the producer on *Thrill of a Romance*. He was a resourceful little Hungarian who had all but single-handedly rescued Universal Studios with a string of musicals starring Deanna Durbin. Before jumping ship to MGM, he'd also been instrumental in resuscitating the career of Marlene Dietrich, casting her as a dance-hall girl with Jimmy Stewart in *Destry Rides Again*.

Pasternak believed in happily-ever-after entertainment, and not surprisingly his orientation fit well with my image. He saw me as the hometown girl next door, and in his films he wanted to use me just that way. It was Pasternak who gave me the longevity I enjoyed in the movies from then on, because he showed that there was a market for me as me, not just as some circus performer diving through hoops and doing stunts. I was quite fond of him, despite his bizarre table manners. Joe Pasternak was the only man in the world I ever knew who ate spaghetti with his hands. He created a scene in the commissary every time he did it, which was often enough—people went out of their way to watch him do it. Others went out of their way *not* to watch.

In *Thrill of a Romance,* my character, Cynthia Glenn, was a swimming instructor at a local playground. Cynthia had married a well-to-do young economist, only to meet the man of her dreams on her honeymoon, after her groom had been unexpectedly summoned away. The leading man was Van Johnson, only this time I was a leading lady. There was no cuter human being in the world at that time, with his freckles and red hair. He portrayed my true love, Major Thomas Milvaine, a war hero recovering from his wounds.

I was delighted at the prospect of working with Van again, because his star had risen even faster than mine. One of the most popular male stars of the day, he was already in the top ten box office with *A Guy Named Joe* and *Thirty Seconds Over Tokyo.* Although I was very much involved with Ben Gage by this time, the studio tried mightily to get us to go out together in public. Van and I were very close on the set, but there was never that kind of spark between us off camera. When someone challenged him about why we didn't date, he quipped, "Because I'm afraid she can't get her webbed feet into a pair of evening sandals."

Pasternak had wholeheartedly embraced Mayer's mandate to include classical music in MGM films. Included in the cast of *Thrill of a Romance* was singer Lauritz Melchior. Melchior was a *Heldentenor* who specialized in Wagnerian opera. I was thrilled because I had been an opera buff for years, starting when I was young enough that my mother wanted to know why I was listening to all those people screaming on the radio every Saturday afternoon.

This was to be Melchior's first film, and I let Sam Katz know that I wanted to meet him as soon as he arrived. Melchior had a Falstaffian figure, and with flowing white hair and a cherubic face, he looked like a clean-shaven Santa Claus. When we met, he put his ample arms around me, and said with that charming Danish accent, "I luff you."

"I luff you, too," I said, mimicking his voice and his twinkle in a way that made him smile. "It's mutual."

Our director Richard Thorpe was famous for bringing his pictures in under budget and ahead of schedule. He was nothing if not efficient, and I soon began to wonder if he hadn't missed his calling as an accountant. He was cranky, especially in the morning, until he'd downed a pot of coffee; it was wise to keep your distance. Dick didn't like people who were too cheerful, which meant that he took an instant dislike to me. He decided to make me the patsy on this picture.

Whatever went wrong was my fault. Esther moved; Esther got out of her light. Esther moved her chair back and it squeaked. Esther flubbed her line—goddammit Esther, again! This daily torrent of blame was quite an adjustment after having worked with George Sidney, and I suppose I wasn't coping very well. Thorpe made me nervous, and of course it's pretty difficult to act natural when you're just waiting for your director to scream at you again.

For one scene, Van and I were sitting at a table and talking. It was a complex set-up, with lots of extras around the pool, and the Tommy Dorsey orchestra playing in the background. Van said his lines to me, and I said mine to him. When I'd uttered my last syllable, Dick hollered, "Cut! We've got that. Everybody go to lunch."

As soon as he called lunch break, I realized that I had left out some of my lines. Usually I kept quiet about missed cues or lines changed, but this time I couldn't. There was a bunch of plot exposition that I had to deliver, otherwise the audience wouldn't be able to follow the story line. I had to speak up and tell him of my missing lines, even though I knew what was coming. "Mr. Thorpe, I'm sorry. I didn't read all of my line and it's kind of important."

"What did you say?" He boomed it out over the microphone, like an accusation.

I summoned what was left of my courage. "I didn't say my whole line. I think we have to do that scene over, because when you edit you're going to need the part I left out." Thorpe did almost every scene in one take—that was how he made the trains run on time. I felt like Oliver Twist asking for more gruel.

He looked at me with those squinty little eyes. Then he spoke again into the microphone. "Wait just a minute. Don't anybody leave." There were groans from about 350 members of the cast and crew, all of whom had headed out the door for the commissary. "Turn the lights back on, boys. The lady wants to act."

That did it. If he'd slapped my face I couldn't have been more stunned. Dick Thorpe had pushed me to my breaking point and beyond—to have said that in front of the entire crew was much too public, much too humiliating. I got up from the table. I didn't say anything to Van, who was staring at me with this oh-you-poor-kid look on his face. On the way to my dressing room I started to cry, and it was as if a dam had burst. I locked myself in Dressing Room B and fell apart.

When actors cry for the camera, their eyes fill with tears and one or two trickle down their cheeks, but they still look attractive. When real people cry, their eyes get red and puffy and their noses run. It's not exactly photogenic. Dick Thorpe kept knocking on my door, trying to apologize. He did it not because he was truly sorry, but to get me to stop crying. Putting me back together was going to take a lot of time and he knew it was going to leave him behind schedule. I refused to see him, but I heard him tell the makeup people, "See if you can get her ready for one o'clock."

At that point I would have been a challenge for Max Factor and all the Westmores combined. Harry Stradling was back behind the camera, but even he couldn't have made this face look good. In addition to the redness and puffiness, there was a lot of collateral damage. Mascara had run in black rivulets down my face. The pancake had smeared, and there were creases and blotches on my face where usually there weren't any. The makeup crew was sympathetic, and it was obvious they'd dealt with this kind of problem before. They put tea bags on my eyes and swabbed me with witch hazel. Eventually they made my face presentable, but what they couldn't do was restore my equilibrium. I was still a mess, at least on the inside. One o'clock came and went, but Thorpe had to shoot around me for most of the afternoon, because I was so fragile that I'd start to cry if anyone said anything to me at all.

Van was sweet about it. At the end of the day he told me, "Well, Esther, you just gave Mr. Thorpe a lesson. I don't think he'll do that to you again, unless he wants to throw his little schedule out the window. From now on, just relax. The thing that's going to make you a star—and this movie will probably seal it after *Bathing Beauty*—is your naturalness. No matter what Thorpe does, he can't take that away from you. Don't let him get you down." He was right—after that episode, Dick Thorpe stopped picking on me. He was still as dyspeptic as ever, but at least it wasn't directed at me personally.

Van was right about the rest of it, too. This was the movie that made me a star. *Thrill of a Romance* was a hit, largely because audiences really responded to the chemistry between the two of us. Van and I matched—it looked like we belonged together as a couple. He was as much the all-American boy as I was the all-American girl. As World War II drew to a close, we also became icons, in a way, symbolizing the virtues that people loved best about America. Van represented all the young men who had gone off to war for their country, and I represented the girls they were fighting to come home to. *Time* magazine said we were as "screwily wholesome as ice cream and toothpaste."

That image followed me for the rest of my career, as did a most unfortunate quote from an interview I gave at the time. Perhaps I was feeling the weight of so much negativity from Dick Thorpe, but I gave a journalist a very self-deprecating assessment of my on-screen abilities. "Let's get this straight," I said. "I know I can't act; I know I can't dance. And I can't sing, but I'm going to keep trying until I get it right." I think that may end up on my tombstone—almost every piece about me has included this piece of pessimism. It's one of the few things I've ever said about myself that I'd really like to take back.

But that was small stuff, relatively speaking. In every respect, life was terrific. I was a star, I was in love, and the man I loved *loved* the idea that I was a star. Unlike Leonard, who thought it unseemly that the wife of a doctor would work in show business, Ben, the band singer, adored the fact that I was in the movies. He delighted in having his picture taken with me—even when he wasn't supposed to be in the shot, he'd find a way to get his face in there. It became almost like a game to him—but that was how he looked at life.

We had so much fun together. There was a kind of joy that I hadn't known in a relationship before. I felt as if somebody had put me on vacation with him, and it was a great time for me to have somebody like that in my life. I didn't see any problem at all between us if we had a relationship that included marriage and children. I thought he'd make a wonderful father, because he was such an overgrown kid himself.

CHAPTER 10

BECOMING A STAR
1946

omeone once said that a reputation is like a lump of wet cement. While it's fresh, it's easy to push around, but as it starts to
harden, it gets a lot more difficult to change; and once it's set up, it's
impossible. *The Hoodlum Saint* is the picture that set my lump of
cement at MGM.

As a black-and-white film in which I did not swim, it was a deviation from the success formula I had established with *Bathing Beauty*
and *Thrill of a Romance*. The plot involved a journalist turned
wheeler-dealer named Terry O'Neill, a hustler who made money for
himself by using a charity for Saint Dismas as a front. William Powell played O'Neill. I had worshiped Powell ever since he paired with
Myrna Loy as Nick and Nora Charles, respectively, in *The Thin Man*.
I played May Lorrison, his newswoman lover. Angela Lansbury portrayed a singer named Dusty Millard. Angela, of course, had made a
big splash in *Gaslight* with Charles Boyer and Ingrid Bergman and
was considered by MGM to be a rising young star.

Norman Taurog, the director, was fine to work with, but right
away I was afraid for the picture. Just a few days into the filming,

Norman and the rest of the crew were all pumped up about how great this movie was going to be, and how it was real Academy Award material. They were so caught up with Oscar fever that they lost sight of the need to make a movie that people would pay money to see.

One of the first scenes called for me to slap Bill Powell after he kissed me without my consent. Norman had told me I was really supposed to let him have it. By this time Bill was in his mid-fifties, and when you're just twenty-two, that strikes you as quite ancient—frail, even. I didn't want to slap that "old man" because I was afraid I was going to hurt him. Swimming develops broad shoulders. I never needed shoulder pads in my dresses, because I had my own built right in; and the same powerful armstroke that helped me in the water gave me quite a wallop on dry land. Norman kept telling me that there was no way to fake it—I had to really connect with Bill's face in order to make that distinctive hollow thwack of palm against cheek.

As the scene began, I had my back to the camera. Bill came up behind me and planted this big kiss. As directed, I put a look of righteous indignation on my face and hauled off and smacked him in the cheek—hard. Then I watched in horror as one side of his face collapsed.

The other side still looked normal. "Oh, my God!" I shrieked. I thought Powell was having a seizure or a stroke.

"Cut! Cut-cut-cut!" screamed Norman. "Makeup!"

"What do you mean, 'Makeup'? Normie, get this man a doctor!"

Taurog glared at me the way a veteran shortstop might regard the team's greenest rookie, which in a way I was. I turned to my costar to apologize. "Oh, Mr. Powell, I'm so sorry. What have I done? I broke your face!"

Bill waved me off with a tolerant but lopsided smile. I tried not to stare at his face—half of him looked thirtysomething; the other half looked like the picture of Dorian Gray. "I'll be fine in a few minutes, Esther. We can un-break my face."

The makeup people came right onto the set and began working on him. To my astonishment I saw an intricate network of rubber bands all around his face, all running into a knot at the top of his head. There was one by the eye, another right below the eye, another along the jawline. I had hit him so hard that I'd broken the bands on one side of his face. When the makeup men were finished, it looked as if somebody had pulled all of his face up toward the top of his head. It was an instant face-lift, which is what they did for older actors instead of plastic surgery back then.

Unfortunately, all the rubber bands in Culver City were not enough to save *The Hoodlum Saint*. Audiences rejected the idea of a romance between William Powell and me. He was much too "December" for my "May," and people were actually offended by it. Because preview comments were so negative, they cut out almost all of our love scenes, and the film became quite disjointed. So much for the Academy Award that Taurog anticipated.

Not surprisingly, the movie was a bomb, but the studio executives blamed the flop on their belief that I had disappointed audiences (a) by not swimming and (b) by appearing in black and white. So it was all my fault, even though I had done exactly what they told me to do. The executives on the third floor were perfectly capable of finger-pointing like that, especially when there was a need for a scapegoat, and I was the handiest candidate.

MGM decided to go back to what they knew worked for me before. The failure of *The Hoodlum Saint* convinced them that audiences wanted to see me in the water and in romantic musical comedies, and they were determined to give the public what it wanted—and what made money—in Technicolor, of course. That sudden popularity of the new color technology had more to do with my success than I had understood at the time. Technicolor brought to life the water, the spectacles, and even my own movie persona in a way that simply didn't work in black and white. Like Betty Grable, I was one of the "Technicolor babies," stars who would have that special glow when filmed in three-strip color. It was not something I felt motivated to fight about. I thought I'd done well enough in *The Hoodlum Saint*. I wasn't fantastically better than I'd been in *Thrill of a Romance*, but I certainly wasn't any worse, either; and the fact that I wasn't unhappy with my performance was enough for me. I reasoned that MGM had been in the business a lot longer than I had, and if they wanted me back in the pool, so be it.

My next assignment was a short one—*Ziegfeld Follies* had me in the saucer tank for a one-song water ballet. The film was a collage of musical numbers showcasing all of MGM's star talent, like a vaudeville revue. Vincente Minnelli directed; Arthur Freed was the producer. Freed played mix-and-match as he went along, dropping some numbers and adding new ones in response to the changing box-office popularity of various stars. After the success of *Bathing Beauty* and *Thrill of a Romance,* MGM felt I would add star power to this revue. Jimmy Melton from the Metropolitan Opera sang "We Will Meet Again in Honolulu" to me while I swam. He sang beautifully, but I had a feeling even as we were filming that his part would be edited out of the finished movie. It didn't make any sense to have this fellow all decked out in a white navy uniform while I was underwater circling through these pink coral fans, unable to hear a thing as there were no underwater speakers. He couldn't see me and I couldn't hear him.

The most Jimmy had seen of me all day was a few minutes at lunch break. For the rest of the shoot, he'd been crooning at poolside while I was blowing bubbles fifteen feet down under. We hadn't even had a decent conversation, but somehow he'd become smitten with me. Perhaps he knew I liked opera and thought I'd be an easy mark for him. In his mind it wasn't that remote a possibility—I'd heard that tenors frequently had a waiting harem of opera groupies at their disposal. Back in my dressing room, there was a note under my door. It said, "We will meet again, but *not* in Honolulu. I am in dressing room 10."

At the beginning that was sort of the way it was for me with dressing room intrigue. Early in my career I kept hearing racy stories about all this hanky-panky going on in the star dressing rooms, but I never saw any of it, at least for a while. By the time I got out of my grease and into civilian attire, everyone had gone home. The suggestive invitation from Jimmy Melton was surely not something I cared to follow up on, but in any event, by the time I'd scrubbed off the body makeup and shampooed the Vaseline out of my hair, he was gone. Apparently he'd waited around for me, but finally left for the airport to return to New York.

My instincts were right. Jimmy Melton and "Honolulu" were

edited out and replaced by an instrumental of "This Heart of Mine" to which Fred Astaire and Lucille Bremer danced in an earlier sequence.

All the same, I was glad I didn't have to explain it to Ben. Ben and I were very much in love and having a wonderful time making the rounds of all the parties. Hollywood parties have come to be publicity events now, but back then they really were times to relax. The stars and executives had beautiful homes where they would entertain lavishly. Money was not an issue. They hired the best orchestras and the best caterers. Of course, the stars never stopped being stars, even amongst themselves.

Many of the best parties were held at L. B. Mayer's house. One evening I was dancing with Ben when Cary Grant cut in. Cary was so gorgeous, and there was always the hint of a little smile in the corners of his mouth.

"You're a wonderful dancer, Mr. Grant," I said.

"Cary, please," he answered, in a perfect imitation of his on-screen persona. Howard Hughes approached us and tapped Cary on the shoulder. Cary graciously stepped aside and I found myself in the arms of Howard Hughes. Hughes was wearing tennis shoes and a rumpled, blue serge suit with a shiny seat. I was not impressed. "I'm giving up Cary Grant for *this?*" I thought to myself.

Before the music ended, Howard led me off the floor to a table in the corner. He already had a legendary reputation as a womanizer. Ben had disappeared somewhere near the bar, and Cary Grant was nowhere to be seen.

"Don't even try, Howard, I'm too athletic," I said looking him square in the eye.

He adjusted what seemed like a hearing aid. "What did you say, Esther? The music's too loud. I can't fix this damn thing."

I shouted, "I'm not your type, Howard." Half the party heard what I said, but not Howard.

"You won't believe this, Esther. I can build airplanes but I can never get these damn hearing aids to work."

"Do you have something important to say? I loved dancing with Cary Grant. At least you could have waited until the dance was over."

Howard just sat there and smiled at me. I wasn't sure whether he heard me or not or what he even wanted. But I figured out the rest. He and Cary were great buddies and they had this little game. Since Howard was so deaf, he was shy about approaching girls for a dance because he couldn't hear whether they're telling him yes or no. So Cary invites them first, and of course no woman on earth would turn him down, then Hughes cuts in. Score one for Howard.

One of the greatest stars of the movies, and one of the richest men in the world carrying on like high school kids at a prom.

A few weeks later, Howard was romancing Cyd Charisse, and I went to dinner with the two of them. Cyd doesn't like to talk, and of course Howard can't hear. It was such perfect symbiosis that I called a cab and went home.

One of my favorite dancing partners at these parties was George Burns. He was outrageous and adorable, and on top of that he really could dance. One evening as we were dancing he looked me in the eye and said, "Have I shown you my dickie? I have a dickie, you know."

"George, you're so bad. Of course I know you have a dickie—you talk about it all the time."

"Would you like to see my dickie, Esther?"

Here we were on the dance floor at the home of the head of my studio. The last thing I wanted was to be party to indecent exposure. I averted my eyes. "George, I'm not going to look. If you unzip your fly and show me what's in there, I'm going to look the other way."

"Esther, turn around. It's okay—really."

Sure enough, there was George, showing me his dickie—the heavily starched, detachable shirt front he was wearing under his tuxedo. He'd removed it from his neck and rolled it into a small white cylinder. "That's quite a dickie, isn't it?" We laughed together and danced some more.

I saw Gracie Allen, sitting by the pool, and of course I sat down with her and told her what had just happened with George and his now-famous dickie. "You sure are married to a wonderful, crazy guy," I said.

"Oh, but you don't know how crazy. Let me tell you about George and what happened before we got married."

She had my full attention. "George and I were on the vaudeville circuit. We had an act together, and little by little I became the comic and he played straight for me. We fell in love working together, and we knew it was forever. He asked me to marry him, but George had this tremendous thing about his pride over making it with women.

"You know, Esther, in those days proper women, even in show business, did not sleep with a man until they were married. There were showgirls, but they were different from us nice girls." When she said that, I thought about the girls in the chorus in the Aquacade, who kept going up the ladder into the diving tower with every guy who caught their fancy, and realized that some things never changed.

"I'd never slept with George, but before we got married he wanted me to know that I was getting a big bargain. He wanted word to get back to me from the girls in the show about what a terrific lover he was; so he took a hotel room and instead of having a bachelor party—a night with the boys—he asked Arlene, one of the showgirls, to come up to the room with him.

"Here was this beautiful girl in his bed, and George came out of the bathroom in his black silk pajamas. She said, 'Oh, George, please don't turn out the lights. It's so dark in here I can't see anything.' And he told her, 'It's better for me in the dark. It's really better. And it will be better for you, too—you'll see.'

"So he climbed into bed in his pajamas, made love to her, and then excused himself to the bathroom. After a short while, he came back out in his pajamas, got back into bed, and made love to her again. He did this seven times in all.

"By morning this poor girl was a wreck. I saw her sitting in the dressing room—she looked awful. 'What happened to you last night?' I asked her.

" 'Are you really gonna marry this guy?' she asked me.

" 'Of course I'm going to marry George,' I told her.

" 'I don't know how to tell you this, Gracie,' said Arlene, 'but he's going to kill you.'

" 'Arlene, what in the world are you talking about?'

" 'Gracie, are you a virgin?'

" 'Yes, I am.'

" 'Then God help you. You're such a tiny thing anyway. I can't imagine how you'll survive.'

" 'Survive what?'

" 'Not only can your fiancé make love seven times a night, but he gets larger every time.'

" 'What?'

" 'You know, *larger* . . .' Arlene refused to say anything more, but she held up her two index fingers six inches apart, and then moved them away from each other little by little until there were fourteen inches between them."

I thought about George and his dickie in a new light.

"But that's not the end of the story," said Gracie. "I didn't learn what really happened until later. George really wanted to impress me, so he had 'auditioned' all the crotches in the show. He chose six guys, and bought six more pairs of black pajamas, one for each of them. He got them all into the bathroom and lined them up in order of their size—so he could have a big finish. Then he sent them out into the bedroom one after another, enjoying himself thoroughly."

"Gracie, how did you find out?" I asked.

"Well, we were on our honeymoon and we had lots of time for lovemaking, because we didn't have the show to do. Finally I asked George, 'Where is the big one?' That was when he told me the story."

We laughed together at this wonderful, ridiculous George. I stood up, walked over to the edge of the pool, and looked back at Gracie who was still laughing. I thought to myself, now *that's* a lady with a great sense of humor!

I was really looking forward to the next film, which was *Easy to Wed*, because I was back working with Van Johnson. The film was a remake of *Libeled Lady*, which had been a hit in the thirties starring Spencer Tracy, Myrna Loy, William Powell, and Jean Harlow. I played the role that Loy had originated—Connie Allenbury, the richest girl in the world, who had sued a newspaper for defamation of character. Keenan Wynn was cast as the editor of the paper, the role that had been Spencer Tracy's. Van had William Powell's role as my leading man. He played Bill Chandler, a man hired by the editor to get me to drop the lawsuit. Lucille Ball inherited Harlow's role as Gladys Benton, turning her from a trashy blonde into a trashy redhead.

Dorothy Kingsley updated the script from the 1936 version for this picture and subsequently worked on many of my other films. She was a chic, attractive blonde, and unlike many of the other screenwriters, she'd actually talk to me before she made any changes. Too often I'd get pink revision pages delivered by messenger the night before we were shooting, which meant you had to unlearn what you'd memorized and learn something else instead that you didn't like nearly as well. Dorothy and I had a mutual respect for one another—we were friends. She had a real feeling for the needs of leading ladies, and she was willing to work with me to get a script we were both happy with.

In *Easy to Wed* I had one confrontation scene with Lucille Ball over being in love with the same man. Lucy's character, Gladys Benton, had been set up to be kind of a bimbo, but the scene didn't work. Both of us were stuck with lines that just didn't sound anything like what women would really say to one another. Her dialogue made her sound particularly petulant and disagreeable. I called Kingsley to talk about it. "We've got to like her," I said.

She agreed and the two of us rewrote the scene together. "Scripts are like men—no one is perfect," I used to tell Dorothy. If they wrote badly for me sometimes, I wasn't going to complain to anybody. I just tried to make improvements with a few changes whenever I could.

That was on-screen. Off-screen, Lucy and I had our troubles. Naturally, it started in hairdressing. The hairdressing department was a great equalizer, an assembly line on which every actor was treated equally. There were not enough hairdressers to send each of us to individual private rooms, so people from different levels of the studio pecking order were all seated in a line. One day, I had Ginger Rogers on my right side and next to her was Eleanor Parker. Marilyn Maxwell was on my left, and next to her was Lucy. Clearly, there was no privacy.

Lucy had married Desi Arnaz in 1940 and was wildly jealous about his exploits as a womanizer. In those days, every woman was a natural enemy to her, because to Desi every woman was a natural target of opportunity. As we all sat there in the hairdressing lineup, Lucy loudly accused me of "stealing" her man. She yelled and gestured and made a scene that would have been very funny on an *I Love Lucy* episode, but I was not amused.

Desi called several times asking me for a date, even though he was already married. I had told him that I was in love with Ben Gage and had no interest in anyone else. I told that to Lucy, too, and added that even if I had not been in love, I wasn't interested in her silly Latin singer. Unfortunately, that wasn't the right thing to say, either. The fact that I didn't find Desi attractive made her cry.

Later, before Fernando Lamas and I were married, Lucy stopped us one night in front of Chasen's. Wagging that curly red head of hers, she attacked Fernando. "You are the reason my husband behaves so badly!" she said vehemently. "He wants to be a Latin lover, like you. You are a terrible example for all Latin men!"

Fernando, of course, loved this sort of confrontation. By now, a small crowd had gathered to witness the scandalous scene, and he stepped back to shoot his cuffs and adjust his jacket perfectly before delivering the verbal coup de grâce. "My dear woman . . ." He addressed a wild-eyed Lucy in withering tones. "No one has to show your husband how to misbehave. He appears to have a natural talent for it."

Easy to Wed varied from *Libeled Lady* in that I had to swim, of course, and also they had added music. Jack Cummings, who was the producer (and still L.B.'s nephew), loved Latin music, and had asked Johnny Green to do the score. He came to me and said, "Esther, I want to ask you something—can you sing?"

"Well," I told him, "I've been working with Harriet Lee, the MGM voice coach, just in case someone might want me to sing sometime."

"I want you to sing—in Spanish."

"Let me see if I get this straight—you've never heard me sing a note, but you want me to sing in a language I don't understand?"

"It will be good discipline for you, Esther."

"Discipline—is that what we do in the movies? I thought this was the entertainment business." I was in no mood for a character-building experience; but I liked Johnny and it seemed like this was going to happen whether I wanted it to or not. At Johnny's behest, Harriet Lee began working with me on *"Acércate Más"* ("Come Closer to Me").

On the day we were to record the song, there was a bunch of guys with violins in the studio. They were busy rehearsing, and I was off by myself in a corner, trying to make sure I remembered the words. Nobody was paying any attention to me; the musicians seemed absorbed in their own little world, and I was getting hungry. I slipped out without saying a word to anyone and headed for the commissary to grab a bite.

Suddenly Marty the unit manager stormed into the commissary. The unit manager is like the policeman—it is his job to see that you're on time in the morning and to make sure the shoot is running as scheduled. Unit managers keep elaborate notes, all designed to find someone to blame when things go wrong. How many minutes are we held up because the star doesn't like her hairdo? How many takes does Miss Williams need to complete her scene? It should have been done by 11:00 A.M. and it wasn't completed until 11:15. Whose fault was that?

"Is Esther Williams in here?" he bellowed. I saw the maître d' point him in my direction, and I practically could see the steam coming out of Marty's ears as he strode briskly toward me. "Are you the dumbest broad that ever lived?" he shouted from about fifteen feet away. "We're holding up the most expensive musicians in the world right now because nobody can the fuck find you and you're filling your fucking face! Come with me now!"

"I don't know why you're so angry," I said as Marty dragged me out of the commissary like a truant officer. He did everything except pick me up by the ear. I felt like a schoolgirl caught playing hooky, or a sailor nabbed in the wrong bar on shore leave. Those "guys with the violins" were virtuoso musicians, and MGM was paying them handsomely to wait for me to finish my hamburger, but nobody had bothered to explain that to me. Like most valuable information on the lot, you more or less picked it up as you went along.

We got back to the recording studio, but Marty wasn't finished with me yet. Having started his diatribe about how stupid I was in front of the entire commissary, he now continued in front of a forty-piece orchestra. Finally Johnny Green had had enough. "Marty— what do you want the kid to do, eat shit?" When he said it into the microphone, it really broke the tension and all the musicians cracked up. I, of course, turned a hot red.

My cheeks were still burning when I entered the recording booth and put my headphones on. Johnny and the orchestra were on the other side of the glass. I think he could tell that I was near tears because he spoke to me into my earphones—no one else could hear him. "Okay, kid. It was a dumb thing to do and you'll never do it again. Everybody has to learn sometime. Let's make some music."

He then proceeded to coach me through the drama of the song— he was far better at bringing out the feelings I was supposed to have than Lillian Burns ever would be—and in Spanish, no less. "Esther, I want seductive . . . I want enticing. You've got all the money in the world, but you want to make this man see you as something more than a dollar bill."

It was just what I needed. Johnny refocused me away from my embarrassment and onto the task we had to accomplish. He was soft and encouraging, praising what I did right and calmly explaining what it was that needed fixing. Unlike the verbal assault from Dick Thorpe, I had someone to stick up for me. With Johnny's coaching I was able to fight for my composure—and regain it. I sang the song over and over, and we did it until every Spanish pronunciation was perfect, and until I got all the phrasing and the emotions the way he wanted them. And we did it within the allotted time frame, so that in the end my ill-advised hamburger hadn't cost MGM an extra dime. We said good-bye to my forty-piece back-up group, and they left for their next gig—they were playing *Flight of the Bumblebee* that night at the Hollywood Bowl.

Ben and I were married on November 25, 1945, at the Westwood Community Church. Melvina Pumphrey, my publicist, was my maid of honor, and we had our reception at her house in Mandeville Canyon. Jane Powell sang "Because." Just before the wedding I went into the little back room of the church to get dressed, and suddenly I started to cry uncontrollably. I cried as if my heart was breaking—it had nothing to do with nerves. In hindsight, of course, it was probably a warning from my psyche that I was making a terrible mistake marrying this great big, fun-loving band singer, but at the time I just put myself back together and walked down the aisle. Right after the reception, Ben and I caught a plane for Acapulco. Although it was the right place for a honeymoon, we were really headed to Mexico for work on my next picture, *Fiesta*.

CHAPTER 11

FIESTA
1946

I should have known my next picture would be trouble as soon as the Mexican tailor demanded that my bosom would have to go. Almost from beginning to end, *Fiesta* was jinxed. By the time it was over, all I could do was thank my lucky stars that it wasn't my first film—if it had been, it would have also been my last.

The plot defied credulity, even by Hollywood standards. I played Maria Morales, a young woman who wanted to become a bullfighter; Ricardo Montalban played my twin brother, Mario, who was supposed to become a matador like our illustrious father had been, only he wanted to be a classical musician instead. When Ricardo disappears on the day of his debut as a matador, I take his place in the bull ring, hoping he'll come out to see who is fighting in his name.

In the sort of larger-than-life way MGM did things, the studio didn't want its costume designers to adapt a bullfighter's outfit for me—it had to be the genuine article. Before shooting began, I traveled to Mexico City to get fitted for a *traje de luces*, the beautiful jewel-encrusted suit of lights that every matador wears in the ring. The tailor who was making my suit was very by-the-book—it never registered with him that this was for a movie, or if it did, he didn't care. When I went for my first fitting, he looked at me, took my measurements for the jacket, shook his head, and said, *"Imposible, señorita."*

He was upset because traditionally the stiff jacket must lie vertically against the chest. Given the measurements he wanted, the only way a woman could wear one "properly" would be if she were constructed like supermodel Kate Moss—perfectly flat. Now I wasn't quite Jane Russell, but I did have a bustline; and this little tailor was just sickened at the sight of me because I was ruining the look of his suit. At that point he refused to do any more work on it unless I agreed to have my bosom surgically removed.

When I realized he was serious, I crossed my arms over my chest. We were at an impasse—a Mexican standoff, as it were. Fortunately, Walter Strohm, the unit manager, had accompanied me to the fitting and intervened. He made a deal with the tailor to pack up the suit and take it back to Hollywood to be fitted. The tailor came along in the bargain, even though by this time he was refusing to speak to me unless I was willing to become a 32AA.

Irene the MGM costume designer and I had a good laugh in the fitting room when I told her what the deal was. A bit later, the tailor arrived to defend the integrity of "his" suit. He sat in a corner and sulked as Irene reworked the darts. The only time he really lost it was when she put hooks and eyes across the fly, so that it would lie flat. Matadors, it seems, like to call attention to their crotches, and the pants on the *traje de luces* are deliberately fitted to emphasize masculine bulges. A bullfighter's fly never quite closes completely, so the world can appreciate what's in there.

The director of *Fiesta* was none other than the foul-tempered Dick Thorpe, the man who had humiliated me in front of the crew on *Thrill of a Romance*. If anything, he was in a worse mood on this picture than he'd been before. He hated Mexico; he hated bullfighting, and above all he hated Ricardo Montalban, who was at least as cheerful as I was. Although this was his first English language film, Ricardo was already revealing the congenial disposition that later characterized Mr. Rourke, his debonair *Fantasy Island* persona. Needless to say, he and I were instant friends. Every morning he'd come on the set with an energetic, heartfelt, "Good morning! God is smiling on us. How is everyone today?" Thorpe really hated that.

Ricardo came from Torrejón, Mexico. His accent was still very heavy at the time, and of course I didn't have one at all. Since we were supposed to be twins, this marked difference in accents was something that troubled me, and I was sure it would bother audiences a great deal as well; so I went to talk to our producer, Jack Cummings, about it. "Jack," I said, "would you explain to me how Ricardo and I could grow up in the same playpen together, with him speaking the way he does and me talking the way I do?"

Jack gave me a reassuring pat, secure in his position not just as a successful MGM producer, but as Louis B. Mayer's nephew as well. He told me, "First of all, Esther, here at MGM we can do anything. I anticipated this question. Your mother is Mary Astor, who speaks perfect English, like you do. Your father is Fortunio Bonanova, who can barely speak English at all."

I liked Jack, but the look on his face suggested that what he'd just told me explained everything, when in fact it explained nothing at all. "Oh, I get it," I said finally. "When we were growing up, I talked only to my mother, and Ricardo spoke only with his father."

"Just so."

"Okay," I told him, "I'll go with that." I didn't really have a choice. After a while, you just kind of have to accept the idea that not everything in Hollywood is going to make sense.

The main location for the shoot was the town of Puebla, about seventy-five miles southeast of Mexico City. Back then, this was still the hinterland, and the clash between traditional Mexican rural values and the demands of a Hollywood production crew generated tension on the set that only mounted over time. We were the first American movie company to come and shoot there in color, and it didn't help that we were making a film about bullfighting, an important part of Mexican culture, and changing the tradition to suit our needs as we went along.

Labor conditions in Mexico mandated that Dick Thorpe carry two full crews, one American, one Mexican. Suddenly there were two of everybody, not always a good thing on a movie set. At the same time, Strohm was riding him hard about spending money.

Meanwhile, Thorpe was coping with production problems that dwarfed anything he'd experienced in the States. There were waves of sickness in the cast and crew, electrical problems, dust on the lenses, horse manure, and honest-to-goodness bullshit. It was a director's nightmare.

Then there was the question of who was going to do the actual bullfighting. I had a coach who taught me to work with the *capote* (the cape) and the *muleta* (the red flannel triangle) that bullfighters used. This worked well for the close-ups, but there was no way the studio would let me into the ring with the bulls. That was fine with me—it was much too dangerous.

We had to find real bullfighters for that. The trouble was that the *traje de luces* fit so closely that everything showed. Someone who was going to be my double had to have a body type like mine, so if a bullfighter had a big ass, everyone was going to know that it wasn't my ass. Swimming gives you a high, flat backside, but the Mexican bullfighters all had nice, rounded bottoms that you could set a cup of coffee on, like a shelf. It just wasn't a good match. Ricardo was tall and slender as well, so Thorpe brought in six matadors from Spain to double for the two of us. These matadors were celebrities in their own right, which meant of course that Thorpe had to coddle six superstar bullfighter egos—not a problem with the usual stunt doubles.

In the middle of this, someone back on the third floor of the Thalberg Building woke up and realized that MGM was making an Esther Williams movie with no water. Quickly, an entirely gratuitous scene was concocted in which I am on a raft in the middle of a lake and swim to shore where I stand around in a bathing suit. Guess which publicity photographs got the most play: the bathing suit or the *traje de luces*?

For my leading man, MGM had cast southerner John Carroll, a rumpled, craggy-faced guy who, like numerous others before him, had been touted as "the next Gable." John was one of those nice guys who never could fathom that someone might not like him, but he'd never worked with Dick Thorpe before. Thorpe, of course, didn't like anybody, but Carroll really put himself on the list when he tried to get Dick to wrap up his scenes quickly so he could get out of Mexico.

Hoping to sweet-talk him into doing this, Johnny knocked on Dick's door late at night (timing was never his strong suit). "Mr. Torp . . ." Johnny couldn't quite pronounce "Thorpe." "Mr. Torp, I got things to do. I'm a busy man. I gotta lot of irons in the fire. I got big money deals comin' my way. I gotta get through with this movie in a hurry—can't really stay in Mexico too long."

Then he sat on Dick's bed, which was another mistake. When someone has been in an accident, you don't sit on the bed, and on this movie Dick Thorpe had been in an accident, all day, every day, since filming began. He was hurting in every bone of his body. Nevertheless, Carroll persisted. "What I'd like you to do for me, Mr. Torp, is to get all my work into one little package and shoot it as quickly as possible. Just free up Esther for those scenes and then we can get all my work done in three or four days, a week at the most. Wouldn't that be great?"

Under the circumstances, I don't think Gable himself could have convinced Dick Thorpe to bundle his scenes together for his own convenience, and now Thorpe was looking at Johnny Carroll like a cobra, through those little slits of eyes he had. "Get out of here," was all he could say.

"Is that a 'yes,' Mr. Torp?"

"Get out of here. I will call the police if you don't leave this minute."

"Well . . . ah . . . I guess I'll catch you when you're in a better mood. Good night."

Thorpe, of course, never had good moods. Following Carroll's departure, he just sat there in his bed and started shrieking. Walter Strohm told me about it the next morning. "I heard Dick screaming and went to his room. I thought he was having nightmares, but it was just the chat with Johnny Carroll that had set him off. It took quite a while to get him to stop."

Shortly thereafter, Thorpe stopped speaking to Johnny. Moreover, he parked him in a backwater Mexican town (not even in Puebla) for the entirety of the time it took to complete the picture. And that was a lot of time; because of the production problems, we were way behind schedule.

Johnny never knew what happened to him. He kept calling Walter Strohm and asking, "When do we shoot my stuff?"

Walter had to keep stalling, saying, "Well, John, we're looking forward to working with you, but it doesn't look like it's going to happen any time soon."

One of the reasons it took so long to complete *Fiesta* was that Thorpe, tighter than a clam's sphincter, decided that he wasn't going to kill the bulls, not when they cost a thousand dollars apiece. In that way he could "recycle" the bulls from one action shot to the next. He thought he was going to save the thousand dollars on each bull; it didn't occur to him that he was also going to kill off his six matadors.

Bulls are cunning animals. It doesn't take them long to figure out not to charge the cape, but to charge the man who is holding it. The first time Thorpe shot a scene with those "recycled" bulls, four matadors ended up in the hospital. Two of them barely survived, since they'd been deeply gored in the groin. Bulls' horns are filthy, and fecal matter is almost always mixed in with the dirt; so the infection can be deadly.

Of course, not killing the treacherous bulls made the Mexicans even more angry with us than they had been already. They also couldn't understand why their own matadors weren't good enough to star in this Hollywood movie—and not good enough to double for a woman, no less. Now we were messing with the essence of *la fiesta brava*, an almost sacred part of their heritage.

Things were tense—you could feel it not just on the set, but in the town as well. The Mexicans were tired of us being there. They were tired of cleaning our rooms, and of having to make lunches for this huge crew every day. It didn't help that the Americans were crabbing about having to boil or peel everything they ate, not without good reason, of course. Several people had come down with bad cases of Montezuma's revenge. Worse yet, a director of photography named Sidney Wagner and one other crew member died of cholera from eating contaminated street food they had bought in town.

After that there was a doctor attached to the film crew. Like the rest of us, he stayed at this little residence hotel in Puebla. One day he walked downstairs and complained about his room to Juan Pablo, the sixteen-year-old boy behind the front desk. The doctor got pretty agitated and called the kid some names, because the boy pulled a gun out from under the desk and fired, wounding him. Puebla had a certain Wild West air to it—many of the local men openly carried guns, but none of us expected they'd be used against us. Needless to say, the tension within the company after that incident was extremely high.

This explosive situation was no place for my boisterous, happy-go-lucky husband, but nevertheless, there he was. We had gone virtually straight from our wedding ceremony to Puebla, with only a brief stay in Acapulco before I started work on the picture. In that sense, Ben and I were still on our honeymoon—what a way to start a marriage!

Ben basically had nothing to do down there except party, and he loved to party. Frequently his companion was my makeup man George Lane, and martinis were the party beverage of choice. One evening, after too much to drink, Ben and George went downstairs to pick up their laundry. Juan Pablo, the shooter, was still behind the front desk. Much to our dismay, no charges had been filed against him for shooting the doctor. The authorities said it was the doctor's fault for picking on the boy and calling him names. For reasons I can no longer remember—perhaps it was a premonition—I followed them to the top of the stairs. When Ben asked Juan Pablo for their laundry, the boy insolently refused to look at him.

Cushioned by the buzz of a couple of martinis, Ben had no appreciation of how volatile the situation had become. My husband wasn't a bully, but he didn't like being treated rudely, either. Ben reached across the desk, took hold of Juan Pablo's face, and turned it toward his own. "Hey!" he said. "Look at me when I'm talking to you." Since Juan Pablo had already opened fire on one member of the company, this was a monumentally stupid thing to do.

For a moment I was afraid that he was going to shoot Ben, too, but at that point Juan Pablo started to scream bloody murder; and it suddenly seemed like Mexican cops were coming out of the woodwork. It was almost like a routine from a Mack Sennett movie, except that there was nothing funny about it. Suddenly there was Ben, all six feet six inches of him, with Mexican policemen literally crawling all over him. Ben had a guy hanging from each arm; another was climbing on his back; another was trying to punch him in the stomach. Ben was a nonviolent person, and he wasn't trying to fight back; but he was covered with cops a foot shorter than he was. He looked like Gulliver in Lilliput. They were all over George Lane, too, and eventually the two of them were dragged off to jail.

I knew enough about Mexican jails to know that nothing good happened to Americans who ended up there. I'd heard stories about the jails in Tijuana, and there was no reason to expect that Puebla would be any better. I started ticking off all the things that could go wrong, beginning with bad food, bad water, and of course the very real possibility that the cops would beat the daylights out of them or just make them disappear.

I found Walter Strohm and told him that I was going to go sit in the jail and keep an eye on Ben and George. Since I was the star of the movie, my decision did not sit well with him. MGM didn't want me any place where I'd be in danger, and in a sense I was Strohm's responsibility. "I'll go with you," he said reluctantly.

I was grateful for the company, because I really had no idea what I was getting into. All I knew was that I wanted to be in a place where I could see Ben all the time and be sure that he was safe. After Walter and I parked ourselves on an uncomfortable bench just outside his cell, I put my head on his shoulder and went to sleep.

The next morning the assistant director came with a fistful of pesos and posted bail for the two prisoners. Once they'd been sprung, it was decided that the safest thing to do would be to get us out of town for a while, so Ben and George and I were spirited away to Mexico City, together with Melvina and a second assistant director to provide "security." Meanwhile, Thorpe started to shoot around me, working on the long shots and the bullfight scenes.

The studio thought it was too dangerous for us to show our faces in public and risk creating another incident, even in Mexico City, so we were put up in an apartment under conditions that amounted to house arrest. We played a lot of gin rummy; all our food was brought in.

In the midst of all this difficulty, my mother arrived. With all the ruckus surrounding Ben's arrest, I'd forgotten that I'd sent her a ticket. I can't say that I welcomed her visit with open arms. She came expecting me to take her around so she could see all the churches, and when my mother had an agenda or something she wanted to do, she had a great deal of trouble understanding anyone else's problems. "What do you mean, you can't go outside, Esther? How am I going to see Mexico City?"

"Melvina will take you, Mother," I told her, mustering as much patience as I could.

"But I don't like Melvina. I came all the way to Mexico City to be with my daughter and now I have to be with Melvina?"

"It's either Melvina or nothing, Mom. We're in a really bad time right now and we just have to get through it."

Things went from bad to worse when Hedda Hopper had picked up the item and ran a terrible column about how Esther Williams's drunken bridegroom had started a fight in Puebla and created an international scandal. There was every possibility that the production company might be tossed out of Mexico before the picture could be finished. All we could do was wait until the Mexicans decided what to do. Ben and George were formally charged with assault, since Juan Pablo was claiming that Ben had slapped him. That was a lie, of course, and I knew it since I'd seen what happened; but this was Mexico and there was no way my word would be taken over that of the "victim" and the dozen or so cops who were now claiming to be eyewitnesses. As often occurs in these situations, "the incident" had taken on a life of its own, to the point where the truth behind it no longer mattered.

Finally the word came down that Ben and George were each to be declared persona non grata and expelled from Mexico. However, the company would be allowed to finish *Fiesta*. It wasn't nearly so bad as it might have been, but it didn't take a genius to figure out that George was going to be fired as soon as he got back to Culver City. I decided to stick up for him. After all, he'd been not much more than an innocent bystander in this entire unpleasant business. All he'd really done was have a few martinis with Ben and try to pick up his laundry. I dug in my heels and insisted that I wasn't going back to work unless George did my makeup.

That brought Bill Tuttle, a top makeup man from the MGM makeup department, down on the next plane. He sat me down in that little gin rummy apartment and Dutch-uncled me about the problem. "Esther, I know you're terribly loyal to George, and I knew you were going to be difficult about this, so I came as soon as I heard. Yes, George will be fired, but don't worry about him. He'll get a job someplace else. Let me do your makeup for the rest of the picture. You can't save everybody."

I saw that there was no point in resisting further and he practically promised to get Lane another job. "Bill," I interrupted, "take 'yes' for an answer. What you're saying makes a lot of sense."

With that, Bill, Melvina, and I headed back to Puebla. Ben and George were put on a plane to Los Angeles. By the time I arrived back on the set, all was forgotten. In my absence, Walter Strohm had very wisely been mending fences with the local populace. Every time they had a bullfight, Strohm threw a big party for the citizenry, including free tequila all around.

He'd also finally convinced Thorpe to kill the bulls, even at a thousand dollars apiece. Strohm then took all the meat and gave it to the poor people of Puebla as a gesture of good will. I had no idea that bulls' balls were such a delicacy—the locals drew chances for those like it was the lottery.

Finally it was time to get Johnny Carroll out of cold storage. Thorpe called him back to Puebla, and almost immediately there were more problems. In its own way, Johnny's oozy bayou drawl was as thick as Ricardo's accent, which is to say that he had trouble wrapping his tongue around some of the dialogue. This, of course, drove Dick Thorpe absolutely wild.

In one scene, I was to run out of an elevator into Carroll's arms, at which point he was supposed to say, "Sweetheart, I got my appointment to the New York Institute of Science."

Try as he might, Johnny couldn't get that sentence to come out right. We started shooting first thing in the morning; at 6 P.M., we were still at it. Next morning, we started all over again. Appointment became "apertment." York was "Yooork." And of course Johnny started to stutter as the takes mounted up. Thorpe was relentless. Eventually the crew threatened revolt, and Thorpe finally said, "Okay, print that one—we can loop it later anyway." Of course, he could have said that after the first or second take, but he was such a sadist that he had decided to put Carroll through hell before he did that. I can only assume that this was his revenge for Johnny's ill-advised late-night chat.

Finally we wrapped the picture and it was time to go home. After all the trouble surrounding Ben's arrest, I knew that I wasn't exactly going to get a warm reception when I returned to Los Angeles, but it was downright frosty in L. B. Mayer's office when I was summoned up to the third floor to see him.

As soon as I walked in, he started yelling and rolling on the floor. One of the legendary Louis B. Mayer tantrums had begun. He got up once or twice, only to fall down again and roll some more.

I said, "Mr. Mayer, come on. You're going to give yourself a heart attack. Get up and let's talk. Tell me what you think."

"I'll tell you what I think!" he thundered, all but spitting the words out at me. "I think you married an idiot, a moron, an ass-hole!"

"Okay, you've got a right to be mad at Ben," I said, trying to pacify him. I didn't want him to start rolling on the floor again. "I have a solution."

"All right, let's hear it."

"We won't come to any more of your parties."

"That's it? That's the solution? An international incident and you just won't come to my house anymore?"

"Yes, Mr. Mayer, that's it."

He was disappointed. He'd clearly anticipated apocalyptic measures from me. What I was supposed to say was, "I'm leaving him," the way he'd expected Lana Turner to divorce Artie Shaw when she'd run off and married him without his blessing. When you got right down to it, he was less angry about the fact that Ben had been thrown out of Mexico than he was that I'd married him at all.

"I still don't like the sonofabitch."

"You don't have to like him, Mr. Mayer. I'm not asking you to sign him to a contract. This is my husband. We are going to have children together."

"You're not going to have any children without asking me." Louis B. Mayer was still the patriarch of MGM, and "his" leading ladies were supposed to consult with "Daddy" on all aspects of their private lives.

"You can be sure, Mr. Mayer, that I'm not going to come and ask your permission about starting a family." And with that I got up and left.

I met Ben at the Brown Derby after my audience with L.B. was over.

"How'd it go?" he asked brightly.

It bothered the hell out of me that he was so nonchalant about all this. "We are not well liked up there," I said. "So we will not cast our pearls before swine."

"What?"

"We are on the outs with Mr. Mayer socially. We will not go to his parties. You will not sing, and I will not dance with Cary Grant and George Burns and Howard Hughes."

"Aw, gee," he said, sounding like a disappointed kid, "those parties were fun!"

"Get some pride, Ben! We—you—are not wanted. Mr. Mayer does not want to see your size sixteen feet any more. He mentioned specifically how you keep stumbling over his furniture, and how much he hates your cigar. Now that I think about it, I do, too. Let's have you pay a little penance and give up the cigar."

"Do I have to?"

Sitting there in the Brown Derby, it started to dawn on me why I'd burst into tears just before I walked down the aisle. I sensed that Ben might be a burden on me. It seemed like he was always dependent on me, not just to be the breadwinner, but to solve all our problems. He didn't appear to have any ambitions of his own. It didn't bother him that he'd spent all those months on the set down in Mexico, essentially doing nothing. Obviously, there was nothing else he thought he should be doing.

"You know," I told him, "it's not so wonderful for me to be the only one making money. I think it would be great if you could reestablish your singing career." I knew that a Broadway musical would be the perfect vehicle for his vocal talent, but he had shown no desire to pursue a career of his own. "We can't just want what the studio wants," I continued. "We have to begin to make our life together. Wouldn't you like to use that beautiful voice on Broadway? I'll go with you to New York."

I was angry enough with the studio that I would have packed up and gone to New York if Ben had shown the slightest bit of ambition, but he wasn't interested. "You have it made and I don't," he told me.

Since I'd always been a competitor, I couldn't understand his attitude. I thought he was giving up too easily. "Don't you even want to audition? Don't you want to find out if you can do it? How are you ever going to know unless you try?"

I was disappointed in him as a man—that he didn't have it in him to go for it, even if it meant falling on his face. In retrospect, I see the truth was that he didn't mind being "Mr. Esther Williams" because he was afraid that he would fail at being Ben Gage. But then we were only recently married, and I was still more or less in love with him.

I had no intention of leaving him, although I knew Louis B. Mayer would have been absolutely delighted.

Just as they told me my next picture would be *This Time for Keeps*, I discovered I was pregnant.

In early July of 1946, Ben began complaining that he didn't feel well. He tried to say it was nothing serious, but he started running a high fever and eventually we took him to Good Samaritan Hospital. The news wasn't good. What had started as an abdominal infection had progressed to peritonitis. Ben's doctor told me that he needed to operate right away to clear out all the infected tissue. He was not terribly optimistic about the outcome.

There I was pregnant, sitting in the hospital hallway waiting for word on whether the father of my unborn child was going to survive. It was going to be a long time before I'd know how Ben was, if he had pulled through the operation okay, or if he'd pulled through at all.

Suddenly there was a commotion in the hallway. Howard Hughes had just been brought in, having crashed his experimental aircraft, the FX-11, into a house on Whittier Drive in Beverly Hills. It was a miracle that he'd escaped the flaming wreckage. With second-degree burns, eleven broken ribs, and a broken collarbone, he'd somehow pulled himself out of the cockpit. Two marines who happened to be passing by had dragged him clear of the wreckage before it was completely engulfed in flames. Howard's chances of survival were even worse than Ben's.

I camped out at the hospital, monitoring Ben's condition. He was touch and go for a week or so, but finally his condition stabilized. After he was out of danger, I went down the hall to see Howard, who was recuperating quickly. I liked him a lot and wished him a speedy recovery, but what I really wanted to see was his bed, which was the talk of the hospital. When I got there, Howard was ensconced in the most amazing contraption I'd ever seen. Because he was so busted up, every movement was painful for him. Within days of his accident, however, he'd designed a special bed for himself that his people at Hughes Tool had quickly manufactured. The bed's platform was made up of thirty-two separate rubber squares, each of which was powered by its own motor. The squares could go up and down and tilt from side to side. One of the squares even had a place for a bedpan.

Using airplane controls, Howard was able to change his position at will. He merrily gave it a test drive for me, and it was like a whirligig—he could turn it completely around so he could look out the window. He could also adjust the shutters, one slat at a time. Being at the hospital every day, it was hard for me not to compare Howard Hughes, the man who had so much initiative that he was designing hospital equipment when his very survival was still in doubt, and my husband, the man who was content to let me support our family.

CHAPTER 12

NAME ABOVE THE TITLE
1946–1947

*D*ammit, not again! As soon as I learned that Dick Thorpe had been assigned to direct *This Time for Keeps,* I went up to the third floor of the Thalberg Building and asked to see Benny Thau. Benny was in charge of contract administration, which was exactly what I wanted to talk to him about.

"Benny, just tear it up."

"Tear up what, Esther?"

"My contract."

"Why?"

"If Dick Thorpe is the only director you're ever going to give me, I'd just as soon not work at all. He seems to have it in for me personally. I don't want to make another picture with him picking on me all the time."

"Sorry, Esther, but there's no way I can tear up your contract. You're not a starlet any more. You're in the top ten at the box office now. Your name is above the title. People pay money to see your movies because of you, not because of your director or the story line or your costars. It's your name that's selling the tickets. Dick Thorpe is efficient; he gets the job done, and he'll be directing *This Time for Keeps*. Make the best of it. Think of it this way: 'If it ain't broke, don't fix it.' "

This Time for Keeps was another movie with a lightweight plot revolving around the comedy of misunderstandings in the romance between my character, Nora Cambaretti, and her true love. The movie was to be filmed at a posh resort, the Grand Hotel on Mackinac Island, Michigan. After the rigors of filming in Mexico, it was nice to have a location where the staff was courteous (and unarmed), the plumbing worked, and you could drink the water, even if it meant dealing with Dick Thorpe's sour disposition yet again. At least Lauritz Melchior was in the cast, so we could talk opera together, as was Jimmy Durante, playing someone named Ferdi Farro. (Where did they get these names?) Xavier Cugat, who for a time seemed to be in almost every MGM musical, appeared in this film as well, playing himself.

Crooner Johnnie Johnston was my leading man, in the role of Dick Johnson. Johnnie was a handsome enough fellow, and a bit of a con man. He'd been making money on the side doing golf tricks. He would show off all his adult life with funny shots and off-kilter swings, like a stand-up comic golfer. He also had invited his fan club, consisting of about ten giggly teenagers up to visit him on location at Mackinac.

One day there was a very proper and elegant foursome behind him on the golf course, waiting with mounting impatience as he went into his golf shenanigans on the first tee. Having paid all that money for a quiet, civilized vacation, they were horrified. I picked up smatterings of their conversation.

"Who is that asshole on the first tee?"

"I hear he's some kind of actor in a movie that's filming here."

"I played golf with him yesterday. We bet on every hole, and I finally beat him. When I asked him to pay up in the locker room, he pulled out this check for five hundred dollars and said, 'Do you have change for this?' The check was all dog-eared—the sonofabitch has probably been using it for years."

While we were filming, Johnnie was carrying on a torrid long-distance romance with soprano actress Kathryn Grayson—they were eventually married in 1947. Kathryn, like me, had gotten her start at MGM in the Andy Hardy movies. While we were at Mackinac, she was making *It Happened in Brooklyn* with Frank Sinatra, but she wrote to Johnston almost every day. One evening after dinner, Johnnie gathered all his dewy-eyed groupies around him and began reading them Kathryn's intimate letters aloud, including the all-too-graphic details concerning what she liked about his lovemaking.

I was appalled. "God," I thought to myself, "that's my leading man! MGM, where did you find him?"

People still ask me, "Who was your favorite leading man?" The answer I give most often is "the water," because the water was really my costar. Technicolor made it so invitingly blue, and with the camera angle at water level as I swam, audiences felt as if they were swimming right beside me.

If the water was my true costar, then the actors who played my "love interest," were often little more than interchangeable parts. Many of them, including Johnnie Johnston in this film and Johnny Carroll in *Fiesta,* had been given roles in my movies so they could get a bit of experience and become better known. I would have preferred stronger leading men, but it's quite possible that a more prominent actor wouldn't want to hold my towel; and sometimes that was literally what happened in the plot. In a way, my movies were vehicles for inexperienced actors on the way up, much like those Andy Hardy films had been showcases for young MGM actresses just starting out.

Audiences didn't seem to be put off by these improbable comedy-of-errors plots, as long as I swam. My films were escapist fare for a country just beginning to put itself back together after the war. They made money, and because they were profitable, MGM took the Benny Thau "if it ain't broke, don't fix it" approach. I wanted to do drama or straight (dry land) comedy, but the studio saw no reason to broaden my range beyond these water musical soufflés. Five years after my screen test with Clark Gable, I was still "the mermaid" on the lot.

I would have loved to have been cast in *Cass Timberlane* opposite Spencer Tracy, and I thought I could do a good job with that role, but the part went to Lana Turner. Like Turner, the other "serious" actresses, such as Ingrid Bergman, Greer Garson, and Katharine Hepburn, who were teamed with good leading men, didn't have to carry a picture alone. Betty Grable over at Fox was the only other woman in the top ten box office, and she had the same kinds of problems I had—cardboard plots and disposable leading men. By the typecasting rules of Hollywood, Bergman and Garson and Hepburn were "drama," and Betty and I were "fluff"; but fortunately for us, "fluff" seemed to be what brought in the paying customers.

A bit later I talked with Ingrid Bergman about the different experiences we had in moviemaking. We were staying at the same small pension in Paris, and I saw her walking up and down in the park, talking to herself. I waited for her to return to the hotel.

"You're learning lines, aren't you?"

"Yes, I'm doing *Tea and Sympathy* in French."

"You know, I really envy you."

"You don't need to envy me, my dear Esther. I can't swim a tenth as well as you can."

"I envy you your leading men," I said. "How did you get them to give you Gary Cooper, Charles Boyer, Cary Grant? Look who they gave me—Johnnie Johnston!"

"It's true that I've worked with the classic leading men of Hollywood, but that's because I needed them. Your pictures are carried by you alone, dear—you and your bathing suit. Nobody has ever tried to ask me to carry a picture all by myself, so take it as a compliment."

In essence, she was telling me the same thing that Benny Thau had said, and as often as I'd think, "If only they'd give me a part with some meat to it," there would be this little voice within me that would say, "Count your blessings. If they make a movie with a lightweight script and without a great leading man and that movie is a success, they've got to assume that it's what you do that works."

Mackinac Island was a tiny resort island located in the straits between lower and Upper Michigan. Irene decided to use a lot of plaid in the costumes and designed a pretty swimsuit for me out of lumberjack plaid flannel. The only trouble was that it absorbed water like crazy. I dove into the pool and tried to swim, but the suit just dragged me to the bottom. It was like trying to swim while wrapped in an old army blanket. I actually had trouble keeping my head above water. Finally I reached around behind me, tugged at the zipper, and watched as the suit quickly sank to the bottom of the deep end of the pool.

On this particular day there were a lot of tourists on the set. They massed behind the cordons in the roped-off area, watching "Hollywood magic at work," and of course their day was made since Esther Williams was swimming in the Mackinac Island pool. Only one thing—suddenly Esther had nothing on.

I swam to the side of the pool and called to my wardrobe woman, Flossie Hackett. I crossed my arms and covered my body as best I could. I whispered, "Flossie . . ."

"Esther, you silly girl, what did you do? You're totally nude!"

"Flossie, this is no joke. That suit was too heavy. It had to go! I had to take it off."

Flossie loved to scold me. "Esther, that suit cost a lot of money to make. Now you just dive down to get it up off the bottom of the pool."

"I can't. Get somebody with one of those skimmers to fish it out. Please find me a towel."

"Esther, a towel isn't going to do you much good. Look at all these people. Even if I hold it for you at the ladder, they're all going to get a pretty good view as you get out."

I had an idea. "Flossie, grab one of those big towels from the chaises and bring me your scissors."

We cut a big hole in the middle of the towel and she dropped it over my head, like a poncho. It clung to me like a wet T-shirt, and I clutched it closed on both sides. As I came up the ladder, applause rang out from the film crew and the spectators.

I learned my lesson. From then on I would sit in on the swimsuit design meetings and participate in the decision making about fabric choice. Once a suit was made, I would get into the pool and swim in it. After that it went back to wardrobe for whatever had to be changed. At the time I didn't realize that this was my apprenticeship in swimsuit design, but that's what it turned out to be.

Meanwhile, however, we had a hell of a production problem. We needed to shoot the pool scene, and I didn't have a swimsuit. Back in Culver City, Irene quickly made up a lighter version of the suit for me, and the studio flew it up to Michigan. There was a lot of screaming about the expense and the delay.

Dick Thorpe was sure that the flannel suit debacle was my fault. Maybe because I was secure in the knowledge of my top ten status, I decided it was time to talk to him about his rotten disposition. I said, "Mr. Thorpe, I'd like to ask you something . . ." He looked at me without a trace of a smile. "Mr. Thorpe, is it just that you don't like actors? Or is it me?"

Apparently I struck a nerve. He responded, "I hate actors."

I said, "You know . . . it shows. Your anger comes through. What is it that makes you so mad at actors? What do we do to you that makes you so angry?"

He said, "Well, you're all so *fucking* beautiful—and you know it."

"But," I said, "the studio wants us to know it. They see that we're dressed beautifully. They make us 'camera ready,' with makeup and hairstyling. It's our job. Your directing and editing is wonderful, and everybody loves your pictures—but nobody loves *you*." He just glowered at me. "We've got a picture to do, Mr. Thorpe, and I'd like to like you by the time we're done. Is there anything you can do about that?"

He thought for a moment and finally spoke. "I could like you if you could not be so cheerful every morning."

I said, "Okay, I can do that. How about if I don't talk to you at all until noon?"

"Make that after lunch," he said.

"Fine."

"And can you not smile so much?"

"Get used to it," I said with the broadest grin I could muster. "The audiences pay a lot of money for that smile! But I'll try to save it for the camera." From then on, there was a kind of mutual respect between Thorpe and me. Those top ten figures were just sheer box office, and that's what put a name above the title.

We finished *This Time for Keeps* uneventfully, before my pregnancy started to show. Throughout the shooting I'd been very careful not to get overtired; fortunately the pool scenes were not rigorous, but I was concerned because I hadn't yet felt the baby kick. When I returned to Los Angeles in early September, I was about four months along. I made an appointment with my obstetrician as soon as I got home.

He seemed unconcerned about the fact that I hadn't yet felt life and said that it was okay when I asked his permission to drive up to Monterey. Ben loved golf, and I wanted him to have a golfing holiday for his birthday, before the baby came. The doctor didn't see a problem, so at the end of October we left for the Del Monte Lodge with Janet Blair and her husband, musician and musical arranger Louis Busch, driving there in their new woodie station wagon. We were close friends. Ben at six feet six inches and Lou at five feet four inches were like Mutt and Jeff on the golf course. Janet's career had taken off in 1942 when she was cast as *My Sister Eileen* at Columbia. Now she was about to begin *Down to Earth* with Rita Hayworth, so we were full of shop talk.

Unfortunately, my water broke just as I got out of the car, and I went very quickly to our room. Janny stayed with me while Lou and Ben went to the bar. There was no way the men could have understood how serious the situation was. I was in pain and I had a strong feeling that the baby was coming; but I knew it was much too soon. I called my doctor at home in Beverly Hills and told him I was having regular pains. "A baby can't survive at five and a half months along," I said.

"That's probably true," he replied, absolutely without emotion.

"I'm going to a hospital right now because I have a feeling that this baby is coming tonight."

"I'd fly up, Esther, but it would probably be all over by the time I got there."

The tone of his voice told me that he really didn't care one way or another. "Don't trouble yourself, doctor," I said. "You can read about it in the paper."

I was taken to the hospital and immediately given a caudal block. My head was awake, but everything below my sternum was numb. I watched as the attending physician removed what had been a baby girl from my body—in pieces. Badly decomposed, she had been dead for over a month. The doctor was furious. "How could your obstetrician let this happen to you?"

At that point the main concern was the potential for infection from the bacteria and the toxins. In addition to the very real possibility that I'd never be able to conceive again, there was a great risk to my own health as well. I told the doctor to do whatever he had to do to keep me from getting an infection.

"That means a full D&C, dilation and curettage. I'll work quickly, but I don't think I can finish before the anesthetic wears off. You're going to be in a lot of pain if I do this now."

"I'm going to be dead if you don't."

"I'll do my best, Mrs. Gage."

It was painful, but the doctor scraped all the remains of what would have been my firstborn child out of my system, then gave me massive doses of penicillin. When I awakened the next morning, I realized that I was in the maternity ward. The Del Monte hospital was tiny, and there was no other place to put me. I had to listen to the joyous sounds of people cooing over healthy newborns in the nearby rooms. It went on all day long.

"Isn't she lovely? . . . What a perfect child! . . . She looks just like you! . . . May I hold her?" Amid so much happiness, I felt absolutely barren. The tears just rolled down my cheeks.

I was devastated, and I wanted my husband to be as devastated as I was about losing our child. I wanted to share my pain with him, but he didn't show up at the hospital until well after dinner. He'd spent the day playing golf. When I saw him, he was in a terrifically happy mood. He'd gotten some sun on his face from his day on the links and had a good buzz from whatever he'd been drinking in the clubhouse at the nineteenth hole.

"Esther, this is the greatest birthday present you could have given me. You should have seen Lou and me out there . . ."

"Did you play nine holes or eighteen, Ben?"

"It was so wonderful that we played eighteen and went back and played another nine. This has been just a dream trip."

He was oblivious to my misery. "For me it's been a nightmare, Ben." I was too exhausted and groggy to express the depth of the hurt and anger that I felt.

"Oh, right . . . right." Then he got this faraway look.

What kind of man could play twenty-seven holes of golf while his wife was lying in a hospital bed having just lost a child? I thought to myself, "There's no point in telling him how I feel—he doesn't know—he just doesn't know." In fairness, the late 1940s were still an unenlightened period regarding obstetrics. Childbirth was regarded as a mysterious process shared only by a woman and her doctor. Husbands were not invited to "share the experience." They were expected to sit in the waiting room and hand out cigars at the appropriate time. Female issues were in the realm of the unmentionable. Still, as I look back on it, Ben was an incredibly insensitive man in an insensitive era.

We returned to Los Angeles. I kept my fears and my disappointment bottled up inside, but I did find a new OB-GYN, Dr. William Bradbury, and asked him the question that was uppermost in my mind. "Will I be able to have more children?"

"Let's get you really healthy before I answer that question. Rest as much as you can before you start your next picture."

I followed Dr. Bradbury's orders and spent a lot of time reading and sunning by the pool of our little house in the Pacific Palisades. Ben's older brother Chuck often kept me company. Before we were married he'd actually tried to warn me about Ben's penchant for buffoonery. One afternoon he asked me, "What happened when you lost the baby?"

It was a delicate question. I'd never really confided the whole story to anyone. Even after we got home, Ben had never asked. As I began telling Chuck the story, starting with the drive up the coast with Lou and Janny and ending in the operating room, I could see Chuck's eyes start to wander off.

"Am I boring you?"

"No, not at all. It's all very interesting, what you said. Tell me, Esther. . . . You were in Lou Busch's new woodie. How did it drive?"

There I was, baring my soul, telling the story of the most painful thing that had ever happened to me, and all he wanted to know about was Louis Busch's station wagon. "It drove fine, Chuck, just fine," I said, fighting off the tears.

By the time I was ready to start my next film, *On an Island With You*, my periods had returned to normal, I was rested, and I had a wonderful tan; but I was severely depressed. The question of whether I'd ever be able to have children still lingered; and I was grappling with the issue of whether I wanted to have children with Ben at all. I didn't know how much energy I wanted to put forth to keep this marriage together, because I knew by then that I was going to be the only one who would make the effort.

We began shooting on location in Florida, using Key Biscayne as Hawaii, in spring of 1947. It was yet another movie with a ridiculous plot, and by now we'd assembled something of a repertory company of actors who kept popping up in my films. I played Rosalind Reynolds, a swimming movie star who had come to Hawaii to make a film, bringing my fiancé with me. His name was Ricardo Montez; not surprisingly he was played by Ricardo Montalban. Cyd Charisse played my friend Yvonne Torro, who secretly wanted Ricardo for herself. Both Cyd and Ricardo had been in *Fiesta* with me. Again in the cast were Jimmy Durante and the ubiquitous Xavier Cugat.

The male lead in *On an Island With You* was Peter Lawford. Peter was a definite improvement over Johnnie Johnston. He had been wonderful in *Good News* with June Allyson, and he was fresh from an affair with Lana Turner. He was still wearing all the gold jewelry with his name on it that she had given him. Peter played the military technical adviser to Rosalind's film, an ex-pilot named Lawrence Kingsley. He more or less kidnaps her and takes her to a remote island so that she will fall in love with him, too. The plot develops around how the two pairs of lovers sort themselves out, so that Peter and I end up together, as do Ricardo and Cyd.

Much to my consternation, Dick Thorpe was directing again. That made three pictures with him in a row, which didn't help my depression. I complained again to Benny Thau, but I got the same response I had the last time—make the best of it. After our détente on Mackinac, Thorpe reserved most of his malice for Ricardo, who he kept referring to as "that damned Mexican." That didn't, however, keep him from trying to kill me.

For the scene in which Peter kidnaps me, I was supposed to fall into a hole in the jungle floor camouflaged by vegetation. Thorpe had the crew dig a hole four feet deep and covered it with palm fronds. I walked into that hole and fell straight down, which was what they wanted. It looked great on camera, but Thorpe had put no

(left) At three. *(below)* My first swimsuit was a hand-me-down. My sister, Maurine, took my brother David and me to Manhattan Beach, where she taught me how to swim.

My big brother Stanton, who died at sixteen. He was a child star at five years of age.

The LAAC Swim Team, 1939 (Los Angeles Athletic Club). Left to right: Gloria Phelps, Billie Steitz, me, Edith Motridge, Ruth Jump, and Edith Pemberton.

(right) In the news at fourteen. *(bottom)* Johnny Weissmuller and I swim together on Treasure Island for Billy Rose's Aquacade. *(below)* I was Class President of George Washington High in south-west Los Angeles.

Tabbed to Make a 'Big Splash'

S. Coach Aileen Allen's new aquatic find, is expected to go places Miss Williams participates in the women's free-style events at ... Athletic Club pool tonight.

San Francisco—after being married to Leonard Kovner—1940.

I took my daily swim at the Beverly Hills Hotel pool despite the presence of onlookers.

(left) Lillian Burns, MGM's drama coach, trying to teach her "method" acting. I wasn't impressed. *(below)* My screen test with Metro's leading star, Clark Gable. He was the first to have called me a mermaid.

(right) The MGM stars all autographed my swimsuit with me in it. *(below)* At nineteen, MGM sent me to visit the U.S. hospitals. *(opposite)* My first bathing suit pinup for MGM at Venice Beach, 1941.

(above) Toward the end of WWII, the U.S. Navy had a competition to "capture the Esther," a waterproof framed portrait. *(right)* With Mickey Rooney in *Andy Hardy's Double Life.*

Six-story marquee of *Bathing Beauty* on top of the Astor Theater in Times Square.

The camera floats on an aerial boom suspended from the ceiling of Stage 30 for the water-spectacular finale of *Bathing Beauty*.

(above) A "water ballet" by Esther Williams, read the title card for Ziegfeld Follies. *(right)* Benny Lane rowed a boat out to the middle of the pool, on Stage 30 to reapply makeup for *Thrill of a Romance.*

(above) Before *Murder She Wrote,* Angela Lansbury and I fought for William Powell in *Hoodlum Saint.* *(right)* My favorite designer, Irene, checks out my pink dress from *Easy to Wed.*

(*above*) My dressing room at MGM when I received my flowers for the first day of shooting on *Duchess of Idaho*. (*right*) Van Johnson and I share a moment with my cocker, Angie, who came to work with me every day on the set of *Easy to Wed*. She never ruined a shot.

Van and I sang in Portuguese in *Easy to Wed*. Carmen Miranda coached us.

(left) Mr. and Mrs. Ben
Gage, November 25,
1945. *(below)* I learned
how to wield the "capote"
in *Fiesta*.

Johnnie Johnston sang his way through *This Time for Keeps* and never got in the water.

The cast of *On an Island With You*. Left to right: Jimmy Durante, Peter Lawford, me, Cyd Charisse, Ricardo Montalban, and Xavier Cugat.

Gene Kelly and Frank Sinatra lift me for a publicity still to disguise the fact that they are shorter than I.

I played a swimsuit designer in *Neptune's Daughter,* and later copied this suit for the Esther Williams Swimwear collection.

(left) My mother and me in my dressing room going over my fan mail. *(below)* An underwater shot from *Pagan Love Song.* I'm four months pregnant with Kim.

(right) I stopped by to visit Joan Crawford making her last film at MGM—*Torch Song,* 1953. *(below)* I wore a glamorous dress in green satin for Palm Beach's elegant Emerald Ball.

(left) Texas Carnival.
Left to right: Chuck
Walters, director; me;
Howard Keel; and
Florence Hackett,
wardrobe. *(below)*
Alan Ladd, Golden
Globe's most popular
male star of the year,
and me, the most
popular female star.

(above) Making the cover of *Life* magazine. *(left)* Fred Cole used this ad in *Harper's Bazaar* and *Vogue* without ever giving MGM credit. *(opposite)* I wore the Cole of California suit in three pictures *Skirts Ahoy!*, *Neptune's Daughter*, and *Dangerous When Wet*. So did all the chorus girls.

(right) Photographer Clarence Bull didn't know how much Victor Mature and I enjoyed posing for this picture. *(below)* I was all in gold sequins for *Million Dollar Mermaid*, fifty feet in the air.

(above) A Busby Berkeley creation for *Million Dollar Mermaid. (left)* I'm pointing out the scenery to Annette Kellerman, on the set of *Million Dollar Mermaid.* I portrayed the famed water queen in the film.

(top) Kim, Ben, and Susie swim at home with Mama Esther. No cameras, please. *(above)* Ben and I christen Susan Tenny Gage at the Community Church in Westwood. *(facing)* Fernando and I swam together even when we weren't filming on the set of *Dangerous When Wet*.

(left) I was chosen "Orange Queen" for the state of Florida while I was filming *Easy to Love* at Cypress Gardens. *(below)* Tom and Jerry underwater in *Dangerous When Wet*.

(left) Fernando and I returned from Portuguese Bend, near Palos Verde at the finish of *Dangerous When Wet.* (below) Cary Grant visits the set of *Dangerous When Wet.*

(above) The Florida-shaped pool in Cypress Gardens, Florida, built for the movie *Easy to Love* by Nick Pope. The pool cost $50,000 in 1952. (right) I lunched with Grace Kelly in Cannes, the day she met Prince Rainier.

(left) I designed my own costume, all in red, for my London appearance at Wembly Arena for the Aqua Spectacular. (below) Hannibal (Howard Keel) begs Amytis (me) not to let this night get away in *Jupiter's Darling*. This was our third picture together.

(above) I posed for Italian fashion magazines during the filming of *Raw Wind in Eden*. *(right)* Ben and I leave with Jupiter's Darling, a 350-pound baby elephant who appeared with me in the film of the same name, on a tour of nine U.S. cities.

Jeff Chandler and I pose for the poster of *Raw Wind in Eden* in
Castelione della Pescaia.

(top) Jeff and I out on the town in Rome. *(above)* Edward and I at dinner at the Desert Inn in Las Vegas. I was soon to be Mrs. Edward Bell.

pillows, no mattresses, no nothing in the bottom of the pit to break my fall. Not surprisingly I sprained my ankle and had to finish the movie on crutches.

Make the best of it, Benny had told me. That had always been my approach to life anyway, so I tried to put my sprained ankle and my aching heart behind me as I finished *On an Island With You*. I thought to myself, That's what being an actress is all about—taking yourself out of your own difficulties to portray somebody else. All the women who were at MGM—Judy Garland is the classic example—were doing superlative work on the screen at the same time that they were going through a great deal of turmoil and tragedy in their private lives. And by and large, they were going through it all by themselves.

It's a lonely business, I thought, this stardom, because you never really feel that it's safe to confide in anyone. Husbands don't want to know, even if they're not the source of the problem. Friends can't keep secrets. Even therapists were known to go to the press. You learned not to trust anyone with your confidences and risk bursting that pretty pink bubble the studio had constructed around you and your outwardly perfect personal life. The public desperately wanted to believe that you lived a fairy tale existence, a projection of all their romantic fantasies, so much so that despite everything, you tried to believe it yourself.

MOVIES AND MOTHERHOOD
1948–49

*M*GM told me that my next film was to be *Neptune's Daughter,* which was to start filming late in 1948—far enough in the future to give me a chance to rest. Then just as I was looking forward to a little down time to sort out my personal life, I got a call from the studio. MGM wanted me to replace Judy Garland in *Take Me Out to the Ball Game,* with Gene Kelly and Frank Sinatra.

Although *Easter Parade* had been a huge success, Judy had barely gotten through the films that followed that one, *The Pirate* and *Words and Music.* Already drug dependent at the age of twenty-six, she was on a pharmaceutical elevator, taking sedatives to sleep at night and Benzedrine in the morning to go to work. MGM's demanding production schedule had contributed to her condition, but the studio hierarchy refused to acknowledge any responsibility, saying that she'd become "undependable." That much was true—Judy was often late, and when she showed up she usually was either groggy or wired. Eventually she checked into a hospital in Boston to detox, but not before MGM removed her from *Take Me Out to the Ball Game,* a situation to be repeated later with *Annie Get Your Gun.*

June Allyson had been slated to replace Judy in *Ball Game,* but Junie had discovered she was pregnant and opted not to work while she was carrying. Like me, she had already had one miscarriage and didn't want to risk losing this baby. When the studio began methodically going down their list of possible replacements, there I was.

We were to start filming in the summer of 1948, with me as K. C. Higgins, who inherits a baseball team from a distant relative. I was excited about doing the picture, a costume musical set in the early 1900s. However, I realized that the historical setting would make the obligatory swimming scene problematic, because the swimsuit as we know it had not yet emerged on the fashion scene. Arthur Freed was the producer. I liked the script, and with Gene Kelly and Frank Sinatra I had two strong leading men. Since this was a role that was not written specifically for me, I hoped that it might be an opportunity to break out of the "swimming star" straitjacket the studio had stuck me in.

I told Lillian Burns, "I'm sick of all these reviews that say I can't act. I'd like to learn something serious . . . like Shakespeare, and I'd like to start with Portia's speech from *The Merchant of Venice*—you know, 'The quality of mercy is not strain'd.' Can we do that?"

Lillian stared at me in disbelief. God knows what She thought. She had not lost her penchant for touching herself as she sat up there in that grand studio of hers. It had a huge picture window, and everyone on the third floor had to walk past it on the way to the commissary. Because of this exposure, Lillian was always jumping up, anxious to curry favor with any VIP who was passing by.

"Lillian, I'm sick and tired of you abandoning me every time you see Joe Pasternak or Jack Cummings walk past here. I'm going to work with a real drama coach—outside the studio." I had no idea that my threat of leaving her would trigger an Oscar-winning Lillian Burns performance. She performed with histrionics worthy of Sarah Bernhardt herself. Lillian started at 4:30 in the afternoon and went on to almost 9:00 P.M., giving herself a most interesting set of symptoms. I sat and watched in astonishment. She faked colic, cramps, and diarrhea. Finally she threatened a nervous breakdown. It was an astounding performance—Lillian was a better actress than I knew.

During that time, Ben and I had been invited to a holiday barbe-
cue at the Mandeville Canyon home of Rex Harrison and Lilli
Palmer, who was under contract to Warner Bros. After everyone else
had left, we stayed behind so that I could talk to Lilli about my
dilemma with Lillian. She recommended her drama teacher to me,
an expatriate Russian named George Schtanoff. Most graciously,
she even offered to arrange an appointment for me. Rex was away
at a rehearsal that evening, so Lilli and I kept talking well after the
fireworks were over. She appeared to be glad to have someone to
talk to, perhaps because she spent a lot of nights by herself.

Rex's nickname of "Sexy Rexy" was well deserved. His affair
with Carole Landis was the worst-kept secret in Hollywood. The
gossip columnists referred to them as the "English star whose
name begins with H and the local glamour girl whose name begins
with L." "Glamour girl" was putting it mildly—Landis was not exactly a paragon of virtue. She was remarkably constructed, with
perhaps the most sensational upper body in Hollywood. People
were surprised that she could stand erect. At the age of twenty-nine
she was already a waning starlet who was separated from her
fourth husband.

Ben fell asleep on a couch, but Lilli and I sat up chatting together, waiting for Rex. I had brought a script I wanted him to consider doing with me, *The Great Indoors*, by Ring Lardner Jr., one of
the Hollywood Ten who had been subpoenaed by the House Un-
American Activities Committee. Lardner was living in exile in London, and MGM had bought this comedy from him before his
troubles in Washington, D.C. I never did talk to Rex about this
script, because he did not come home that night. I gave up waiting
for Rex when the clock struck 2 A.M.

The following morning the scandal broke—"Miss L" was dead.
Carole Landis had committed suicide by taking an overdose of
sleeping pills. The newspapers conjectured that she became despon-
dent because Rex Harrison had told her that their affair was over.
There was some factual underpinning for the speculation—Rex was
leaving Hollywood for New York to appear as Henry VIII in Maxwell
Anderson's new play *Anne of the Thousand Days*.

Lilli knew, as I did, that Rex must have been with Carole the night of the suicide. There was no doubt that he was not home that night. Lilli knew that her husband had been having an affair, but she kept her head high through the maelstrom that followed. In the process, she gave one of her finest performances. She answered questions from the press and stood by him through the coroner's inquest. The two of them denied that there was any romantic relationship with Landis at all. Rex and Carole were just "good friends." Lilli appeared arm-in-arm with him at the services for Landis, wearing a navy blue dress she borrowed from Mary Fairbanks, who had told her, "One doesn't wear black to the funeral of one's husband's mistress."

The official alibi, orchestrated by the studio, was that a platoon of people could account for every minute of Rex's time on that Fourth of July. Lilli was alleged to have been staying with her sister in New York on that holiday. Supposedly, Rex called her in New York after he found Landis's body, and she hopped the first airplane back to Los Angeles. She claimed to have arrived at Los Angeles International at 6:00 A.M. on the morning of July 6, and to have been picked up by Leland Hayward. (Lilli repeats this story in her autobiography, *Change Lobsters and Dance.*) Curiously, no reporters saw her get off the airplane at LAX, but there were hordes of them at the front door when Palmer and Hayward supposedly arrived from the airport.

How powerful were the studios in those days? How close was the "Hollywood club"? Despite a barrage of speculation in the newspapers, no one cracked. No one who attended that Fourth of July party denied that Lilli was in New York. Including me. I knew "the rules." That's how thorough the protection was that studio lawyers and publicists arranged. It could not happen with today's scandal-loving media.

In the midst of this scandal, Lilli remembered to call George Schtanoff for me. When she phoned to tell me that she had set up an appointment, I thanked her warmly and said nothing about the events of that night.

For my first session, Schtanoff asked me to bring something to read. After my debacle with Lillian, I certainly wasn't going to perform Shakespearean soliloquies in front of a Russian drama teacher. I brought my script for *Take Me Out to the Ball Game*. He read through it quickly and asked, "Do you have to wear a uniform like the rest of the team?"

"No," I said, "it's a musical and I'm the girl, the owner of the baseball team. I'm in ruffles and lace."

"Would you please explain a musical to me?"

"What part of 'musical' don't you understand, Mr. Schtanoff?"

"Esther, I want to work with you, but I don't know how to begin," he said seriously—Russians are *very* serious. "Why are you in the pool if you are singing *Take Me Out to the Ball Game*? Lilli tells me that your movies are very popular, but I don't understand how can you do that."

"Do what?"

"How can you sing while you're underwater?"

"I don't sing while I'm underwater. I sing when I'm on top of the water. I may sound as though I am changing the subject—because I am—but what I want to learn from you is how to perform Portia's speech from *The Merchant of Venice*. I know you understand Shakespeare. Please help me."

He looked at me with a blank stare. But then he said sweetly, "Anybody can do Portia, but I don't know anyone except you who can sing and swim at the same time. I'm afraid I should not tamper with your successful career." He handed me back my script and said, "I'm looking forward to seeing this movie. Please let me know when it will be released."

It sounded very much to me as though this fine acting teacher was telling me the same thing that Benny Thau was telling me: "If it ain't broke, don't fix it." Clearly, it was time to confine my lessons to the rehearsal hall. Figure out how to make a turn-of-the-century swimsuit, get it just right for the song in the pool, and get on with the movie.

Although it turned out to be pure misery, I was looking forward to doing this picture with particular excitement because I was a Frank Sinatra fan. I had been a bobby-soxer in the early days of Frank's singing career, and although I didn't go to the Paramount Theater in New York and scream like millions of other girls, I bought every record he made. I not only adored the way he sang, but admired his underrated natural approach to acting. He had done *Step Lively* with Gloria DeHaven, which wasn't a big success; but then he did *Anchors Aweigh* with Gene Kelly, and his film career really took off.

We were instant friends. He told me that both of us approached acting the same way, speaking like you'd talk to a friend, as if the camera wasn't there. Frank loved his new place in the film industry, but he also loved to party. While we were making this picture, he was a Roman candle shooting off in all directions. As soon as the day's filming was done, he went rushing off to one bash or another. He often grabbed catnaps on the set because he'd been out all night. Sometimes he showed up fighting a hangover. The unit manager reported every one of his infractions to the third floor. When Frank told me that he had heard the rumor that he was getting bounced off the picture, I tried to reassure him.

"Frank," I said, "they're not going to let you go. You have too much talent."

"So did Judy. Tell that to the kid on the Yellow Brick Road."

"This is different. Take a look at the dailies. Your voice sounds wonderful. You're even matching Gene step-for-step in the dance numbers. So you're painting the town after work, but it's not affecting what you do on film." Frank remembered my remarks, and thereafter I was the beneficiary of his legendary loyalty to his friends. Whenever I saw him perform, I sat at ringside with my elbow on the stage.

I was glad to have a friend on the set—I needed one. Gene didn't make much of a secret about how disappointed he was that I was playing K. C. Higgins. He'd come up with the idea for *Take Me Out to the Ball Game* with his pal, dancer/choreographer Stanley Donen. The two of them had collaborated on the musical numbers for *On the Town* and *Anchors Aweigh*, which had costarred Kathryn Grayson, and Kelly had developed the role of K. C. Higgins with Grayson in mind. Producer Arthur Freed substituted Garland for Grayson, but what I was good at was obviously very different from either of them; and Gene never let me forget that in this case he thought "different" meant "not in his league."

Kelly played a character named Eddie O'Brien and Sinatra was

Dennis Ryan, two winter-season vaudevillians who were also the shortstop and second baseman on a baseball team called the Wolves. O'Brien and Ryan were two-thirds of the most famous double-play combination since Tinker to Evers to Chance. Originally Kelly had wanted real-life baseball manager Leo Durocher (who was married to MGM star Laraine Day when Kelly and Donen first developed the idea) to play O'Shaughnessy, the first baseman. However, when Freed brought in the rubber-faced Jules Munshin (who had been terrific in *On the Town*), the double-play infield trio became the unforgettable "O'Brien to Ryan to Goldberg."

Arthur Freed tapped Busby Berkeley to direct, but Kelly and Donen were fully in charge of the musical numbers, not Buzz, even though Berkeley's name remained on the credits as director. Kelly was a dancer who thought more like a producer/director. He was a forceful rising power within MGM who wielded a lot of clout with Freed. He was also a notorious perfectionist, and Esther the swimmer wasn't exactly what he had in mind as a dancing partner.

A dancer I was not. There's a clean tightness to dancers. Their movements are sharp and precise. Swimmers, on the other hand, are all fluid motion; there's no sudden stopping and starting in the water. As graceful as I was in the pool, I felt clumsy on dry land. It was one thing to jitterbug with a bunch of GIs, quite another to perform for the cameras with Gene Kelly, and his mounting aggravation with me just made it worse. I read a book on psychocybernetics, which explained how to break each step in my dance number into component parts. According to the book, it was the same technique that golfer Ben Hogan had used to reconstruct his golf swing after a terrible automobile accident. I rehearsed every movement in my sleep, according to psychocybernetics principles. However, those flippers that worked so well in the water remained just two left feet on the dance floor. Kelly, one of the most winning and likeable of men on-screen, was nothing less than a tyrant behind the camera—at least with me. He had to see that I was doing the best I could—and suffering through it.

As much as Kelly resented the fact that I was not a dancer, he resented my height even more. There was no hiding that I was half a head taller than he was. Looking at the two of us side by side in front of that rehearsal hall mirror, I thought back to my first meeting with Louis B. Mayer, when he talked about all the techniques the studio used to make short men look taller. "You can put Charles Boyer on a box and dig a hole for Loretta Young's horse, Mr. Mayer," I grumbled under my breath, "but for a dance number, the box won't work."

I wore flat shoes and curved my spine so deeply it felt like I had scoliosis, but still it didn't work. Kelly just looked at me as though I was hopeless. If he could have made me dance on my ankles, he would have. In one scene, we were supposed to sit on an old-fashioned loveseat in a hotel lobby. Just as we were about to say our lines, he looked at me, then looked out at Stanley Donen behind the camera and said, "You know something? This sonofabitch even *sits* tall!"

"Gene," I said, "I was born with long legs and a long waistline. Swimming gave me broad shoulders. I have perfect proportions in a swimsuit, and that's why I'm here making movies at MGM. I'm sorry that my physique doesn't fit in with your plans—you'd like me to be petite, with short little legs and narrow shoulders, but there's nothing I can do about it. I can't make myself five-two, and I can't make you six-three, either. For this scene, it would help a lot if you'd just sit up straight. If that's not enough, try tucking one foot under your ass."

Gene looked at me and then turned to Stanley Donen behind the camera. "Gee, the way you just said that, you surprise me, Esther. I think you really *would* like to learn how to act."

That's how it was with Gene. There was always that little zinger. He and Donen made me the butt of their jokes. The two of them were quite a pair; it was as if they were joined at the hip—and the mouth.

Shortly before production began, I'd ordered a brand new powder blue Cadillac Eldorado convertible. With everything on it custom-made, it cost $5,200. This was the first new car I had allowed myself. For the kid from Orchard Avenue, it was a big deal. The salesman called to say that he wanted to bring it to me on the lot, and when I walked out of the rehearsal hall to take delivery, Stanley and Gene followed me out. The two of them were merciless, mincing around the car, dripping sarcasm with every step.

"Oh my!" said Gene, with make-believe admiration. "Stanley, do you see what Esther has?"

"Look, Gene," said Donen, parroting Kelly's tone of voice. "See what you can get from splashing around in the pool!"

"She just does what she does in the pool and it buys this!???"

They went on and on, right in front of me. Obviously, I was getting their special treatment.

A meeting was set up with Busby to see what he could do to ease the situation that was developing between me and Kelly and Donen. Busby had done *Footlight Parade* at Warner Bros. way back in 1933, which included the water extravaganza "By a Waterfall," so he knew about the kinds of numbers the audience expected from him and from me. He'd also staged the fabulous production numbers in *Ziegfeld Girl*, the movie that Leonard Kovner and I had seen at Grauman's Chinese the night before he chased me through the streets of Silver Lake. As it turned out, Arthur Freed sat in on the meeting because Busby had conceived a water dream sequence to add to *Take Me Out to the Ballgame*.

Earlier in his career, Busby had gotten into difficulties over his alcohol consumption. He was still known to drink a drop or two, but he was one of the most creative individuals in Hollywood, maybe the only true genius I would ever work with. I could see that at once. More than that, he loved what I did in the water. At the meeting, he came up with an imaginative concept where I was swimming in a rushing river and Gene was reaching out to me, but couldn't quite grab hold of me. Buzz saw it as a kind of catching and losing and catching and losing—very sexy and very pretty. Freed was enthusiastic about it and told him to put it on storyboards in time for a follow-up meeting.

When I saw Berkeley's storyboards, I could foresee my liberation. I could envision the two of us going on together from one movie to the next. I knew I needed someone with a real sense of showmanship if my movies were to continue to be successful. Other writers and producers were coming up with only the most contrived excuses to get me into the pool, but Buzz had all kinds of marvelous ideas, not just for this film, but for others as well.

Kelly took one look at the boards for the dream sequence and vetoed it flat out. As we were rehearsing in front of the rehearsal hall mirror, and as I bent my spine, I challenged him about it.

"You heard me. The dream sequence is out, Esther," he said. His tone was patronizing and arrogant.

My smart mouth took over. "Are you sure it isn't because you don't know how to swim, Gene?"

He gave me a death-ray look and said, "I know how to swim, smartass."

Instead, we had to do what Gene called "The Baby Doll number." I hated it, but luck was with me when it came time to film. Good old Stage 30 had been set up as a park with a fountain in the middle. Gene and I had been doing these little hippity-hoppity baby steps round and round the pool singing, "Cause you're my baby doll, my beautiful baby doll."

The song had obviously been written for five-foot-two-inch June or Judy, not for Esther, who was nobody's "baby." At the end of the number, both Gene and I were to lose our balance and fall in the fountain. Somehow I got through the number, but as we were shooting, something wonderful—disastrously wonderful—happened. The camera operator did about the worst thing you could do while filming: He froze about a third of the way through the song. He got behind in the moves and captured nothing on the film from a point early in the song. He never told us to stop before we fell in the water, and of course our costumes were now dripping wet. In order to keep the film on schedule and on budget, they decided to cut the number rather than reshoot. I went up to the cameraman and gave him a big wet hug. The picture was completed. Finally I was done with Kelly and Donen. In retrospect, Gene was right. The movie does just fine without an Esther Williams aqua special. Even swimming while singing "Take Me Out to the Ball Game" is a stretch. It was a box-office hit, a classic Gene Kelly movie. However, at that time in my career, I wasn't used to a back seat, and Kelly and Donen knew how I felt.

Neptune's Daughter was still the next film on my schedule, but during the break after *Take Me Out to the Ball Game*, I turned my attention back to the idea of having a baby. When I thought about it, I decided that becoming a mother was more important to me than the question of whether or not Ben was a good husband. I put aside all my reservations about our marriage because I wanted so much to have a baby. I needed to erase that aching feeling of barrenness that had weighed me down ever since the miscarriage. Even though I was married, I knew that in many ways I would like to have been a single parent. I was just ahead of my time.

I did what the doctor told me and took my temperature every morning to determine when I would be most fertile. Because of the miscarriage, he told me it might take awhile to conceive, and I figured I could get through the making of *Neptune's Daughter* without a problem. I was wrong. Early into the shooting, I realized I was pregnant.

Neptune's Daughter was another frothy romantic comedy about mistaken identity and how the pairs of lovers eventually get sorted out correctly. It reunited me with what had become my "repertory company"—Red Skelton, Ricardo Montalban, and of course Xavier Cugat. Coincidentally, in two ways this film also foreshadowed the future of my life after the movies. I played Eve Barrett, a champion swimmer who becomes a swimsuit designer and businesswoman. Ricardo played my love interest, José O'Rourke, a dashing South American with a reputation as a Romeo, not unlike Fernando Lamas, a man who was soon to enter my life for real.

Neptune's Daughter was my third film with Montalban. The first time he played my twin brother. Next he was my fiancé, but lost me to Peter Lawford and ended up with Cyd Charisse. This time MGM made him a wealthy polo player and let me keep him. This was the film in which we introduced Frank Loesser's Oscar-winning song, "Baby, It's Cold Outside." Betty Garrett (who'd been great to work with in *Ball Game)* was cast as my sister, Betty Barrett. (There go those corny names again.) Red played Jack Spratt, a masseur whom Betty mistakes for a well-to-do Latino. Keenan Wynn portrayed my partner in the swimsuit business, and the man I leave in the lurch in favor of Ricardo. If you pay close attention, you'll see Mel Blanc in his very first on-screen appearance (as one of Ricardo's sidekicks). Even if you don't recognize his face, you'll know that voice, because over at the Warner Bros. animation department, this man was already a star. Blanc was the voice behind Bugs Bunny, Porky Pig,

Daffy Duck, and Sylvester and Tweetie Pie, and the man who brought you "What's Up, Doc?" and "Th-th-th-th-that's all, f-f-f-folks."

It was a happy set. I was relieved to be back with my own style of film, and, of course, I was overjoyed to be pregnant. I ignored the fact that my "condition" was against studio policy and I did not tell the producer Jack Cummings. He was inclined to have fits of nervous hysteria, and I knew this bit of news would send him over the top. I stayed small, but my shape did give Irene, my costume designer and coconspirator, some extra headaches in her struggle to keep my swimsuits fitting properly.

One day Junie Allyson had an appointment for a fitting right after me, but Irene was running late because we were struggling with a gold sequined glamour suit for the final water carnival scene. June was working on *The Stratton Story* with Jimmy Stewart at the time. Perpetually cast as the perky wife or girlfriend, she was always in those demure white blouses with little round Peter Pan collars. We were friends, so she walked in while Irene and I were still working. She cast an admiring eye on my sequins and said, "Do you suppose I'll ever have a swimsuit like that in a picture?"

I said, "Junie, honey, they don't make swimsuits with Peter Pan collars. Be glad they don't. You don't have to get wet. You have *your* identification, and *this* is mine."

This was true. I was still "the mermaid" on the lot, sequins and all. I was very aware that my public image was that of an actress in a swimsuit, but I never knew when audiences would tire of the simple plots in my movies. I had enough business sense to realize that I should capitalize on my reputation while I was still strong at the box office. Hollywood is notoriously fickle, and most actors never get to decide which picture is going to be their last. I had been approached by Fred Cole, who had built Cole of California into one of the top swimwear manufacturers in the country. Cole talked to me about putting my name on one of his suits. Of course, I'd appear in print ads showing off "the Esther Williams suit." First, however, I had to get the studio's—meaning L. B. Mayer's—approval.

The fan magazines were already crammed with ads of actresses endorsing products for women, such as soaps, lotions, or nylons. One typical ad (in 1953) read, " 'Your legs need glamour, not glimmer,' says Ava Gardner." In small type under her photo it said, "Ava Gardner, star of MGM's CinemaScope production in color, *Knights of the Round Table,* wears Bur-Mil Cameo nylons with the exclusive face powder finish."

The PR department scheduled us for all our photo sessions, but no one ever mentioned whether they were shooting for a magazine cover or for an advertisement. My likeness had already been used to promote any number of products. When the ads appeared in print I was always surprised to see what I was selling. Celebrity endorsements are very lucrative today, and those earnings unquestionably belong to the stars. Back then it was all part of our workload, and whatever money changed hands between the product manufacturer and the studio was not shared with "talent."

The way I looked at it, my deal with Cole wasn't anything the studio wasn't already doing. I just wanted to keep the money. Fred Cole had offered me a 5 percent royalty on sales of a suit, which would carry my name, and had made a commitment with me to begin a subsidiary line for juniors and children. The deal could eventually net me about $150,000 a year, roughly what I was making at the time from MGM.

Before we began work on *Neptune's Daughter,* I went to Howard Strickling, head of studio publicity, to tell him what I had in mind. I figured that Howard would see the PR benefits for MGM of my deal with Cole right away and put in a good word for me with Mayer. "Mayer loves you more than that; he's crazy about you, Esther," Strickling said. "The thing to do is go and ask him yourself." There it was again: Do it yourself, Esther.

Whether he knew it or not, Howard Strickling was sending me into the den of Leo the Lion. I went up to the third floor, said hello to Ida Koverman, and was ushered into the great office with the white crescent-shaped desk. Tucked under my arm I had the artwork for a beautiful full page ad that Cole had done up, which—if approved—would run in *Vogue* and *Harper's Bazaar.* The illustration showed me coming out of the pool in a red suit, looking like a Varga girl. I loved the suit, which was one of the first ever made with latex, an early precursor of spandex. With that stretch fabric we finally would be rid of those damned zippers up the backs of the suits.

The ad copy read, "Like Esther, this suit has everything." What it didn't have was the customary plug for the current film—"Esther Williams, whose latest MGM release is . . ." That was considered too crass for the well-heeled clientele we were trying to reach through the fashion magazines. I thought it was the prettiest publicity that had been done on me, and even without the hard sell I believed that the studio would reap the benefits of all this free promotion for one of their stars.

As soon as I saw Mayer, who knew about the whole thing, I should have recognized the storm signals and put off the meeting for another time. He was already throwing telephones and kicking things, and I was anxious to get his approval.

Before I really got started, he hurled himself to the floor. Here was this grown man, with his white-on-white tie and his beautifully tailored suit, rolling around on the rug like a rotund penguin. He was kicking his heels and actually foaming at the mouth, as if he'd stuck an Alka-Seltzer under his tongue.

He seemed to forget that I'd seen this act before, right after the debacle in Mexico that ended with Ben getting the heave-ho out of the country. "Mr. Mayer, you have to stand up and talk to me. This is ridiculous."

He sat up on the carpet and looked at me like the petulant child that he was. It was obvious that he needed someone to mother him through this tantrum. I was pregnant, which was close enough to motherhood, so I grabbed a Kleenex from his desk and handed it to him.

"Now wipe the sides of your mouth and be a good boy. This is ridiculous. You were yelling at the top of your voice. I'm sure that everyone up and down the hall has heard you. I'm embarrassed for Ida Koverman, who had to listen to this out there."

"Ida Koverman has heard it many times before."

"Well, Mr. Mayer, I have to tell you that you must not yell at me."

"Why not? I yell at everyone else. Everybody knows this is what I do."

"Your tantrums are legendary, complete with these performances on the floor. But you must not yell at me."

"Why?" He was already yelling again.

"Because you can't get to the end of the pool first."

He blinked at me in disbelief. "I can't do what?"

"Get to the end of the pool first."

His voice quieted a bit. "You'll have to explain that to me."

"We'll be on the starting platform and they'll say, 'Swimmers take your mark.' I'll dive in and you'll dive in; and then I'll be at the end of the pool, but you'll be on the bottom because I'll bet you don't know how to swim."

"That's true."

"It's a metaphor, Mr. Mayer. Until you can get to the end of the pool ahead of me, you can't yell at me anymore."

It was just the kind of logic that would appeal to a sulking child, and it worked. He got up off the floor and sat behind his desk. "Okay," he said. "What is it that you wanted?"

"I want this swimsuit company deal. We're about to make *Neptune's Daughter,* in which I will wear this suit. So will all the girls in the aqua chorus. I'll be wearing it in red, like in this beautiful ad; I had Fred Cole make them in white for the girls."

"You had this done without my permission?"

"Mr. Mayer, Cole of California is giving the studio these suits for free." "Free" seemed to be the magic word that finally punctured his outrage. His features softened, and he slumped a bit in his chair, like a deflating inner tube.

"I'm in a terrible mood," he admitted.

No surprise there. "Is something wrong, Mr. Mayer?"

I didn't think he'd confide in me, but he did. "I went to the Hollywood Bowl last night, and Jane Powell was singing. I opened up my program, and there was the very thing you've been asking me for, which is not to have an MGM credit. All it said was 'Miss Jane Powell.' The studio's name didn't appear."

"Mr. Mayer, everyone knows that she's . . ."

"I want it in the program." He looked at me as if he wanted to tell me something more.

"That can't be the only thing bothering you. What else is the matter?"

"Well, you'll be reading about it anyway. I asked Lorena to marry me. She turned me down."

Lorena was Lorena Danker, Mayer's love interest. She was the widow of Danny Danker, a successful Hollywood advertising executive, and Mayer, a widower, had been appearing with her at his parties, the same parties to which Ben and I were no longer invited. Lorena may have been reluctant to remarry because Danker hadn't died all that long ago; and she had a ten-year-old daughter. It also didn't help that Hedda Hopper had tried to poison the romance by reporting (falsely) that Mayer's intentions were not strictly honorable.

I left the dispirited Mayer and went back to see Howard Strickling. "Thanks for the warning, Howard! Before you sent me in there, you might have told me about the Jane Powell thing and his problems with Lorena."

"What did he say about your deal with Cole, Esther?"

"In a way, the timing was wonderful, because I don't even think he remembers what I asked him for. So I'm going to do it anyway."

Shortly thereafter, Lorena Danker had a change of heart. She and Mayer were married in December of 1948.

The filming of *Neptune's Daughter* went smoothly and we were finally working on the last production number. The girls in the chorus were going off the high platforms into the water. They looked marvelous in those white suits. I was already in the pool when suddenly I began to feel a little funny. I went to my dressing room and discovered I was spotting. I called Dr. Bradbury right away.

"Do you want this baby?" he asked.

"More than anything, doctor," I answered truthfully.

"Have you done enough of this number for them to finish it without you?"

"Yes."

"Then go home, go to bed, and stay there."

For the rest of my pregnancy, Dr. Bradbury let me do only one extracurricular activity. He allowed me to continue teaching blind children to swim. Swimming was an ideal form of exercise for them—many seeing adults swim with their eyes closed anyway. We taught the children in the heated pool of the Loew's Hotel in Santa Monica and began teaching them to swim. At first we had to go very slowly, since the kids didn't have much muscle tone. Because they didn't do much running or other physical activity, they had skinny little pipe cleaner legs, and we had to build them up so they had some stamina.

I bought some inner tubes with narrow openings so they could begin to feel secure in the water. Then I got them racing in their little tubes. Because their ears stayed dry, and they could hear their friends nearby, they began to relax and enjoy themselves. Once they were at ease in the pool, I started to encourage them to go underwater. I went under with them and invited them to feel my face while we were below the surface.

They progressed very quickly and soon were swimming without the tubes. The kids discovered that they could "hear" the end of the pool, so they'd put their hands out just in time or know when to turn for the next lap. The change in the children was remarkable. Not only did they learn to swim, but they became less clingy, more robust, and had a great deal more confidence.

Meanwhile, my tummy got rounder and rounder. Back then stars who were expecting were hidden away. Ironic, since the country was in the midst of this huge baby boom, and there were pregnant women everywhere. Hollywood was anxious to keep its stars out of sight when they were in this most "unglamorous" condition. Sleazy magazines such as *Confidential* delighted in publishing unflattering photographs of celebrities, and since I made my living in a bathing suit, I was a prime target. I asked everyone associated with the project not to take any pictures of me, and they honored my request.

Looking back on it now, I wish I had a photo or two, because teaching these children was one of the most gratifying experiences I'd ever had. Just as I was beginning my eighth month, Dr. Bradbury told me I had to stop. He was afraid one of the children might accidentally kick me. I had followed the doctor's orders to the letter up to this point, but this time I declined. "No one's going to kick me, doctor," I reassured him. "Come see for yourself."

I was so confident, that Dr. Bradbury allowed me to work with them for as long as I was able. I continued teaching until just before Benjamin Stanton Gage (Benjie for short) was born on August 6, 1949, weighing in at just over eight pounds. Finally, I was a mother.

CHAPTER 14

DUCHESS OF IDAHO AND PAGAN LOVE SONG
1950

*I*n my era of Hollywood, the studio owned everything, including the baby. Despite the fact that motherhood disrupted the production schedule and placed competing demands on stars' time, MGM realized that a new baby offered promotional opportunities they could exploit, so there was a *quid pro quo*. They waited until the baby no longer looked wrinkled, like Winston Churchill, and then they got everyone into the act. The MGM publicity department showed up at our home exactly three months to the day after Benjie was born. With the studio's blessing, the nursery was invaded by a reporter, camera crew, and a small army of men holding lights and reflectors, so that we could appear on the cover of a fan magazine.

Not much has changed. When Alec Baldwin and Kim Basinger were coming out of the hospital with their first child, they were accosted by the press. Kim didn't want to be photographed so soon after having had a baby. The new parents didn't want their baby photographed either, but the cameraman was stubborn. Alec hit him. I happened to watch *Court TV* as Alec Baldwin was explaining his feelings. He is apparently a sensitive man who feels that his privacy is very important to him, his wife, and his children. However, photographers have never felt that we movie stars have a right to a private life.

That attitude began with the studio system. When the studio invaded your home, you and your baby were both on display—and on trial. That baby was reporting for work, just like you were, and his unpredictable needs could never intrude on your role in the publicity machine. Basically, your child was a prop. Despite all the promises that the photographers would be very tasteful and respectful of your privacy, you knew you had to have the prettiest nursery in the world or it would look bad. You knew you'd better have an adorable child ready for the camera, and that baby better not be having a bad day. It was your job to see that he was in a good state of mind, and that he wasn't throwing up on everybody. If the baby was crying or tired when the press arrived, that was your fault. You should have seen to it that he got a nap earlier.

Looking back, I realize how unnatural it was, but at the time I didn't find it hard to accept. By then I had been in the movies long enough to know that there was no logic—no human logic—to the way stars were treated. The studio crossed all of the humanitarian lines and made it part of your work, even though they didn't pay for anything. They didn't pay the doctor, and they didn't pay for the nurse when the baby had colic. I accepted it because it was just part of the job.

Louella Parsons was the first person to interview me after Benjie was born, and I decided that an old-fashioned colonial cradle would be picturesque and make good copy. As a matter of fact, it was one my dad had made for one of us. Benjie was lying there in this beautiful old cradle, and I was rocking him. Louella said, "Oh Esther, you went to all of this trouble for me!"

I said, "You mean having the baby, Louella, or the cradle?"

She said, "Well, it's all so quaint."

She drank like a fish, and knowing that, I had brewed a pot of tea. She said, "Is that the strongest thing we're going to have while we talk about the baby?"

I said, "Yes, Louella, I think tea is appropriate to the cradle."

She didn't like the rules much, but I was ready for Louella and her photographer. I was dressed in a pinafore, with ruffles, eyelet embroidery, and all the appropriate maternal gear. Everyone wanted pictures of a sweet baby and a pretty mother, preferably one who's got her figure back already.

Even friends were anxious to exploit the situation. I had a close friend at the time Benjie was born, and I had mentioned to her that I had arranged to have a sitting—just portraits of mother and child. This was to be for the family only; it had no PR angle. Without my knowledge, she sold a story to *Modern Screen* magazine with the promise that she would get a cover for them of me with the baby, and a story by her on the inside. When she showed up for my private sitting along with a cameraman from the magazine, she was all dressed up, because she thought she was going to get her picture taken with me.

I was surprised to see her. "What's this about?" I asked. "Why are you here?"

She said, "Well, I've sold a story about your new baby to *Modern Screen* magazine."

I asked, "How much did you get?"

She said, "Five hundred dollars."

I said, "You've just told me what our friendship is worth. Only five hundred dollars? I think you've underpriced yourself, for one thing. This is a scoop, and you're going to do a lead story with a cover. I guess it will have to be enough, because we won't be seeing each other any more after today." She's in her nineties now and we haven't spoken since; and she still doesn't know why I don't come to her parties.

After an all-too-brief maternity leave, you were expected back on the lot, "camera-ready," which in my case meant looking good in a swimsuit, so I got in the pool right after Benjie was born. As always, it was my answer for getting in shape. I was already swimming my way back into condition to begin work on my next film, *Duchess of Idaho*.

There were no ruffles and long skirts in this one. I was to play Christine Duncan, a swimming star in a night club (of all things) who goes to Idaho to help the faltering romance of her roommate,

Ellen Hallett. Paula Raymond was cast as Ellen, long-suffering secretary to Douglas Morrison, wealthy playboy. Ellen had long har-
bored a crush on her boss, played by John Lund, who had
remained oblivious to her charms. To bring the jerk to his senses, I
headed for Sun Valley and pretended to be romantically interested
in him, in order to drive him back into the arms of Ellen. On the
way there I met my true love to be, brash young bandleader Dick
Layne, played by Van Johnson. However, out of loyalty to my roommate, I put my feelings aside and continue with the charade of pur-
suing John. Not surprisingly, in the end Van and I end up together,
as do Paula and John.

Wait a minute! Hadn't I already made this movie at least once?
As soon as they gave me the script, I realized it was yet another rehash of what was now the Esther Williams formula: the mis-
matched lovers plot. It was enough to give one a case of cinematic
déjà vu. Delete Mackinac Island; insert Sun Valley. Delete Peter
Lawford; insert Van Johnson—again. As happy as I was to be working once more with Van, the recycled plots were getting to me. At
one point I turned to Van and said, "Didn't we do this scene before
in an elevator?"

He laughed. "Esther, this is our fourth picture together. We've
done this scene in an elevator, at the side of the pool, and we've even
done it swimming in the pool together, with you holding me up so I
could say my lines and not go blub-blub underwater." He was not
exaggerating. Van was getting better at swimming, but when we
made *Thrill of a Romance*, while swimming the backstroke together
I had to put my hand under his back to keep him afloat. He was
properly grateful.

We could laugh about it, but the truth was that there was a definite predictability to the plots of my films. Audiences had come to
expect a certain kind of film from me, and these movies were im-
mensely popular. The Hollywood term "bankable" hadn't been
coined yet, but I was part of a group of reliable MGM box-office
stars whose films were counted on to make a certain amount of
money for the studio. To moviegoers and the studio alike, I was a
known quantity. *Neptune's Daughter* and *Duchess of Idaho* were "Esther Williams movies," just like other films were "Clark Gable
movies," "Judy Garland movies," and "Tracy and Hepburn movies."

People stood in line to see these films not because of the title or the plot, but because we were in them, and the revenue from these "predictable" movies financed the production of a lot of turgid drama and bad comedies that nobody stood in line for.

This status brought me a lot of respect on the third floor of the Thalberg Building, which was crazy about box-office power. The critics and the acting community, however, took a different view. They were snobbish toward musicals. Deborah Kerr and I were in hairstyling getting ready for the day's shoot when she decided to broach the subject with me. Other than in hairstyling, you really didn't see much of any of the other stars on the lot. Makeup was done in private. Joan Crawford and the other divas were not about to let anyone see how much paint and time it took to make them look glamorous. The hairdressing department was like a salon, the theory being that once you've got your face on you wouldn't mind being seen. Consequently, it was there that you'd run into all the actresses who were working that day.

Like Greer Garson, Deborah Kerr was an English import, a serious dramatic actress typically cast as a cool and well-bred lady. Anna, the governess in *The King and I*, was the most famous in a long line of these classy women she played, and although that film was very entertaining, many of her earlier pictures were clearly boring, at least at the box office. When I saw her, she'd just finished *Edward, My Son* and *If Winter Comes*, both of which had gone quickly to double feature status. As we were being curled and coifed she said, "Esther, I really love what you do on the screen. You're so pretty and you swim so well. Your pictures are light and beautiful, but I wonder . . . isn't there anything you can do about getting a good story? You know, a good script?"

There it was again, just like in the reviews, the distinction between "drama" and "fluff." It seemed as if the only people who liked my movies were in the audience. I stopped Sydney Guilaroff in mid-pincurl and turned slowly in my seat. I heard myself saying in defense of "fluff": "Deborah, look at it this way. If I make one *Neptune's Daughter*, you can make two *If Winter Comes*."

Deborah thought for a moment. "Now that I think of it, you have a point."

In *Duchess of Idaho*, tap dancing star Eleanor Powell was doing a guest appearance. She had starred in the popular *Broadway Melody* films before the war. Although she had chosen to retire from the screen when she married Glenn Ford in 1943, there were those who whispered that it was just as well, since her popularity had been waning at the time. MGM liked to use what they considered "fading" stars this way—they gave them guest-star billing. I saw her in wardrobe. She'd been rehearsing so long for her upcoming number that her feet were bleeding.

I said, "Eleanor, it's only a guest shot. Is it really worth it?"

"If they're filming it, it has to be better than good. It must be perfect. My feet will be all right."

I pondered what she said. I was still at the top, but I could see how quickly the bottom could drop out, even when you are still giving your all. There had to be a better way to go than this. Seeing her made me more aware than ever that someday—maybe sooner than I'd know—there'd be no more ways to get me back in the water.

Arthur Freed had purchased the rights to a book called *Tahiti Landfall* and had decided to base a musical on it. He wanted to call his picture *Pagan Love Song*, so he could reuse a song of the same title that he'd written in 1929 with his frequent collaborator, composer Nacio Herb Brown. Freed didn't let any music go to waste, particularly his own. A year later he very successfully recycled several other songs that he and Brown had previously written together for a new film, including "Good Mornin'," "You Are My Lucky Star," and the title tune "Singin' in the Rain."

As far as *Pagan Love Song* was concerned, the problem was that *Tahiti Landfall* was essentially an armchair travelogue. It had a thin love story, as some critics said after the movie was released. The first script was drafted with Cyd Charisse and Van Johnson in mind for the leads, but Cyd was pregnant and that story line was thrown out. A new screenplay was being tailored for me.

I was to play Mimi Bennett, a half-Caucasian/half-native girl who falls in love with Hazard Endicott (oh, those names!), a midwestern schoolteacher who has come to the island to take over a rundown plantation left to him by his late uncle. Howard Keel, who had just finished playing Frank Butler in *Annie Get Your Gun*, was cast as Hazard. Though basically a singer with a powerful baritone,

Howard radiated a roguish virility. He was terrific in the big production of *Annie,* and a great choice for *Pagan.* To my mind, at least, a less-great selection was Arthur Freed's choice of director, Stanley Donen, who as Gene Kelly's assistant on *Take Me Out to the Ball Game* gave me such a nasty time. This was to be his first solo directing assignment.

Over my dead body.

I went to see Dore Schary, who had become MGM vice president of production in July of 1948. Nick Schenck, the "general" who ran the Loews/MGM corporate empire in New York, had originally brought in Schary with Mayer's approval, but the relationship between the two men had become increasingly contentious. As VP of production, Schary had control over stories, stars, and directors, but Mayer was still VP in charge of the studio as a whole; and Schary was theoretically answerable to him. It was literally The Clash of the Titans. Unless Schenck intervened, there was always a question of whose word was final.

Mayer and Schary had diametrically opposite approaches to moviemaking, so the animosity between them became personal. They had already locked horns over *Battleground* and were still *mano-a-mano* over the making of *Quo Vadis?* L. B. Mayer loved spectacle and he loved movie stars. If you had star quality, he'd spend all the money in the world to showcase it, confident that this expenditure would come back to the studio with the box-office success of blockbuster hits. *Titanic* would have been his kind of movie, because he understood A pictures in a way that Dore Schary, an owlish intellectual, never did.

Schary had been a B movie producer at RKO, and he came to MGM with that mindset still intact. He didn't like movie stars. Small movies with featured players like Nancy Davis (eventually Nancy Reagan) and Jim Whitmore were more to his speed. He'd just produced a bizarre message film with these two "stars" called *The Next Voice You Hear,* in which the voice of God came over the radio. If you had told Louis B. Mayer to make that movie, he'd have started rolling on the floor in one of his famous tantrums.

For the first year or so of his tenure, Dore Schary's arrival didn't really affect me, since my production schedule had already been set.

Now an appointment was set for me to see Dore Schary to air my
protest over working with Donen. I'd never met Schary, but I had
heard a lot about him. He seemed to be part of a clique that existed
in Hollywood and moviemaking that could best be described as
"the elite." You didn't just hang out with people like that. You bore
their scrutiny. "Were you from a good family?" "Did you come
from money?" "Was your talent intellectual or even avant-garde?"
Schary's parties were attended by the chicest, most well-bred members of the Hollywood A-list, like Cary Grant and his elegant wife,
Betsy Drake; Lew and Edie Wasserman; Alfred Hitchcock; Vincente
Minnelli and his beautiful little Judy Garland; Joan Crawford and
top show business lawyer Greg Bautzer.

My friend and director Chuck Walters attended one of Dore
Schary's parties, but he was not invited. He was summoned and ordered to bring the day's rushes with him. The experience was not A
in nature. It was C for cruelty.

Chuck arrived with his rushes from that day in cans under his
arm and was told to wait in the entry hall until the eminent folk in
the dining room had completed their gourmet repast. He listened as
they nibbled their dinner with considerable gaiety. Some had had a
little too much champagne and there was a lot of joking, with everybody talking just a little too loud. Finally they filed out of the dining
room with the ice in their fresh drinks clinking. They headed for
Schary's luxuriously appointed projection room with the deep-
cushioned chairs. Schary gave a curt nod, and Chuck was commanded to hand over his cans of film to the projectionist. Then he
had to sit off to the side like an outsider or one of the help and have
his work of that day shown as after-dinner entertainment.

In the film industry, dailies are considered sacrosanct. That raw,
unedited footage is a deeply private matter. All of the flaws and fail-
ures, all of the mistakes and bloopers, are included along with takes
ready for editing. No one is invited to the screening of dailies except cast and crew. Sometimes just the director and the producer
look at them.

That evening, as the actors on the screen made the usual false
starts and attempts at perfection in pursuit of a scene, their efforts
were laughed at by some in Schary's screening room and critically

admired by others. But it wouldn't have mattered if every take had been perfect. Those scenes should not have been shown to any group until the film was ready for the theaters, and certainly not to this assemblage of worthies. The last people you would invite to see dailies would be a group of industry-wise colleagues, particularly when they were a bit drunk and raucous.

Schary didn't care. What Chuck described to me is totally unprofessional and unethical in the motion picture business. I felt Chuck's humiliation. I was forewarned.

I got right to the point in my first meeting with Schary. "Mr. Schary, we haven't met before. But now I think it's important for us to talk."

"What's on your mind, Miss Williams?"

"I can't do *Pagan Love Song* with Stanley Donen."

He looked at me with surprise and said, "But . . ."

"Stanley Donen thinks I'm ridiculous."

Schary shot a look to a spot in his office over my shoulder. I turned and followed his gaze, but saw nothing, so I continued, "Mr. Schary, I'm sure you are aware that Gene Kelly holds a very important place in this studio. At one point in the production of *Take Me Out to the Ball Game,* Busby Berkeley was shoved aside as director in favor of Gene. He literally directed the last half of the movie, with constant asides to Stanley—about me. They both thought I was ridiculous in a role that, in their minds, should have been Judy Garland. It was all right by me to be second choice in *that* film, but I have no intention of being Donen's second choice in my own movie.

"I will need all the help and confidence and support from my director in this difficult location in Hawaii," I continued. "I don't feel I will have it with Stanley Donen."

Mr. Schary stood up, beckoned to the corner behind me, and smoothly said, "Stanley, come out, please." Stanley Donen appeared from behind some drapes and stood looking at me with a hurt little boy smile. He had been eavesdropping.

He said, "Oh, Esther, how can you say I think you are ridiculous? You are so beautiful. I love you."

Too little, too late, I thought. I stuck to my guns, leaving them both unmistakably impressed with my feeling that I didn't want Donen on my picture.

After that, I went home to a nightly ordeal of telephone harassment. The studio would call with someone saying, "Mr. Schary on the phone for you, Miss Williams." Then Dore would launch into a pitch for Stanley Donen. It got down to outright begging for me to change my mind, and it continued for ten days.

Finally, I said, "Mr. Schary, please don't call me any more about Stanley Donen. I'm not just being stubborn. I feel very deeply that this decision to put him on this picture with me is very bad for the movie. That camera is a lie detector, Mr. Schary, and if I'm going to be continually angry because Stanley Donen's smug face is behind that viewfinder, it's going to show on film and this movie is doomed. I'm not going to change my mind, so if you want to take me off this film and put me on suspension, that's fine."

Dore said, "It's impossible. You must do the picture."

"Then you just have to give me another director—*any* other director."

"What about Bob Alton?"

"Bob Alton has never done a location movie," I said.

"I know. Will you accept him?"

"Yes, anybody but Stanley."

Robert Alton was first and foremost a choreographer, and I had worked with him on the dance numbers in *Bathing Beauty*. He'd gone on to choreograph *Easter Parade*, *The Barkleys of Broadway*, and *Annie Get Your Gun*, but his only other directing assignment was the unsuccessful *Merton of the Movies*. In accepting him, I was up against the wall, but I knew he would try his best. *Pagan Love Song*, I hoped, would be a harmonious experience.

Wishing didn't make it so. *Pagan Love Song* was supposed to take place in Tahiti, but the logistics of shooting on a French-speaking island, with no airport, were too complicated, so the studio decided to use the Hawaiian island of Kauai instead. When they chose Kauai, somebody wasn't thinking, and that somebody was the unit manager, O. O. "Bunny" Dull. Short, fat, with either drink in hand or a hangover, Bunny didn't move easily. Bunny Dull started the day off by saying, "This is my first drink today, and boy, do I need it." Of course, he would say it at 9:00 in the morning.

Weather is probably the most important element to study when choosing a movie location. Just ask Kevin Costner about what happened during the filming of *Water World*. Reading weather reports and statistics about wind, rain, and tides obviously didn't concern Bunny, but it concerned everybody else very shortly as the rains came that April, and kept right on coming.

At least three or four times a day, the entire company—actors, camera crew, makeup, etc.—was all huddled together under a tin roof, listening to the pounding rain. We couldn't even hear each other complaining how stupid it all was. To prove that he was on the job as director, Bob Alton sat on the set under an umbrella, desperately searching the script for a way to use rain in some future sequence.

Day after day we ended up with no shot film in the can and returned dripping wet to our little makeshift houses in the small town of Lihue. We ate poi, which no one could digest. We had temporarily joyous little luaus, where everyone got quite drunk. Love affairs began (and sometimes ended) in one night. I went home each evening to Ben, who had been playing golf all day in the rain. He took to the golf course with umbrella, gloves, and raincoat. He never considered the possibility of going home to LA to work. I enjoyed my seven-month-old Benjie, more than anyone could possibly imagine, and to complicate matters even more, I discovered I was pregnant again. I knew it was too soon, but there it was.

One day I woke up with serious morning sickness. It was clear that pregnancy was a reality. Now I had a big problem. I had to tell the studio—certainly not just Bunny Dull—that the shooting schedule would have to be changed to accommodate my newly discovered condition. I had to tell the studio and I had to tell them that night. Ben was a "people-oriented" fellow ("Hey, I know a guy!"). On Kauai he played golf with a ham radio operator, who went through his address book and came up with the name of a ham radio operator he knew in Culver City, which is where MGM was located. We got in the car, drove over winding roads through the rain, and went to his house at the tip of the island. He got on the radio and contacted Culver City, then handed Ben the mike.

"Hello?"

"Hello? Culver City? Can we talk to Bud?" Ben's booming voice could have been heard on the mainland without the ham radio.

"Hello? Who's there?"

Ben put me on the microphone.

I said, "This is Esther Williams."

A voice on the other end said, "No shit. I'm Errol Flynn."

"No, really. I need to talk to a producer at Metro-Goldwyn-Mayer by the name of Arthur Freed. Would you please call MGM and tell Mr. Freed to get in touch with Esther Williams in the city of Lihue on the island of Kauai?"

"This is some kind of joke."

"This is no joke; I'm pregnant. I'm Esther Williams and I have to talk with someone at MGM or there'll be big trouble."

The guy laughed and said, "OK lady, whoever you are. I'll do it." I don't think he believed it was me until he read the morning papers.

What I didn't know was that our ham radio signals went out over the airwaves to the entire coast of California. Anyone could have been listening to my baby news. And apparently many people were. Someone called Louella. Arthur Freed read the news in his morning paper. He was not amused.

When I saw Bob Alton the next morning, he was nearly hysterical. Approaching him carefully, I said, "You heard?"

"Everybody heard! What do you mean you're pregnant? What are we going to do? What are *you* going to do?"

Not for one moment did Ben and I consider abortion. All of these decisions about choice were to come in the years ahead. "Now Bob, we just need to make a few schedule changes. Anything that is too athletic can be moved up to the beginning of the picture. We've already done some of that. We only have a few more scenes that could be called chancy. We'll be back at the studio soon and we'll be protected by all those skilled people."

"Oh, God, let this rain stop!" he said as it began to pour down on our heads again.

The next day was finally bright and clear, and we were scheduled to film one of those "chancy" shots, with me in a double outrigger canoe in the ocean. The scene was to be shot at a beach where the ocean floor fell away sharply from the shoreline. The steep drop created a powerful shore break, which was dramatic to photograph but tricky to negotiate in the outrigger. What made it even more dangerous was that the ocean bottom was covered with abundant black coral, which was jagged, like broken glass.

Getting dumped would be dangerous. Coral is a living thing, and if I made contact with it, not only would I be badly cut, but pieces of coral would become embedded in the wounds, causing serious infections. The conventional treatment was to paint the skin with bright purple Gentian Violet, but even so, the infection from the coral was very hard to cure and often left terrible scars.

Alton wanted to shoot at about 4:30 in the afternoon. Local beach boys had been teaching me how to handle the outrigger, and they knew it was risky for a novice to be out there at that hour, when the big sets of waves came in. I learned later that they had actually tried to warn Alton and Dull about the danger, but they had interrupted an "important" conversation about overtime and were ignored. Even though I hadn't heard those warnings, late in the afternoon I sat there in the canoe, wishing that I'd had the foresight to ask for a beach boy to lie in the bottom of the outrigger to guide me in, staying clear of the coral. But the beach boys were on the shore, playing cards and ignoring all of us "stupid" mainlanders. Polynesians are a proud people. If you brush them aside, they go back to their own company of friends and leave you to your problem—whatever the outcome.

I heard the assistant on the beach yell through the microphone, "Silence, we're rolling!" As I began paddling I saw Bob Alton, my director, sitting safely under his umbrella on the dry sand, a good distance from the shore break. Quickly the calm ocean changed to a series of curling waves, each climbing higher and higher. Meanwhile, the force of the ocean propelled me rapidly toward shore. Perched on the crest of a wave, I looked down and saw that there was no water beneath me at all, just the dreaded black coral on the ocean floor.

I rolled myself up into a ball and clung to the side of the outrigger, holding on for dear life. The canoe cracked against the coral, splintering the lower outrigger. At a moment like that, your life does not pass before you. Instead, all motion seems to stand still. You are frozen in time. You can't even pray. I looked down at that mutilating glassy rock and figured I'd be lucky if I were only scarred for life. I would lose my baby. With the next wave, I was thrown into what I was certain was my death. My eyes closed and I said good-bye.

Suddenly, I felt a plume of refreshing Hawaiian water all around my body. I wasn't torn or shredded by the coral. I was floating. I looked down and realized that I had been tossed out of the canoe right over one of those blowholes in the coral. A geyser of water from the blowhole had shot me up and away from the bottom, allowing the wave to come in under me. By the time I was set down, I was back in the safe, warm ocean again. I looked to see if I had hit the coral anywhere with my body. I found to my amazement only a tiny scratch on one finger that the Gentian Violet could easily cure. Thank you, God!

I strode as quickly as I could to my tent dressing room on the sand, tears of rage filling my eyes. Luckily, I couldn't talk when Bob Alton yelled outside my tent with high-pitched hysteria. "What happened? You ruined the shot. We were rolling!"

"I can't talk to you now, Bob," I said. "When you see the rushes, it will be self-explanatory." I lay on my cot and sobbed with relief.

The pregnant movie star crying on the beach in Kauai was just ten years older than the champion swimmer who cried when they canceled the 1940 Olympics in Helsinki. Whether it was diving out of trees or handling an outrigger, it took every bit of the courage and discipline of a champion to do all the things the studio kept inventing for me to do. MGM figured anything that had to do with water was swimming, and that therefore Esther could handle it. No problem.

Because there was no one else who could do what I did, it was obvious that it would be extremely difficult, probably impossible, to replace me. Oddly enough, what I felt most of all about my unique situation was not added power, but added responsibility. I felt the burden of all those people depending on me to complete the film.

I was looking forward to having another baby, but I did feel a little bit guilty because I had gotten pregnant so soon after Benjie; so I took the responsibility, such as it was, on myself. What was I going to do about the studio's indifference? How was I going to keep them from killing me next time? As I collected myself, I heard the voice of my mother Bula in the back of my mind. "Esther," she asked, "what part of the problem are you?"

"Okay, Mom. I won't be so eager to cooperate, to please everybody. I'll take more responsibility for checking out these stunts. I have to so I can continue with this work. The producers and directors don't understand. They don't even get wet. I've got to take care of myself from now on."

I stopped crying and pulled a towel over myself. I knew that my baby and I would be fine in the morning. "Thank you, God! Just don't let it rain," I prayed. "I've got to get back home to my baby doctor and think about the two of us."

We wrapped up location shooting on Kauai at the end of May, but there was still a lot of work to be done. Howard Keel had broken his arm while we were there, and there was one scene that called for him to ride a bicycle. They tried to camouflage his cast with a towel, but it was awkward; Alton wanted to reshoot back in Culver City.

By this time they were photographing me behind palm fronds and bunches of bananas. Because this was my third pregnancy, I was showing a lot sooner. There was one underwater number that called for a great deal of ingenuity. The crew got the underwater banana leaves moving in such a way that you barely glimpsed my protruding tummy from the side, which was a good thing, since I was clad in silver lamé. Silver lamé is very chic underwater: It makes you look like a mackerel but shows every bump and lump, and I was now quite pear-shaped. As soon as shooting was finished in July, I went straight into maternity clothes.

Back in the days of silent movies there was a star named Pearl White, best known for *The Perils of Pauline. Pauline* was an adventure serial, like *Flash Gordon* or *Buck Rogers,* and Pearl was a true heroine—she wasn't dependent on men to rescue her from danger. In her day, her fame rivaled that of Mary Pickford, in part because Pearl performed her own stunts. As we finished *Pagan Love Song,* I felt as though I'd inherited Pearl White's mantle. Part actress, part stuntwoman, I knew I was doing all this on my own, and that's how it was always going to be. No guys were going to save me. I had to do it myself.

CHAPTER 15

THE END OF AN ERA
1950–1951

*M*y baby wasn't due until December, but just before Halloween I went into labor. Kimball Austin Gage was born on October 30, six weeks early. Even so he weighed six pounds ten ounces; he would have been a real bruiser at full term.

The studio gave me a couple of months to nurse my baby and make my figure "camera-ready." As always, I swam myself back into condition, and in early 1951 I began work on my next film, *Texas Carnival*. This movie reunited me with some of the "usual suspects," including Red Skelton, and some of the usual plot points as well. In *Neptune's Daughter*, Red had been a masseur who impersonated a wealthy South American polo player. In *Carnival*, he played a carnival dunk-tank performer who impersonates a wealthy oil baron. My character was named Debbie Telford, Red's assistant, who is mistaken for his oil baroness sister.

For the second time in a row, Howard Keel was my leading man, and we had one rather sexy underwater fantasy sequence, which began with Howard falling asleep and dreaming of me. He was lying on his bed when, thanks to a process shot, I came swimming into his room through what looked like midair, weaving my body over and around his bed. I was wearing a diaphanous white negligee, with a flesh-colored bathing suit underneath. (Years later, when they showed this scene at a charity event, I was going to call it "Howard's wet dream," until someone reminded me that it was a fund-raiser for little children.)

Today, no one would think twice about this scene, but in 1951 it was considered fairly daring. We got away with it because I was wet. Dry, I never would have been allowed anywhere near a man's bed in that state of undress. The straitlaced 1930 Hays Code, which protected the morality of moviegoers by forbidding such prurient offenses by the studios as "indecent or undue exposure," was still very much with us. The Breen Office, which was responsible for code enforcement, was ever vigilant, but inconsistent. The water "protected" my virtue as well as the filmgoer's. I was allowed to cavort around a bed underwater, clad in a see-through negligee deliberately designed to look like I had nothing on underneath.

The on-screen effect we achieved in that number was not delivered without some off-screen drama. In fact, I almost died. I'd had an accident on the set of *On an Island With You* when no one thought to cushion my fall into an animal pit, but so far my underwater on-set experiences had been free of similar screw-ups. Despite my vow after *Pagan Love Song*, I'd grown complacent, because otherwise my strong survival instinct should have alerted me to an immediate problem when we first began to work on that number. The underwater "set" was a replica of Howard's darkened bedroom, with walls, a floor, a window—and some idiot put a ceiling on the room. I had gone through a small trap door to get into the room, and for a while I was enjoying trying different underwater swimming maneuvers; because the white chiffon was moving nicely, making lovely swirling patterns.

To highlight the drama of the white chiffon, they had made the interior of the underwater set all black, which suddenly became a problem when I needed to resurface for air. The black walls made it impossible to see the hatch in the trapdoor from the inside. I kept swimming around, trying various spots in the ceiling, but every place I tried, I hit solid wood. I couldn't see any way to get out because it was wall, wall, ceiling. I was trapped with no air, and I began to panic. The panic is terrible—it's terrible because when there is no more air, you have no more strength. The fear sets in that there is no way out. You are using up your reserve and time is running out.

Meanwhile, on the other side of the tank's glass window, the crew was oblivious to the fact that I was in serious trouble. As I kept bumping into the ceiling, I could see one guy on the phone not looking in my direction; another was eating a sandwich. I was frantic, hitting and hitting and hitting on the black walls and ceiling. "I can't get out and they don't know," I thought. I saw somebody looking through the underwater camera, but he didn't see my distress. I was going to drown. Finally, Pete, the prop man, saw what was happening, dove through the hatch, and pulled me out gasping and fighting for air. A hush had come over the set as the crew realized the danger I had experienced and its potential consequences. He was the only person on the set who realized the crisis. I was working with people who knew nothing about the dangers of swimming underwater. None of them except for Pete had ever been down there.

I was enraged! This made two movies in a row where somebody's stupidity had nearly killed me.

When I had recovered sufficiently, I set out to corner the set designer on the picture. I asked, "Where is he? Where is that sonofabitch who locked me in a wooden crate down there? Where is the dumb bastard who put a ceiling on a swimming pool?" There was blood in my eye. I had every intention of shoving him in the pool and letting *him* try to find his own damned way out of that black set. When I came back the next morning to finish the number, the ceiling was gone.

I was distracted about everything during the filming of *Texas Carnival*. I couldn't be at home to nurse Kim, so I had to express my milk several times a day for him, which was a time-consuming process. Kim was a difficult baby, at least for a mother working full time. He never slept at night. He had colic. He had fevers and convulsions. His eyes would roll back up into his head. I had a hard time finding and keeping nurses for him. He would rock back and forth in his crib night after night. One night, I was awakened by a terrible clatter, like a wood pile collapsing. Kim had literally rocked his crib into kindling wood. Bleary-eyed, I was on the set every morning at 6:30, on time, ready for hair, makeup, and a "swim." And there were lines to be learned. I needed more than twenty-four hours in the day.

Louis B. Mayer's former lady love, tap dancer Ann Miller, was also in the cast of *Texas Carnival*. She had been introduced to Mayer by her agent, Frank Orsatti, during her years at Columbia. She cut quite a figure on the dance floor at Ciro's with Mayer, and playing hostess at his guest ranch in Perris. We became friends working on the film together. Years later, when I was married to Fernando Lamas and was watching a video of *Texas Carnival* with him, he turned to me and asked, "Why did you just give this picture to Ann Miller? You're the star, but she's on the screen much more than you are. Didn't you notice that she had more scenes than you did?" Fernando would actually clock screen time in order to calculate which star had dominated the film.

"I was just glad somebody was sharing some of the work," I told him quite honestly. "I had a difficult kid at home."

With two little boys in diapers, I had to keep it simple if I were going to have a life at all. I had heard that Barbara Stanwyck was famous for coming to the studio in the early morning before her call and hanging out with the crew; she was like one of the guys. How I envied her. She must not have had any little ones at home. I had babies I had to spend time with before I went to work, because that was the only time of day when I had enough energy to enjoy them. By the time I got home late at night, my eyes were so chlorinated I saw rings around every light.

Which, in a bizarre way, explains how I ended up buying a restaurant. Virtually every night when I got home, Ben would be waiting in the house with "someone I just had to meet." Usually it was a new "best friend" from the nineteenth hole, and invariably it was someone who desperately wanted to sell me something, often stocks and bonds, or real estate. Ben would go on and on about what a good deal it was, and finally I'd say yes. When you're that tired, you just say yes so you can get that stranger out of your house, give the babies a bath, hold them, sing them to sleep, then learn lines and go to bed. Already we had invested in a gas station and a metal products plant. This time I invested in a restaurant called the Trails, another deal "too good to pass up."

The Trails was located at Sepulveda Boulevard and Centinela Avenue in the Westchester section of Los Angeles. It was close to MGM in Culver City, but even closer to Hughes Tool Company, which was by now a powerhouse in the burgeoning defense electronics field. The company had become an employment mecca for innovative scientists and engineers. The men here—and by and large they were all men—had blueprinted Howard Hughes's casual sketch of a hospital bed, then quickly built the ingenious contraption that Hughes had demonstrated for me. The Trails was where they gravitated for lunch, and some of them never left until closing time.

There was a policy at Hughes against drinking at lunch, but these men ignored it. In fact, they not only drank at lunch, they drank after lunch into the cocktail hour, and then past that until dinner. The Trails, which really was a great place, had a huge bar, a dance floor, and a bandstand where Ben sang with a combo. But the most original attraction at the restaurant was a glass-enclosed miniature zoo, complete with parrots, fish, and a group of very active monkeys. There you'd be, eating dinner, with four monkeys masturbating behind you. Nobody ever complained, but somehow, I never thought this kind of action went with food.

Notwithstanding its popularity with the gang from Hughes, the Trails was about to go into receivership when we bought it. We didn't change a thing, except the sign: I was still trying to make Ben feel like a breadwinner, so the new sign over the door said ESTHER & BEN GAGE'S TRAILS. There was also a giant guest book in the entrance way, and everybody wrote the same thing: "We like the birds. We like the fish. And we sure like the monkeys. But where's Esther?" The Trails became Ben's headquarters and gave him a place to go every day, other than the golf course.

Howard Hughes himself was a regular at the restaurant, and in a way it became his headquarters, too. Howard had recently relocated his own base of operations to Las Vegas, so when he wanted to do business in Los Angeles, he went into the back of our restaurant to use the telephone at Ben's desk. One month he ran up $1,700 in long-distance charges. Ben, reluctant to confront a billionaire and ask for the money, left it to me to call a halt to his excesses. One day when I came into the office, there was Howard on the phone.

"Howard, hang up the phone!" I said.

"What did you say, Esther? I couldn't hear you—I'm on the phone." Howard's hearing hadn't improved. (Neither had his taste in clothing—I think he was still wearing the same blue serge suit with the shiny seat that he had on the night he cut in to dance with me at Mayer's house.)

"That's what we need to talk about. Get off the phone, Howard," I shouted.

"No. I'm talking . . . I'm talking to Paris."

"I know, Howard. Hang up the phone—now."

He looked up, glowered at me as if I were the most unreasonable woman he'd ever seen, then told Paris, "I'll have to call you back."

I showed Howard our phone bill and said, "Do you see what you've spent in the past month on our telephone? I'd like the money, please."

"How much of it do you want?"

"What do you mean, how much of it? I want it all—seventeen hundred dollars."

"I don't have any money, Esther," he told me.

This was a man who had been lavishing flowers and diamonds on Lana Turner, Terry Moore, and Kathryn Grayson—simultaneously. "Goddammit, Howard, you're a billionaire. We are not going to keep subsidizing you. If this keeps up, we'll soon be eating the monkeys."

"Okay . . . Okay." And with that, he picked up the phone and called his aide-de-camp, Noah Dietrich. Dietrich held the purse strings at Hughes Aircraft, and Hughes told him to bring a checkbook.

Dietrich arrived quickly and asked Hughes, "Who's the check for?"

"It's for Esther . . . seventeen hundred dollars."

Noah looked at me, and I could tell that he was thinking the worst. Howard, the intrepid womanizer, had young women stashed in rented apartments, houses, and hotel rooms all over LA, keeping each captive with the promise of a movie career. It gave a whole new meaning to "ladies in waiting." Dietrich must have thought that I'd gone to bed with Howard and now was blackmailing him. "What has she done for us for seventeen hundred dollars, Howard?" he asked.

I waved the phone bill under his nose. "See for yourself."

"Who do I make the check out to?" Dietrich asked me.

"Esther Williams," I said.

"It says outside that you're Esther Gage. I'll make you a deal—I'll make out the check to Esther Williams if you give me an auto-graphed picture." With Howard's people, it was always "a deal," no matter how stupid it was.

Imagine having to haggle with a billionaire and his sidekick to get what was really owed me. We exchanged signatures. I don't know where my signature ended up, but his went directly to the bank. At a recent celebrity auction, I learned that a signed Howard Hughes check sold for $25,000.

In April of 1951, *Life* magazine celebrated my entrepreneurial activities with a cover story entitled "Mermaid Tycoon." They pre-sented me as "Aquatic Esther," "Garagewoman Esther," "Restaura-teur Esther," and "Industrialist Esther" (looking over a group of models wearing "my" Cole of California swimsuits, like a general re-viewing her troops). They showed me as everything but "Exhausted Esther," which is who I really was much of the time.

Back at the studio, I was doing fine; MGM publicity chief Howard Strickling was happy about my good publicity. But things there were becoming increasingly tense as the hostilities between Schary and Mayer mounted. Just after the new year, Schary had va-cationed with his family in Boca Raton, Florida, and had used the occasion to confer with Loew's president Nick Schenck, who was there playing golf and waiting out the New York winter. At their meeting, Schenck bestowed a new seven-year contract extension on Schary. Schary, Benny Thau, L. K. Sidney, Eddie Mannix, and the rest of the men on the third floor also were offered Loew's stock op-tions, but when the news hit the papers, there was no mention of Mayer's name. Not surprisingly, Mayer took the slight personally.

Mayer came to believe that Schenck and Schary were conniving to push him out. From then on he behaved as if this were true, and his behavior precipitated a final showdown that ensured his departure. In February, Mayer attended a public preview of one of Schary's pet projects, the Civil War drama, *The Red Badge of Courage*. Mayer had vigorously opposed the making of the film as a waste of money, and as the screening proceeded he loudly disparaged the movie. He happened not to be alone. The audience laughed openly at one of the battle sequences, which showed World War II Medal of Honor winner Audie Murphy fleeing headlong in cowardly retreat from the enemy. Most of the seats in the theater were empty by the time the end credits rolled; nevertheless, it was boorish for the studio head to ridicule an MGM product so openly. Worse yet, his remarks were overheard by a woman sitting across the aisle. She was journalist Lillian Ross, who was chronicling the making of *Red Badge* for *The New Yorker* magazine.

By the time Mayer was given an honorary Academy Award at the end of March, rumors were flying that he was on his way out.

Mayer saw the writing on the wall. Ben and I were having dinner at Chasen's to celebrate the *Life* cover story. By coincidence, Mayer and Lorena were also there. In those days, Chasen's was the neighborhood eatery to the stars—you always saw people you knew. Mayer came over and said, "They're kicking me out, Esther. If I start up another studio, would you come with me?"

There was nothing bullying about his request. I'd never been afraid of Mayer, and there certainly wasn't anything scary about him now. Partly by standing up to him, partly by mothering him through his fits of temper, and partly by making hit movies, I'd gained his respect. He'd stopped trying to be my "Daddy." I liked our mutual respect. I heard that Katharine Hepburn also enjoyed that kind of relationship with him.

I didn't want to turn him down flat, but I also had no intention of going with him. From a family standpoint, I couldn't risk it, since I was still the primary breadwinner in my household. The "mermaid tycoon" businesses kept Ben occupied, but they didn't bring in much revenue. Financially, I had to keep working, and the truth was that my pictures really couldn't be made anywhere but MGM.

Notwithstanding the moron who built the black coffin underwater set on *Texas Carnival*, over the years we'd assembled a team of people who had learned how to make swimming movies, and it had become a specialized branch of filmmaking. We'd attracted a group of cameramen who'd done scuba work and who liked to shoot underwater. (Jon Hall, who'd made a bunch of Arabian Nights movies in the forties and later became TV's *Ramar of the Jungle,* pioneered the manufacture of underwater camera equipment.) We kept a roster of chorus girls we'd trained who could swim in the production numbers. Most of them doubled as dancers, because we found that it was easier to teach dancers to swim than it was to teach swimmers to dance. (After *Take Me Out to the Ball Game,* I knew that all too well!) With the making of *Neptune's Daughter,* we'd formed the first swimmer-dancer union within the Screen Actors Guild. Sydney Guilaroff and his assistants in hairstyling had perfected the mix of Vaseline and baby oil to keep hair in place all day underwater. Bill Tuttle's crew in makeup had found the right body paint and face makeup so that I could stay in the pool all day long.

Together we were an efficient production unit for making movies that made money, and the odds of enticing all of these talented individuals to defect from MGM were not good. The prospect of training another group of swimming-movie specialists was daunting, and Mayer's ability to secure financing for another studio was completely unknown. And of course there was another major consideration: MGM owned my greatest "prop," the $250,000 pool on Stage 30 that Sam Katz had built for me. I wanted to find a way to let Mayer down easy (and without him making a scene in Chasen's), so I fastened on the pool as an excuse and tried to lighten things up. "Thanks, Mr. Mayer, but where are you going to find a pool like the one on Stage 30? How can I go with you if you don't have a pool?"

"I'll build one," he answered unconvincingly.

"No you won't," I said. "But call me if you do."

He looked at me, crestfallen, and it was painful to see him like that. Mayer had always been short; now he looked small, which was very different indeed. He seemed quite vulnerable as he wished me well and returned to his table.

Shortly thereafter, he gave an interview to Lillian Ross, during which he explained his distaste for grim little message films—Dore Schary–type films, like *Red Badge of Courage.* "Andy Hardy . . . senti-

mentality! What's wrong with it? Love . . . good old-fashioned romance. Is it bad? It entertains. It brings the audience to the box office." His words summarized his approach to moviemaking. He may
as well have been describing my movies. No wonder he wanted me
to go with him.

Back on the lot, I ran into PR chief Howard Strickling. Howard
looked pale and tense, and when he was nervous, he stuttered.
"H-h-h hello, Esther," he said. "What do you hear?" Although Howard
was a powerful man at MGM, he was also a very frightened man.

"Howard, you know what's going on. They want L.B. out."

"I-I-I know." Of course he knew. He *had* to know. And he also
knew the behind-the-scenes story of Mayer's ouster.

According to Howard, Mayer had forced the issue of the dif-
ferences between himself and Schary with "the general," Nick
Schenck. He'd sent Schenck a letter lambasting Dore Schary for his
small-time movies, his snobbism, and his lack of understanding and
appreciation for movie stars. As far as I knew, he was right on the
money there. Then Mayer essentially had flung down the gauntlet,
telling Schenck that he had to choose between the two of them.
Schenck responded with a letter of his own, telling Mayer that
Schary had been good for the studio's bottom line, and that if a
choice had to be made, Mayer was out. Mayer was outraged. With
Schary sitting across the white crescent desk from him, he refused
to take Schenck's phone call, telling Bob Rubin, the New York–
based Loews/MGM corporate counsel, that Nick Schenck and
Schary could "take the studio and choke on it."

The old lion resigned on June 22, 1951. The man who had built
MGM, and who had first envisioned me as a star, departed through
the gate that still bore his name. It was the end of an era.

Mayer left MGM at the height of the Communist "Red scare" that
was gripping the country. Six months earlier, the Chinese had joined
the Korean War; the espionage trial of Julius and Ethel Rosenberg
had just ended. It was an ugly and fearful time in the country, and in
Hollywood in particular. There was talk of requiring everyone at the
studios to sign a loyalty oath. The American Legion threatened to
submit lists of alleged film industry Communists to the studios, demanding that they "prove" their writers and stars were loyal to Old

Glory, and they vowed to picket any movies with actors who had not been cleared by the legion. Senator Joe McCarthy and the House Un-American Activities Committee (HUAC) were summoning a parade of Hollywood witnesses to answer the question, "Are you now or have you ever been a member of the Communist Party?" Some, like Sterling Hayden and Elia Kazan, named names. Others, like Charlie Chaplin, told them to take a hike and paid the price. The witch hunt ruined the careers of many actors, including that of my *Neptune's Daughter* costar Betty Garrett and her husband, Larry Parks.

MGM thought it was a good time to wave the flag. My next film, *Skirts Ahoy!*, was part of the effort to convince the public that Hollywood was not Red, but red, white, and blue. At a time when men were getting called up to fight in Korea, the movie was to be all but a recruitment film for women to join the navy. The government needed women to take over the administrative jobs so that they could free up the men to fight. In *Skirts Ahoy!* I played one of three women who run away from various troubles at home and enlist in the Waves. My costars were Joan Evans, who had the ingenue role, and Vivian Blaine, who had starred as the adenoidal Adelaide in the Broadway hit *Guys and Dolls*. (She later repeated the role in the film version opposite Frank Sinatra.)

Screenwriter Isobel Lennart, who would go on to write *Funny Girl*, was assigned to the project. She told me that in its dealings with MGM, the navy had specifically requested that I star in the movie. They wanted an all-American girl, one with no Communist skeletons in the closet.

Isobel wrote quickly, and she soon had a treatment for me to look at. I was to portray socialite Whitney Young. Rich but not snooty, Whitney had a sense of duty and patriotism. Having fled Mr. Wrong on her wedding day, she wasn't joining the navy just to look for Mr. Right. Isobel also had imbued her with a nurturing, almost maternal quality in the way she befriended the other two women. I liked the fact that the story lines of their loyalty to one another, and of the way they adapt to life in the navy, took precedence over romance. (Barry Sullivan played Lieutenant Commander Paul Elcott, the navy physician who finally turns out to be my Dr. Right.)

By this time, whenever I looked at a script, I made sure there were swimming sequences. As *Skirts Ahoy!* was about the navy, the producers thought the proximity of water would suffice. But I knew what the audience expected from me. I had to be in a swimsuit and in the water. Isobel had written one scene where the three of us were part of a fitness class doing calisthenics on a big outdoor field. I suggested that we move the exercises into the pool as part of a beginners' swim class. We made the women played by Joan and Vivian nonswimmers, and had capable swimmer Whitney, me, sign up for the class just to be with her pals. When they start sinking, she does a racing dive and rescues them, revealing her expertise to the exasperated instructor, who orders her out of the class. Isobel saw something nurturing in me that is attractive in women—the way they treat their friends, their children, their husbands. I never could just let people come into my life and service me; I had to be "serviceable" to them. That's what Isobel captured in this role. She asked me lots of questions about how I felt about loyalty and love, and she wove these ideas into the script.

As for wardrobe for the movie, we had to go by the book about official navy attire. There would be no adding extra sparkle, or substituting high heels for sensible oxfords. I was happy to wear the crisp navy blue or white dress uniforms, which were quite attractive. When I saw what we'd be wearing to shoot the pool scene, however, my heart sank. Regulation U.S. Navy swimwear for Waves was all but prehistoric. The outfits were made out of shapeless gray cotton knit and looked something like a sleeveless T-shirt. They were the saddest bathing suits I'd ever seen. They had no internal support; for women who were at all well endowed, their bosoms would either be flattened or jammed down to their waists. There was no way we could shoot a swimming sequence in those suits. When they got wet, they clung like an old sweater. Regulation outfits or not, I didn't want to be seen on-screen in that suit.

Dan Kimball, Secretary of the Navy, was the only man who could solve the dilemma. I'd met him on a prior trip to Washington, and we'd hit it off well. I had no problem picking up the phone and asking to see him, but the aide who took my call asking for an appointment with the secretary of the navy couldn't believe his ears ("You're *who?* And you want a meeting with *him?*"). Nevertheless, he must have delivered the message, because Kimball's personal adjutant very quickly returned my call and set up the appointment.

The publicity department piggybacked my trip to Washington with a promotional junket for *Texas Carnival*. Melvina Pumphrey was contacted and put in charge of arranging my trip. She was asked if there was anything else I wanted to do while I was there. Well yes, there was something—I wanted to swim in the White House pool.

Eventually, Gerald Ford built an outdoor pool on the White House lawn somewhere. But in 1951, the pool was in the basement, and I don't think Harry or Bess Truman used it much. When I went into one of the changing rooms, there was a bathing cap hanging on a peg. Of course, Esther couldn't resist peeking inside, and my curiosity was rewarded. There in block letters around the back of the neck was the name of the owner who had left it behind: the previous first lady, Eleanor Roosevelt. I thought of my mother; Mrs. Roosevelt had been her heroine ever since FDR took office. Because of her crusading stand on civil rights and rights for women, she had become a role model for me as well. With a great sense of pride, I put Mrs. Roosevelt's cap on my head and dove in to swim some laps.

It was just the morale-booster I needed for my meeting with Secretary of the Navy Dan Kimball. Kimball was a handsome, strapping fellow with a fine sense of humor. He looked like Hollywood's idea of what a secretary of the navy should be—he may as well have come from Central Casting. As I was ushered into his office he said, "It's so good to see you again, Esther. What did you want to talk about?"

"Do you have a powder room, Dan? I'd like to show you something." I'd brought the regulation suit with me in a tote bag, but I knew it was no good just taking the suit out of the bag and holding it up. It would be far more effective to physically demonstrate the problem, so I popped into the powder room and came out wearing the suit.

Kimball's jaw dropped. "What the hell is that?" he asked.

"This, Mr. Secretary, is what you have your female navy recruits swimming in . . . and you oughtta see it when it's wet!"

"I'm going to swim in the movie, but no woman wants to wear

this, Dan, whether she has a terrific figure or not. If we're making this film to boost the recruitment of women and they see me in this, it's gonna backfire."

"What do you suggest?"

"If you'd excuse me again for just a moment . . ." I went back into the bathroom and emerged wearing my Cole of California Esther Williams suit. I'd asked Fred Cole to run it up in a snappy bright navy blue specifically for this occasion.

"Wow!"

"Wow indeed. I'm glad you appreciate the difference. Mr. Secretary, could you make this the official swimsuit of the U.S. Navy?"

"Consider it done. What happens next?"

"Well, Dan, I'd like to take your order for fifty thousand swimsuits right now." That was my first big selling job. I left his office triumphant and headed straight for a phone to tell Fred Cole.

My success in Washington buoyed me through the making of *Skirts Ahoy!* I'd never worked with Sidney Lanfield, our director, before, but I took a disliking to him early on, not for how he treated me, but for how he treated Vivian Blaine. He singled out Brooklyn-born Vivian as the one who could never do anything right. It was almost as if he was trying to take her down a peg for having been the toast of Broadway in her role as Adelaide in *Guys and Dolls.* Even when she started falling apart, he didn't let up on her. Lanfield was a small-time director who was now given a chance at a major production, and he took out his own insecurities on a nervous actress.

I knew how that felt. I'd put up with abuse like that from Dick Thorpe for far too long. Joan and I tried to provide some moral support for Vivian, but it wasn't enough; so I went to Lanfield. By this time I was a star, and safe from his caustic remarks. "Can't you see that Vivian is disintegrating before your eyes? What you're doing is cruel. It's hurting the film. If you keep this up, she won't ever be able to give you what you need." He stared at me in stony silence. I took my star power one more step. "And if it continues, I'll make sure you're taken off this picture." Clearly, no love was lost between us. It was too late to calm Vivian down. I thought she'd have a nervous breakdown by the end of the picture, and I never spoke to Sid Lanfield again.

Once we wrapped up the filming, the now-familiar pattern proceeded into the next phase and we moved into publicity. The studio
shot the stills that would be used for lobby cards and posters, then
they sent me out to the beach for the swimsuit shots. After that they
arranged for the parade of fan magazine writers and photographers
to come to the house for interviews and the obligatory home can-
dids with Ben and the boys. By this time they had practically run
out of subject matter, having already thoroughly covered my interest in cooking, my favorite sports, my reading habits, and my taste
in clothes and home decor. Finally in desperation they asked me
whether I had any new ideas for story angles that hadn't been done
yet. That's when we decided to do a layout on teaching fourteen-
year-old Elizabeth Taylor how to swim.

Barely a teenager, Elizabeth Taylor was already more beautiful
and voluptuous than Miss America. When she arrived at the Beverly
Wilshire Hotel for our magazine shoot, I was bowled over. I couldn't
believe she was only fourteen. She filled out a swimsuit better than I
did. We did the pictures, including one shot of me teaching her to
float. With that superstructure of hers, she floated just fine. What
she couldn't do was sink. The photographs in *Holiday* magazine
were spectacular and memorable. The layout resides in my scrap-
book, but no one who sees it believes that Elizabeth was only fourteen at the time. She was in a hurry to become Elizabeth Taylor who
a couple of decades later riveted the world with her beauty, love affairs, marriages, and scandals.

Just as publicity for *Skirts Ahoy!* was wrapping up, MGM sent
me the script for my next movie. At first it was called *One Piece
Bathing Suit*, a title that didn't sound at all promising. Before its release, the title was changed to something that was much catchier:
Million Dollar Mermaid.

CHAPTER 16

MILLION DOLLAR MERMAID
1952

$\mathcal{T}$he MGM executives on the third floor thought they were giving me the *crème de la crème* when they cast me in *Million Dollar Mermaid*. My producer Arthur Hornblow Jr. was a patrician gentleman who had been married to Myrna Loy at the peak of her popularity in the late thirties and early forties. He was always dressed to the nines in a blazer and scarf. He was a former lawyer with an Ivy League education who fell into show business after World War I. Behind that dignified exterior, however, was a tough producer with an eye for the box office, who had brought to the screen films as diverse as *Ruggles of Red Gap, Gaslight,* and *The Asphalt Jungle.*

My director for the film, Mervyn LeRoy, and his wife Kitty were prominent members of the Hollywood "aristocracy." They were among the most sought-after guests for every A-list party in town. But Mervyn's background was as rough and tumble as Hornblow's was genteel. A school dropout at the age of twelve, he earned his living as a singing newsboy and graduated to doing Chaplin imitations in vaudeville. LeRoy learned the movie business from the ground up, coming to Hollywood when he was still in his teens and becoming a jack-of-all-trades, working in the wardrobe department and the lab, and as a cameraman, screenwriter, and actor. When the movies learned to talk, he started directing. His early films at Warner Bros. included such lighthearted fare as *Gold Diggers of 1933* and *Tugboat Annie,* as well as *Little Caesar,* the original gangster movie that launched both a film genre and the career of Edward G. Robinson. It was Mervyn who rechristened Julia Jean Turner as Lana when she was just fifteen and gave her her first role (in *They Won't Forget).* When he left Warner's for MGM, he brought Lana with him. In the mid-thirties he began producing as well as directing, and in 1939 he solidified his already prestigious reputation by producing *The Wizard of Oz.* Between him and Arthur, I felt as though I was being graced by the Hollywood Royal Family. You don't fool around with people like that.

I liked Mervyn, and not just because he loathed Dore Schary as much as I did. He was *so* Hollywood. I always drove with the top of my convertible down, and one day a limo pulled up beside me at a traffic light on Sunset Boulevard. The tinted rear window rolled down, and Mervyn LeRoy's head popped out.

"Esther!" he shouted. "Put the top up! Don't get too tan for the movie. Let's take a lunch together soon." And with that, he rolled up the window, the light changed, and he was off.

We never did "do lunch," but before we started work on *Million Dollar Mermaid,* Mervyn, Arthur, and I "took a meeting" to talk about the film. LeRoy filled me in on the original story of my movie character, Annette Kellerman, an Australian who had been a champion long-distance swimmer at the turn of the century. She'd had polio as a young girl and began swimming to regain the strength in her legs. Swimming competitively in distance events, Kellerman pioneered the wearing of masculine style swimwear for women, rather like a sleeveless wet suit or unitard. This was revolutionary, since "proper" ladies at the beach in her era still covered up from head to toe, decked out in ruffles and bows, just like my costumes in *Take Me Out to the Ball Game,* except that they were swimming in them, even in shoes and stockings. It's a wonder anyone could even stay afloat.

While preparing for a long swim, Kellerman was arrested on a beach one day near Boston and charged with indecent exposure. The racing suit exposed her arms and legs, which in Massachusetts back then was deemed nearly as lewd as going topless. After a highly publicized trial (Kellerman was acquitted), she put together a swimming and diving act and began working summer carnivals in the East, clad in her infamous one-piece swimsuit, but now with stockings attached to avoid being "indecent." She became the first professional woman swimmer. Her shows were increasingly popular, and eventually she became the star attraction at the Hippodrome Theater in New York. Finally she came to California and made movies in the earliest days of Hollywood, before she retired to become a wife, mother, and owner of a health food store in the Pacific Palisades.

Hornblow showed me several old photographs of her, and one really grabbed my attention. I thought, "My God, I wish I could meet her!" When she had visited California, in the early twenties, they had strung a tightrope between the bluffs of the Palisades, the beach, and the Santa Monica pier. The photo showed Annette Kellerman with her parasol, balancing above what is now Pacific Coast Highway. Shades of Pearl White *(The Perils of Pauline)!* Here was a woman whose career foreshadowed my own, who started out as a champion swimmer but ended up in the movies on the high wire.

Victor Mature costarred opposite me as Annette's lover, carnival hustler Jimmy Sullivan. Vic was a big man; he had a great swagger. I liked him and I knew we'd be good together on screen. He'd already done *Samson and Delilah,* but I got him and his well-developed pectorals before the peak of his "Biblical loincloth period," when he did *The Robe, Demetrius and the Gladiators,* and *The Egyptian.* How he maintained his muscular physique, given his peculiar diet, I'll never know. Vic was the only person I ever knew who could—and would— eat anything at all. He'd knock on my dressing room door at the end of the day and ask, "Do you have any ketchup?" Then he'd put it on a piece of cardboard and eat it, like an hors d'oeuvre. Literally.

Like Bob Mitchum, he was one of Howard Hughes's hard-drinking buddies. Vic called Hughes "The Phantom," because no one ever knew when he'd show up on the lot. Working on a scene, Vic would suddenly catch a glimpse of Howard out of the corner of his eye. Howard would stay on the set for a while, but never spoke to anybody. Then he'd disappear as quietly as he'd arrived, like a skinny ghost.

Vic also had a strange affliction. Having a lot of lines to deliver often made him anxious, and his hands and feet would swell up. He was a large enough man to begin with, but when all the blood in his body rushed to his extremities, they became huge. He had to take off his shoes because they hurt so much, and of course the swelling made it very hard to film him.

Aside from that, Vic was like an overgrown boy, like Peter Pan— or Johnny Weissmuller. He did as he pleased and never felt responsible to anyone. In a way, I, who usually felt responsible for everything and everybody, envied him his freedom.

When shooting began, Vic was rather aggressive about what he thought the personal payoff should be for being my leading man. This is not unusual in Hollywood. Attraction between actors working on a movie are inevitable. You're portraying strong emotions, many of them sexual if not romantic, and you're thrown together all day, every day, for as many as forty or fifty days. Partnering in a film is very much like a marriage—in fact, you spend more time with your leading man than you do with your spouse.

I felt a powerful attraction to Victor Mature. I was married, but all the passion and most of the love in that marriage were gone, or going. Vic, I knew, was entangled in a similar marriage. Still, I had been raised with conventional values in which I believed at the time, and in which, for the most part, I still believe. So I tried to stay away from Vic.

But he was my first leading man who really lived up to the title, and it's hard to stay away from a charismatic guy who's constantly whispering, "You're fantastic. I love you," on the set and off.

It might look better, here, if I said that Victor Mature seduced me, or that I didn't know what I was doing until it was too late, or that he battered down the gates and conquered the city. Nothing of the sort. I knew that he wanted me, and I wanted him. We were on equal terms. We didn't have to play games any more.

One night, after doing a steamy love scene that was more than adequate foreplay, we went to my dressing room, locked the door, and unleashed our hunger, our passion for each other. Vic was a strong and fulfilling lover. Even better than I had fantasized. That first night, we made love over and over and into exhaustion. He adored the romance of it, too, offering me a surprisingly vulnerable and gentle side that was irresistible.

It didn't take long for the MGM gossip mill to begin rumbling about our affair, and the Hollywood columnists dropped subtle blind items, like: "What two married stars at MGM are making beautiful Million Dollar music together?" I assumed Vic's wife—they'd been married and fighting only a couple of years—had learned to endure his affairs. My Ben, as usual, was oblivious.

Fictional desire and real desire blended during the making of *Million Dollar Mermaid*, and it's obvious, to me at least, in every scene of that film. Some days, I stood trembling with excitement, waiting for Vic's secret knock on my dressing-room door. We were shameless and happy.

Million Dollar Mermaid was going to be an extraordinary experience, on and off the screen. For once, swimming was really part of the story and didn't have to be shoehorned into the rest of the plot. I loved the idea of playing Annette Kellerman, a real person, rather than a superficial character created to give me an excuse to swim. It was a good script (even Deborah Kerr would agree), and I knew I'd have some challenging scenes to play. With Walter Pigeon playing my father, and Vic as Jimmy Sullivan, I had actors of substance opposite me. In addition to being lovers, Vic and I became friends, and he made the filmmaking process more exciting than it had ever been.

Because of the historical basis to the film, the set designer had taken care to recreate the original Hippodrome, which had been the jewel in the crown of the vaudeville circuit. One day as we were getting ready to shoot a scene, I saw Arthur Hornblow escort an older woman onto the set. They crossed to where I was standing and Arthur said, "Esther, I'd like you to meet Annette Kellerman."

Although she was sixty-five, there wasn't a wrinkle on her face. She was wearing a scarf with a hat and visor, and what she'd done was pull her face up into her hat. (This was another variation on the "rubber band" instant face-lift I'd first seen on William Powell seven years earlier, when I made *Hoodlum Saint*.)

Annette Kellerman looked around the set and nodded her approval. "This is very accurate," she said. "This is what backstage at the Hippodrome was like."

The two of us posed for a picture and then I asked, "How do you feel about me playing your life?"

There was an awkward silence. "Do you have a problem with that question?" I asked.

"It's not that," she finally answered in a pronounced Down Under accent. "It's just that I wish you were Australian."

"I'm the only swimmer in the movies, Miss Kellerman. I'm all you've got."

"I know. I know," she said. I wasn't sure she ever approved. She stayed and watched the shooting for a bit, and then left. I thought maybe she'd come to the premiere, but I never saw her again.

I had been looking forward to having Mervyn LeRoy's expertise behind the camera. Because of the movies he'd done before, such as *Random Harvest* and *Waterloo Bridge,* I had expected great insight and sensitivity, especially in dealing with the romantic part of the story line. It didn't happen. He wasn't the perceptive director I thought he would be. There's one dramatic sequence near the end of the movie where the glass wall of a diving tank shatters, and my back is broken as I'm pushed through the jagged opening in a surge of water and broken glass. As we got ready to shoot, all Mervyn said was, "Let's have a nice little scene."

A nice little scene? I had no idea how that "direction" was supposed to help me play the scene, but the truth is that was all the direction Mervyn *ever* gave me. It didn't matter whether we were doing a love scene, a fight, or an action sequence, he'd always say the same thing—"Let's have a nice little scene." Eventually I realized that he simply was tired, or more likely burned out. He had just directed *Quo Vadis?,* a troubled marathon costume epic with the proverbial cast of thousands, shot in Rome over the better part of a year. The film was successful, but it drained him; and I suspect that was why he wanted to do my movie. Mervyn knew we had a formula, and that we had a team of professionals who understood the art and science of making swimming movies. The fact that we knew what we were doing gave him license to sit back in his director's chair and talk about having "nice little scenes."

He realized that I'd figured it out, too, and so he tried to make it up to me. In the last scene of the film, I'm lying in the hospital, severely injured from when the tank shattered. Getting ready for the scene he told me, "This is a love scene. Jimmy comes back and he's found you at last. I'm going to do something for you. I'm going to put black flaps all around, so the crew doesn't distract you."

"The crew doesn't distract me, Mervyn. I don't want some black things around. I'm used to it. It's okay."

"No, Esther, I insist. I'm going to give you the same respect I would give Vivien Leigh or Greer Garson."

Obviously this mattered to him, so I said, "Well, if it makes you happy, Mervyn, go ahead." Somehow these kinds of situations never seemed to be about me; it was always about them and what they wanted.

But there was another masculine ego to be dealt with. When Victor Mature arrived to do the scene, he promptly blew a gasket. "What the hell is this? Who put all this black crap up around everything? I can't breathe in here!"

"Vic," I said, hoping his hands didn't start to swell up again, "we have to humor Mervyn. This is what he did with Greer Garson. I have to cry, so he figures I won't want anybody to see me do that." Victor was in no mood to humor anyone, least of all Mervyn. All those black cotton drapes that were giving him allergic fits came down. Mervyn, without missing a beat, leaned over to Vic, and in his usual confidential whisper, said, "Alright now, let's have a nice little scene." Vic and I looked at each other and tried not to laugh, because we knew we had to cry.

We used Stage 30 for our swim scenes. Today there's a little placard that identifies it as THE ESTHER WILLIAMS STAGE, but back then we just called it "Pneumonia Alley." The water always had to be warm for the swimmers, but hot air rises, and the crew up in the scaffolding above the stage were always complaining about the heat waves, the humidity, and chlorine fumes, which sometimes made them lightheaded or nauseous. Occasionally, one of the guys would pass out and fall into the water. To compensate, the air temperature of the soundstage was kept at sixty degrees, so the crew in the rigging wouldn't get the vapors. This meant that the swimmers all caught colds, because we were coming out of the eighty-five to ninety-degree water into the arctic air. My solution was to never get out of the pool. I'd just stay in there all day long.

I even took naps that way. I'd hook my heels on the coping, take short, quick breaths to keep myself afloat, and just drop right off. The lungs are like pontoons, and I was able to program myself to take little sips of air while I was sleeping. I found that if I leaned back and put my hands under my neck, the water wouldn't wake me up by leaking into my ears. People who came looking for me were told, "Esther is taking her nap in the pool. Look for a floating person that's asleep."

Staying in the pool for great lengths of time had its dangers, not on the surface, but below it. When we were shooting an underwater number, we followed a storyboard, and each segment of the number was timed. Through the windows the crew held up index cards for me that said how long the segment was: 45 SECONDS UNDERWATER was pretty typical, but what they meant was forty-five seconds of actual filming. I spent a lot more time underwater than that. What I had to do was get down, get set, make sure I was on my mark in front of the underwater window, match my position to the previous shot, and then do whatever it was that they wanted me to do for the camera. And after that I had to shoot back up to the top again. Eventually I began to put those "45 Seconds" cards together, combining the storyboard takes to make the action more fluid (you should excuse the expression) and to save time. As the day wore on, my lungs would expand and I could stay down longer and longer. Whatever I could do at 9:00 in the morning, I could do double that by 4:00 in the afternoon.

On one particular shot I was going feet first into a big scallop shell on the bottom of the pool that opened to reveal a huge pearl inside. I went down and down and down, and I swam around the pearl. I knew from the storyboard that I was supposed to go around the pearl one more time, but instead I lay my head on it, like a pillow, and sort of went into a trance. My eyes glazed over; I didn't know where up or down was, and I didn't care. This feeling is something like "the rapture" experienced by scuba divers. It's a very dangerous dreamlike state caused by excess carbon dioxide in the body, and when it takes over, all you want to do is go to sleep even as the oxygen is running out. Rapture may be what the anteroom of death feels like—you just want to fade off into the ozone.

Mervyn LeRoy was directing this "nice little scene" from the chamber in front of the underwater window. He didn't know he was watching his star drowning, but he knew that this shot didn't call for me to fall asleep. The pool had an underwater speaker, and suddenly I heard him calling my name. "Esther! Esther!! Get your head off that pearl! It's just been painted and the paint may come off. Get off it!"

I began to try to find his voice, but I was still dazed. "Esther, what the hell are you doing? Get off the pearl!" he repeated. I thought I already had. Mervyn's insistent voice, however, started to bring me out of my stupor, and it probably saved my life. I sat up and looked up toward the surface and thought, "This is what my mother talked about—survival. There has to come a time when you know more about what you've got to do than anybody in the world." I summoned what mental and physical resources I had left and swam to the surface. I never did that napping thing again.

The script for *Million Dollar Mermaid* included two water extravaganza scenes, and I pleaded with Merve to bring in Busby Berkeley to stage them, because I knew he'd bring a real sense of showmanship to the film. Busby hadn't directed a picture at MGM since Gene Kelly had him fired from *Take Me Out to the Ball Game,* but he'd continued directing flashy musical numbers within films like *Call Me Mister* with Betty Grable and Dan Dailey, and *Two Tickets to Broadway,* with Tony Martin and Janet Leigh. Fatigued as he was, Merve knew it was better than trying to do them himself and finally said yes.

Busby still drank, but not at work. On the set he was as wonderfully creative as ever. Before we did a take, he would gather everyone around him and chalk-talk his way through the scene. He stood in front of his blackboard, like a football coach diagramming a play, and told each of us on the team what our assignments were. Then we'd break the huddle and shoot.

Busby didn't give much thought to my safety. He just expected me to do whatever he dreamed up for me. Because I was the star, he said I had to do it better than anyone else. As a result, I risked my life every time he said, "Roll 'em." For the recreation of the water extravaganza at the New York Hippodrome, Busby pulled out all the stops. He suspended trapezes over the pool from which divers plunged into the water. I had my own trapeze, which was held in place by a pin at the very top of the soundstage until it was time for me to swing. I was like a parrot holding onto a perch, except that I was horizontal way up there, just under the ceiling of the stage. Face down, fifty feet above the pool, I gripped that trapeze so hard with my feet I broke a toe.

To signal everyone so they'd know when to dive in, Buzz fired off a pistol. Pinned to the ceiling like that, the sound of gunshots echoing through the soundstage rattled the hell out of me. We had a couple of rehearsals. Mostly they were for the crew snapping the release pin, so they'd know which gunshot was theirs. When they let loose, I was to swing forward over the pool, then back again. On the second swing, Buzz was to fire again, which was my cue to dive in.

What Busby had neglected to tell me was that he had rigged up four hundred electrically controlled smudge pots on both sides of the pool. As the chorus members dove in, the pots began to discharge thick, gorgeous plumes of red and yellow smoke fifty feet into the air. All of a sudden this smoke was billowing up, and soon it was so thick I couldn't see through it, but he wanted me to swing through this surrealistic universe of Technicolor smoke. It was typical of Buzz that he never mentioned the smoke. He just assumed it was a production detail that I didn't need to be concerned about. On the second great swing across the pool, I was to do a half gainer off the trapeze, but I couldn't see the pool below. I was afraid I was going to dive headfirst into the cement. Of course, being nearsighted didn't help. "I don't see any blue down there, Buzz," I called out. "What's with all this smoke?"

Buzz was up on a crane, armed with a bullhorn. "What's your problem, Williams?" he yelled into the horn. "You know where the water is. You already looked. Just don't dive in crooked." Then he fired off one round from the pistol and the crew snapped my pin. Down I swept like a circus aerialist, across the pool and back, smiling as if it were a backyard swing. As I came forward again, Buzz shot off another round and I did my half gainer through the billowing smoke, praying that I would hit warm water instead of cold cement. It was over in a matter of seconds. I sank deep into the pool and felt the incredible safety of being underwater. As I pushed my way to the surface, Buzz called, "Print it!" And I knew I wouldn't have to do it again. Years later, fans would tell me it was their favorite scene in all of my movies. It wasn't one of mine.

That dive into swirling smoke cost me only a broken toe. I wasn't so lucky on the next stunt, which almost killed me.

Designers Helen Rose and Walter Plunkett fitted me in an extraordinary swim costume—much like a diver's body suit, only covered, including the soles of the feet, with gold sequins, fifty thousand of them—like chain mail. Atop a gold turban, which was wrapped around my head, they perched a gold crown. And it was the crown that held the danger.

In the middle of the pool on Stage 30, there was a hydraulic lift. Busby had fitted it with a Lucite disk, a platform just big enough for me to stand on. A slender pipe on the platform steadied me as it rose in the air, with a fountain of water cascading all around me. When the lift took me fifty feet above the pool, I was to do a swan dive into the water below.

"Okay. Let's do it, Esther," Busby shouted.

I took my position on the disk and the hydraulic lift started rising. Up . . . up . . . up I went, the pool, the crew dropping away.

The lift finally jolted to a stop. I was perched on the height of a six-story rooftop.

Acrophobia! Dizziness! My equilibrium was gone because my inner ear had never fully recovered from the seven broken eardrums I'd suffered through years of living underwater. I suddenly couldn't tell if I was leaning or standing straight, and my mind—as well as my body—must've frozen up there.

"We're waiting, Esther!" Busby barked. "Jump!"

I forced a smile for the camera and swan-dived from that tiny platform. Hurtling down, I muttered a silent, "Oh, shit." I suddenly realized what was going to happen next. *The gold crown on my head.* Instead of being made with something pliable like cardboard, it was lightweight aluminum, a lot stronger and less flexible than my neck.

I hit the water with tremendous force. The impact snapped my head back. I heard something pop in my neck. I knew instantly that I was in big trouble.

Totally unaware, Mervyn called out, "Great . . . time for lunch."

Magic words. You only had to say it once. Everyone—Mervyn, Busby, the crew—trooped across the soundstage and within seconds vanished. Only Flossie Hackett, my wardrobe lady, remained, and only because it was her job to get my costume off for later shooting.

I could kick my legs, so I desperately treaded water; but my arms and shoulders were virtually paralyzed. The back of my neck was in screaming pain. In my mind's eye I saw the headlines: "Esther Williams Drowns in MGM Studio Pool." I cried out, "Flossie, you've got to get some help for me."

She thought I was joking. "C'mon, Esther, you're such a kidder. I want to go to lunch. I'm hungry."

"Flossie, I'm really in trouble," I gasped. "Find two guys who can lift me out of the pool."

Finally she believed I was serious. She ran to the big soundstage door and shouted, "I think Esther Williams is dead. She can't get out of the pool."

Some men came running in, quickly stripped off their shoes and shirts, and jumped in to pull me out. I was crying by that time, because the pain was so intense. They carried me to my dressing room. While we were waiting for the ambulance, Flossie carefully removed my gold fishnet bodysuit, rolling it down my body like pantyhose, and those fifty thousand tiny metal sequins were like little knives, nicking and cutting me. (Flossie was supposed to keep my costumes in good repair, so I'm sure the absurdity of peeling off the suit, instead of swiftly cutting it off, never crossed her mind.)

At the hospital, I blacked out from the pain. The X-rays showed that I had broken three vertebrae in the back of my neck. I'd come as close to snapping my spinal cord and becoming a paraplegic as you could without actually succeeding.

The doctor gave me a shot for the pain, then put my head in a brace to stabilize it. He put the rest of me in a full body cast, from the back of my neck all the way to my knees. My arms were encased down to my elbows; he left my lower arms free so once I regained movement, I could feed myself. As I began to come out of the painkillers, I realized that no one at the studio was aware that I'd been injured. For all I knew, Mervyn and Busby were still swearing at me for not reporting to the set after lunch. I told Flossie, "Take me back to the studio. Let's show them what happens when every-one is in such a hurry for lunch."

I didn't have to stay in the hospital; that body armor *was* my hos-pital. While I was out of commission they had to shoot around me. They couldn't replace me because too much of the film had already been done, including most of the big numbers. Besides, there were no other Hollywood swimming movie stars. The fact that they had to wait for me was, in its way, quite a compliment as well as a comfort.

Busby visited me at home. He was very sweet and wished me a speedy recovery, but it wasn't long before my cast was not just a hos-pital, but a jail as well. Imprisoned in my plaster of Paris, I got down on myself a little. I had time to think about what happened, and I realized that this near-death experience was partly my own fault.

I once again heard Bula's voice telling me that I hadn't really learned the lesson I should have after the incident with the outrig-ger in Hawaii. I hadn't paid enough attention to what it would mean to make that dive with a metal crown on my head, at least not until I was in the air. This was not something that Helen Rose or Walter Plunkett—or any costume designer, for that matter—would have known to take into consideration. I didn't think it out in advance, and shame on me, because I was the only one who would under-stand something like that. Take care of yourself, I thought. No one else can really do that for you.

I lived in that cast for six months. With youth and good condi-tioning on my side, I healed, but those three broken vertebrae fused together. I had headaches for a long time afterward. I still do. When-ever I'm stressed out, I get a headache from that solid piece of bone that I grew in the back of my neck. I was just lucky that it didn't turn out worse. Many years later, when I saw what happened to Christo-pher Reeve, I thought, "There but for the grace of God . . ."

After the cast was removed, I went back and finished the movie. Although we remained friends, Vic and I were no longer lovers. He had been exceptionally sweet during my convalescence. Vic was one man I never had to teach anything, not even how to swim! But I had never thought for a second that our affair would last past the mak-ing of the movie. In some part of my heart, I knew that I was just one more in his long list of conquests. But I don't regret a minute in his arms. Romances with beautiful leading men don't last forever, but don't knock it until you've had one.

My six-month hiatus was not long enough to restore Mervyn's zest for directing; he was still calling for "nice little scenes" right to the end. As we were wrapping the picture, I confronted him about it—nicely. I really did like him, even if he didn't really direct his actors. "Mervyn, why did you take on this project at all?"

"Frankly, Esther, I needed a hit, a top grosser," he said. At least it was an honest answer.

As it turned out, we gave Mervyn what he wanted. We even made it a Christmas present. *Million Dollar Mermaid* opened on December 5, 1952, as the holiday attraction at New York's Radio City Music Hall, and it was a major hit. It played there for eight weeks, and with lines around the block spilling into the side streets as people waited in the snow for tickets.

In January of 1953, while *Million Dollar Mermaid* was still doing big box office, the Hollywood Foreign Press Association voted me the number one female movie star in fifty countries. For that I was awarded the "Henrietta" statue; today they call it the Golden Globe. It wasn't an Oscar, but I had no expectation of ever receiving that kind of acknowledgment from my peers in the acting profession. And in a way it didn't matter, because I knew that the people out there in the audience still loved my movies. I felt validated, at least by the fans. On this film more than on many others, I really felt as though I'd earned their accolades, because I'd done it the hard way (and it had nearly killed me).

The awards ceremony took place in the ballroom of the Miramar Hotel in Santa Monica. Today for these events the stars make a big to-do about having big-name designers coordinate their "look," but for that night I made my own outfit. I never went to couturiers; if there was an outlet store, I'd find it. The fact that I could look great on less money added to my enjoyment. Penny-pinching was a lifelong habit left over from growing up in a depression family in southwest LA.

That night I wore a champagne-colored strapless evening gown, and before I got dressed I climbed up the hill behind my house in

Mandeville Canyon and secretly picked some cymbidium orchids from my neighbor's collection. Now, I suppose this was burglary, but my neighbor had more orchids than he knew what to do with; and these were growing right outside my bedroom window. The orchids matched the color of my dress perfectly, and I wore them as a long spray that trailed all the way from my waist to the floor. Everyone raved that this was a sensational way to wear orchids, and I did think my appearance made a classy counterpoint to Marilyn Monroe, who was named "Best New Personality."

Marilyn made quite an entrance that night, having poured herself into a skin-tight red sequined dress. Next day in the gossip columns, Joan Crawford tut-tutted that Marilyn was the embarrassment of the evening. Marilyn fired back by having her picture taken in nothing but a burlap sack. The caption under the picture of this equally revealing outfit was a perfect Marilyn line: "Is this better, Miss Crawford?"

A champagne gown trailing a spray of orchids . . . a box-office smash . . . the world's number one female star . . . two wonderful little boys at home . . . I had it all. But there was something wrong with the plot. Even though I had a lucrative contract with MGM, I had a husband who was drinking and gambling our money away faster than I could make it.

CHAPTER 17

DANGEROUS WHEN WET
1953

*B*en had very expensive vices. By this time he was not just an alcoholic, but a compulsive gambler as well. Whenever we'd go to Las Vegas, I watched how much he gambled, because I saw that fever. There was always a slot machine in a gas station, always a place to pull the lever; he could just drop the coins in, pull the handle, get back in the car, and keep going. It seemed at every corner there was a gimmick waiting to grab some of your hard-earned money—actually, in this case, waiting for *my* hard-earned money. And Ben was really easy prey. He would drink and start gambling, then get loaded and lose all his common sense. I would stand by sometimes, helpless, just waiting for the end—either the end of the evening or the end of the chips.

It's a funny thing about having been born without any money—it never becomes the end-all, be-all of your life. I was never into the conventional big-ticket trappings of stardom anyway—the furs and the fancy cars. I'd always invested in things that I felt would appreciate in value. I'd buy real estate in expensive residential neighborhoods such as Sunset Boulevard, or the Riviera Country Club in

Pacific Palisades. I remember saying to somebody once, "I don't care about having real jewelry; I'd rather have a lot on Sunset."

The real estate, however, was a great temptation to Ben, because he could borrow on the properties without telling me. It wasn't until the 1960s that a husband could be stopped from taking a loan against community property without a wife's signature. That was too late for women like Doris Day and me, who had been the big breadwinners of our families. Doris, after working brutally hard since she was a teenager, was wiped out, left broke and in debt by her husband/manager, Marty Melcher, a wheeler-dealer who, in league with a shady lawyer, sank Doris's millions into high-risk ventures that went belly up. I read that Doris hauled them all into court and won a multimillion-dollar judgment, which she couldn't collect. Like Doris, I found out that my husband had spent everything and then some, but only after the money was already gone.

I probably should have done a better job of policing our family finances and our "Mermaid Tycoon" enterprises; I had no idea that Ben was going through so much money. Looking back, I suppose that when you find yourself using the word "policing" in connection with the activities of your spouse, it should be a red flag. But you judge others by yourself, by what you would do. That was something I hadn't assimilated yet. This "big, sweet-faced, overgrown boy" had a different morality about taking than I did. What had first manifested itself in the early days of our marriage as a lack of ambition had developed into something more sinister. Ben was completely capable of letting me be the sole financial support of our family and had no compunctions whatsoever about spending everything I earned. And when he wasn't at the bar or on the golf course, he was at the racetrack.

I didn't know it then, but he and his gambling buddies, like Desi Arnaz, Lucille Ball's husband, were going to the races every day. That was a big mistake because no matter how much money we had, Desi and Lucy had more; and there was just no way Ben could keep up with the wild Cuban, although God knows he tried. He completely neglected The Trails and our other businesses, which were quickly going down the tubes. We had a joint checking account, and he had free access to everything.

Was I too trusting, or too focused on my career to see what was going on? It never occurred to me to be the family bookkeeper as well. There were plenty of warning signs, but for whatever reason— my career, my income, a reluctance to engage in heated marital conflicts—I tried to ignore the signals.

It was during those awful days of money madness and booze, when I was struggling to keep my second marriage together, that Fernando Lamas strode into my life. Here's how:

With the financial success of *Million Dollar Mermaid*, MGM was anxious for me to start preparing for my next picture, *Dangerous When Wet*, with me as Katy Higgins (the country cousin, I suppose, of my character K. C. Higgins from *Take Me Out to the Ball Game*), an American girl who swims the English Channel. William Demarest and Charlotte Greenwood were cast as my parents; Barbara Whiting was my teenage sister, script by Dorothy Kingsley, and Chuck Walters directing. Chuck and I had a good rapport from having done *Texas Carnival* together, so I looked forward to this one.

We discussed who would play André Lanet, my love interest, and Chuck asked whether I knew Fernando Lamas. I told her that I'd seen him on the lot coming and going from Gertrude Fogler's voice studio. I knew he had starred in movies with Jane Powell, Greer Garson, and Lana Turner, and I knew that he was romantically linked with Lana. And I heard he could swim. Yes, Fernando Lamas sounded like good casting.

He was contacted through the production office about *Dangerous When Wet*, but word came back that he didn't want to do the picture. That was a new one for me. I couldn't imagine why he'd turned it down. It was a good script, and the name Esther Williams on the marquee was a guaranteed solid draw. I decided to find out why.

On my way to the commissary one afternoon, I ran into Fernando as he was leaving Miss Fogler's studio. She had been helping him smooth over his Latin accent so it would be more understandable. He was wearing gray slacks, a blue blazer, and a yellow silk scarf around his neck, and with his dark hair, bronze tan, and flashing white smile, he was ridiculously gorgeous. Even by MGM standards—the studio of Clark Gable, Robert Taylor, and Co.—Fernando was a knockout.

Feigning a casual indifference, I said, "I'd like to talk with you, Fernando. Join me for a cup of coffee?"

The commissary was fairly empty, which meant we wouldn't be interrupted by the usual patter of table hoppers.

"Why don't you want to do *Dangerous When Wet?*" I asked.

"I have come all the way from Argentina to be a *star* at MGM, and I know what I want to do. I want to act in important pictures."

The emphasis on "star" caused me to wince just a bit. "This will be an important picture. That's the only kind I do," I said.

"No," he said, and with great panache, proclaimed, "I don't want to play Nelson Eddy to your Jeanette MacDonald in a swimming pool."

I laughed at this spirited assessment of my movies, and even more at his analogy. "But it'll be great entertainment," I responded.

"I read the script. I don't have enough good scenes."

Ah, so that's what was bugging him. Spoken like the true *star* he wanted to be.

Despite this gaucho charisma, I wasn't quite sure I wanted to deal with this package. At least not yet. Still, I needed a strong leading man, and I didn't want to let this one get away. Besides, he could swim, which was a big plus for me. I had propped up Van Johnson during our swimming sequences with my hand under his back, and Ricardo Montalban and John Bromfield, and struggled through the routines walking on ramps concealed underwater. And as for Johnnie Johnson? No thank you! I decided to take the plunge.

I set the hook. "We'll rewrite your part and make it bigger. Much bigger."

Now I had to reel him in with a little flattery. "Tell me something—is it true that you were a swimming champion in Buenos Aires?"

"My dear Esther," he said suavely, "at one time I was one of the five fastest men in the world."

Fernando's reputation as a Casanova had preceded him, and my smart mouth could not resist the opening he left me: "I know all about that," I said, smiling, "but can you *swim?*"

Fernando leaned over as if to share something in confidence with me. At that moment he was the very epitome of the debonair lover

I'd seen in *Merry Widow*. "I'm trying to keep it a secret," he said in a conspiratorial whisper, "so I don't end up in *all* your movies."

With that, I knew we'd get along just fine. Fernando had a wonderful sly sense of humor, and after we made some changes to the script to beef up his role, he agreed to do the movie. We settled into a comfortable, easy relationship. We joked, we kidded, and at the start, it was professional and uncomplicated.

Fernando had a beautiful baritone voice. In *Merry Widow* he was given practically the entire Franz Lehar score because Lana Turner, with whom he costarred, couldn't sing a note. Now, for *Dangerous When Wet*, André (Fernando) was to sing three songs. The first was a duet with me in a dressing room/swimming sequence, which takes place at his mother's house. André and I sing, "Ain't Nature Grand" while we change into our swimsuits—in separate dressing rooms, of course. In this scene, André talks me into swimming with him, but since I have no swimsuit with me, he asks me to wear his mother's suit, which is hanging on a peg in the dressing room. The idea is that I'm to look frumpy.

I thought I'd have some fun with Fernando. I had Helen Rose make me up a black-lace lingerie teddy. We began the song, changed into our swimsuits, and when we came out of the dressing room, I was wearing this sexy black-lace teddy instead of his mother's swimsuit. Now, Fernando loved his own singing voice, and when I appeared, he stopped the scene, stared at me, stunned, that I would upstage his song with this seductive swim costume. He demanded that we redo the shot because it "interrupted his concentration." Chuck Walters redid the scene to please Fernando, but clever Chuck kept the stunned look on Fernando's face in the final cut.

Fernando was not to be outdone. In a swimming race in which André is to lose to Katy, he could not bear the idea that Esther Williams would reach the end of the pool first despite what was called for in the script. In a mad race to the end of the pool Fernando gets there first with his ear-to-ear grin. The orchestra was forced to pick up the pace of the song to match his swimming stroke. This rather sweet melodic ballad now sounded like "The Flight of the Bumblebee."

I understood Fernando. This was to be a test of wills.

One of the best-remembered scenes from *Dangerous When Wet* is a cartoon sequence with Tom and Jerry. William Hanna and Joseph Barbera, their creators, had successfully put Jerry the mouse into a live-action dance number with Gene Kelly in *Anchors Aweigh* (which was a first), and I was delighted when they suggested that I do a scene with Tom and Jerry underwater. It was a comic dream sequence intended to parallel the conflict that my character was experiencing between her commitment to swim the English Channel and her attraction to André. In the dream, a sexy cartoon character representing Fernando was supposed to tempt me to get involved with him and distract me from my goal of swimming the Channel. Hanna and Barbera, searching for the right cartoon metaphor for this romantic Frenchman who Fernando portrayed, made him an octopus.

"Perfect. I've heard his tentacles are everywhere," I said.

Once we reviewed the sequence on storyboards, a French bistro table was built at the bottom of the pool, with a little chair and Lucite cleats for my feet to keep me seated at the table so I wouldn't float to the surface. Helen Rose designed a one-piece swimsuit in white, which played beautifully against the Technicolor blue of the water. Helen experimented with weights in my swimsuit to keep me from floating to the surface; clearly a dangerous idea. Besides, the weights showed on camera, and in order to keep me down, she would have needed enough weights to virtually sink me. The Lucite cleats were a far better idea.

I dove in, sat down at the underwater table, put one foot in the cleats, and wrapped the other around the leg of the chair to anchor myself at the bottom. I played the scene with the imaginary octopus that would later be drawn in by Hanna and Barbera (while Fernando sang off camera, "In my wildest dreams, I never thought we'd meet," a gurgling, underwater sound added to his voice). This was all done in pantomime, as I was alone underwater. I also swam with Tom and Jerry, was chased by a cartoon shark, and was followed by a family of singing seahorses. It looked as if I swam and acted effortlessly. Hardly. It is quite a challenge to swim the crawl and backstroke *underwater*. For swimmers out there, try to lift your elbows while swimming underwater. You'll find your body is propelled to the top. In order to keep yourself under the surface, your toes must be pointed downward (an unnatural and ungainly position), and your arms must stroke laterally, a technique that demands a power-ful upper body. Oh yes, don't forget that while you're doing this, you've got dialogue. And don't forget to smile!

Acting underwater is something quite different from swimming. In previous films, I swam, smiled, and danced, ducking behind ba-nana leaves so I could shoot up to the top of the tank for air. For the first time, I had lines, gestures, movements that I would have had in any scene, dry or wet—only I had *no air*. After a while, it seemed so normal that even the crew forgot I was underwater. Whenever I came to the end of my breath, and shot up to the surface, the assis-tant director would shout, "What's the matter, Esther, we haven't fin-ished the scene yet."

By the time *Dangerous When Wet* was filming, underwater pho-tography had improved immeasurably. The sequence with Tom and Jerry is crystal clear, unlike the murky underwater scenes of my first film, *Bathing Beauty*.

When the movie came back from previews, the response cards indicated that the audience didn't believe I was underwater during the Tom and Jerry sequence. Joe Barbera was concerned. He couldn't figure out the problem. As we were discussing the promo-tion for the movie, Joe blurted out, "I've got it! There are no *bubbles*, Esther. People expect *bubbles* underwater."

So for the following preview, Joe and Phil had drawn $50,000 worth of pink underwater bubbles floating from my mouth when-ever I spoke.

"Joe, you didn't need to spend all that money," I said, "I could've blown the bubbles for free. All you had to do was ask."

"Yeah," sighed Joe, "but they wouldn't look real."

They returned from the next preview and called me at home, "Es-ther," they said, laughing, "it works! They *loved* the Tom and Jerry part. The audience held their breath for the entire length of the number. You wouldn't believe it. When it ended you could hear a collective gasp in the theater. They just sat there breathing!"

One evening, during the filming of *Dangerous When Wet*, Ben and I attended a fund-raiser at the Crystal Ballroom of the Beverly Hills Hotel. Studio executive Benny Thau was at our table, as were Fer-nando and his lady of the moment, Lana Turner.

During the making of *The Merry Widow*, he and Lana had begun a hot—very hot—affair. On the surface, at least, it looked like a great matchup. Fernando was very much a ladies' man, and Lana certainly liked men. Lamas had taken just one look at the blond-and-creamy Lana, liked what he saw, and started showing up at rehearsals wearing a skin-tight brown dancer's leotard, which made no secret of his masculine charms. Lana was obviously impressed— and Lana had been impressed by the best, including seven husbands and a legion of lovers, among them Errol Flynn, Clark Gable, Victor Mature, Mickey Rooney, Frank Sinatra, Peter Lawford, and Robert Taylor. Fernando was now about to join those distinguished ranks.

The first delicate hint I had of their affair came one afternoon as Fernando was on his way to the makeup department, situated next to the stars' dressing rooms. I heard Lana shout from her dressing room window—and I mean shout—"Fernando Lamas! Get your Argentinean ass in here!" Fernando, who was always accompanied by an entourage of adoring sycophants, needed no further encouragement. With the grace of a Latin cavalier, he bowed to his gentlemen friends and scooted into Lana's dressing room, which was situated right next to mine.

Like the dressing rooms of most MGM stars, mine was furnished with a couch, a table, and a couple of chairs. Lana, however, had demanded—and got—a huge bed with pink satin sheets and pillows, plus there were mirrors everywhere. From the sounds coming through the wall between Lana's dressing room and mine, I could tell that she and Fernando weren't going over lines.

I'm afraid that I was a bit curious, but then, how could I resist? I placed an empty glass against the wall between our rooms and pressed my ear to it. The sound I heard, magnified by the water glass, was rather like listening to a symphony. The first movement began with gentle strings and sighing woodwinds. The second movement, which started with mounting rhythm, brought in the whole brass section, with trumpets and tubas blowing like crazy. The third movement was filled with pounding kettledrums and marimbas (the Latin touch), which reached a wild and ecstatic crescendo. What followed was diminuendo—back to the sighing woodwinds.

"Oh, Fernando, oh, Fernando," Lana moaned.

Oh well, I thought to myself, At least she remembers his name.

Many years later, after Fernando and I were married, I hesitantly confessed to him that I had eavesdropped on his matinee with Lana. "My dear," he said with a grin, "I am flattered."

During the dinner at the Beverly Hills Hotel, I was talking to Benny Thau, who was seated to my right. Lana and Fernando were next to Thau. Ben was seated to my left, but when I turned to say something to him, he was gone. I figured that I'd been so caught up in my conversation with Thau that I hadn't seen him leave; but then my shoe brushed against something bulky and soft on the floor, and I came to the dismal realization that Ben hadn't gone to the men's room after all. As casually as I could, I looked down. There he was, out cold. He'd gotten so drunk that he'd slid under the table.

Fernando saw me peeking under the tablecloth and asked, "Is Ben under there?"

"I'm afraid so," I replied. It had happened rather suddenly, but I was not completely surprised. This was just the most recent in a string of humiliating incidents in which Ben got drunk in public. I realized that he must have had quite a head start on the booze before we left home and that he'd already been drunk when he got behind the wheel to drive us to the hotel. For the moment, however, that was not the issue. When a man who is six feet six inches slides under the table, people are bound to notice when you try to drag him out. So now I had this sticky problem of what to do. We were seated at a ringside table right next to the dance floor in the Crystal Ballroom, so it was impossible to smuggle him out without creating a scene. I felt as though everyone at the gala was watching this tableau unfolding, as if we were the floor show.

"Would you like to dance with me and we'll discuss the problem?" Fernando asked, helping me to my feet.

"We have to get him out of here," I said. "How many guys do you think it will take to carry him?" With all his drinking, Ben had put on a lot of weight. He now weighed almost three hundred pounds.

"At least three," said Fernando. "There's got to be one under his feet, one under his head, and one under his middle or he'll cave in."

"That's going to be a lovely sight," I winced.

"And you're not going to want to see it," said Fernando. "I'll find some men to carry him out."

"Thanks. I'll get the car."

"Put the top down," he said.

Fortunately, in those days the paparazzi left before the events were over. Otherwise there would have been a horde of photographers out front, waiting for tabloid fodder just like this. As it was, there was no one there but some valets with nothing to do. I got into my pretty blue Eldorado convertible and drove around behind the hotel to the loading dock. Ben, still unconscious, was carried out through the back door of the kitchen like a bag of cement. It took four—not three—waiters to carry him, one under his head, one under his shoulders, one under his ass, and one under his size sixteen feet. They stretched him out in the back seat, and I drove home.

There was no way I could get him out of the car and upstairs by myself, so I put the top up on the car and left him there overnight. In the morning, Benjie came to me and said, "Mommy, there's a man in the back of the car."

"It's just Daddy. He got sick last night," I said, shielding my little boy. "We'll let him sleep and I'll give him some medicine when he wakes up."

Next day on the set, I thanked Fernando for his help. Coming to the studio was a welcome escape from my troubles at home. I had found a valuable and empathetic friend.

Toward the end of the summer, one of the biggest parties of the year was given by Marion Davies. Her longtime paramour, William Randolph Hearst, had died the year before, and Marion had since married Horace Brown. It was quite a bash. Davies had turned her huge Beverly Hills mansion into five nightclubs with five different orchestras—there was a Stork Club, an El Morocco, a Coconut Grove. Everybody in town was there. People were dancing and drinking and having a great time.

Ben and I were already seated when Fernando arrived. He made quite an entrance. Dressed in an impeccably tailored tuxedo, he arrived with Lana Turner on one arm, and Ava Gardner on the other. Everything in the room came to a halt when they walked in; people stopped in mid-sentence just to stare at this ravishing trio—beauty personified. Fernando seated Lana and Ava at the table with Ben and me. Arlene Dahl and her husband, Lex Barker (the Hollywood Tarzan of the early 1950s), were there, too.

This grouping may still hold Hollywood's all-time record for marital musical chairs and tangled libidos. Fernando's two decorative ladies had each been married to bandleader Artie Shaw. Ava and Lana were pals, and Ava at this time was in the midst of her stormy marriage to Frank Sinatra. About six years earlier, however, Lana had been labeled a "homewrecker" over her involvement with Frank, when he was still married to his first wife, Nancy. Both Lana and Ava had been ardently pursued by Howard Hughes, and Lana had had a brief affair with Victor Mature. That was just the back story; it got a lot more confusing from then on as the various couples at the table later played mix and match. Lana and Fernando broke up and she married Lex Barker, after he divorced Arlene Dahl. Following his affair with Lana and Arlene's divorce from Lex, Fernando married Arlene, who became the mother of his son, Lorenzo. Eventually, they divorced and Fernando and I were married. In this group, only Ben was the odd man out.

Evidently, Lex's marriage to Arlene was already rocky. He was seated next to Lana, and it wasn't long before the two of them were getting a bit cozy. When Lex asked Lana to dance, Fernando stood up, threw his keys on the table, and said, "Why don't you do what you really want to do? You don't want to dance with her. You want to fuck her. Here are the keys, Lex. Take my car and go." Then he turned to me and said, "Come on, Esther, let's dance."

"What did you do that for?" I asked, trying to ignore the hubbub he had created at the table behind us. Understandably enough, Lana was in a snit over the whole thing. "You don't care what Lex Barker says to Lana," I told him. "You're not insecure. What's your problem?"

"Well," he said with a shrug, "the party was dull, so I thought I would liven it up."

At the end of the evening, Lana was still not speaking to him. Having made the Lillian Burns exit (chin up, shoulders up, head thrown back), she was walking along the swimming pool in the direction of the car. The problem, of course, was that she had arrived with Fernando and was more or less stuck with going home with him. (I guess if you're Lana Turner you don't call a cab or bum a ride with friends.) Fernando was right behind her, followed by Ben and me and Lex and Arlene. At this inopportune point, a young woman named Joan Denier, who eventually played Dulcinea on Broadway to Richard Kiley's Don Quixote in *Man of La Mancha*, came up to this daisy chain on parade. She was very pretty, and on the make for Fernando. "You look divine," she said as she threw her arms around him. That much was true, but at this point in the evening it wasn't what he wanted to hear. He picked her up and threw her into the pool. The incident made the papers the next day; there was a photo of her with her dress all wet and clinging to her fabulous body.

I looked at my costar and wondered what he would do next. He reminded me of perennial bad boy Errol Flynn, who had a reputation for pulling stunts like that. "You're some piece of work," I said to him. "Why do you do these things?"

"This is how I have fun, Esther," he said with a mischievous twinkle in his eye. By this time Lana was so angry that she was absolutely rigid. She got into the car next to Fernando without saying a word, and the two of them drove off in stony silence.

The next day was a work day. Fernando and I were supposed to shoot a picnic sequence on the rolling hills of Lot 3, where there was a mansion that we were using as André's family chateau in the Champagne region of France. The crew had a picnic hamper and a blanket all set up on the lawn in front of this chateau, but Fernando was nowhere to be found. Chuck Walters said, "Somebody please go find out if Mr. Lamas is sick. If he's not, bring him in. We're ready to shoot." Just as he said that, we saw Fernando coming across this vast lawn. He was limping badly, and he looked terrible.

After the Lex Barker incident at the party and the frosty ride home, he and Lana had had the fight of their lives. As Fernando reported it, Lana turned on the TV as soon as she got in the door and still wouldn't talk to him, so Fernando got mad and kicked the set in. "The problem with kicking a television set," he explained to me, "is that your foot goes in easily, but it's very hard to get it out again without cutting yourself to ribbons. I had to call for help to get my foot out. When I got ready to leave, I slammed the door and said, 'You'll not see me again, Miss Turner.' But as I left the front porch, I missed the top step and sprained my ankle."

I had to laugh. All I could think was that this handsome Latin had really put his foot in it this time—literally. As bad as Fernando looked, Lana apparently looked worse. She had a black eye and a cut lip and assorted scratches and bruises from all the pushing and slapping after a knock-down-drag-out fight. Fernando told me, though, that he was not entirely responsible for all of her injuries. Many of the black-and-blue marks she now sported had been self-inflicted.

Apparently, Lana had a little knotted rope that she used to hit herself on the legs and arms. If you bruise easily, it's very effective. Fernando said that on other occasions when they had disagreements she would take the rope, smack it repeatedly against her leg, and tell him, "You'd like to be doing this, wouldn't you? You'd like to hit me. Go on, hit me! . . . Hit me!!"

She kept egging him on, as if somehow she'd misbehaved and was inviting him to punish her. "I knew one day I would hit her," he confessed to me. Needless to say, Fernando's great romance with Lana was kaput. "It's over," he said simply. "I can't go back. We said too many terrible things that can't be taken back."

While it lasted, their affair had been a public relations bonanza for MGM, but now that it was over it gave the studio a big headache. Fernando and Lana were supposed to start shooting *Latin Lovers* together as soon as *Dangerous When Wet* had wrapped, but when Fernando told me about the fight, I knew what was going to happen next. Lana went upstairs to Benny Thau, showed off her welts and bruises, and told him that Fernando had beaten her up. Fernando was bounced from *Latin Lovers;* my former costar Ricardo Montalban (a devoutly monogamous Catholic) took his place. (In hindsight Fernando was just as well out of that one; this was not destined to be one of the "important pictures" he said he wanted to appear in when he came from Argentina.)

One of the problems with *Dangerous When Wet* was that it didn't have a good ending. The movie just seemed to trail off, and I knew we needed to rev up the finale, which was the Channel swim. One day I turned on the television and saw news coverage of my friend and long-distance swimmer Florence Chadwick, trying to break her own record for swimming the Catalina Channel. At this point in the swim, however, she was in trouble. The water was very choppy and

she'd swallowed too much salt water, which had made her nauseous. She was ready to quit. Her coach, together with my old Aquacade costar Johnny Weissmuller, was in a boat beside her. When she
signaled that she wanted to come out because she was too sick to go
on, Johnny tore off his jacket and pants (I was relieved when I saw
that he had a pair of trunks on underneath) and dove into the water.

"Florence, come on. Get ahold of yourself," Johnny told her.
"You'll be all right. I'll pace you."

"You can't touch me," she cautioned him. In distance swims like
this, no one could touch the swimmer, because it could be seen as
helping her along.

"I know." And there was Johnny, swimming beside Florence with
that powerful stroke of his. He was pulling her along with his sheer
energy.

I quickly picked up the phone and called Dorothy Kingsley,
Chuck Walters, and our producer George Wells. "Turn on your TV," I
told them. "We've got our ending for the picture." Everyone agreed
that this was what the film needed, and Dorothy rewrote the ending
of *Dangerous When Wet* based on what happened with Florence and
Johnny.

When Fernando and I got ready to shoot the scene, we went
down to Portuguese Bend at the end of the Palos Verdes Peninsula
and used the beach there as the shore where Katie Higgins com-
pletes her crossing of the English Channel. Like Florence, I had to
get out of the water under my own power, but after I was on the
beach, the scene called for Fernando to scoop me up in his arms
once I'd crossed the finish line.

It was May. Even though I was slathered with protective goose
grease like a real Channel swimmer, the water was freezing. The
camera followed in a boat as I thrashed through unexpectedly
rough sea and high swells, gulping mouthfuls of salt water. I spent
most of the afternoon in that water, fighting the Pacific Ocean, and I
began to understand what my character was supposed to feel while
swimming the Channel—the exhaustion, the pain, the lungs and
muscles pleading to give up.

When night fell, the scene was set where I was to finish the swim,
having finally conquered the Channel, cross the finish line, and try

to stagger to the beach. André (Fernando) is riding in a boat beside me, pacing me to the finish. He sees me weaken in the last 100 yards and leaps into the pounding surf to rescue me. I signal him to stay away until I reach the finish line. Once I cross the line, I collapse at the water's edge and Fernando scoops me into his arms and carries me to dry land. Perfect scenario.

The cast, camera, crew are all gathered on the beach in the glare of the huge arc lights waiting for the final shot. By now, the water was not only paralyzingly cold, but inky black. And the waves were still pounding.

Take One: Fernando jumps from the small boat into the surf, struggles to my side, and just as the script reads, scoops me into his arms—only thanks to my protective goose grease, I squirt out of his grasp and slither into the foam. Not good.

Take Two: Fernando jumps into the Pacific again, but this time he grabs me more firmly, intent upon holding me no matter what. Once again I slide through his hands—Laurel and Hardy, meet Esther Williams and Fernando Lamas.

It wasn't until well after midnight that an exhausted Chuck Walters (not to mention a completely debilitated Esther and Fernando) called, "Cut! That's a wrap!"

We got out of our wet swimsuits, bundled ourselves up in terry cloth robes, and practically collapsed from the sheer fatigue of the day's work in the icy cold ocean, falling into the back of a waiting limo for the ride back to Culver City. As we left Portuguese Bend, I was curled up in the car, still shivering from the cold water. Fernando reached over, took my hand, and placed it on his crotch. He was fully erect. I looked at him sitting there beside me, and asked myself, What kind of blood does this man have in his veins? So much for cozy fireplaces and candlelight.

Up until this time Fernando and I had been just friends, but in the car, with our terry cloth robes on and nothing else, I guess he figured it was time to break the ice between us. I sat there with my hand on his crotch and wondered, Do I want to move my hand from this man? Actually I don't think I even had a choice. Fernando placed his hand on top of mine and never let go—all the way back to MGM, a forty-five-minute ride. It was perhaps the longest I ever experienced an erection (or the longest erection I ever experienced!).

When we arrived in front of my dressing room he said, "Well, we're here," and he turned to me.

And I said, "Can I have my hand back now?"

"Yes," he said. And he took my hand, which had been warmed mightily through the trip, kissed it, and said, "Good night, Miss Williams."

I got out of the car and that was all there was to it. I went inside, sat down on my couch, and said, "Well, I guess that's the Latin way of making a pass, leaving the woman hanging, wondering what happens next."

The next day we were shooting at the Stage 30 pool, where we were doing the close-ups of the distance swim. They had put giant clapper boards in the pool that went back and forth to recreate the wave action of those large swells. The effect was like a giant washing machine, and the waves were almost crashing over my head. Fernando was such a good swimmer, and the two of us swam well together. We owned the water—a good swimmer owns the water— and you're not in danger because you know exactly what you're doing. We rode the swells up and came down and rode them up again; there was an exhilaration to it. It must have felt like that when Ginger Rogers and Fred Astaire danced together; it was just so good to be comfortable with what you are doing. And of course the secrets we had from the night before were delicious.

After we finished, we were wrapped up in the intimacy of our terry cloth robes again and the fun of being with someone who does something as well as you do, and he said, "Should we repeat the experience of last night?"

"No," I said. "You had your chance." I didn't want to be the next Lana in his life.

"Well, I'll tell you what. Let me come in and we'll have a martini together."

"Okay, but I get to keep my hands, right?"

"Yes, Esther," he said with a grin. "You can keep your hands."

Over martinis he said, "When we finish this picture, why don't we go away together. Let me take you away from all this."

I almost suggested he hire a writer to come up with better lines. Instead, I said, "Away from what? I'm in the top ten at the box office. I'm treated like a queen here."

"I'll take you to Europe. Have you ever been there?"

"Yes."

"Only on a personal appearance tour, right?"

"Yes, but . . ."

"This time, dear Esther, I'll take you to meet the crowned heads of Europe. It will be like royalty meeting royalty."

"Do you know any crowned heads?"

"I know two of them, Juan Carlos and Sofía of Spain. All I have to do is ask for an audience."

He had an air of nonchalant grandeur about the whole prospect, but I knew that if I was going to take such a momentous step, it was time for me to be serious, to test him.

"What are we going to do with my two little boys?" I asked.

"Boys?" Fernando's eyebrow raised.

"Yes, my children."

"I would rather you didn't bring them along. We want to have a good time."

Had he said something different, had he even hinted at the kind of serious commitment I was hoping to hear, my marriage to Ben might have ended that night, and my love affair with Fernando Lamas might have begun years sooner than it did. But as drawn to him as I was, as much as I wanted him, I didn't want him merely jumping from Lana Turner's bed to mine.

"Fernando," I said, locking my eyes on his. "You have a terrible reputation. Do you still have a lot of fooling around to do?"

Silence. Then he said, "Such an honest question deserves an honest answer. I am afraid so . . . I do like the ladies."

"Well, I would probably have a problem with that, because I would be faithful to you and you have no intention of being faithful to anybody."

"I never said *that*," he protested.

"I'll tell you what. Much as I'd like meeting the crowned heads of Europe, I think I'd better go on taking care of my little kids, because I don't think you're going to be the family type. Let's let the world take a couple of turns and see how everything comes out."

"Esther," he said, reaching for me, "I want you now."

"I think we better not do this," I said, pushing him away.

He left. And so he was gone out of my life—for all I knew, gone forever. And I thought about him all the way home.

The next morning, I picked up my *LA Times,* and there he was in a photo at some kind of night spot with Arlene Dahl. After we'd had that serious talk about being together and doing Europe and dining on gold plates with the King of Spain, Fernando had gone right to the phone and made a date with Arlene. Frankly, I suspected that he'd been secretly seeing Arlene even while carrying on with Lana. When he said, "I do like the ladies," it was one of the few understatements of his life.

Well, I told myself, That's the end of that.

I was wrong.

CHAPTER 18

EASY TO LOVE, MY QUINTESSENTIAL MGM FILM
1953–1955

I returned to my home and tried to figure out how I was going to stay married to a man whose self-destructive behavior—drinking, gambling, lack of interest in work—was destroying our family. For a while I didn't think that I could do it. Ben and I agreed to a trial separation, but we kept it a secret. I thought our best chance, if we were ever going to get back together again, was to keep it quiet. That had become my way of handling things whenever I went through bad times.

From a publicity standpoint, MGM was relieved that I wanted to hush up my problems with Ben. We lived under the protection of the great god Public Relations, because the studio had set it up that way, with a kind of army all around us to keep scandal out of the papers. Of course some stars needed more protection than others. Whitey Hendry was busy on the telephone, making nightly protective calls to star dressing rooms, and Howard Strickling was a genius at damage control. The whole idea was to buff up the public image of the stars, airbrushing us into these perfect people for audiences to idolize.

The major partners of the studio in peddling these fantasies were the fan magazines, which were the exact opposite of today's tabloids. Back then they didn't make up bad stories about you, they made up good ones. The fan magazines portrayed your love relationship as a dream state—what could go wrong between two people if at least one of them was a movie star? One issue of *Photoplay* ran a cover story entitled "Esther Williams: The Truth About Her Marriage." The article debunked the allegation (which had been floating around Hollywood for a while) that "Ben just sits around and waits for her to come home, that he lives on the fringes of Esther's career." That, of course, was the truth, but the story went on and on about how hard Ben worked and what a brilliant job he was doing with our businesses, even though I knew many of them were faltering. The article ended with a fictional quote from me saying, "It's incomprehensible that anyone should think I could be having trouble with my man." The whole thing was a lie, but we were keeping up appearances.

While we were living apart, I tried to cope with the problem of taking my children's father away from them. Ben was like a big kid with them, and they loved him very much. They were still preschoolers, and there was no way to explain about responsibility to two little boys who were thinking about baseball and bicycles. They wouldn't understand the drinking problem either. The night he had to be carried out of the Beverly Hills Hotel was not the only time Ben got falling-down drunk, and I'd already slipped into the classic pattern of hiding the extent of his drinking from Benjie and Kim.

We were still separated when I was invited to Eisenhower's presidential inauguration, which would take place in January 1953. I really wanted to attend, but there was no way I could go stag to Washington and not open myself up to all the questions I preferred not to answer. Going with a "date" would be worse. Either way, the great public relations myth of me as this happily married woman would be unmasked as the charade that it was, so I called Ben and asked whether he'd like to go with me. We sat there in the stands in front of the Capitol for the swearing-in ceremony. Later we went to all the parties—five inaugural balls in all.

To my surprise, we had a wonderful time, and for a brief interlude I was reminded of how much fun Ben Gage could be. That trip rekindled the dying embers of our marriage. Ben already had moved back home by the time I was ready to begin work on my next film.

Easy to Love was produced by Joe Pasternak and directed once again by Chuck Walters, with Busby Berkeley slated to do the big production numbers. For the fifth time, Van Johnson would be my costar. By this time Van and I were as synchronized as any two swimmers in the pool. The last time we worked together had been *Duchess of Idaho,* and even there we had been comfortable enough with each other to improvise most of the script. We were family. Through the years, I swam with Van, married him, fought with him, and made love to him—all on camera. We knew our lives, our secrets, and our public and private personas, even though off camera we had little or no contact. I was aware of his marital difficulties, but none of that ever came up on the set. Nor did mine. We were a sweetheart couple who had that MGM *look* that was so "American," with no ethnic traces whatsoever.

The plot of *Easy to Love* was by now all too familiar—once again, only the names changed. My character was Julie Hallerton, and Van played my boss, Ray Lloyd. Although he had no idea she cared about him, Julie was so smitten that she was both the star of Ray's aquatic show and his secretary, for the lavish salary of seventy-five dollars a week. In order to get Van's attention, I encourage two other guys, played by John Bromfield and crooner Tony Martin, to go through the courtship motions to make Van jealous. If you can't guess how this comes out, you haven't been paying attention.

The movie was to be shot in Florida at Cypress Gardens. I went there soon after the inauguration—and promptly missed a period. When I realized what was happening, the first person I thought of wasn't Ben, but poor Joe Pasternak. This would be the third picture I did for him when I was pregnant. Under the best of circumstances, making a movie and making a baby are a head-to-head race against time. When you have to consider the bathing suit factor and the daredevil stunts associated with Busby's water extravaganzas, it gets even more difficult. I picked up the phone to make the call, knowing Joe would not be happy to hear what I had to say.

"Joe, I'm sorry to do this to you again, but I'm going to have a baby."

"My God, Esther, what's the matter with you?"

"There's nothing wrong with me, Joe. Everything's running like clockwork, obviously."

"What are *you* going to do?"

Just as it was in Hawaii with *Pagan Love Song*, since it was my baby, it was my problem. Knowing that there was no swimmer on the lot to replace me, I had to get everybody on the film rallied to finish the work before I started showing. We revamped the production schedule to film all the water sequences up front; there was no way I'd fit into a bathing suit by the time my fifth month came along.

Naturally, the hardest things to do would be Busby's big numbers, including a waterskiing grande finale. A reviewer once described my movie performances as one impossible daredevil stunt after another, and Busby was setting me up for yet another series of high-flying athletic feats. He had already rounded up sixty-eight of the greatest water-skiers from all over the world. They were already under contract and rehearsing together so they'd be ready to ski with me, the star.

This posed a minor difficulty—I'd never water-skied before in my life.

I had no choice but to start learning and practicing, but I was probably the only person associated with this picture who understood that waterskiing really has nothing to do with swimming and demands an entirely different set of muscles and skills. When you ski, your whole body is tensed and held together by an arched back. You need very strong arms, but those long, smooth muscles and powerful leg kicks you develop as a swimmer aren't much help. While I was making *Easy to Love*, I could barely swim at all. I'd go to lift my arms and sink like a stone, because my upper body was too tight from holding on to the tow rope.

But waterskiing was wet, so MGM assumed that this was

Esther's department and that of course it would be no problem for me for pick it up—fast. The studio got me a coach who wanted me on one ski, but I decided to stay on two skis. I knew that I would lose the baby if I skied slalom, there would be too much strain on my stomach muscles. "You'd better learn quickly, Esther, because you can't fall," Pasternak warned. "These champions are so good they've forgotten that everyone can't ski. If they're behind you going at thirty-five miles an hour, they won't expect you to fall, so stay up or they'll chop you to ribbons."

With that comforting thought, I brought my boys to Florida and enrolled them in nursery school. Dick Pope, who owned Cypress Gardens, found me a house, since I didn't want to stay at a hotel. I brought along Jane, my housekeeper and nanny, so I knew the boys would be safe and sound. At least that part of my life was under control.

Things were not so great on the husband front. Ben and I had reconciled, but our relationship wasn't exactly rosy. After he moved back home, his behavior reverted to type—a lot of golfing and drinking and not much working. We still had a restaurant to take care of, but Ben smelled a free trip to Florida and asked his brother Chuck to watch over The Trails. We called a truce. Whenever I started a movie, all domestic fights were put on hold. I had too much other business to worry about to be squabbling with Ben. I had to keep my mind on the work, with a minimum of distractions, especially since the baby inside me was going to get bigger every day.

While we were filming, the rest of the Cypress Gardens theme park remained open for business. Dick Pope was still running three or four water shows a day, and crowds of people would gather all over the lawns and up on the verandas to watch the colorful spectacle. One day a member of the crew told me that Ben was going to be in the ski show that day. Although I couldn't believe that he would really do anything that stupid, I went to see for myself. (He had not mentioned his new career over the dinner table.) Ben had gained quite a bit of weight and didn't look good in a swimsuit anymore. In fact, he looked like a buffoon. But there he was in boxer trunks, a big walrus with a girl on his shoulders.

Everyone knew he was my husband. I was appalled at this exhibition. Golf was one thing, but now he was up on water skis in front of a crowd at Cypress Gardens with some show-skier's crotch at the back of his neck and her thighs around his ears.

When he came back to the house after the last water show of the day, I said, "Ben, go home and take care of the business. I can't stand your being here. You're making a fool of yourself and of me." I may have shamed him into going back to Los Angeles, but at least I wouldn't have to watch him be an object of ridicule. Mercifully, Ben left for home the next morning.

Now all I had to do was survive Busby Berkeley.

Busby, of course, was in his element—liquid. He designed a synchronized swim routine that featured a chorus of a hundred swimmers in a brand new pool that was shaped like the state of Florida. It was built just for the movie, with my signature set in mosaic tiles and installed on the deck of the pool. Busby created a lovely water duet for John Bromfield and me, which involved swimming through a cove blanketed in flowers and rotating languidly on turntables placed just below the surface. As I lay on the turntable, I was covered with white gardenias because the baby was beginning to show.

The number in the pool, however, turned out just to be a warm-up for Busby When he really let loose was on the lake. Freed from the confines of the pool, he went wild in the wide open spaces of Lake Eloise. He had so much more room to work with, and with sixty-eight of the world's greatest water-skiers, plus the girls from the Cypress Gardens water show (the Aqua Maids), he had over a hundred troops to command and lots of chances to shoot off guns to cue them. He felt like King of the World. The finale was nine minutes long. Like Patton going into battle, Busby mapped out elaborate maneuvers for the speedboats and the skiers, whizzing them across the lake in formation, weaving them in patterns in and out of the cypress trees, whooshing up ski-jump ramps and past geysers of water sixty feet high.

When Busby described the geysers, I thought that skiing over them was to be devoutly avoided. I knew that the needle jets that created them were made out of brass and stuck up just six inches out of the water. Accidentally hitting them could be fatal, impaling both me and my baby. I was nearsighted. The ski boats would be speeding at thirty-five miles per hour. Would I be able to see those jets in time to avoid them? I studied the layout very carefully in rehearsal to make certain I knew exactly where those things were. After the diving accident with the metal crown in *Million Dollar Mermaid*, I'd finally learned (the hard way) that no one was going to look after my safety but me. Certainly the possibility that I might be injured was never a factor when Buzz was dreaming up his routines; he just assumed I could do anything.

Busby was both a showman and a show-off, and he liked to load the camera boat with friends so that everyone could appreciate his marvelous creativity. All those extra people weighed the boat down, but as far as he was concerned, it was a case of "the more the merrier." On the first day we were shooting the ski sequence in which I was supposed to head for the geysers, then whip around them. Busby was busy with his artillery, shooting off guns to cue various members of the tech crew. As I skied, I looked at the overloaded camera boat and saw that it was getting dangerously near me. Busby, however, was oblivious. He was in hot pursuit of a closer shot, yelling at me through a bullhorn, "Esther! Esther!! Turn to me! Turn to me!!"

Meanwhile, the boat kept getting closer and closer. Wedged between the boat and the geyser jets, I was running out of water to ski on. I tried to recall exactly where those needles were, and when I turned to look at him, the camera boat was just ten inches away from my ski. With all those people in it, it was kicking up a huge wake, with a trough that looked like the Grand Canyon. If I caught the edge of the wake with a ski, I'd fall into the propeller of the boat. My face wouldn't be on many fan magazine covers after that.

I began shouting, "Buzz, you're too close!" but he didn't hear me. I was so mad at this crazy man because all he cared about was getting his shot, and he couldn't see that he was putting me in terrible danger. As with the near disaster on Kauai with the outrigger, a director's carelessness was endangering my life.

I had no choice but to fall, which was the one thing I'd made up my mind not to do, because I was afraid I'd lose the baby. I fell toward my right leg, away from the boat.

Once in the water, I kicked off my skis and began swimming for shore like I was anchoring on a 4-by-100 Olympic relay. The camera boat was waiting for me, but I steamed right by it. I knew I couldn't get in the boat because I'd have to hit the side with my tummy to pull myself up and in; and anyway I was much too angry. If I'd seen Busby's damned starter's pistol, I'd have shot him with it.

But Busby still didn't get it. He was yelling at me as I headed for the beach. "Esther, come back! Why did you ruin the shot?"

I was shaking with anger when I got out of the water, and I was still shaking when I got back to my little cottage. An hour or so later, Busby sent over someone from the crew to talk me into returning to the set, but I said, "Tell Mr. Berkeley I have to speak to him, and he's got to come here; because I'm not shooting anymore today."

He was still clueless when he sat down in my living room and asked, "Why did you go home? We were having a great day!"

What stupidity! It wasn't enough that I had a husband in my life who I had to send home for being a drunk and an idiot. Now I had a director who'd almost killed me and didn't even know that anything was wrong.

"Shut up, you goddamn fool!" By this time I was screaming at him. "Don't you know how close that boat came to me? That was like a precipice beside me, that deep wake. It would have been so easy to slide into it and right into the propeller. Did it ever cross your mind that my life was in your hands?"

Slowly the enormity of what might have happened registered in his mind. "God, Esther, I didn't know all that was going on."

"Shoot around me for a couple of days so that I can see if that fall did me any harm," I said. I wanted to give my body a chance to calm down.

A few days later I was sound asleep when the phone rang in the middle of the night. It was Busby. "I've gotta talk to you about the number we're doing. I have a great idea for the ending."

"Buzz, it's two-thirty in the morning. Where are you?"

"I'm in the tub."

"With a martini, right?"

"Right."

Busby was prone to drink martinis well on into the night. "Buzz,

I've got to get up and go to work in the morning. I need my sleep . . . So do you. Couldn't we talk tomorrow?" I started to hang up.

"No, wait! This is where I get my greatest ideas. I have to be wet. The creative juices are flowing."

Yeah, and they've got an olive floating in 'em, I thought to myself.

"Esther . . . can you dive from a swing hanging from a helicopter?" he asked.

I should have known that this was the early wake-up call for Pearl White. I was still furious at him, but I couldn't help myself. I was also more than a bit intrigued. "Gee, Buzz, has *anyone* ever done it?"

"No, but I'm not coming to you for what other people can do. If you are going to be my star, you have to do things nobody else has done."

"Just how does this work?"

"Well," he said, "you're skiing along and we drop you the swing from the helicopter. You kick off your skis, and the chopper pulls you up out of the water. You climb up onto this trapeze swing, and we fly you over eight speedboats that're pulling the skiers in V-formation. Then you dive into the lake and hit right in the center of the V."

"How fast would the V be moving?" I asked.

"Thirty-five miles per hour, more or less."

"How far above the water would the trapeze be?"

"Eighty feet."

By comparison, Pearl White was a wimp. "Ah, Buzz . . . what about wind drift?"

"What do you mean?"

I said, "Wind drift, Buzz. Even if it's calm at the surface, between the tropical breezes and the chop from the helicopter, it could be a lot windier a bit higher up. The winds might push me off center and make me land on one of the skiers."

"Well, you mustn't, Esther, because these are all champions. If you hit one of them, we'd have a lawsuit that would kill us. You're not going to do that."

"I'll tell you what. I'll do the ski part, but I'm not diving from a helicopter with this baby in my tummy. There's a really nice girl who was a platform diver in the LA Athletic Club when I was on the

team. You're going to call her—her name is Helen Crelinkovich—
and Helen will do it. You've got to pay her handsomely; you pay her
each time she does the dive if you do it more than once."

He said, "We don't have to do that—there's no union rule covering this."

"Never mind the union rule. She's my friend. If you get her,
you've got to pay her each time; because you're a perfectionist and
you might do it twenty times. And each time you do it, you pay her
three thousand dollars."

"Three thousand dollars?" he repeated.

I said, "I'm being her agent because that's a very dangerous dive
you're asking for."

"I hate doubles."

"Not as much as I hate miscarriages. I'll do everything else you
ask of me, Buzz—I'll even do the ski-jump over the orchestra at the
end—but not the dive. I want to hang on to this baby." Whatever my
problems with Ben (and they were many), I already felt very close to
this child inside me. It was as if we were on the same wavelength,
right from the beginning.

So I did the skiing and the helicopter swooped down with the
swing, which I grabbed, and it pulled me out of the water. Then they
cut away and put Helen up on the swing. She made a perfect dive
three times from eighty feet, and she got herself nine thousand dollars. And I was still alive and safely pregnant.

The baby girl who was to be my little Susie was most considerate. She kept her knees and elbows tucked in until we got home. I
was still a size ten when we finished filming at Cypress Gardens. We
had one water comedy sequence left to shoot back at MGM, a circus
number for which I wore clown face and a blousant clown outfit
that I finally needed to hide my pregnancy. Busby had done his special sequences, and now Chuck Walters was back directing.

One day I was sitting in my dressing room in my clown suit, removing the last of the clown white from my face when in walked
Joan Crawford. She didn't bother to knock.

Joan had just returned to MGM after an absence of a decade. Ten
years earlier, Louis B. Mayer had labeled her "box-office poison"
and canceled her contract, after which she landed at Warner Bros.

and turned in an Oscar-winning performance as *Mildred Pierce*. (There were those around town who still called her "Mildred Fierce.") Now she was back at MGM to make *Torch Song*, ensconced two doors down from me in Dressing Room D.

She was an unbelievable sight as she paused for effect in my doorway. She looked like a big turquoise parrot, with a great sparkly headdress of turquoise feathers. She was wearing a low-cut leotard, all gossamer and bare to the tail that swept up in back of her, with turquoise high heels and fishnet stockings. It was very sheer—probably because she wanted it that way. Joan still had a wonderful figure, even this late in her life, and loved showing her body, with her broad shoulders, that long waist, and very long legs. Her makeup was as wild as the rest of her. It was very dark, almost copper, and there was lots of it, with turquoise sequins on her eyebrows and pulled up in her hair.

"Joan? Is that you under all that?"

"Esther, I simply *have* to talk to you!" she said in that deep, dramatic voice of hers. She made her entrance into my room and struck a glamorous avian pose.

I was eye-to-beady-eye with this fantastic creature as she leaned over toward me. What I thought was, "Oh, Joan, I do believe we've been in the vodka bottle," because it was that time of the afternoon; but what I said was, "That's quite an outfit. . . . What's on your mind, Joan?"

"Today was a wardrobe test for *Torch Song*, and this . . ." she gestured toward her plumage, "is for the finale. It's a big production number, and I dance and I do it divinely and isn't it wonderful?"

"It's beautiful."

She looked rather marvelous in a bizarre way, this sequined bird-person, and there I was, pregnant in my clown suit. I'd never felt so matronly in my life.

She put her face close to mine and said, "I've come to ask a favor of you. . . ."

I was a little worried about what was going to happen next. She was leaning even closer, coming at me with a mouthful of gooey red lipstick, and I thought, Oh God, please don't let her kiss me. Just don't let her kiss me with that lipstick on. "What favor is that?" I asked.

"Esther, please let me have your director."

"Chuck Walters?"

"Yes. I have a mad, mad crush on him. I know it's an infatuation that I'll have to get over; and I think he's gay, but I don't care. I just want him and I've got to have him do my movie; and he's perfect for it. I know he was a choreographer on Broadway . . . I want him to hold me in his arms for this big dance number at the end while I'm in this outfit."

It sounded to me like she wanted to make it with him a lot more than she wanted him to direct the movie, but that was Chuck's problem, not mine. "Joan, you've got him. He's yours."

"But I want him, I *want* him." She was so busy still trying to convince me that she didn't hear what I'd said.

"Joan . . . Joan . . . Take 'yes' for an answer. You've got him. He's yours. We still have some work on this clown number to do, but I'll do it by myself or we'll get Busby to finish it."

"Oh! Thank you! You dear, wonderful woman!" And with that she took my face in her hands and pulled me even closer—Joan was very strong. Then she planted a big wet lipsticky kiss on my mouth. I reached for a Kleenex before she could do it again and then she was gone.

That was Joan Crawford at her best—when she wanted something.

Once she'd made her grand departure, I got myself together to go home, but as I was leaving I heard some noises coming from Stage 4. It sounded like yelling, so I walked over to take a look. Stage 4 was where they did all the show business pictures, because it was set up like a theater. The house was dark; no one was in the audience. There was nothing on but the work light in the center of the stage; in the far corner a janitor was sweeping up. Downstage under the middle of the proscenium arch was Joan, still in her bird outfit, talking to the empty seats.

I stood there and listened in the darkness as she cried out, "Why have you left me? Why don't you come to my movies? What did I do? What did I say? Don't turn your back on me!" Joan had been a star since the 1920s, with an Oscar and a fine body of work behind her, but here she was, almost fifty, reduced to begging an imaginary audience not to forget her. Tears were streaming down her face, streaking her copper makeup. Suddenly she looked old and pathetic. I slipped away without her noticing.

What a sad, sad lady, I thought as I got into my car. Like watching Eleanor Powell rehearse till her feet bled. Seeing Joan like that was a shot across the bow for me. "Get out when you're still on top," I told myself. "There's life after Hollywood." Without quite thinking about it, I patted my unborn baby in my stomach and headed home to play with my two little boys. Suddenly "matronly" didn't seem so bad at all.

CHAPTER 19

JUPITER'S DARLING AND FAREWELL MGM
1953–1955

A few weeks after I bestowed Chuck Walters on her, Joan Crawford was finally ready to start *Torch Song*. Like the launching of a battleship, the beginning of a movie was always commemorated at MGM. We all got flowers on the first day of our picture. The producer sent a big bouquet of roses; sometimes your leading man would even send you candy. It was a happy kind of day, but Joan always demanded a monumental celebration that was much more grandiose than normal.

By this time in her career, she had acquired quite an entourage, and whenever she started a picture, her sycophants sent her flowers. Of course, these were not just ordinary bouquets—Joan saw to that. "Stanley the Florist knows what I like," she'd tell her pals. Stanley's was a floral design boutique that catered to the movie colony. Good old Stanley knew what the drill was; Joan had trained him well. He always included a bunch of nonfloral extras in his bouquets—like cashmere sweaters, vodka, cheese, or gold jewelry. These flower arrangements were more like lavish Christmas presents. An unsuspecting friend who ordered flowers for Joan, expecting to pay fifty dollars or so for one of Stanley's "bouquets," was floored to receive a bill that might run as much as a thousand dollars.

The day that Joan started *Torch Song*, a steady stream of delivery boys from Stanley the Florist began to arrive at Dressing Room D. I watched this parade for a while and thought to myself, Well, she certainly makes a big deal about being Crawford. I'll do something that'll be fun.

I found a bottle of vodka in my closet that was down to about a thimbleful and wrapped it in toilet paper. Then I hung one of my old beat-up wax gardenias on the throat of the bottle. I took a funny old card that someone had sent me, crossed out the "Esther" on the envelope and wrote "Joan." The whole thing had a very shabby look to it; it was the very antithesis of Stanley the Florist. I hoped she'd think it was funny.

I waddled down the hall to her dressing room. The door was open, and Joan was holding court to an adoring group, a full house, everyone clutching martinis, gazing up at the queen. They were all guys—no one got into Joan's inner circle unless they wore pants—and they were hanging on her every word, or pretending to. "And then what happened, Joan? . . . Oh, that's hilarious, Joan . . ."

I stood in the doorway, handed her what I thought was this charming joke, and said, "I brought you something. Happy picture, Joan."

Joan was nearsighted, so she put her glasses on to get a better look at what I'd given her and at me. For a moment, I didn't think she recognized me. By this time I was well into my eighth month and not the bathing beauty of an Esther Williams movie. She peered at the bottle like a hair in her soup, and said, "What the hell is that?"

"Well," I said, "you've got so many gorgeous things here that I thought you might like a tacky little present for the start of your movie."

"I don't like tacky," she announced. I stared at her imperious pose with which she dismissed me.

"I . . . I'm sorry," I stammered, almost stumbling as I backed out of her dressing room.

"Keep your tacky present and go," she commanded. Everyone in the room was still; not a sound. I left and took the gift with me.

Without meaning to, I'd done about the worst thing you could do to her. Joan loved being in the movies. She loved the makeup and the costumes and everything about it, and she'd convinced herself that this bubble was real life. When I came in there with that sad little toilet paper-wrapped, almost-empty bottle of vodka, I'd stuck a pin in that bubble. My gag gift was a chilling reminder that her bubble world wasn't real, and she never forgave me for it. She didn't speak to me again, ever, when we were coming and going. Two weeks earlier, I'd been the most wonderful person in the universe when I gave her my director. Now I was on her shit list for life.

After that encounter, all I wanted to do was go home and have my baby. Susan Tenney Gage was born October 1, 1953. Just as she'd been all the time I carried her, Susie was very considerate and was born very easily and right on time.

After three months of maternity leave, I reported back to the studio, and hard on the heels of the lesson I learned observing poor Joan Crawford, I learned an even more bitter lesson. I had assumed that my next movie would be *Athena*. It was a premise that a writer named Leo Pogostin, my friend and director Chuck Walters, and I had come up with about a reincarnated goddess who comes back to life in the twentieth century, with all her goddess instincts intact. We'd worked up a treatment together over lunches in the commissary during the making of *Easy to Love,* and Leo had finished the script while I was out with Susie.

I was excited about the film, and as soon as I got back I met Leo and Chuck for lunch. The first thing Chuck did was "thank me for my generosity" in giving him to Joan Crawford to do *Torch Song*. As Joan had guessed, Chuck was indeed gay, but apparently that did not discourage her in the slightest. Neither did the fact that Chuck was essentially a married man—he'd had a stable relationship for some time with a man, a real estate developer. They'd been living together in Malibu for years, but Joan was not an easy person to deny.

One night she appeared at their house on the beach, Chuck said, and demanded to come in. "She just plunked herself down and announced, 'I'm spending the night with you.' "

"How did you get rid of her?" I asked.

"How do you get rid of Joan Crawford when she wants to go to bed with you? You don't. She'd been drinking and she wouldn't leave," Chuck said. "It was a nightmare!"

Over coffee I started bubbling on enthusiastically about *Athena*, until I realized that both Chuck and Leo had become uncharacteristically silent. "What's wrong?" I asked.

"*Athena* is already shooting," said Leo, fiddling with the silverware.

"Excuse me?"

"Jane Powell is doing it. They took all the swimming sequences and made them singing scenes." Chuck was unable to meet my gaze. "Dick Thorpe is directing."

That last piece of information twisted the knife. "Well," I said, "I haven't seen Dore Schary in a while. I guess it's time for another visit."

I stormed up to the third floor and was shown into his office. "What happened here?" I asked. "I come back all ready to start *Athena*, and I find that you've given it away. You knew this was my picture. You knew that I had written it with Leo and Chuck. You saw our names on it, including mine." Leo had assured me that he and Chuck had set it up that way, so that all of us shared credit for the story.

Schary nodded, then said brusquely, "We have a studio to run here."

Schary's actions were absolutely indefensible, which may have been why he didn't have the decency to tell me himself. What he'd done was "legal" since we were all under contract, and everything we did on company time belonged to the studio; but it went to the heart of my sense of values about fair play. I felt like something had been stolen from me. It was yet another omen that the time to get out of MGM was fast approaching.

I went home to my children, distancing myself as much as possible from the MGM that had been my home away from home for the past twelve years. To be treated so shabbily by the head of the studio, and with such a lack of dignity, seemed unjust. Word filtered through the studio of my confrontation with Schary. The gossip wags wrote: "The Mermaid on the Lot has been beached." I thought MGM and I were both on the same team. I was learning otherwise.

However, I was not one to sit home and lick my wounds for very long, and I was still under contract. So when my old friend Dorothy Kingsley called to tell me she was working on a new script that would be perfect for me, I was able to put my feelings in my personal storehouse and get on with it.

Hollywood scripts are like fashion statements. Once a designer finds a style that works, all the others follow suit with or without any originality. The fifties and into the sixties was the Age of Antiquity for the Hollywood studios. Any story that had its foot in Athens, Rome, or Jerusalem was part of the Hollywood mindset—*Samson and Delilah, Hercules, The Robe, Spartacus.* My script of *Athena* had been right on the money. When Dorothy called me, MGM producer George Wells had just purchased *The Road to Rome*, the 1927 Broadway comedy by Robert E. Sherwood. I wasn't sure whether Schary had okayed this project to pacify me or that Dorothy had come to my rescue. Despite how Schary felt, I was still one of their big moneymaking stars, and that carried weight in the front office.

The plot revolved around the threatening presence of Hannibal and his legions of elephants poised on the outskirts of Rome, waiting to sack the city. Improbable as it may sound, Dorothy Kingsley was able to tailor two swimming sequences into this Roman farce, and probably the most intricate numbers I have ever done. Dorothy was comfortable writing scripts for me, as we had been a team since *Bathing Beauty.*

I came back to the studio ready to work, assiduously avoiding any encounter with Schary. George Sidney was set to direct, and Howard Keel was cast as Hannibal. I'd have my friends around me. I played Amytis, the fabled vestal virgin betrothed to Fabius Maximus, emperor of Rome, who was played by George Sanders, married at that point in real life to Zsa Zsa Gabor. When Amytis sneaks into Hannibal's camp, she is captured and eventually falls in love with him and convinces him not to attack Rome. Hermes Pan was brought in from 20th Century–Fox to do the choreography. Cedric Gibbons did the art direction. The set for Fabius's pool was designed after the outdoor pool at San Simeon, near Santa Barbara, the fabled estate of William Randolph Hearst, invitations to whose extravagant weekend bacchanals during the thirties, hosted by his paramour, Marion Davies, were coveted by all Hollywood royalty.

By the time *Jupiter's Darling* was being made, San Simeon was being turned into a national monument.

The underwater sequence to the song "I Have a Dream" tells the story of how Amytis, who is Greek, and now promised to the Roman emperor Fabius, dreams of finding true love with a Greek warrior, represented by underwater statues. Over a dozen stuntmen, posing as Greek statues in Stein's clown-white makeup, were planted at the bottom of the pool and secured by Lucite cleats. Amytis swims around and through this underwater sculpture garden as she breathes life into each statue. The Crystal Scarborough School of Swimming, in West Los Angeles, sent two of its baby swimmers to the studio to play underwater Cupid statuettes, poised to shoot their arrows of love through the heart of Amytis. At the bottom of the pool, Amytis seals her fate with an underwater kiss, but, alas, as she returns to the surface, each statue turns back into stone. For the first time, the sensuous quality of the water, coupled with the near-nude muscular stuntmen, caught the attention of the Hays Office. I assured the censors that it was just another Esther Williams all-American movie and my kiss was no more seductive than the first kiss I had given to Mickey Rooney back in 1942.

More troubling than the watchdogs of virtue from the Hays Office was the fact that while lying on the floor of the pool, twenty-five feet deep, surrounded by these handsome underwater creatures, I broke my left eardrum, which had already sustained breaks in five movies. In order to continue swimming, I was fitted with an ear and nose prosthesis made out of French latex and glued on with eyelash adhesive that completely covered my aural and nasal openings. It was glued on the first thing in the morning and removed after the final shot at six o'clock. I felt like the Man in the Iron Mask. I couldn't hear, I couldn't smell, and I couldn't taste.

The final underwater swimming sequence was the first time that swimming was used as an integral part of the story and no longer as dream sequences with underwater fantasies. Now I, as Amytis, swam for my life, to escape the clutches of Hannibal and his soldiers.

This scene was as complex as any of the fountains and flames that Sam Katz had designed for me. The script called for Amytis to ride a horse over the edge of the cliffs of the Tiber River, 200 feet above the water's surface. The problem was that horses don't dive, and in this case neither would I. George Wells was so convinced that this stunt "would bring in the audience in droves," he refused to consider a suggestion that we cut the scene. I told George Sidney that I remembered having seen a diving horse as an attraction on George Hamid's Steel Pier, in Atlantic City. The horse would dive from a high tower built on the Pier into a large and deep saucer tank with a rider riding bareback—and the rider was a woman. Hamid and his wife were friends of mine, and perhaps he would "loan" the horse to the studio. Within no time, I was on the phone, and George Wells had his horse on a truck bound for Culver City.

The cast and crew moved to location at the isthmus, on Catalina Island, a rugged series of cliffs and caves above a not so pacific ocean. The trick now was to find a stuntman who could dive who would risk his life on the back of the horse as they dived over the precipice of one of the cliffs into the ocean below. Hamid's diver refused to leave New Jersey. I had done stunts before, but this was beyond the call. Maybe I had to be pregnant to gather the courage I had in those Busby adventures. Edie Motridge had been with me on the set, and she suggested a platform diver who swam with us during our competitive days at the Los Angeles Athletic Club. We found Al Lewin through the club, and, sure enough, he thought it would be a kick to be in one of my movies. Yes, he said, he could dive from a horse. "How do you know if you could pull off this stunt?" I asked. "Did you ever dive with a horse before?" "Es," he said, "remember all those pratfalls from the high towers during those swim meets? It's no different with a horse. You just use the horse as if he were a springboard, separating yourself once you're over the cliff. As long as it's high to split from the horse in mid-air." "Don't worry, Al, it certainly will be high enough," I said, jittery. "Besides," he said, "I've always promised my kids that I would be in one of your pictures." Sweet Al Lewin.

George Sidney brought him to Catalina, and high above the ocean, Al, now dressed in red chiffon, galloped over the cliffs, freed himself from the horse, just as he said he would, and dove into the sea. One take. George has the shot. And Al has broken his back. I panicked as I watched the scene. I felt so responsible. Edie and I huddled around him as the ambulance arrived on the set to begin the trip back to LA. "I told you, Al," I said as I held his hands as he lay on the stretcher. This is not just jumping off the high board with Aileen Allen coaching you. This is tough stuff." He looked up at me through his pain and winced a smile. "D'ya think the audience will know it's not you on the horse, Es? Did I look good?" "Oh, Al," I cried, "you were wonderful!" Al recovered months later and wrote me how proud he was to have been in one of my movies. Although I was flattered, I couldn't help think of what risks a production will take to "get the shot."

The rest of the underwater chase was filmed in and around Silver Springs, Florida, because the water was clear enough for the matching shots of the horse flailing underwater, only this time with me. I was warned to keep clear of the horse, since its kick could be lethal. And to top it off, we returned to Catalina to film the final scenes inside the caves of the isthmus, which were filled with over two hundred bats. As the lights were turned on, the bats swooped toward my bobbing head, forcing me underwater, without a camera. This simple MGM musical comedy with Marge and Gower Champion, hoofing around on dry land with pink and purple elephants, turned into an action/adventure epic for me worthy of my old friend, Tarzan.

Howard Keel was cast as Hannibal. The first time he walked out of makeup for *Jupiter's Darling*, I didn't recognize him. Suddenly Howard had become Hannibal the hunk. He'd been given a beard and this curly wig of great-looking hair. He also looked like he'd been pumping iron; the man who'd played a lanky schoolteacher on Kauai now sported washboard abs. But Howard hadn't touched a barbell. They'd outfitted him with this amazing body armor—snap-on muscles—sort of like what Michael Keaton wore when he played Batman.

Jupiter's Darling was a great hair picture. George Sidney insisted that all great historical women were redheads, so Sydney Guilaroff found me a lovely shade of mahogany. Then he gave me a parade of elaborate hairstyles, with braids and chignons. In every mix there is a thorn. MGM drama coach Lillian Burns was being a true pain in the ass, using her position as George's wife to insist that I would benefit from her coaching. Early on she came to me and issued what was essentially a thinly veiled summons. "I really want to work with you on this picture; but you haven't been coming in often, and my husband is the director. I especially want to go over this love scene at the walls of Rome. . . . Let me know when you and Howard can come to my room for a session."

In the scene, Hannibal sings, "I'll never trust a woman," takes me by the hair, and throws me around in what is almost a tango. Howard had never taken Lillian on, so he was all set to meet her demands and go see her; but I thought it was pointless to rehearse something so physical in her office. I wanted to do it on the set and told her so. Lillian refused, and it became a test of wills in which I won the battle that sparked a greater war. At my insistence we did the scene on the set on a Saturday afternoon, when no one was around to see her dominance over my director. She never forgave me for forcing the issue.

Lillian's way of teaching acting hadn't changed since I was doing *Andy Hardy*. It was still all about exaggerated gestures tied to bits of dialogue, with no greater vision of whether any of it fit the character or the overall plot. Working with her again, I felt the way I'd always felt—that her eyeball-rolling, nostril-flaring, snap-your-head-back style was not only hammy but possibly contagious. She was doing me more harm than good.

When I was still a starlet I had to suffer through these sessions with her, but at this point in my career, I didn't. "Lillian," I said, "I'm not learning anything, and I wish you wouldn't make me watch you act out my scenes so I can copy your movements. I'm about ten feet taller than you are, and you're doing things I shouldn't even see you do, because I'm afraid I'll do them, too. So if you'll just leave me alone, I can handle this role."

She was so infuriated that she went running to George. She could really turn it on when she wanted to. "Geoooooorrrrge! Esther has to come in and be with me because you're the director and you need to tell her that she needs my help. Geoooorrrrge, do something!"

Poor George just put his head in his hands. He was overloaded already and didn't need another crisis. He was still working through his grief over the recent death of his father, L.K., and you didn't have to be Dear Abby to see that he and Lillian were having marital difficulties.

George started hiding in his work. He began keeping us longer and longer on the set, well after quitting time. He didn't want to go home at night, because he'd have to listen to Lillian go on and on about what a bitch I was because I wouldn't work with her anymore. Late in the afternoon he'd begin setting up a complicated shot with five or six camera moves, knowing that it would surely take at least till midnight to finish it. We had labor rules about golden time, which meant golden paychecks for the crew for all these extra hours. On Friday nights he'd have drinks brought in for everyone. George wanted all of us to stay and party, but the crew also had lives of their own. Even if they were being paid handsomely to have free drinks with the director.

I *wasn't* being paid extra, and I wanted to go home more than anyone. I was missing the fun of those first months with Susie—time that could never be recaptured. I told George that with a new baby at home I wasn't willing to stay at the studio till midnight anymore. For the first time in my life in the movie business I was labeled "uncooperative" and "difficult."

Things got worse when George stalled production for three months to wait for Marge and Gower Champion to join the cast after finishing *Three for the Show* over at Columbia with Betty Grable and Jack Lemmon. Gower was to play Varius, a slave, and Marge was Meta, my lady-in-waiting, and they and their wonderful dancing were perfect for the picture; but until they were available, we were just marking time. George didn't want to confess the real reason for the delay and risk being forced to recast the roles, so he had the crew, the musicians, and the rest of us called in for rehearsal every day. The reason he gave for these endless rehearsals was that Esther Williams wasn't learning a major musical number.

This was absurd. In nineteen previous movies I'd done stunts and musical numbers a million times more difficult than this one, but never had I rehearsed the way this one little song was being rehearsed, not even with Busby Berkeley when he was trying to kill me or with that notorious perfectionist Gene Kelly, who fervently believed that with enough rehearsal he could make me shorter.

As those late nights and extra months mounted up, my mental cash register kept ringing, and it told me that the tab for *Jupiter's Darling* was beginning to run way up there. I also realized that my name on the marquee was going to have to earn that money back. Until now, the genre of films known as "Esther Williams movies" had always been profitable, but we'd never had a problem keeping production costs within reason. As the waste dragged on, *Jupiter's Darling* was starting to carry so much financial baggage that it was becoming clear that it would never get out of the red.

With the picture doomed to lose money, I could see who would be held responsible, and it wasn't either of the Georges—Wells the producer, or Sidney the director—and, of course, Dore Schary was more than ready to believe anything negative about me. After the run-in over Stanley Donen and the theft of *Athena*, I could just see Schary making a private collection of unfavorable reports on *Jupiter's Darling:* "Esther refused to work with Lillian." "Esther refused to stay late on the set." "Esther needed three months to learn a number." A new kind of patsy was emerging, a box-office patsy.

Not surprisingly, when the film opened to a disappointing box office, I took the rap. When things go wrong in Hollywood, finger-pointing becomes a blood sport, but this time I was not alone in being gored. While I was saddled with the blame for *Jupiter's Darling*, everyone was condemning Lana Turner for the fact that *The Prodigal*, her costume epic, was a turkey.

There was a badly concealed glee in the industry over the failure of both films. Everybody was a little too eager to show me to the door, and Lana wasn't treated any better. It didn't matter how much money our other films had made for the studio; the disappointing grosses from these movies somehow "proved" that the fans had abandoned us. The trades ran pieces saying we had come to the end of the line. These stories were picked up by regular news organizations, and soon *Time* magazine reported that Lana and I were Hollywood has-beens.

I was one step closer to my farewell, and I knew the next would follow soon. By 1955, TV had made great inroads in movie revenues. The entire studio system was falling apart, and MGM had really lost its luster. Dore Schary's penchant for small films with small stars was killing off what was left of MGM glamour. Many of its most established stars were jumping ship, including Greer Garson, Van Johnson, and the King, Clark Gable.

It was just a matter of time until I would decide I wanted out. I knew it had come to the end when they told me I was going to play the part of Mary in the remake of *The Women,* a brittle, bitchy comedy written by Clare Boothe Luce. It had first been produced as a Broadway play. Then Anita Loos did a brilliant job with the 1939 screenplay adaptation, and George Cukor directed a perfect cast, with Norma Shearer as Mary, and Joan Crawford as Crystal, the gold-digging, husband-stealer. Roz Russell, Joan Fontaine, and Paulette Goddard were terrific in supporting roles. It still holds up, and you'd be hard-pressed to improve on it even now.

Fay Kanin, doing the new screenplay, called me to talk about the role of Mary, and I knew almost immediately that Dory Schary with his uncanny instinct for failure, had greenlighted another really bad idea. The film was to become a musical called *The Opposite Sex,* with Joan Collins, Dolores Gray, Ann Sheridan, and Ann Miller in the cast. There was nothing particularly wrong with that group of actresses, but they were definitely second-string when compared to the originals. The studio was also going to add men to the plot, an unfortunate decision since the most intriguing thing about *The Women* was that it was a magnificent film without men. Worse yet, the character of Mary was to be rewritten to suit me. Instead of her being a conventional wife and mother with a wealthy but wandering husband, she would become a swimming star in an Aquacade. Was this a surprise?

I wanted no part of this bomb, and I went to Dore Schary to tell him so. He looked at me archly and said, "Since when do you know about plays?" He was very smooth, almost snide, and very condescending, but in one way we were equal. I didn't respect the pictures he made (and he knew it), and he didn't respect the pictures I made (and I knew it).

"I'm not doing this movie," I told him, knowing full well that this would lead to a suspension.

"Very well, Miss Williams."

I went back to my baby and my house in Mandeville Canyon to figure out what I should do next.

Jupiter's Darling, I suspected, was not a problem in a vacuum. The Esther Williams swimming musicals had probably had their run. A great run, but still, all things come to an end. Broadway was already, or soon would be, turning out shows that would become the next generation of Hollywood musicals—*My Fair Lady, The King and I, West Side Story, The Sound of Music, Funny Girl*—and there was no place in such properties for a mermaid.

I called one of the smartest men in Hollywood, my friend Lew Wasserman, who at that time was still an agent, and asked him to give me some advice. He came over to my house and sat with me under the giant sycamores in my yard. I told Lew that I was thinking about walking away from my contract.

I had no money worries. Like many stars, I had what was known in Hollywood as a deferred payment contract, money extracted from my salary over the years and set aside as a retirement nest egg. This was a tax dodge, as well as a way to hedge your bets against a time when maybe you weren't making so much money.

"How much do they owe you on the deferred payment contract?" Lew asked.

"Just under three million dollars," I said.

"Then they'll be happy to let you go," he said simply.

I was stunned. I'd been so busy thinking about what a hard time MGM was going to have giving me up that his words hit me like a wet flounder, right in the face. I suddenly felt very vulnerable and very small—smaller than Abe Lastvogel, my agent at William Morris, who had advised me to accept this contract.

"Happy?" I asked. "I don't follow you."

"If you leave," he continued, "they don't have to pay you that money, and they will be delighted to be rid of that obligation."

"But Lew," I protested, "it's money I've already earned. . . ."

"And I can assure you the fine print says they don't have to pay it out to you unless you stay at MGM and fulfill your contract."

"But I don't want to do the scripts they're offering me."

"Of course you don't, but you have to if you want that money."

Suddenly I could see how it would go from then on. Dory Schary was going to force-feed me a steady diet of lousy scripts, and it didn't matter to him whether I liked them or not, as long as I kept churning them out. He'd let me die a slow death at the box office, making garbage just for the privilege of collecting what was right-fully mine, the money they owed me for hits like *Million Dollar Mer-maid*. For someone like me who wanted and needed to be happy in her work, this was a definition of hell.

"It's over, isn't it, Lew," I said. It was more of a statement than a question.

"Yes, Esther, it's all over," he said.

CHAPTER 20

GOING, GOING . . .
1955–1956

*T*he suspension that Dore Schary threatened was inevitable, so I set about coordinating my departure before he could stick me with another dreadful film, and I knew there was one thing I had to do before I left.

I got the okay from the money men on the third floor and went to see Henry Grace in set decoration about redoing my dressing room. I chose an entirely different color scheme from my red, white, and blue chintz, which by now had seen far too much Nivea oil and Vaseline. I selected a beautiful seafoam green for the walls, a muted aqua for the floor, and a pale green velvet couch with moss green pillows. I also picked out a chandelier of Swedish crystal to replace my dinky early American light fixture. Henry started squawking about how pale everything was and how easily it would show grease and dirt, so I had to promise him that I'd sit on a hard chair, not on the velvet couch if I was still in my body makeup. Of course, he didn't know that I wasn't planning to spend much time there.

When the dressing room was done, I thought it looked like the perfect retreat for a cool blonde. Grace Kelly had been a contract player at MGM for years, but she'd become a star working for other studios. Although she'd made *Mogambo* for MGM with Clark Gable and Ava Gardner, Schary had loaned her out (foolishly, most said) to make a series of box-office bonanzas, including *Rear Window* and *The Country Girl*, for which she won an Oscar. Now she was coming back "home" to MGM to do *High Society*, a musical, with Frank Sinatra and her costar in *The Country Girl*, Bing Crosby.

Star dressing rooms were at a premium at the studio, and I knew she would be in line for the first vacated space. The year before, we'd done a publicity photo together at the Cannes Film Festival, in which I'd nailed a star with her name on it to a door. I took a star and attached it outside Dressing Room B. Then I wrote a note that said, "Dear Grace: Enjoy!" and fastened it beneath the star.

I packed all my terry cloth robes, my tired saggy bathing suits in which the elastic had died, the old wax gardenia and beat-up ornaments that I'd worn in all those films. I threw the whole bunch of stuff into my station wagon and drove toward the East Gate. *Bathing Beauty, Million Dollar Mermaid*, and all the rest seemed a lifetime ago.

At the gate, the guard on duty—with the improbable name of Ken Hollywood—smiled at me as he had for fourteen years, every morning I came to work. Ken peered at my overloaded station wagon and asked, "Esther, where're you going with all that stuff?"

"I'm leaving, Ken," I said.

And off I drove. I didn't say good-bye to anybody else. There was no point. Everyone I cared about was already gone. I heard Gable left the same way. The only two stars who lived out those deferred payment contracts were Robert Taylor and Cyd Charisse, and what happened to them was exactly what I'd feared for myself. Bob was badly cast in a couple of tired westerns, and Cyd made a few movies that nobody ever saw.

Strangely enough, I was very calm about it. Lew Wasserman's words, "Yes, Esther, it's all over," kept ringing in my ears. I was leaving behind almost $3 million in deferred income, but my mother Bula had helped me look inside myself to understand and accept the idea that it was the right thing to do. She told me, "Esther, you have always had a thing in your life called 'consciousness of supply,' and nobody can take away your good when you have consciousness of supply. You will get all that money back, and more."

But I wasn't leaving entirely empty-handed. There was still my fifty-thousand-dollar "signing bonus," a "gift" from that old lecher Sam Katz.

That fifty thousand dollars had an odd history. When I arrived at MGM late in 1941, Sam promised that I would appear in a swimming movie. Even though I was already married, I was still naive enough that I didn't know what a "casting couch" was. Dear, departed Ida Koverman, Mayer's first lieutenant, had felt obliged to tell me that the real reason I'd been brought to the studio was to sleep with Katz.

But *that* was never going to happen, although I don't think he ever believed that. These men had great confidence in their ability to bed down women, whom they pursued endlessly.

Within a couple of weeks of my contract, Louis B. Mayer had ordered up my screen test with Clark Gable in a fit of pique because Lana had run off with Artie Shaw. At that time Mayer's direct involvement had been unusual; this was a period when he was so sidetracked with his racehorses that he left the day-to-day running of the studio to Katz. No one anticipated how accidentally successful my screen test would be or that I would refuse Mayer's demand that I costar opposite Gable in *Somewhere I'll Find You*. My insistence that I not be cast in a film before I'd been at MGM for nine months, coupled with Mayer's diversion into Thoroughbred racing, turned out to be providential for me. It gave Katz time to start building my $250,000 pool in the hope of keeping me around long enough to be "useful."

Sam Katz had put aside fifty thousand dollars as a signing bonus for me, to be collected at the end of my contract or whenever I left the studio, whichever came first. It was a "goodwill gesture," one more piece of his campaign to convince me that even though I was nineteen and five feet eight and he was fifty-three and five feet three, he was not *that* old and not *that* short, especially if we were both horizontal. This was when I didn't show up for those intimate little lunches and told him that I thought of him like my father.

Hidden within these signing bonuses, there was a little fund for him, too. The formula that allotted me fifty thousand dollars was keyed to a sliding scale based on salary, which entitled him to put $3 million in a pension fund that he set aside for himself. The knowledge that this $3 million was waiting allowed him to shelve his pride when Mayer kicked him downstairs. His last years at MGM were spent doing nothing at a small desk in what was essentially a broom closet on the first floor, but he came in to work every day in his pearl gray suit so he could eventually collect that money.

Finally, he'd served out his "sentence" down there and got to say good-bye, taking his windfall with him. By coincidence I had an appointment with L. B. Mayer the day Katz took his leave of the studio. I was waiting for Mayer in front of that big white crescent desk in his office, which adjoined the executive conference room. There was no door between them. As Mayer left the conference room, I could hear Sam Katz calling after him, "I'm leaving. I'm going to take my money and go. I just want to tell you one thing. You guys have all thought something went on between Esther Williams and me. And I want to tell you, she never let me touch her with a ten-foot pole. So I'm on the record, just so you know . . . that lady is not only chlorinated, she's clean."

Meanwhile, "real life" continued, and at home Ben Gage's drinking spun further out of control. It didn't matter whether he was out on the town—like that night at the Beverly Hilton Hotel when Fernando had the waiters carry him out—or at home. We had pool parties at the house on Mandeville Canyon where he'd go swimming and strip off his trunks because he'd get an erection and wanted to wave it about like a banner. He was extraordinarily hung and down would come his trunks and there it would be. He almost always did this in front of a young woman, who'd come up to me in the house and say, "My God! Do you know what your husband just did?"

And I'd try to gloss over it, saying, "Oh, haven't you ever seen one before? Get over it. It's nothing." But the score begins to add up after a while; and you become a joke, and your marriage becomes a joke. Ben never stopped playing the fool, and I never stopped apologizing.

While I was still at the studio, incidents like this one had kept Howard Strickling and the MGM PR department busy. Whenever

Ben disgraced himself, Howard got the call from Louella Parsons or Hedda Hopper. L. B. Mayer had those women in his pocket, and they never wrote anything derogatory about an MGM star without checking with the studio first. Howard would then call me and ask, "Did this really happen?" Almost invariably I confirmed the worst. Then he'd say, "Don't worry, we'll quash the story." The studio did the same thing that I was doing with the children, hushing up how much of a problem Ben's drinking had become.

Now, of course, the protective shield that MGM had provided was gone, yet somehow the fable of Ben and Esther Gage as one of Hollywood's happiest couples lived on. There was the lovely fan magazine myth that we had the greatest marriage in Hollywood, but Ben kept hacking chunks out of it, until one day there was almost nothing left to keep it together. We reached the stage where we were more like roommates than husband and wife. All those erections weren't inspired by me. The only reason I stayed married to him was because of the children. As unhappy as I was, I still thought my kids were too young to grow up without a father, and I tried to make sure they never saw him drunk. This meant that there were evenings when, after dinner out or after a party, I couldn't bring Ben home.

One night I left him in Bette Davis's bathtub. The day had begun at our place. Bette and her husband, Gary Merrill, had a daughter, Beadie, who was a little older than Benjie, and we invited them to our house for an Easter egg hunt. We put the children's names on the eggs, but Beadie had raced ahead, found all of them, and refused to part with any of them. Not surprisingly, Benjie came to me tearfully to complain. "Let's go talk to her mommie, Benjie. She'll straighten it all out."

I said this, of course, not knowing that there was nothing reasonable about Bette Davis. "Bette," I said, "Beadie's got all the eggs and she won't give them up."

Bette, the consummate actress, sang out cheerily, "Oh, Beadie, Beadie . . . come here!" When the child got close enough, Bette yanked the basket roughly from her, at which point Beadie bit her mother on the hand, drawing blood. I rushed for a towel while Gary and Bette scooped up their daughter and headed for the door. (Talk about omens: Beadie bit the hand that fed her—then and later. She eventually wrote a nasty little book called *My Mother's Keeper* that did for Bette what *Mommie Dearest* had done for Joan Crawford, except that Bette was still alive when it was published.)

Since the egg hunt had ended on such a rotten note, I wanted to smooth things over with Bette and Gary later that evening. The Merrills (of course, no one ever called them that) lived in a big brown shingle house in Hancock Park, and Ben and I dropped in to chat. I never knew precisely how drunk Ben was from day to day but by now I'd learned to watch him carefully for telltale signs.

So when he went to the bathroom and didn't come back, I went to look for him. I found him passed out in the bathtub, fully clothed. Bette, not masking her irritation and contempt for Ben's behavior said, "I don't have to put up with this. I'm going to bed—this is disgusting." I knew it was no use apologizing to Bette. I lived a life of apologizing to people, but apologies aren't any good; the moment happened and you just have to go on from there. So, I thought, There goes another lady who will never be a friend of mine. I lost a lot of friends and potential friends that way over the years. But the evening was far from over.

Gary and Bette had what might euphemistically be called a difficult marriage. He was a bit younger than she was, and they argued all the time, sniping at each other in front of guests, like Martha and George in *Who's Afraid of Virginia Woolf?* He wasn't much interested in dealing with Bette when she was in one of her moods, so he stayed at the bar out in the pool house, downing one Scotch after another. He then decided, as men so often decide when they're alone with women and they've had too much to drink, the woman they're with looks a lot better than what's waiting for them upstairs.

So now I had a drunken Gary Merrill making indecent proposals to me at the bar in the pool house, a husband out like a light in the bathtub of the bathroom off the bar, and Bette Davis screaming from her bedroom window, "Gary, get up here, you sonofabitch! I know what you're doing!"

Gary looked up warily at the window. "Happens all the time," he said thickly, taking a big swig and putting his arm around my shoulder. Edward Albee himself couldn't have done any better.

I began to suspect that this was a scene they'd played many times over, but I didn't want to be part of it. "Gary, go on up to her . . . please," I begged as I disengaged myself from his clumsy embrace. "You can't even pretend to go on the make when you've got a wife like Bette. She'll get a gun and shoot us both."

I had to get out of there, but of course Ben was still in Bette's bathtub; and Gary was in no shape to help me lug him to the car. He was so afraid of Bette's wrath that he was getting more smashed than Ben, and it occurred to me that he might climb in the tub, too. I had no choice but to leave Ben behind. I drove home alone again, wondering how I could live with this for the rest of my life. Ben was delivered home in the morning, complete with the usual hangover. He shuffled to the bed and collapsed again.

I often wondered how women like Bette and myself, who rose to the top of our professions and were so successful in our public lives, could have such disastrous private lives. I haven't found the answer yet.

Ben often stayed late at The Trails, drinking up the profits until he was no longer physically able to drive home. The cops brought him back to Mandeville Canyon many nights. I'd get up early in the morning and see him slumped over in the front seat. Then I'd have to figure out how to get him back in the house before the children saw him.

When *Jupiter's Darling* opened, I was obliged by contract to trudge through another publicity tour, this time accompanied at several theaters by a baby elephant. Because there were elephants in the movie, the MGM publicity geniuses thought it would be a good gimmick to send me around with an elephant that did a few tricks and attracted attention. (I was reminded of a bit of actors' wisdom: "Never get on the same stage with animals or small children.")

The *Jupiter's Darling* tour was to be my last obligation to MGM. I told Ben that he wasn't coming along with me because I couldn't trust him anymore. The drinking had gotten too far out of hand. I was not about to be caught in Albany, New York, with a six-foot-six liability. Poor Ben, he wanted to go on tour so much this time, perhaps to revive a singing career. Although he had dubbed the voice of Dana Andrews in *State Fair*, and later for Victor Mature in *Straw-*

berry Blond with Rita Hayworth (a Hollywood twist of irony), Ben's career was practically nonexistent.

He cried, apologized, and promised he wouldn't touch another drop, vowing that he'd be there for me. How strange. I was coming to the end and he was treating it like a beginning. Too little too late?

No matter, Ben tore at my heart. He was still my husband, and the father of our children. I felt guilty about how difficult it must be for him to be married to a movie star, and one who was continuously in the spotlight. It wasn't an easy task.

This, however, shouldn't have been an excuse for Ben's drinking or gambling or lack of ambition, but I'm sure it was a contributing factor. When there are so many demands in your life, a relationship must adjust itself to meet those demands. Each partner must carry his or her weight if the relationship is to reach any level of success. If I were to have nursed Ben's life and career throughout our marriage, it would have been at the cost of mine with no guarantees of how successful his might have been.

I decided that if he would agree to stop drinking, we would have a go at the tour, together. We went into rehearsal for three weeks before we left, with Ben and me, five dancing boys, and a baby elephant. Ben stayed sober.

It was common in the forties and fifties to have live shows before a movie in big city theaters, and in this one, Ben and I appeared in a little variety show onstage before the movie was shown. I was all for this tour. I was still clinging to some futile hope that Ben would finally be discovered. I had agreed that if the act were any good, we would take it to Las Vegas. We could use the MGM tour as an "out of town" rehearsal. We left the children at home with our nanny, Jane. We brought a small orchestra with us and traveled by bus—Albany, Atlantic City, Michigan, Wisconsin—and it was pretty bad. Not that the act was bad, but it really put a marriage that was already floundering to a terrible test. All the things that were wrong got worse.

Late in September of 1955 we were on the road with the tour, and I sank into a deep depression. October 1 would be Susie's second birthday, and I wouldn't be there to celebrate with her. In Madison, Wisconsin, I started crying and I just couldn't stop. Ben sent for the children, and I made arrangements for them and Jane to stay the entire run of the show.

But it was just a good moment in a very bad time. Ben's promises melted with the ice in his Scotch, but somehow we got through the show. He still had this beautiful voice. He sang "The Girl That I Marry" from *Annie Get Your Gun,* and we danced to "I Don't Know Why I Love You Like I Do." It was four shows a day, starting at 11:00 in the morning, and there were days when I didn't feel like being there at all.

We signed to bring the show to the Sahara in Las Vegas, opening just a few days after Marlene Dietrich completed her three-week engagement. Marlene had once again reinvented herself, this time as a cabaret entertainer. We were in dress rehearsals, and as I looked out into what should have been an empty audience, I was a little rattled to see her sitting there in the second row. She stayed through the entire rehearsal and afterward she said, "Dahlingh, can I talk to yooh?"

And I said, "Yes, Miss Dietrich." Of course, she didn't remember that I'd modeled for her at I. Magnin's when I was still hoping to become an assistant buyer and she'd stretched out on the chaise in the dressing room, completely naked.

"Call me Marlene."

She'd also forgotten that I'd often been sitting next to her in the hairdressing department very early in my time at MGM, when she insisted on getting her hair done in the nude. Sydney Guilaroff always did Marlene himself, and she took particular delight in driving him crazy.

No matter how grand Sydney was, he was also a prude; and Marlene amused herself by twitting him about it. She would sit in his chair, wearing her salon drape with nothing whatsoever underneath it. While Sydney was working on her hair, braiding and pinning and fixing, she would gently tug on her cover-up until it came away and she'd be sitting there before him totally nude.

Nudity didn't bother Marlene in the slightest, and she did it because she knew Sydney hated it. He'd scold her in that prissy way of his, shaking a hairbrush at her, "Marlene, that's the third time you've done that, and it's making me very nervous."

"Is it, dahlingh? Is it makingh yooh nehrvous?"

Finally he tried to cinch the drape around her neck so it would stay on, but she said, "Dahlingh, yooh ahr chokkingh me." He had no choice but to loosen the drape and finish her hair while she sat there entirely naked.

Now she was a gorgeous grandmother, playing to a packed house every night. "Esther," she said, "yoohr shoes vhen yooh dahnce must not be the sahme color as the dress."

"But Miss Dietrich . . . Marlene . . . I had them dyed to order, and . . ."

"No. The audience must not be avare of yoohr feet—yooh must haf shoos the color of yoohr skin, so that it looks like yooh ahr dahncing in high heels in yoohr bare feet." I was struggling to keep my life together, and Marlene was talking to me about shoes.

The children came right along with us to Las Vegas. In the daytime, I could be there for their meals and take them swimming in those beautiful pools. There was no reason that they shouldn't be with us all the time now that we were staying at the Sahara Hotel. Or so I thought. The Sahara thought otherwise.

My nanny, Jane Boyd, was black. Actually, she was sort of café au lait, but that distinction was lost on the management of the Sahara, who declared that no blacks could set foot on the premises. I had heard all these stories about Lena Horne, Sammy Davis Jr., Count Basie, Louis Armstrong, and other entertainers who were not allowed to stay at the hotels where they were headlining. I was amazed to find out that Vegas casinos never let black people even gamble. I had thought they would take anybody's money. The police in Las Vegas would step in and ask those who were black to leave the casinos. It was an ugly policy that was rigidly enforced, and the Sahara was not making any exceptions for me or my children.

If Jane were to take care of my three children, they would all have to stay across the tracks from the Sahara Hotel in an apartment complex that was clearly designated for the "help." Jane was not at all happy to be treated as "help." In my home, she was family.

I had told her, "When I hand my children over to you, I don't want them to feel any difference in the warmth of our arms. I want you to love them and care for them in the same way I do." And she did. We became good friends, and when I went through some tough

times, she was there for me. We shared holidays and vacations together, and because we wore the same size, we even shared clothes.
She was a strong, assertive woman, and I liked that in her because it
was good for the children. It almost broke my heart to send the children to a building away from me. There was no way I could explain.
It was either that or back to Los Angeles, where I wouldn't see them.
I explained that "across the way" meant sleeping rooms because
mommy and daddy came home so late at night. I was furious at the
Sahara.

Jane agreed to tolerate the "other side of the tracks" treatment
because she knew how much I missed the children. One day, near
the end of the engagement, I came to her and said, "Jane, I know
you've been treated rotten and I appreciate that you've endured it
for me. I've got an idea about how we can get back at the Sahara in
a small way and have some fun." Her face brightened into a big
smile for the first time in weeks.

"I want you to try on this Indian sari that I brought along and see
if you like it." The sari was a beautiful shade of turquoise with gold
accents. Jane looked gorgeous in it. I asked her to invite her
boyfriend, George, to come to Las Vegas for the last weekend of our
show at the Sahara. We called a tuxedo shop to order his outfit and
spent the rest of the afternoon trying to find someplace that would
make a glamorous-looking turban. Jane and I researched the proper
attire, jewelry, and makeup for Indian royalty.

Next, I called Steve Parker, the manager of the Sahara showroom. "I've just had some exciting news," I gushed. "My friends the
maharajah and the maharani of Jodhpur are in Los Angeles, and
they are coming to Las Vegas for the last performance of our show!"
The name was ridiculous, but I was improvising. "They're Indian
royalty, and I want them seated at a ringside table and given every
courtesy of the Sahara."

Parker was so enthusiastic about his showroom being graced by
royalty and the possibility of their losing a small fortune at the tables, I considered putting a little heavy tan makeup on the kids and
having the maharajah bring his whole family. But I realized the kids
would start yelling "Mommy" and "Daddy" when we came onstage
and blow the whole thing.

"Oh, by the way," Parker asked, "are the Jodhpurs going to be *your* guests?" This was Las Vegas code for "Are you picking up the tab?"

"These people are royalty," I said indignantly. "Any hotel on the strip would be honored to have them. If you prefer, I'll entertain them somewhere else." He was still apologizing when we hung up.

When Jane in her sari and George in his turban arrived at the showroom that night, Steve Parker was there to greet them personally. Jane looked radiantly beautiful. The orchestra played a fanfare when they entered and the audience applauded as Steve escorted "the royal couple" to a ringside table. As he promised, they got the A treatment, from flowers to Dom Perignon. When I came on stage, I introduced them as dear friends who had entertained me so lavishly in India and I dedicated the show to them. When the show was over, Ben and I went down and sat ringside with them. The tourists couldn't take enough snapshots of us, and Jane and I were kept busy autographing programs.

At the end of the evening, Jane and George went back to the little apartment across the tracks where my children were waiting up for them with a sitter. The next morning, Steve thanked me very warmly for bringing them and assured me that the Sahara was honored to have had them as the hotel's guests. He even complimented me on what a special night I had arranged for them. I said, "Yes, wouldn't it be wonderful if we could do this for all of our friends." He missed my double meaning. The Sahara Hotel never knew that they were the first establishment in Las Vegas to break the color barrier.

All in all, the engagement in Vegas was a success, I suppose, if you don't count Ben's drinking and gambling. We had been paid top dollar, twenty-thousand dollars a week, and the world came to see Esther Williams, in person, and Ben knew it. He felt like a lounge act, an opening number for the headliner. It just didn't happen for him. I tried. I got us there. Perhaps it was too late. Esther Williams was too much of a marquee name.

Each night, after the show, we'd stop at the hotel lounge and mingle with friends who had come to see us. I always knew when Ben got that look in his eyes, waiting for the moment that he would excuse himself and head over to the crap tables. He was like a wolf to a

baited trap. In the middle of a conversation, Ben would casually announce, "I feel lucky tonight."

That was the signal for him to pull his big frame up and head
over to the tables. I would panic slightly as the familiar scene played
out before me. I would quickly end any conversations we were having with our friends and follow Ben to the tables. The pattern was always the same. The hostesses would supply the drinks—always free;
Ben would open with a "lucky streak," and within an hour, I was
stuffing whatever was left that I could salvage from the table down
the bodice of my strapless gown. Quietly, I would sneak over to the
cashiers' windows, dig into my cleavage, and convert the chips into
dollars. I had my own hotel safety deposit box where I'd stash what
remained of the losings. I'd beg him to quit, but between the
booze and the dice, it was a losing battle. There's always a crowd
when someone wins or loses big, and Ben certainly did not go un-
noticed. I'd lean over and whisper, "Ben, that's enough. We're losing.
Let's go."

"You go to sleep," he'd say, slurring his words. "I be up soon. I
love ya."

So I'd stay there, watching the chips dwindle faster than I could
retrieve them, until finally they were gone, and I was back to my
normal C-cup. I could barely hold him up as he staggered away
from the table. There I was, the most recognizable face in the hotel,
dragging this oversized behemoth across what seemed like the Gobi
desert back to our suite, feeling completely humiliated.

There is nothing quite like making twenty thousand dollars a
week, and seeing your husband blow the whole thing in a couple of
nights—all under the same roof. Trust me. It's a near-religious experience.

We returned to Los Angeles, and I felt slightly unhinged. My
fifteen-year tenure at MGM had ground to a halt. As I always knew,
it was just a matter of time before the swimming musical would
come to an end. The only swimming that I'd be doing now, I
thought, would be in my backyard pool in Mandeville Canyon. I resisted the deep feelings of depression that spun about me. The
William Morris Agency assured me that my name had value. I had
to move on, but Bula had always told me, "When you don't know

what to do, don't just do *something*. Stand there and wait upon the action of your Lord." I could wait.

I got a script to do a picture at Universal called *The Unguarded Moment*. The role was that of a high school teacher threatened by a student who is sexually obsessed with her. I thought it was a curious choice for Universal to offer me the lead in a "dry" psychological thriller, and I wasn't sure the public would accept me without my glittering crowns and sparkly swimsuits. Nonetheless, Universal offered me $200,000, which was more than I ever made for a single film at MGM in or out of the water. I wasn't sure if this was a result of William Morris's or Bula's philosophy. George Nadar was the male lead, and the film introduced newcomer John Saxon as the obsessed high school student. Later, after we had started shooting, Roz Russell came up to me at a party and said, "I hear you're doing my script." I looked at her blankly until she explained that she had written it under the pseudonym C. A. McKnight. "I wrote the part for me, but I got too old."

Universal may have been satisfied to take me out of the pool, but not so the public. For them, the name Esther Williams was synonymous with water. When Universal premiered *Unguarded Moment* that summer, in Atlantic City, my good friend George Hamid, who had lent MGM the diving horse for *Jupiter's Darling*, phoned and asked me to attend the premiere at a theater he owned on the Boardwalk. "We'll have a big party for you, Esther. It'll be just like old times."

I told him this movie was different from what he was used to seeing. There were no fountains, no underwater ballets, no girls in gold lamé. However, George was a showman not unlike Billy Rose.

"Come on Esther," he said, "don't be such a sad sack. Let's give 'em a show!"

I looked at him, remembering the excitement when he came to MGM with his horse. "I think those days are over, George."

"Not for me they ain't. You got a lot of fans around here and I'm giving a big party for the opening of *Unguarded Moment*, gold lamé or no gold lamé. I got a seaplane and I got a movie house on the boardwalk. And I bet you can't swim from my plane to the movie house."

"George," I laughed, "it sounds like a stunt from one of my old films." I didn't want him to think that having made a dry movie was the end of my swimming career. "Of course I can," I continued. I must have been crazy. It *was* like a stunt from an MGM movie, only this was New Jersey, and not Stage 30.

I flew to New Jersey and George met me in Atlantic City. Everything was planned. We would sail out to the seaplane from the Steel Pier where it would take off and circle the city. Once the plane landed, I would climb out on the wing, dive into the ocean, and swim to shore, where I would be met by fans and the press. I would then be taken to the theater, where I would change and greet the audience. I was up for the party.

Earlier that afternoon, a banner had been stretched across the beachfront, announcing my swimming arrival. The plane took off as scheduled; we circled the city, landed in the ocean, and taxied to about a quarter of a mile from the shore. I changed into a one-piece, two-tone swimsuit, pink on one side and purple on the other.

I scrambled out of the cockpit, climbed up on the wing of the plane, and looked down at the dark ocean and toward the shore. The pilot looked at me as if I were insane and asked me to sign my seat before I got out. Was he just a fan or did he think he wouldn't see me again? It was a hot summer afternoon, and the water temperature was warm. I paused a moment with my toes curled over the edge of the wing. The plane bobbed up and down in the waves. Did I hear Busby shoot off the gun? I took a comfortable swan dive, so as not to enter the water too deeply, and quickly surfaced for my swim to shore.

As I approached the shoreline, I caught a wave, which carried me toward the sand. Suddenly, what seemed like a mass of arms and legs, all shapes and sizes, came rushing toward me into the ocean. I turned as if to swim back toward the plane, but a wave washed me in further toward the shore. I must have panicked, because the next thing I knew, three powerful lifeguards scooped me above their heads and held me like a trophy surfboard as they carried me to the shore and onto the boardwalk. Thousands of screaming fans reached out to touch me, but other lifeguards formed a barrier to keep them clear of me. I was carried into the theater, where flashbulbs were popping and fans were screaming. George was waiting for me in the dressing room. "See, I told ya you could do it. Thanks, champ. I love you, Esther."

"Yeah, George," I said, smiling weakly. "I love you too."

I left New Jersey thinking, "Well, if I ever need a job and they ever need a replacement for the horse . . ."

After *Unguarded Moment,* I devoted more attention to the business side of my career now that there was no more MGM payroll. I thought the William Morris Agency should have protected me better in that deferred payment contract. I knew they were happy to take their 10 percent cut and run.

I began exploring the idea of doing some television. I did an appearance on *Milton Berle* and a mystery guest spot on *What's My Line?* The show paid a five-hundred-dollar contribution to your favorite charity for appearing, which in my case was the foundation that had been set up to teach blind children how to swim. When William Morris took 10 percent of that five hundred dollars, I picked up the phone and called their comptroller, Morris Stoller.

"The agency must be really hard up, Morris," I said, "to take fifty dollars from a blind baby. Aren't you ashamed? Send them a fifty-dollar donation to make up for it." Stoller refused, pleading company policy, thus proving (once again) that agents have no shame whatsoever.

I was also paying more attention to our "Mermaid Tycoon" businesses, because the money was disappearing fast. The Trails Corporation was our business entity that owned The Trails restaurant. Even though business at the restaurant was doing well, through Ben's mismanagement it had racked up some sizable loss-carry-forwards.

In the middle of this financial turmoil, a London-based organization approached Ben about the possibility of producing a water show at Wembley Arena, outside of London, similar to the Billy Rose Aquacades. Ben approached me with the idea. I had some grave doubts. The idea of London with Ben seemed out of the question. The terrain was all too familiar. I told him to bring the deal to Abe Lastvogel, the head of William Morris whom I could trust to set it up honestly, less ten percent of course. Abe sparked to the idea and took it to Pat Weaver, then head of NBC. I flew into New York to meet with Pat who was ecstatic about the idea. He suggested that Ben produce, I would star, and NBC would bring the show to New York after London, and if things went well, we would then tour the country, with a grand opening in Toronto, Canada. It would be much like the old Sonja Henie Ice Shows. I was eager to capitalize on my image as the "Million Dollar Mermaid." I knew that there would never be another series of aquamusical films, and if by some chance there were, I would no longer be the gorgeous swimmer of twenty. Let's face it, no one loves a middle-aged mermaid.

I was very nervous about Ben producing. I couldn't handle any more broken promises, any more nights on the bathroom floor. However, I knew the show had the potential to make some real money, and given our situation at the restaurant, we needed it. We could designate The Trails Corporation as the producing entity, thus being able to check off the profits against the loss-carry-forward of the restaurant. Before I agreed to go ahead, I had NBC put a clause in the contract that stipulated that if for any reason I felt I needed to cancel the tour, I alone could make that decision. I was hedging my bet more against a husband who might leave me at the sight of the nearest pub than against a difficult network. All I had to do was to notify the network before we opened in Toronto. It was an exit clause for me.

Did I think Ben and I could make a success of this? What was I imagining!

Ambitiously, we designed a show that would duplicate many of the sensational musical numbers from my movies, complete with two hundred swimmers and dancers. We were scheduled to open in London on August 9 in the gigantic, ten-thousand-seat Wembley Arena. We would rehearse in Los Angeles and work out the knots overseas. As we planned to tour the show afterward, everything was designed to be movable. There was a vinyl pool with an aluminum structure, ramps for the dancers and swimmers, and a wooden stage. Ben designed a portable ski arm that would thrust out across the pool for a swimming number from *Easy to Love*. It all broke down into Erector set modules, which could be loaded onto flatbed trucks for transport. Key members of the cast and crew would travel with the show and we would pick up other dancers and swimmers from town to town as we needed them.

Ben and I packed up all the kids, Jane Boyd, and Melvin Pumpfry and left for England.

In London we had leased an estate in Saint John's Wood for the run of the show, a gorgeous three-story mansion with beautiful oil paintings, elegant furnishings, and a resident maid and butler. The house overlooked a tube station on the main line to London, and I recall looking out of my bathroom in those early, gray London mornings (I don't think it ever stopped raining that summer), watching people politely filing into the tube station, and thinking what a contrast it was to the mobs shoving each other in New York City.

The grounds were manicured in the English style. Ben, who had continued to drink, would sometimes wander unsteadily around the garden of this mansion, glass in hand, peering in the windows like some kind of inebriated Peeping Tom.

I was relieved when my parents arrived in London at the end of the tour of Europe I'd given them as a present. I was very glad they were able to stay in the house with us instead of a hotel, since it meant I wasn't the only grown-up in the family. I especially welcomed the comforting, down-to-earth presence of my mother. Because the emotional load I was carrying was pretty heavy, I needed someone to talk to about it.

Once we began performing at Wembley, I realized how precarious the set was. It had to be carefully monitored so that each set piece would not loosen from the previous performance. Each nut and bolt was to be checked. Ben was in charge. The most dangerous part was the wooden stage, which was screwed into the aluminum supports. The danger signals were everywhere. Preceding one of my big swim sequences was a troupe of acrobats who balanced on one another's shoulders in a human tower, then jumped down and bounded across the stage. As soon as they were done, Ben was to send out the stagehands to check the stage since the bouncing worked the screws out of their holes. This was a task that was to be performed every day at every performance.

During our last matinee at Wembley, I was doing my stage routine with two male dancers just before I dove into the pool. The boys lifted me, then set me down so I could run. I was barefoot, of course, since I was getting ready to swim, and as they set me down I

pushed off right on top of one of those screws that had been loos-
ened by the acrobats. I tore a huge hole in the bottom of my foot;
blood was spewing everywhere. "Lift me up and carry me to the
top," I told the dancers. "I think the bleeding will stop when I hit the
water."

That was the understatement of all time. When the heavily chem-
icalized pool water rushed into that wound, the pain was so terrible
that I momentarily blacked out on the bottom. Then that same survival instinct that took over when I was about to succumb to the underwater rapture during the making of *Million Dollar Mermaid*
kicked in. "This is what they mean about 'the show must go on,' "
said an insistent voice inside me. I knew I had to get to the surface
and stay in time with the music, but with every kick that huge flap
of skin opened up and all that chlorinated water rushed into the
wound.

I made it through one number, but now there was a real question
of how I was going to get through the rest of the show. One of the
stagehands was resourceful enough to come up with a surgical rubber glove, which kept the loose skin in place over the crater in my
foot. It hurt like hell, and it looked like I had five condoms dangling
from the ends of my toes. After the matinee was over they called an
ambulance and got me to the hospital, where they taped up my foot
and gave me a shot of cortisone so I could perform in the last show
that night. They also gave me a pair of crutches to use for the next
several weeks.

Like the outrigger on Kauai and Busby in the speedboat, it was
another one of those times when I became the victim of someone
else's negligence. In this case that someone was my husband. Ben
was the producer, and he should have been out there checking the
stage. God knows he didn't have much else to do. This was our next-
to-last show in London, and he surely knew that those screws
worked themselves loose during every performance.

Now, however, I had a decision to make. The show was not well
received by the newspapers, despite sell-out houses for the complete
run. The critics invariably compared the live show to my movies and
found it wanting. They were used to seeing an Esther Williams million-dollar smile, close-up, underwater, on a forty-foot-high screen

at their local movie houses. What a disappointment seeing me in the show must have been for them. From any distance in Wembley, my head appeared to be about the size of a floating tennis ball. It could have been anyone in the water. In the days of the Billy Rose Aquacade, no one had as yet seen me on the big screen, so there was no point of comparison.

The response was a disappointment, as was the lack of critical acclaim, although I was used to that by now. Swimming musicals were fun and beautiful to look at and were clearly adored by the public, but they didn't win any Academy Awards.

The contract with NBC stipulated that I had to notify the network three weeks before we were due to open in Toronto. As we got ready to pack up and head for New York, I was hit by waves of anxiety over the prospect of taking this show on tour. I was on crutches with a hole the size of a half dollar in the bottom of my foot, and I kept thinking about all the other things that could go wrong. I spent sleepless nights conjuring up disaster scenarios, with flatbed trucks getting lost, a sea of empty seats in the stands, or drought-induced water rationing that would prohibit us from filling the pool.

I had a continuing nightmare that we couldn't get all the parts to this Erector set structure into New York on time, and then there would be no way to hold the water. No water—no show. I woke up with the dismal picture of an audience looking at this big empty pool. The image was too hopeless for words. Once again, being the star gave me more responsibility, not less, and I felt the weight of the expectations of the two hundred dancers and swimmers who were doing the show and depending on me for a paycheck.

That was another sore subject. The dancers had come to me complaining that Ben wasn't paying them regularly. I had no idea whether he was skimming the money or just careless, but a few weeks earlier I'd had to ask Sonny Howe, my assistant choreographer, to handle the payroll. I know the feelings of hostility when people don't get their money on time, and there was no way I could juggle that task along with all the rest.

Ben was lost in the bottom of his martini glass. I couldn't get rid of this sick feeling in the pit of my stomach that this tour was going to be the worst mistake I would ever make. In desperation, I had called the William Morris Agency to request a business manager to help me. The agency, unfortunately, acted as though I was just being demanding. "Your husband is the producer, isn't he?" they responded. "Let him take care of it." I recalled with a bitter sense of irony the manner in which agents are always portrayed in Hollywood movies: guys rushing around solving problems for the star. Where were all those wonderful agents now, I wondered?

At the eleventh hour I called Pat Weaver at NBC and pulled the plug on the tour. I hated to disappoint all those performers who had switched their lives around to be in the show, but my premonition of failure was just too strong. We would not open in Toronto, but we were still committed to do the live TV special in New York. I only had to wait for my foot to heal. I sent my parents home from London with Malvina, and Ben, Jane, the children and I left for New York.

If anything, Ben's behavior was worse in Manhattan than it had been in London. Early in rehearsals, he'd gone into the wardrobe department and found a pair of oversized terry cloth shorts in a bilious chartreuse. He wore them with a loud flowered shirt, a big scarf around his neck, and a baseball cap. He wandered around backstage in this get-up, holding his drink in one hand as if it were another fashion accessory, and in the other hand he sported a large Cuban cigar. It was tough explaining to people that this garish apparition was not only my husband but the producer of the show, and I could no longer tell whether he was behaving this way to spite me or because he thought it was funny or if he just couldn't help it.

For the telecast, I was the host as well as the star, which meant I went back and forth between wet and dry. I had to get out of the pool after doing a swimming number and jump into formal attire to do my part as MC. The evening gown was easy in/easy out, with no niceties like hooks or eyes, just a big industrial zipper up the back. It was the hair that was time-consuming. I brought my hairdresser with me from London to New York. Her name was Norma Friday, and she had a thing about men. She worked her way through the entire backstage crew, going to bed with everybody on the tech roster before the show aired. I asked her once, "Norma, you've got circles under your eyes. What's the problem?"

"No problem, Esther. You like to do what you do, and I like to do what I do, and I'm having fun so just leave me alone."

As long as she pursued her hobby on her own time it was fine by me, so I said, "Well, don't ever just not show up," because she was absolutely essential to getting me out on the stage.

I needed Norma and one other assistant working on me simultaneously to unfasten those "crowbars" that held my braids from the swim number in place and replace them with a tiara. We used a stopwatch during rehearsals, timing how long it took us to make the change—sometimes we were down to seconds. I had a little dressing room with a piece of canvas for privacy, but I had to jump over a bunch of cables just to get to it; so most of the time I changed in the wings. Reasonably private about such things, now I just couldn't care. Often I darted around in the nude just off camera, since I had barely enough time to shed one set of clothes and get into another. Billy Rose should only see me now.

We got through the live broadcast successfully, even though there was one break where I completely missed my change of clothes and had to come out as MC clad in just a towel. Sadly, the end of the show meant it was time to say good-bye to my cast of swimmers and dancers, since the tour was not going to happen. As Sonny and I paid their last checks, all the talking was about the farewell party. I wanted to go, but Sonny told me it would be too depressing. I understood and went sadly back to the Plaza, where Ben and the children and I were staying.

I found him there, passed out again in the hotel room, still wearing the chartreuse shorts. I left the hotel, crossed the street, and limped into Central Park. I was lonely, and the work and the injury had really taken its toll. It had been a terrible summer, and I felt like throwing in the towel. I climbed up on a rock by the lake, and as I sat looking at the beauty of New York at night, I realized I couldn't be married to Ben anymore.

I don't know what time I returned to the hotel. It seemed as if an eternity had passed. The next morning I had Jane take the kids to the park. Ben and I ordered some breakfast and sat alone in the suite; he was nursing a hangover. I looked at this sad creature in front of me, this man who was my husband.

"Ben," I said, trying to see if he could focus clearly on me, "you have to go home." The words were simple and direct; it was my tone of voice that said it all.

"Aren't you coming, too?" he asked, raising his head to look at me.

"Not this time."

"What'll you do?" he said as if he meant both now and forever.

My voice began to break: "I don't know . . ."

"Com'on, Es, we're such a good team. Don't give up on us." He could barely get off the couch.

I began to sob uncontrollably. My thoughts rushed in too quickly. I had no more words; there were only tears. Ben, I thought, How could you ever think of yourself as part of a "team"? You don't really care about me, about us, about the kids, about anything. You couldn't. You never have.

He came over to me and took me in his arms, and I leaned my head on his big shoulder . . . for the last time.

That afternoon I called the travel agent and made a reservation for Ben's return to Los Angeles. As for me, I really didn't know what the next step would be. For the moment, at least, Jane and I would remain in New York with the children. I had to have time to think.

Years ago, when I was still at MGM, Ben and I had gone on a junket to Cuba with Caesar Romero and a group of wealthy MGM investors. Julio Lobo, a wealthy sugar plantation owner, had been our host. These were the pre-Castro days when Fulgencio Batista was still in power. Julio had a magnificent villa on Havana's Veradero Beach. There had been some great parties, and Julio had extended an effusive, open-ended invitation to come back whenever I wanted and to bring my family. I remembered his offer, and right now I needed a refuge, a place to lick my wounds. Julio was ecstatic when I called. "Yes," he said, "you're more than welcome." I packed up the children, and along with Jane Boyd hopped a plane for Havana.

What a relief when I saw that beautiful Cuban plantation and the beach and the turquoise sea. I hungered for a rest and the kids were glad to have their mom to themselves again in whatever my condition. We spent the days horseback riding and swimming. We rode bareback through the fields, chewed sugar cane, and got sunburned on the beach. I was beginning to feel a bit better, but I couldn't shake the immense feelings of failure.

I hired a tutor for the kids, and we stayed through October and November. News was slow filtering in to Cuba from the States; in early December I got word that on Thanksgiving my favorite turkey, Dore Schary, had gotten the ax at MGM. It was too late for me and for the studio, but at least some measure of justice had been served.

One afternoon, the beach boys began boarding up the windows. They said a hurricane was headed for the island. That night, as the wind moaned against the windows, I made sure the house was secure and the kids were safely tucked in and asleep in bed. Then, dressed in slacks and a sweater, I stepped outside. The sky was black—no moon, no stars. The wind began to whip my hair. I strode across the beach and stared at the churning ocean; the roar of the waves drowned out the sound of the approaching hurricane. I stripped off my clothes, and with the wind-driven sand stinging my bare flesh, I plunged into the heaving sea.

All my life I had tried to do my best. I had tried to be strong like Stanton. I had tried to take care of everybody—parents, friends, children, husbands. I had worked hard, done what was demanded of me, saved my money, became a movie star. But it was never good enough. Now almost everything had fallen apart around me, and I didn't know whose fault it was. I was also tired of fighting. Now it was between the sea and me. The sea I could fight. Waves and tides I could fight. If they beat me, if they carried me away, I could accept that. But they would have a fight on their hands. Strong strokes took me straight out, then I turned and rode the waves in as they crashed and foamed against the shore.

I reached the beach and dashed along the sand, propelled by the wind at my back; cutting into the surf again, I knifed into the waves and began swimming again. I went farther out this time, testing my will against the ocean's roar. Then I turned once more and rode the crest of another wave hurtling toward shore. Suddenly I felt a power, a freedom—almost like that felt by that eight-year-old child who so long ago had surfed the waves in Manhattan Beach for the first time in her life. I knew she was still inside me—that child of promise, that child of hope who had taken so much on her strong shoulders.

She could never be beaten; neither could I.

I don't know how long I would have stayed in Cuba, but late in 1956 I got the phone call that brought it all to an end. Ben's father, Benjamin Emmons Gage, had died. I had no idea what was in store for Ben and me, but I thought it was my duty to come home with the children for the funeral; so we packed up and returned to California.

CHAPTER 21

GONE
1957–59

After his father's funeral, Ben and I sat down for a serious talk about how we would deal with what was left of a marriage and the children. His father's death had a sobering effect, but not sobering enough. Although Ben vowed to change, he had no control over keeping his promises. Alcohol had become the most important thing in his life, and his word was only as good as the drink in his hand.

I had contracted to do another film at Universal, *Raw Wind in Eden,* which was scheduled to begin filming in Italy in June of 1957. Jeff Chandler and Carlos Thompson (who had married Lilli Palmer after her divorce from Rex Harrison) were to costar with me. *Raw Wind* was a strange picture, in which I was to play a fashion model who ping-pongs back and forth romantically between Jeff and Carlos. Because this was sort of a "fallen woman" part, the conventional wisdom said that this was more of a Lana Turner movie than an Esther Williams movie. However, they offered me $250,000, which was certainly enough for me to come to a quick decision. I agreed to do the film.

I didn't trust Ben to look after the children while I was in Italy, so

I enrolled Benjie and Kim in summer camp. Susie was just three and a half, so I planned to take her with me. There was a lot to do before I left, including outfitting two active boys with enough clothes for a summer away from home. I headed for the May Company, a local department store, and picked out an assortment of shorts and T-shirts for the boys. When I presented my charge card to pay for the purchase, however, the credit department called down and said, "Would you mind coming upstairs?"

"Yes, I mind!" I said with exasperation. "I have a lot of shopping to do." I had no intention of getting into an elevator and cooling my heels in line at the credit department. Movie stars get kind of testy at things like that, and besides, I was certain it was some kind of screw-up on their part. I had no credit problems. I was financially very secure.

When they insisted, I finally went upstairs. They told me that I couldn't charge anything anymore because my bill hadn't been paid for two years. I was stunned. "What do you mean, my bills aren't paid? My bookkeepers have been taking care of my bills for years. Do you know who I am?"

"Yes, we do, Miss Williams. Your bookkeepers may have taken care of your bills, but not at the May Company. Your card was cancelled last year."

I was silent. I left the May Company in a daze. I ran home and began phoning other stores where I had charge accounts. Saks, Bullocks, I. Magnin—none of my department store accounts had been paid.

If that were not enough, I got a call from my brother-in-law, Bob Sherwood, who was married to my sister June.

"Esther, what time is the meeting?"

"What meeting, Bob?"

"The creditors' meeting . . . you mean you don't know about it?"

"Tell me more."

"For the creditors of The Trails. I'm still owed for the menus I printed."

"Ben never paid you for them? Why doesn't he just write you a check?"

"Doesn't Ben tell you anything? Esther, The Trails is bankrupt. We've all been asked to settle for twenty cents on the dollar for what the restaurant owes us."

First I was denied credit to buy the children clothes for summer camp, and now this. Like a sleepwalker, I had drifted deeply into debt without knowing it. I phoned our accountants and was waiting for an answer when I got a call from Santa Monica Hospital. A patient named Al Scarcella was asking for me.

Ben had two bookkeepers. One was Joe Baldecchi; the other was Al Scarcella. The two of them took care of the books for The Trails and the rest of the "Mermaid Tycoon" businesses and all our personal bills. Al had a beat-up little airplane that he kept at Santa Monica Airport. Al was a smoker, and he did something that everyone knows not to do—he lit a cigarette while he was working on the plane. Somehow he had ignited his gasoline-soaked overalls, and he became a flaming torch.

I hurried over to the hospital, terrified of what I would see. I liked Al, a sweet Italian fellow who had always struck me as a bit sad. I entered his room, fearing the worst. What I found was more horrible than anyone could possibly imagine. All the skin was burned away from his face—his cranium and skeletal mask were completely exposed.

He was like a cinder, and now this cinder began to speak to me in a very hoarse whisper. "Esther, I have to talk to you. I have to tell you what's going on." He managed to wave the nurse out of the room, and with me holding his burned, bony, blackened hand, he continued, "I'm so ashamed that I. . . ."

I knew I was hearing his last words. He was burned over 85 percent of his body, and there was no way he could survive what had happened to him. He said, "We've been terrible to you. We've betrayed you. We've stolen from you and played with your money as if it was Monopoly money . . . and it's gone. I have to tell you . . ." Al knew that Ben was gambling. He knew that he was going to the racetrack every day, and he knew what he and Ben and Joe Baldecchi had done to cover it up. A few hours later, the hospital called me to say that Al had died.

Al's deathbed confession overcame any lingering notions I had about my staying with Ben for the good of the children. Ben had obviously squandered my future and the children's future to gratify his addictions, but I still had only the barest outline of what had happened. I had to figure some means to get the truth out of him, a way in which there could be no evasions, no lying, and no backpedaling. I called my attorney Paul Ziffrin, and Morris Stoller, head comptroller at William Morris, to set up a showdown. Armed with Al's disclosures, I asked Paul to interrogate Ben, just as if he were on the witness stand, until he divulged what happened to the money and where it all went. As hard as I knew it would be, I was prepared to sit there until he told the whole story.

The day of the meeting, Ben came in blithely cracking jokes, behaving as if he hadn't a worry in the world. He had no idea what all of this was about. I hadn't mentioned anything to him about the creditors' meeting or my embarrassment at the May Company. As planned, Paul began interrogating him about the finances. It was terrible. It was terrible to see him lying and being evasive, because he'd been caught off guard and didn't have anything made up in advance. Paul just kept hammering at him, and Ben couldn't invent new lies fast enough to keep them all straight.

Eventually he confessed that he had lost something like $250,000 on the restaurant. He'd also made a series of bad investments and loaned money to a lot of his friends and cronies. Both Al Scarcella and Joe Baldecchi had been treated to a couple of nice vacation junkets at my expense. Ben even owned up to the fact that he'd become a regular at Santa Anita and Hollywood Park. By the time Ziffrin got done with him, he was on the floor. Millions had sifted through his hands. And I was broke.

I was so furious I wouldn't let him see Susie and me off at the airport when we left for Italy. When I said good-bye to him in the doorway of 2077 Mandeville Canyon Road, I was happy to be putting a continent and an ocean between us. I never wanted to see him again.

I was still furious when I arrived in Rome. I felt bleak about everything. I'd been in the movies since 1941, and now I had absolutely nothing to show for it. Nothing. Everything was gone. All the saving and investing and frugal living I'd done, choosing to give up the jewelry and fancy cars to live like a normal person instead of like a movie star, had all been for nothing.

I decided to make up for all that self-sacrifice in one fell swoop. I suddenly went all "movie star." It was ironic—now that I was broke, I decided to live like a diva. I made demands. Clothes became very important to me. I was introduced to Italian couturiers who wanted nothing better than to have Esther Williams wear their latest fashions. They were happy to give me free clothes to wear, just for the promotional value. I had the studio buy me a wardrobe for the movie; then I talked them into letting me keep it. I *had* to have a house on the beach, and I *had* to have a boat take me to location. They found me a wonderful house, right on the Mediterranean, and I commuted to the set by my own private water taxi. The house had no electricity, so they *had* to bring in a generator for me.

I made up my mind that I was going to have a good time and went out to seek it with a vengeance. The studio threw a party to kick off the production, where I met Giorgio. Giorgio Pavoini was an attractive advertising executive whose agency was doing all the promotional work on *Raw Wind*. When I was introduced to him, I did something that I'd never done before. I said, "Giorgio, you don't speak much English and I speak practically no Italian. Let's not even bother talking. Let's just go to your apartment." It was an offer he couldn't refuse, and most of our communication after that was nonverbal.

That was the beginning of a marvelous affair. Giorgio was so *very* Italian, so *very* romantic, and extremely handsome. We'd go speeding down the Autostrada in his Lancia, basking in the glory of the Italian countryside. He was a wonderful dancer, and we went places in Rome that I never would have known about because it was his city.

Meanwhile, on the set my costar Jeff Chandler clearly was very attracted to me and told me so. Jeff was six feet five with strong features and distinctive curly gray hair. He was a good actor who had developed something of the same typecasting problem I had. I had been pigeonholed in swimming musicals; he was stuck in westerns and action/adventure movies, often as an Indian (no one knew to say "Native American" yet). His most successful film had been *Broken Arrow*, in which he played Cochise. The portrayal brought him an Oscar nomination, and for what it's worth, you could say he really owned the role. He was cast as Cochise in two more films after that. In a way, we arrived in Italy like two of a kind. Jeff's marriage to his wife, Marge, was already shaky, and both of us were trying to escape the ironclad typecasting box that Hollywood had stuck us in.

So now I had this delicious problem. Two men were vying to put their heads on my pillow, and sometimes it was a little awkward. When I finished my work on the set, Giorgio was often waiting for me at the beach house. This was fine until Jeff would tell me he was coming by. I was juggling these two gorgeous guys at night, and then getting up in the morning and going to work. It was a great boost to the ego. Although I arrived in Italy feeling as if life had kicked me in the teeth, my situation quickly took a turn for the better, or so it seemed. Suddenly, I was an American movie star living the glamorous life in Europe, wearing gorgeous designer clothes, making love passionately and often. I was so ready for that, to be treated like a prima donna and be so ardently pursued. It helped ease a lot of the pain.

It never occurred to me at the time that I was drifting dangerously close to the kind of lifestyle at which I had cast a jaundiced eye during my early years in Hollywood—the carryings-on of Lana Turner, Marlene Dietrich, and so many others. Or if it did occur to me, I didn't dwell on it. Nor did I worry very much that my personal life had become as different as it could be from my All-American screen image.

After the film had wrapped, Giorgio took me to luncheon at the Palazzo, then the hottest restaurant in Rome. It had been Mussolini's house during the war. I was feeling very chic and a bit *La Dolce Vita* in my Italian couture clothing. I liked Giorgio, and I loved the exciting, sweep-you-off-your-feet romantic streak in him. He followed me to the Venice Film Festival and filled my room with flowers. He spent a great deal of his time traveling about with the Beautiful People. He certainly didn't appear to have to work for a living. I thought it would be wonderful to be part of the jet set with him, head off to Acapulco for the season, and stay at Merle Oberon's villa there.

Over luncheon at the Palazzo, however, he told me that his wife had just called. She'd been sent to a sanitarium after having a nervous breakdown and had threatened suicide. Suddenly it was like coming back from Mount Olympus to ground zero. I had this little pang—more than a little pang, actually—wondering what this jet-setter was going to do with me and my three American children. When I conjured up the absurd image of Benjie, Kim, and Susie lolling poolside at Merle's villa, I realized that this self-indulgent life was not me at all. Italian lovers are wonderful for a summer affair, but reality intruded on my grand fantasy.

With the filming concluded, it was time for Susie and me to go home. Despite my hectic schedule of assignations, this had been a wonderful summer for her, too. She finally had lots of quality time with Mom, carriage rides in the park, and plenty of days at the beach. We booked passage on the farewell voyage of the *Ile de France*. It was a lavishly decorated art deco ship, and I spent considerable amounts of time on its stairways, running up to the radio room. In those days that was the only place a passenger could receive phone calls, and I had Giorgio calling me from Italy and Jeff calling me from New York.

On board a luxury liner, we all "dressed" for dinner, and one of my suitors was sending me orchids every day to wear with my evening clothes to dinner. Lavender, white, cymbidium . . . sometimes a whole spray to wear in my hair. The extravagant flowers were very glamorous and it made me feel quite desirable. I thought that things must be a little jumbled at the shipboard florist, because I never could find a card to determine whether the orchids were from Jeff or Giorgio.

Jeff had left Italy a few weeks ahead of me, declaring his undying love. He promised to meet me in New York to pick up where we'd left off. He knew all about Giorgio and was just waiting for it to blow over. "What're you doing with that rhinestone, when I'm the real thing?" he asked me. "I'm going to be waiting on your doorstep when you come home and we're getting married." I had been deliberately noncommittal toward Jeff during my double summer idyll with him and Giorgio. However, I had no doubt that his offer of marriage was sincere, and it was beginning to sound pretty good as I looked into the future. He had already told Marge that he wanted a divorce.

By the time I reached New York, the only piece of the "Mermaid

Tycoon" empire that was still standing was the Esther Williams swimming pool business. Don Preuss, the entrepreneur who had started marketing "Esther Williams" aluminum above-ground backyard swimming pools, was planning a big publicity event in connection with my return to the States. Don was selling franchises to install and service these pools. For two hundred thousand dollars, a new distributor received exclusive rights to a particular sales territory, basic inventory, plus training on installation and service. He also received a free promotional visit from me—or so I thought. Only later did I discover that Don was gouging the franchisees another five thousand dollars for the pleasure of my company on these junkets and pocketing the fee. I was killing myself traveling around the country, whistle-stopping from one middle-sized town to another, counting on the goodwill my trip would generate to boost sales. But Don was making me a mercenary in their eyes, and with each visit the distributors were gritting their teeth because they'd paid through the nose.

Don may have been the ultimate con man (after he'd skimmed all the profits he could from the swimming pool business, he went straight into electric toothbrushes), but he certainly had a knack for PR. He'd arranged press coverage of my return from Italy and was ready to greet me with a load of photographers on a tugboat in New York Harbor as we came into port. As I got onto the tug, there was a sign behind me saying WELCOME HOME, ESTHER and a big cake and . . . wait a minute . . . who's that standing behind Don?

It was Ben.

I could hardly believe what I was seeing. I didn't want to see him, and most of all I didn't want him acting as if everything was all right between us, especially since there had been all kinds of items in the gossip columns about my romantic summer in Rome—how I'd ". . . fallen in love under the melon moon." There was a good reason why Italy was the birthplace of the term "paparazzi," and I'd made no particular effort to hide my affairs with either Jeff or Giorgio. I'd pretty much assumed that my behavior would announce to Ben that I wanted nothing more to do with him. (I later discovered that the orchids on the *Ile de France* had been sent by Ben, wasting whatever money he could get his hands on.)

The night I arrived in New York, Jeff Chandler and I had a date to see *West Side Story* together, and I was absolutely flabbergasted when Ben asked me to get him a ticket so he could go with us. I refused. He wanted to tag along, he said, so that "we" could refute all the stories that Hedda Hopper and Louella Parsons had been running about me in Italy. As far as I was concerned, however, the two of us were no longer a "we." I was looking forward to the end of our marriage and already thought of him as my ex-husband.

"Don't you have any pride?" I asked. "Don't you care that maybe I'm serious about Jeff? Aren't you even angry if I tell you that what they said in the papers about me was true? Can you live with that?"

"It doesn't make any difference. Let's not even talk about it."

"Ben, that's impossible—after all I've gone through with you, after what you finally confessed to the lawyers in the William Morris office. I've blatantly enjoyed two other men in Italy all summer . . . and you don't want to talk about it?"

"What time is the curtain?"

The man had no shame. Somehow he scrounged a ticket for himself right next to Jeff and me, and there we sat, a very strange ménage à trois, third row center.

Ben's presence didn't dampen Jeff's ardor at all. Jeff and I did Manhattan together, indoors and out. By the time I left New York near Labor Day, Jeff was totally in love with me, and I was feeling rather warm and fuzzy, despite some inexplicable nagging doubts. In California, I faced financial problems that were even bigger than the ones I'd left behind in June. Ben's financial finagling had generated an IRS audit, and I returned to discover that the federal government had slapped a lien on the house in Mandeville Canyon. I was going to lose it unless I paid the government $750,000. That still sounds like a lot of money today. Forty years ago it was a fortune.

My attorney Lew Goldman arranged a meeting with an Internal Revenue agent to try to work out a settlement. He warned me that I would probably have to sign a collateral agreement promising to pay off the $750,000 in full, little by little, even if it took the rest of my life to do it.

I realized I had no choice. "Who do I meet to talk about it?"

"The agent's name is Walter Wunderlicht."

"You've got to be kidding. Nobody's name is Walter Wunderlicht."

Special Agent Walter Wunderlicht came to Goldman's office, and I figured it couldn't hurt to try a little charm. So I started telling him the whole sorry story of how I'd been so frugal and how my irresponsible husband had thrown it all away. When he started yawning, I asked, "Am I boring you? There was all this money I thought I had in the bank, and now it's gone."

"This shouldn't come as news. It happens all the time with husbands in Hollywood."

"I just didn't think it could happen to me."

"I've seen all your movies. Miss Williams, you should be a millionaire. This is a very tragic story."

And with that, I began to laugh.

"What's so funny?" he asked.

The truth was that there was nothing I could do *but* laugh. What Ben had done to provoke the audit was so dumb it was breathtaking. He hadn't reported my salary for *The Unguarded Moment* to the IRS. It was a move guaranteed to get its attention. He might as well have shot off a gun at the Treasury Department. And now I was looking at the wall. My career in the movies appeared to be over. With nothing on the horizon, I had no idea how I was ever going to repay $750,000 to the government.

I signed the agreement with Wunderlicht. From that point forward, I would be allowed to keep a small percentage of whatever I earned, to be used for living expenses. Everything else went to Uncle Sam.

My separation from Ben became official in November of 1957, and I took a lot of flak from the two gossip queens, Hedda Hopper and Louella Parsons, who couldn't understand why I wanted to break up this deliriously happy marriage. Somehow these harpies, who should have known better, had bought into the fan magazine fairy tale. I got a call from Louella, who scolded me saying, "Esther, how could you do this to Ben? The two of you are just the perfect couple."

Louella should have been able to figure it out better than anybody, because she had a husband who drank even more than Ben. His name was "Docky" Martin, and he really was a physician, even though his hands shook so badly I doubted whether he could actually hold a thermometer. In his early years he'd made a living curing VD in Hollywood hookers. Eventually he became the chief medical officer for 20th Century-Fox. One famous night during a large party at L. B. Mayer's, he passed out under the piano, but when someone started to rouse him, Louella pushed him away, saying, "Don't wake him. He has surgery in the morning and needs his rest!"

Both Hedda and Louella talked to you like they were pals and insinuated that you should confide in them, but you did so at your peril. The memory of what they had written about me while I was in Italy was all too clear, so while Louella was lecturing me about how ungrateful I was, after Ben had made me a rich woman because he was such a terrific businessman and how I owed everything to him, I just bit my tongue and didn't respond.

We separated, and I felt like a free woman and acted like one. I was invited on a date by Clifford Odets, the playwright and screenwriter who had written *Golden Boy* and *The Country Girl*. (He was considerably older than I was.) We went to dinner at Chasen's. He had been depressed because he'd been ill, but he was interesting to be with because he really wanted to talk about life's larger issues. We developed a wonderful rapport very quickly. It had been a long time since I'd had a conversation with a man who was intellectually stimulating.

I think the fact that I had so much zest for life was something he'd been missing and wanted to connect with. As he drove me home, he told me, "I very much want to see you again, Esther. You're good therapy for me. I think spending time with you will help me snap out of this melancholy I seem to be stuck in."

When we got to my front door, there was a box. I opened it and found a fire-scorched black wreath with dead flowers and a black ribbon. A card read: "Happy Anniversary to you. Ben." It was November 25, 1957—what would have been our twelfth wedding anniversary. Maybe Ben thought it was funny—he surely thought almost everything else was a joke—but it was a mean-spirited thing to do when he knew his children were sleeping in the house. What if Susie had found this hideous thing on the doorstep?

I carried it inside, and as I sat with Clifford Odets in my living room, suddenly all the uncried tears came. "You throw it away," Odets told me. "What a cruel man." And the two of us sat on the ottoman in front of the fireplace and tossed the wreath into the flames. Before this I just thought Ben was a big overgrown kid who didn't want any responsibility and had no concept of self-discipline. But Odets was right—he was also a cruel bastard.

As far as the divorce settlement was concerned, I wanted to keep it all as civil as possible. We met for dinner at a little out-of-the-way place on Pacific Coast Highway called the Santa Inez Inn. We sat there having a martini, and I wanted to limit it to one so I wouldn't be talking to somebody who couldn't hear anymore or who was under the table. "I really hope we can do this without any acrimony—the children must come first. . . ." I launched into the little speech I'd prepared, but as I looked at Ben I saw that his eyes were glazed over. He was staring past my ear into space, and I feared that this was going to be tougher on him than I'd previously thought. "Is this hard for you to hear?" I asked.

"Well, actually . . ." Ben's voice trailed off, so I turned around in my chair and followed the direction of his gaze. At a table behind me was Hermes Pan, Fred Astaire's choreographer.

"Ben, are you looking at Hermes in back of me?"

"Yes, I am. I'm a Fred a stare at Hermes Pan." He smiled broadly, very pleased with himself. "Pretty good pun, don't you think?"

"Oh Ben, you've just put the last nail in the coffin!" I'd always hated Ben's dreadful puns, but never more so than now. "Ben, do you have no sense of occasion or are you really stupid? Here we are, talking about the future of our children, and you are playing word games?" I was granted an interlocutory decree on April 8, 1958.

We had to work out the details. I received custody of the children; back then that was almost automatic. It was the money—or the lack of it—that was at issue. We owed $750,000 to the IRS. I gave Ben $75,000 in cash from my salary for *Raw Wind in Eden*, which I had stashed in an Italian bank. The price for freedom had jumped. Leonard had been only $1,500. Whatever had prompted Ben to send that wreath was still bottled up inside him, and I was afraid that he would lash out at me publicly, especially if he saw some way to make money from the tabloids. It would get ugly fast if he decided to spew forth about my "wanton ways" in Italy, and how now *he* had to divorce *me*. Our collateral agreement stipulated that he would not do an unauthorized biography, and that he would not talk to the press. Consistent with Ben's lack of reality, he got some friends to shill the $75,000 as a down payment on a marble quarry in Yucca Valley, a business in which he had no experience whatsoever, and it was gone in two months.

This was a rough time emotionally for the children, and for me as well. I felt very vulnerable and exposed, and although I didn't want to be married to Ben any more, I continually wrestled with my guilt feelings over what the divorce would do to the children. I tried psychotherapy, which didn't help much, and I don't think it was really my fault. I'd pour out my innermost soul, and the analyst would say, "I can't believe Esther Williams is in this room talking to me." It was as if I were making a fifty-minute celebrity appearance before an audience of one and paying for the privilege.

The night before my final court date I meditated a bit before I went to sleep, in the hope that my dreams would give me insight into what to say. I'd done the same thing in 1944, when I went before the judge to divorce Leonard Kovner. When I woke up the next morning, the words had come to me. When Judge Orlando H. Rhodes of the Santa Monica Municipal Court asked me the reason why I was seeking a divorce, I told him, "Your honor, I'm really tired of being what my husband does for a living."

The divorce was granted on April 20, 1959.

He banged the gavel and said, "Divorce granted on the grounds of mental cruelty."

I was single again, and at a crossroads in my life. I was deeply in debt, with a career on the ropes, and I had three small children I was going to have to nurture and support. It was at this time that I read about Cary Grant's use of LSD under a doctor's supervision, and how it had given new direction to his life. A new direction was exactly what I needed, so I gave him a call.

That phone call led to the LSD session I had with Cary's doctor. It was then, under LSD that I understood for the first time that at the age of eight, I'd taken on the mantle of the oldest son after my brother Stanton died, that I had to become strong and responsible for my siblings and parents, and then by extension for whatever life or fate brought my way.

There was another issue that I had not faced, and perhaps it was a part of the desperate need I felt for answers. No matter how many times he asked me to marry him, I didn't understand why I always said no to Jeff Chandler. We were perfect together in many ways. He loved me passionately, and I loved him back—with unspoken reservations. One evening, after an especially romantic dinner, he confronted me with painful honesty, "Esther, I love you and you love me. We're both divorced and free. I've told my kids how I feel about you. But every time I ask you to marry me, you turn me down. I don't understand. I want an answer from you."

The truth is that I didn't have one. I looked into his beautiful face and those gorgeous eyes and admitted, "I'm not sure. Give me time and see if I can give you a really honest answer."

I feel so guided all of the time by something within me that knows all the answers if I just ask for them. That night, I closed my eyes and went to that place in me where the truth lies. I call it my center, my Christ center. The next morning, I reached over to Jeff and said, "Jeff, now it's clear to me. This may sound crazy, but I have never known you before. You are a total stranger to me. I've known all of the other men in my life as reincarnations from other lifetimes. But I have never met you before and I need to know you better." It was an admittedly strange, but honest answer.

I may not have known him from other lifetimes, but I knew a lot about Jeff. He was a good-hearted, generous man who treated me with a love and respect I had never experienced before. He was manly and responsible, and sweet with my children. Unlike Leonard, he was proud of his Jewish heritage and respected his family. He was serious, too. He wanted to sweep me into his life and give me everything I had worked so hard for. He wanted to make me his wife and even pay off my debts.

These thoughts filled my mind one night as I prepared another dinner for us. I was downstairs in the kitchen. This was the kitchen of the house that Tony Curtis and Janet Leigh had owned in their early years of marriage, and Jeff had bought it from his friend Tony to be *our* house. I loved it and reveled in that GE kitchen. We had already talked about which rooms the children would stay in and which curtains I wanted to replace.

The house had a big swimming pool, and Jeff was struggling with swimming lessons, racing back and forth in the pool as if he were training for competition. I tried to explain to him that it was too late for him to be a serious swimmer. They would never make those movies anymore. "Well, at least I won't drown," he said. I guess they didn't have pools in Brooklyn when he was growing up.

There were other things about him that were so endearing and so oddly bonding. When he was in the service right after World War II in the Aleutian Islands, he saw me in *Easy to Wed*. Van Johnson's name in that movie was Bill Chandler. Later, when he got a break as an actor in the movies, he changed his name from Ira Grossel. Because he had such a crush on me on the screen (he said that I was his kind of girl—the athletics, the height, everything) and because Bill Chandler got me at the end of that film, he changed his name to Jeff Chandler. Talk about devoted. He told me that after filming *Raw Wind in Eden* with me, he felt just like Van Johnson, he fell so in love with me, and that the only possible ending was marriage.

So there I was in his kitchen, preparing dinner, dressed in a little pink and white, short-skirted sunsuit. I was cooking his favorite meal, chicken cacciatore—we both learned to love Italian food after filming in Tuscany. Suddenly, I realized that he had been upstairs a long time and dinner was ready. So I called, "Jeff." There was no answer. He was upstairs in his huge bedroom and evidently didn't hear me. So I called him again, "Jeff, dinner's ready. Come down and we'll have dinner out on the patio."

"You come up here," he called down.

I knew that tone of voice. It meant that there might be lovemaking instead of dinner. I said, "Okay, I'll be right up."

"Aaaaaaaaaaaaaaaaaaaaaaaaaaaaaaaahhhhhhhhhhhhhhhhhh!"

I froze at the bedroom door and started screaming. I couldn't stop myself. There's a high-pitched scream that you make when you see a mouse. It's a scream that has no logic. It is sheer, uncontrolled panic. I just stood there in the center of the doorway and screamed. It was the kind of scream that doesn't really mean anything. It has one tone to it. It doesn't go into any bars of music. It's not a movie star scream, but the kind you make when your mind shuts down.

Jeff was standing in the middle of the bedroom in a red wig, a flowered chiffon dress, expensive high-heeled shoes, and lots of makeup.

I just kept screaming.

He shouted, "Esther, take it easy! Don't yell!"

I couldn't help myself. I screamed and screamed and screamed with shock and disbelief and refusal to comprehend. While my heart was screaming, part of my brain was calculating the extremes he had gone to for this outfit. This wasn't Kmart clothing. Were those Gucci shoes? I had seen that dress in *Vogue*!

Jeff was terrified by my reaction. "Please, Esther. For God's sake, stop screaming. I beg you."

"Take that off! Take that all off now!" I yelled and started screaming again.

He retreated into his dressing room in a panic and undressed as fast as he could. He threw the wig, the dress, the shoes, the bra, the stockings—*stockings*!—into a heap. I was regaining my composure when I heard him running water at his sink. "Please, come in," he said in a frightened, tentative voice.

I still couldn't believe what I was seeing. "Put some more cream on and get that makeup off, Jeff. You look like Betsy Bloomingdale."

He looked up sheepishly, "She's a very good-looking woman." At least we both laughed.

I wasn't laughing inside. Suddenly, I couldn't make sense of a large piece of my life. Here was my lover—a strong, manly figure by anyone's estimate—who had just been standing before me in high heels and a dress. This was no joke. He enjoyed that kind of thing. He was a cross-dresser.

My head was spinning with questions to ask him, but I knew this wasn't the time to ask them. Jeff was still in shock from my reaction. Suddenly I could see how fragile he was. He had just revealed the most sensitive secret of his life to me, and I hadn't taken it well. To spare me any more upset, he had returned to his more-or-less masculine self, wearing the handsome robe I had bought him in Rome. He *looked* like the man I loved, but I really didn't understand what else was going on.

I had to go to bed with him. I had to see whether his cross-dressing appealed to me in some way I didn't want to admit to myself. I had to see if it was a turn-on for me. We hardly spoke at all that night and, fortunately, Jeff had an early call at Universal for *Thunder in the Sun,* another cowboy movie in which he was starring with Susan Hayward and playing a big rugged trail boss all in leather, on a wagon train. I pretended to be asleep when he left. When I heard the door close, I sat bolt upright, wide awake.

Had it all been a bad dream? I got up and with a sense of fear I went to find out. The closets in his bedroom were all filled with beautiful men's clothing, as I had seen before. I went through this large house, room by room, but it didn't take me long to find what I was looking for.

The room that he had converted to his painting studio, where he kept his canvases and easels, had a large walk-in closet. I opened the door and it was like the designer department at Saks Fifth Avenue. It glowed with wonderful women's suits and dresses and beautiful negligees. The lingerie was from Jewel Park, one of the most expensive shops in Beverly Hills. He had swimsuits in every color. He had foundation garments. He had lots of shoes, and fabulous hats, all on the hat stands that a wardrobe department would use. And wigs, lots of different colors and hairstyles.

Conflicting emotions washed over me. Jeff was dead serious about this dress-up game and obviously had been at it for a long time. The investment in clothes was staggering. I studied the pearls on the hats and had some second thoughts about his fashion sense. I found myself becoming his girlfriend as I inspected this huge wardrobe—a girl with her girlfriend.

I grew uncomfortable being alone in the house with those clothes and drove away to spend a troubled day thinking. When I picked the boys up later from school, I dropped them off with Jane and I went back to Jeff's. He had just returned from the studio and was glad to see me. He admitted that he was afraid he would never see me again after last night's performance. I went in the house only long enough to get some of my things, and I went right out. I didn't want to be in the house anymore—suddenly, it wasn't my house.

I got back in the car and waited for Jeff to join me.

Desperately, he tried to explain the childhood influences that had made him the way he was: a father who had deserted him and his mother; a home in which maleness was held in contempt; a mother and an Aunt Sophie who told him whenever he did anything wrong, "You're just like your father"; two angry women who made a little boy hate his own sex. A compulsion to don Aunt Sophie's underpants, which gave him his first orgasm; growing up and feeling happy and secure only in women's clothing.

I listened to Jeff as sympathetically as I could, but I still couldn't understand where all this left me and our relationship.

"I've been thinking very hard all day long and I have to understand this," I said. "You're going to have to explain to me: When you make love to me, who are you making love to? What roles are we playing in your mind?"

"I'm a beautiful woman making love to a beautiful woman," he said.

"But I wasn't aware that you were a beautiful woman. How was I supposed to come up with that picture?"

"I was hoping that your neuroses would match mine," he said.

"I don't think I have any neuroses that unusual. I like men. And I didn't like seeing you dressed like that."

He sagged and sighed. "Well, I wasn't lucky. Your neuroses didn't match mine."

"Jeff, are you getting help? Are you seeing a therapist?"

"Yes, of course."

I felt a strong intuition and blurted it out: "Your therapist is a cross-dresser, too. Isn't he?"

"How did you know?" he asked in amazement.

"Very convenient," I said. "During therapy you can both sit there in your evening gowns while you are having a therapy session."

"I knew you'd have a sense of humor about this, Esther," he said with a look of hope.

"Jeff, that's not humor. That's bitterness. Twenty-four hours ago I was having happy fantasies about our marriage. You've ruined all that with your little secret. I can't see you again after tonight. It's over between us."

"Why does it bother you so much? Why couldn't you get used to it?" He was pleading. "It makes me feel closer to you."

"Did you dress up like that for your wife? Has she seen you in your dresses?"

"As a matter of fact, yes."

"Why would you want to leave her and try to start all over with somebody who might not like it? You had acceptance from her. I don't know why she didn't mind, but you should have appreciated it."

"Because I love you. I fell madly in love with you!"

"Not enough in love to get rid of the print chiffon," I said cynically.

"That's true," he said with a shrug.

I thought for a moment. "And that's why my bra and panties would disappear sometimes when I stayed overnight. . . ."

"Oh, yes," he admitted. "That was the best turn-on. I would put those on . . ."

"And then you would masturbate. Right?"

"Of course."

"Jeff, you have a secret love life that doesn't include me at all—unless you count my lingerie. I'm just a part of your fantasy. I loved you as a real person, as a man. When you dress up like that, do you know how ridiculous you look?"

"You said I looked like Betsy Bloomingdale, and she looks wonderful."

I couldn't believe what I was hearing. "If you found comfort in that, then I'm sorry. I find your aberration very, very sad. This doesn't work for me at all. I didn't feel anything when you made love to me last night. I didn't think of you as the man in my life. You were a nice matron. I can't be married to a matron."

"Esther, please don't . . ."

He saw what I was holding out to him and began to cry. He had written me some very beautiful love poetry and had told me that if we ever split up for any reason, it was the only thing he wanted back. I was crying, too.

It was a situation I could never have imagined, but I knew I had to leave the house before it became any more emotional. I looked up at him through my tears and said, "Jeff, do you mind if I give you a fashion tip before I leave you forever?"

"What's that?" He smiled a confused smile.

"When I looked in your closet, I saw blouses with polka dots, dresses with polka dots, even hats with big polka dot bows."

"So?" he said.

I opened the car door on my side and looked at him lovingly for the last time. "Jeff, you're too big for polka dots."

It was time to circle the wagons. I gathered my family close around me. Just to get away, I agreed to appear at a big fund-raiser with Jane Russell in Honolulu, and I took the children and my parents with me. I was a basket case. I replayed over and over the three years of my relationship with Jeff. He was such a wonderful lover, a strong masculine presence. I saw him as my husband, a substitute father for my children. This was too hard for me to comprehend. Still I never shared my secret.

Fortunately, work came to my rescue and helped me take my mind off my broken romance. NBC wanted me to do another TV special. A good thing, too, because the IRS's Walter Wunderlicht was always breathing down my neck, and somehow I had to keep chipping away at that $750,000 mountain of debt.

The TV special, *Esther Williams at Cypress Gardens*, played another role in my future as well. By one of those strange turns of fate that reads like a Hollywood movie—almost like an Esther Williams movie—it brought Fernando Lamas back into my life.

CHAPTER 22

THE RETURN OF FERNANDO
1960–1961

*W*hen Pat Weaver, then the head of NBC, approached me about doing a television special, they were hoping to duplicate—or exceed—the very impressive ratings that the live telecast of the Aqua Spectacular from New York had gotten four years earlier. The first thing I told them was that we had to do it at a beautiful, exotic location, and the best place I could think of was Cypress Gardens, Florida, where I'd made both *On an Island With You* and *Easy to Love*. Dick Pope, that little Napoleon, still ran the place as if he owned not just the land but the performers as well—me included. When we were doing *Easy to Love*, he would bring a steady stream of glad-handing visiting firemen to my dressing room, promising them all autographed pictures.

Some quirk in his personality had allowed him to think this made him my friend, so doing the special at Cypress Gardens gave me a chance to make good use of him. I talked him into putting up one of my Esther Williams backyard pools in a meadow, surrounded by all kinds of tropical flowers, so I could have a beautiful backdrop for all the publicity and advertising stills for my swimming pool business. With the name "Cypress Gardens" in the title of the special, I was also able to cajole him into building a beautiful new pool for the show. It was 80 by 165 and cost $500,000—bigger and more expensive than the pool on Stage 30 at MGM. It was so wide that it looked like it flowed right into Lake Eloise. We installed nine big underwater windows in the sides, so the camera could pan the length of the pool and not lose continuity. Pope was counting on the publicity from the show to bring in more tourists. In addition, he planned to make money by leasing out the new pool as a place to shoot commercials, which turned out to be a good move for him.

The commercials in *Esther Williams at Cypress Gardens* are a reminder of how much TV has changed, and how much it has stayed the same. For many years Hugh Downs has been Barbara Walters's avuncular, urbane cohost on ABC's *20/20*, so it's a bit of a jolt to see him hawking beer at the breaks in my special. What he's selling is beer in general—no specific brand. The show was sponsored by the United States Brewers Foundation, and at first they wanted me to be part of the commercial. I was supposed to dive into the pool, retrieve a bottle from an underwater refrigerator, bring it to the surface, and then open it while treading water.

I refused. There would be no refrigerators at the bottom of my pool. For twenty years I'd made being underwater glamorous—a place for beautiful, languorous fantasies, with coral fans and pearls. I wasn't about to wreck that image.

The arm wrestling with the ad agency over the underwater refrigerator went on for some time, but I finally prevailed, in part because NBC gave me carte blanche. I was the producer of the show, so the Brewers Foundation had to settle for Hugh in a bright yellow sport coat, extolling the virtues of a glass of beer on a hot summer evening and reminding the audience to "pour one for your wife, too."

Being the producer also meant that I was responsible for the whole deal. It was impossible to bring the children with me. So I left them once again at home in California with Jane. I couldn't quite trust Ben yet. I was now responsible for coming up with the concept for the script. I had clipped an article from the newspaper about the visit of the Shah of Iran to Cypress Gardens. The Shah had been dazzled by the place and like Ben, my ex-husband, His Royal Highness had ended up in the waterskiing show with a girl on his shoulders. (I guess it's just a guy thing.) This became the inspiration for the script.

The Shah, whom we would call the Prince of Persia, would come to Cypress Gardens with his entourage, where he'd meet Esther Williams, who was putting together (surprise) a swimming show. The network gave me a couple of writers to flesh out my treatment, and they also gave me a director named Alan Handley, who somehow missed the concept of TV as a collaborative medium. When I asked to meet with him, he declined, and sent word back, "I'm sure Miss Williams is a very nice person, but I just can't think of what we'd have to talk about."

I suppose that should have been a tipoff that this would be a difficult relationship. Handley had done a bunch of variety specials on indoor soundstages with dry actors. Handley didn't understand wet. He didn't know where to put the camera for the divers; he didn't know to be low on every shot for people in swimsuits, to make their legs look longer. He had no idea how long swimming numbers took. He couldn't even audition cast members because he couldn't tell who could or could not really swim. However, he had a contract with NBC, and they were firm on their commitment. They wouldn't budge and I wasn't about to take on Pat and the network the way I had Dore Schary and MGM. I needed the Special.

When we got to Florida, Handley just wilted. We started in May, and everything there was 102°—the humidity, the water temperature, and Handley's disposition. I was prepared for it because I'd worked at Cypress Gardens on those two earlier films, but Handley took refuge in his trailer and whined incessantly of heat exhaustion.

By the time we got to July, he was completely discombobulated. He would come to work clad only in boxer shorts. And I had to point out to him that he was exposing himself, and that it was unnerving everybody. If he didn't know his private parts were hanging out, there was no way he was together enough to direct the special. At that point I was already doing most of his work for him, so it wasn't that much more effort to do the rest. I finally put two airmail stamps on his forehead and sent him home.

From then on, everything was my responsibility. I put up a calendar in my little office with one of those Plan Ahe$_{ad}$ signs over it and backed everything up from the August 8 airdate so I could schedule out what had to happen and when—something Handley hadn't bothered to do. Everything had to be finished by August 2; I needed those last six days to edit in Los Angeles. Time was short, and I still had no one to play the Prince of Persia. Those nine big underwater windows that showed how beautifully you swam would also expose anyone who was klutzy. If I had to hold up my leading man, everyone would be able to see it, and there was no room in the schedule for me to teach someone how to be graceful and competent in the water.

I needed someone who could sing *and* swim. I thought of all the leading men I had worked with—Red, Van, Ricardo, Howard Keel, John Bromfield, Peter Lawford, even Jimmy Durante. Not a swimmer in the bunch. And then there was Fernando Lamas, the Argentine swimming champ. I remembered that he had been one of the five fastest men in the world. It was perfect casting—he was handsome, he had a beautiful baritone voice, a charming accent, and that regal princely air about him. He was also rather Persian-looking. In 1960, no one worried about matching an actor's nationality to the part, and at a time when audiences had no problem with Jeff Chandler (who started out in life as Ira Grossel from Brooklyn) as Cochise, passing off Fernando as Persian wasn't a stretch.

I hadn't spoken with him since the making of *Dangerous When Wet,* when he wanted to whisk me off to meet the crowned heads of Europe. The closest I got was when I'd seen him onstage in New York in 1958. I was just back from Italy, and he was appearing on Broadway with Ethel Merman in a musical called *Happy Hunting.* Before the curtain, he sent a provocative note to me in the audience, saying, "Don't leave town without seeing me. I'll clear everything off my calendar if you'll just come backstage." He was still married to Arlene Dahl—how was he going to clear *that* calendar? Fortunately I had a plane to catch. I think I knew that if I'd gone to his dressing room, I never would have made the flight.

Now he was separated from Arlene, and there were eight years of unfinished business between us. I held off his arrival until July 28 so I could get all my other work as star-producer-director out of the

way. I taped all my swimming sequences that didn't involve him before he got there. I guess I was "clearing my calendar," because I
knew he had the power to disrupt the hell out of my routines. He
certainly had during *Dangerous When Wet,* when he offered me his
crotch as a hand warmer on the ride back to the studio from Portuguese Bend. There was no doubt in my mind what was going to
happen when he arrived in Cypress Gardens.

It was time to send for supplies; Plan Ahead applied to my love
life as well as my professional life. I called the pediatrician, Dr. Ray
LaScola, who took care of Benjie, Kim, and Susie. I liked and
trusted him. I said, "You're the only one who's going to understand
why I want you to go into the house and look in my bedroom on the
nightstand near my bed for a round, white box."

"Your diaphragm? . . . Are things getting romantic in Florida?"

"Not yet, but I think I should be prepared."

"Anything else?"

"Well, in my closet there's a tiara on the shelf I'd like to use in the
show."

"Of course."

A few days later, a very festive package arrived for me. Ray had
put the tiara and the little round box into bubble wrap and elabo-
rately gift wrapped the box with a card that said, "Enjoy." Only afterward did I realize he probably assumed I'd be wearing both of
them at the same time.

Fernando arrived as promised on July 28 and came straight to
the set. As always, he looked very smart and dapper, but it seemed to
me that he was a great deal thinner than he had been before, and a
little bit tentative. He plunked himself down beside me and said,
"Come here." He opened his arms and held me very close. "I remember how good you felt, and you feel even better now than you did
then."

"There's less of you now than before," I told him. "What happened?"

"I'm just coming out of a nervous breakdown," he admitted. "But
you're going to make me well. I need the love of a good woman."

"Well, I think I qualify, but we have work to do. Let me show you
what we've been working on, and you can watch while I run
through the number with your stand-in."

"Why don't I do it with you?" His eyes caught mine. "Just tell me what you want . . . and I'll do it." He hadn't been there more than five minutes and the air was already heavy, not just with humidity but with innuendo.

We rehearsed the finale in which we swam to "And This Is My Beloved" from *Kismet*, and it was excruciatingly sexy. The undulating motion of the water gave an intimacy to our most casual moves. As we swam side by side, Fernando pulled me slowly toward him until our lips met and our bodies embraced. I swam away and he caught me by my feet and drew me back, running his hand over my legs. Every time my body went past him, his other hand was underwater caressing me. At one point I more or less coiled myself around him. We were touching each other all over in a way that the censors would not have permitted if we'd been dry.

When the rehearsal ended, I calmed myself down and went back to dealing with the minutiae of production. At the end of the day, I was totally engrossed in giving everybody their call times for the morning until Fernando came up behind me, put his arm around my waist, and whispered, "If you had any class, you'd invite me to dinner."

"Seven-thirty."

"Seven."

"What do you want to eat?"

He undressed me with his eyes before he said, "Loin chops, tender, juicy Loin chops."

I drove to my rented home and warned Melvina that I'd have company that evening. Melvina Pumphrey, who was still with me from MGM, quickly gave the maid the evening off; she wanted no witnesses to what she knew was going to happen. Then she started clearing her throat. Melvina had a nervous tic, and when she got anxious she had a habit of clearing her throat, over and over; I guess her nerves kicked her salivary glands into overdrive. She was quite apprehensive about the arrival of Fernando, because she was afraid I would be out of commission for the duration. She was also aware of Fernando's reputation, and her concern for me was as humorous as it was touching. "Don't burn the lamb chops," I warned her.

Fernando arrived on time. He wore blue jeans as I did, but I don't think we said more than ten words before those jeans were off both of us and we retired to the bedroom. While Fernando and I were in the throes of passion I could hear Melvina ahem-ing compulsively in the hallway outside the bedroom door . . . "The lamb chops are ready . . ."

A bit later she tried again, "Ahem . . . ahemahemahem . . . the lamb chops are burned . . ."

And finally, "Ahem . . . ahemahemahemahemahem. Ah—Ah—I'll just throw them out."

We never did have dinner that night, and I don't remember that we slept much either. We consummated this long-promised some-thing—this chemistry that had existed between us for so long. The sex was a thrilling rollercoaster ride. Fernando certainly lived up to his advance billing; God knows he'd had enough practice to have earned a black belt in the bedroom arts. What was surprising was that between passionate sessions of lovemaking, we got into these very deep conversations. I could sense that there had been a tremen-dous change in him. Eight years earlier he was a suave Casanova—charismatic, glib, and confident, but absolutely untrustworthy as a partner. Back then he was sure that every new romantic conquest was a notch in his gunbelt. Now he was more mature and not quite so sure of himself, which added an appealing vulnerability to his Latin-lover facade.

His marriage to Arlene had been a disaster, although it had pro-duced a son, Lorenzo, now two years old. The quick affairs he'd al-ways fallen into were no longer satisfying, and he was finally bored with the kind of women who could be bedded on a first date. His movie career was in disarray. He'd gone five years without making a picture after *Rose Marie*, which came out in 1955, until *The Girl Rush* earlier in 1960, which had bombed. He was now forty-five years old, and he faced the prospect of having to reinvent himself, both personally and professionally. He'd long suffered from chronic back trouble and had been foolish enough to take painkillers and then get behind the wheel of his car. He then drove into a wall at the Bel Air Hotel. After the accident, Fernando's doctor, Omar Farid, had introduced him to Science of Mind, the same set of teachings that I'd grown up with.

My training in Science of Mind had begun with my mother. She took me to a different church every Sunday, and she encouraged me to question the minister afterward when he stood at the door shaking hands as people were leaving. If I didn't get an answer or didn't like the answer I got, we didn't go back. We went to "conventional" Protestant churches, but she also took me to black gospel churches in Crenshaw and Holy Roller Baptist revivals in Long Beach. Science of Mind was the cornerstone of my mother's commonsense psychology, which I found both comforting and helpful whenever I faced problems of my own.

Where Fernando's gothic Catholicism had failed him, Science of Mind offered him a framework for reexamining his life, and a way to begin pulling himself out of the psychological trough he'd fallen into. It also provided some basis for the meeting of our minds, not just our bodies. Sometime that night I asked him to tell me about how he got the way he was. It didn't all come out at once, but the more I listened, the more amazed I was that he was not confined to an institution.

He was born in Buenos Aires in 1916, but both of his parents were from Spain. His father was from Galicia in the north. There were a lot of Celts in that area, and Fernando had that angular, wiry look that was almost more Scottish than Hispanic. His mother was from Córdoba in the south, an area with a pronounced Moorish influence, and it was from his mother that he got all that passion. They had emigrated to Argentina, but both of them had died when he was very young.

Fernando was raised by his two grandmothers; his paternal grandmother, Carmen, was a matriarch. She had lived in a big house in town, where Fernando grew up with three aunts and an uncle living under the same roof. They all deferred to her. Carmen was a force to be reckoned with, and she had a will of iron. She was also a screamer and yelled at her little grandson—and indeed at everyone else in the household. There was a great deal of bowing and scraping and walking on eggshells in that home, just to keep Carmen's feathers from being ruffled. Everyone was frightened of her, and no one wanted to set off one of her tantrums.

Fernando was a clever little boy, however, and learned to manipulate her at an early age. Carmen's house was filled with valuable antiques, and when she'd start on one of her screaming jags, he'd pick up a ceramic heirloom and threaten to drop it if she didn't shut up. It was the only means he had to defend himself from her wrath.

Fernando's maternal grandmother, Generosa, was as loving and generous as her name and lived in a little cottage by the El Tigre River, where she made hats. He visited her on weekends. Generosa encouraged him to swim and then to swim competitively. She herself couldn't swim, but she wanted him to learn; so she tied one end of a rope around her waist and the other end around his waist and walked along the river bank while he went into the water. On Friday nights when school was let out for the weekend, Fernando's heart would soar because he could head for that little cottage, but on Sunday evenings a black depression descended as time drew near to go back to Carmen. This weekend pattern of light and dark mood swings was so powerful that it followed Fernando into adulthood, long after both women were dead.

Carmen wasn't simply mean and vindictive. When Fernando finally told me what she did to him when he was twelve, I came to the conclusion that she was certifiably insane. The Lamas family mausoleum was located in the heart of Buenos Aires, in the same cemetery where Evita Perón was eventually buried. After a certain number of deaths in the family, the tomb was full, and the people who ran the cemetery approached Carmen and told her it was time to make more room, which they did by removing the dead from their caskets and cremating them. Carmen had decided that Fernando's parents were to be cremated. She forced him to go to the crypt and be present when they opened the coffins, since a family member had to identify the remains.

It was ghastly, of course. Fernando's mother had died just eight years earlier, and he still had a strong memory of how beautiful she'd been. When they opened her casket, there was this grisly skull, with the white hair that had continued to grow. Then they opened his father's coffin. Since he'd died when Fernando was just a year old, he had no real memory of his father until now. The adolescent Fernando ran screaming from the cemetery, fleeing that place of death and the hideous visions of his skeletal parents. The indelible horror of that day haunted him for life. Even as a grown man, he told me he could be talking to someone at a cocktail party, when suddenly the skeleton inside that person's head was all he could see. These gruesome X-ray images never went away; he just got used to them.

So here was this man who was, for all his bravado, obviously damaged goods. Behind that Latin-lover facade was a needy child, and what he needed was love. I had always had a strong maternal, nurturing side. I could just picture that little boy and what he had lived through—I was no stranger to childhood wounds—and I wanted to reach out and be what he needed me to be. In addition, of course, I had always found Fernando magnetically attractive. Now, I thought, it would be exciting to be with someone who was that handsome, that interesting, and who had troubles I felt I could deal with. I needed Fernando Lamas as much as he needed me. At some level, "trouble" had a hold on me. I was attracted to difficult men, knowing deep in my heart that there was always a price to pay.

Sometimes in relationships you get married before you ever go to a church and say the words in front of somebody. That first night a kind of commitment was made by both of us. When he told me, "I need the love of a good woman," I knew it was me he was talking about. I've always believed in the healing power of love, and I took him on as a reclamation project, confident that if I just loved him enough, he would become well. From that point on, I began my job of trying to heal the needy boy within. Sisyphus had it easier than I did.

As soon as we returned, I dove into the editing process to get *Esther Williams at Cypress Gardens* ready to air. Fernando, who had already developed a leaning toward directing, jumped right in to help. Editing arguments about which takes to use and where the cuts should come can be endless, but whenever I had a discussion with the editor, Fernando would say, "The lady told you how she wants it. Don't argue; just get it done."

I also had to face the backwash from the Alan Handley problem. Not surprisingly, he had run whining to the network, and now the NBC execs wanted to hear from me about why I sent him packing. Fernando took on the assignment of protecting my schedule, saying, "Esther has no time to talk to you now; she'll talk to you later," and making it stick. This was an entirely different feeling from having Ben hanging on me when I had worked on previous productions; I carried that alcoholic albatross through the Aqua Spectacular in London and again in New York. All of a sudden I had a bright, strong man who knew the business, wanted to help, and was on my side. We were a team.

Fernando knew how to ask for something and get it. "Tell NBC to give you a big party the night they run the special," he told me.

I felt a bit awkward making the request, but it *was* my birthday; and on August 8 I got not only the party but also a very nice birthday present—a fifty-two share, meaning that more than half of all TV sets in use in the country were tuned in to *Esther Williams at Cypress Gardens*. If NBC had any reservations about the party, they vanished when the ratings came in.

At about the same time, Fernando asked Arlene for a divorce. Predictably, she didn't take it well and vowed to fight tooth and nail. In a strategy session, Fernando and I sat in my rose garden with his lawyer who said, "Arlene is going to sue you for divorce and take everything you got."

"Too late," said Fernando. "As soon as we got back from Florida, I took everything out of the bank. It's all in a numbered account in Switzerland."

Arlene was quite prepared to play the role of the jilted wife and paint me as a homewrecker who had lured Fernando away from his loving spouse and small son. It wasn't that way, of course, but the press had gleefully meted out exactly the same scarlet woman treatment to Elizabeth Taylor a year earlier, when Eddie Fisher had left Debbie Reynolds to marry her.

I offered to let myself be named as corespondent in the divorce proceedings, but Fernando had a better idea. He was going to blame his back trouble on Arlene. He was prepared to say that she was frigid, and that all of his back pains came from grinding away on this unresponsive, undersexed woman.

It was a very daring gambit. Arlene had begun marketing herself as a sex symbol. She was getting involved in the manufacture of negligees and had just posed in *Playboy* wearing one of her diaphanous creations. If Fernando, whose reputation as a virile Latin lover was undisputed, publicly declared that she was a cold fish in bed, it would be very bad for business. The magazines would have a field day.

The ploy worked. As soon as Fernando told Arlene what he planned to do, she withdrew her lawsuit and jumped on a plane for Mexico; in a matter of days the divorce was final.

Fernando rented a little guest house on a large estate on Sunset Boulevard not far from my house in Mandeville Canyon and began to take up space in my life. My bedroom had a sliding door, so it was very easy for him to crawl into my bed at night and leave without seeing the kids in the morning. I assumed at the time that he did this to spare my children the shock of seeing their mother with another man. Only later did I realize that he didn't want to see them. I should have noticed a signpost somewhere along there when I asked him, "Do you like my kids?"

"Am I supposed to?"

"Well, I think of them as my most attractive accessory. I love the feeling of when I've got my two boys and my little girl beside me, don't you?"

"They have no relation to the way I feel about you," he told me. "They've had you for eleven, ten, and six years. I just want you for one year to myself."

I didn't know it then, but he didn't mean one year; he meant one lifetime. This was Fernando's way of letting me know that he had to come first with me, ahead of my children, ahead of everyone.

Fernando was passionate about so many things—he cared about what I did (which was another big difference from Ben, who looked at me as little more than a meal ticket). At a cocktail party if I casually put my hand on the shoulder of a fellow I was talking to, Fernando came over and removed my hand, saying, "You don't touch other men." I wasn't even aware I was touching the guy, and yet it mattered so much to Fernando. It was more than jealousy; it was possessiveness, and compared to Ben it was flattering—at first.

Although my love life was going well, my financial problems continued. While I was in Cypress Gardens I'd been offered a movie called *The Big Show*, which would film in Munich, Germany, in the spring and summer of 1961. Even though I had top billing, I was

only going to be paid one hundred thousand dollars. Had it not been
for Mr. Wunderlicht, my IRS overseer, I probably would have turned
it down, but I needed the money; so I agreed, even though it meant I
had to leave my children during the filming. I put Susie with my sister June, who lived at San Juan Capistrano, and let the boys stay
with Ben out by the marble quarry in the desert community of
Twentynine Palms.

My brother David and his family lived nearby. My sons would see
their cousins every day, and David could monitor Ben. If things
got really bad, he was prepared to step in and bring the boys to live
with him.

Benjie and Kim were old enough now that I thought it was important for them to understand why I had divorced their father; I
probably did too good a job hiding Ben's addictions from them
when they were little.

There was another reason to farm them out that spring. When I
got back from Germany, our home would be gone. The house in
Mandeville was to be sold to pay part of what I owed, and I didn't
want the children to have to be there for that. This way they'd go
away for the summer and then come back in the fall to a new (and
more modest) home.

There were a lot of tears at the airport when I left. I was losing
my house, leaving my children and Fernando behind, and flying to
Germany. As an eighteen-year-old girl, I had seen the war-ravaged
faces of those sweet boys in the veterans' hospitals. I was left with
that permanent image of the devastation wreacked on the world in
World War II.

Even before I left, I already knew that *The Big Show* would be a
second-rate film. The script dealt with an autocratic father who
bosses his sons around. The plot was a rehash—it had already been
made twice, once as *House of Strangers* in 1949, and again as *Broken
Lance* in 1954. This time the setting was a circus family, with Ne-
hemiah Persoff as the patriarch and Cliff Robertson (soon to play
JFK in *PT 109)* as the son I fall in love with. The production company Lippert showed every indication of treating me like a hired
hand, not like a star. My contract guaranteed me the right to make
changes to the script. I gave them nine typewritten pages of revi-

sions, but when I arrived I was told that they weren't going to use them. I complained to the producer and got "so sue me" as a response, and of course I was in no position to do that.

The director, Jim Clark, was a former editor who had made the critically acclaimed *A Dog of Flanders*, about a boy and his dog. Lippert probably hired him because he was so good with animals. As far as actors were concerned, that was another matter. He had everyone in costume and on the set at 7:00 in the morning, regardless of when he needed them or even whether he needed them at all. I sat around all day in full hair and makeup and a cocktail dress, shivering in the tent of the cold, damp Cirque d'Hiver, breathing in the rancid smells of horses, elephants, and bears. I was miserable.

Fernando flew in to lift me out of my gloom, and this time when he offered to take me away from all this, I gratefully agreed. I left the production and headed for Madrid with my Spanish-speaking lover. (Actually Fernando spoke five languages—Spanish, English, Italian, French, and Portuguese—and he could lie to you in every one of them.) We had a great time in Spain and went out to visit Fernando's friends who were working on *El Cid*, with Charlton Heston and Sophia Loren.

Technically I was playing hooky from *The Big Show*, but I wasn't completely irresponsible. I did ask a member of the crew how soon they planned to use me and was assured I wasn't needed for a few days. Nevertheless, they sent the unit manager, Clarence Urist, to Spain to retrieve me. I was in violation of my contract, which meant that they could withhold my salary, unless I was "sick."

We had to make me look like I was at death's door. Fernando wadded up some Kleenex and stuffed them in my cheeks so they looked swollen. Then he put some white makeup on me to give me a deathly pallor. He even made me a "fever blister" out of library paste and a few breadcrumbs. By the time he got done with me, I was a triumph of stagecraft.

When Clarence arrived, he threw a fit because at first Fernando wouldn't let him see me. I'd been throwing up all night, Fernando explained, and was very weak. Finally he admitted Clarence into the darkened hotel room, where I was moaning softly. Dr. Rodrigo Díaz de Vivar was in attendance at my bedside. "She looks terrible," admitted Clarence.

"I know," said Fernando. "We're really worried about her."

"Is it catching, Dr. Díaz?" Clarence asked.

"He doesn't speak much English," replied Fernando.

Dr. Díaz was in fact Luis María Casaras, the assistant director on *El Cid,* and an old pal of Fernando's from Argentina. Rodrigo Díaz de Vivar was El Cid's real name. Luis María spoke perfect English.

"We think Esther has a nasty case of food poisoning from bad paella," Fernando continued gravely, "but we can't be sure. There's also a contagious bug going around. People who get it are vomiting for weeks."

Clarence took two giant steps backward and headed for the doorway. The three men continued their conference in the living room. "What shall I tell them back in Munich?" Clarence asked.

Fernando and the "doctor" had an earnest conversation in Spanish, after which he explained to Clarence, "Well, her physician says she can't fly until she's feeling better, and of course you're not going to want to film her with that blister on her lip. Today is Friday. Monday is the earliest she could make it back to work."

Now Fernando and I had a weekend to play together, but of course as sick as I was supposed to be, I couldn't be seen out and about. I couldn't go to all those marvelous flamenco clubs; I was a prisoner in the hotel. However, the room service was good and the company was attentive, and staying in bed with Fernando was a damn sight better than shivering amidst the elephant turds in Munich.

Has anyone ever said to you, be careful of what you wish for? As I got on the plane that Monday to go back to Germany, I started feeling sick for real. By the time we landed in Frankfurt, I had a high fever and the terminal was spinning. I was so ill that all I wanted to do was get back to my hotel and climb in bed.

The hotel in Munich where we were staying had a very pompous night manager who was on duty when I returned. To my surprise, he wouldn't let me into my room. Even though I could barely stand up, I tried to reason with him. "But . . . but . . . all my things are still in my suite."

"Not any more, Fräulein Villiams."

The night manager had taken it upon himself to remove every-thing from my room, put it in boxes, and stash it in the basement. "Nobody notified us that Fräulein Villiams was going away for the weekend. The policy of the hotel is that you must notify us if you are going to be out." Essentially they had thrown me out on the street because I hadn't kept them informed of my movements.

And they said the Gestapo was dead.

The production company found me another hotel, but the old one refused to release my baggage until they were paid for the three days that I was in Spain. By this time I was trembling and throwing up. The company found me a doctor—a real one this time—who di-agnosed me with a case of amoebic dysentery. Served me right, I guess, for telling my fib. I took the vile green liquid he prescribed and eventually felt well enough to continue shooting.

I was weak but better when Fernando arrived from Spain. "I'm moving in," he announced.

"Of course you are," I said. "I'm not surprised."

"I really think it's time for us to get serious about each other," he said, "but there is something I have to ask you."

"What is it?"

"Do you think you could stop being Esther Williams?"

CHAPTER 23

ESTHER LAMAS
1961–1964

"Yeah, I think I could stop being Esther Williams," I said. "But can you stop fucking around?"

"For you, Esther, I suppose I could do that." After a pause, he added, "Anyhow, I'm getting a little tired," he said, protecting his pride.

"That's good to hear," I said, "because there's only one thing worse than a middle-aged mermaid, and that's a middle-aged Latin lover. But tell me, how do I stop being Esther Williams?"

"Well, you've been on that pedestal for a long time now. I'd like you to get off of it."

I knew him well enough to realize that he wasn't just asking me to give up being a movie star. For Fernando, a pedestal had room for only one person. If I stepped down, there would still be a perfectly good pedestal—one with a vacancy. "Let me see if I understand how this is gonna work," I continued. "I get off the pedestal and put you on it?"

"Exactly. That would make me very happy."

"And from now on, we don't talk about Esther Williams any more. We just talk about Fernando Lamas? Is that the deal?"

"Yes. Precisely . . ." There was a note of surprise in his voice, as if he could not imagine it any other way. "That would make me very happy."

"Well, I guess it would make anybody happy. You know, if I stop being Esther Williams, you don't get any of my perks, like joint photo spreads in the magazines, or other kinds of publicity about how happy we are."

"I don't want you doing publicity. I want you at home."

"So this would be something like a hiatus?"

"No, this would be for good. You will be my wife."

Fernando needed me, and I was at a point in my life where I needed to be needed like that; so there was a kind of symbiosis at work. The other unavoidable fact, however, was that Fernando looked like a port in the storm for me. The IRS had a lien on my five-bedroom house in Mandeville Canyon. The only good thing about losing it was that I wouldn't have Ben hanging around any more. Even after the divorce, I would return home and find him there, pretending to be spending time with the children or even cleaning the pool. Fernando and I would have to find our own place if I were to become his wife.

"If I become your wife, can I show you my bills?" Despite the sale of the house, I still had a mountain of debt, a legacy of Ben's mismanagement.

"Sure, but I'm not going to pay them."

I had been Esther Williams for about thirty-seven years by this time, and my career was in the doldrums. After I finished this not very good movie in Germany, I was seriously considering making something called *The Magic Fountain* in Spain, another no-frills/bad-script independent film. As long as I owed my soul to the IRS, I had to keep working, and although I wasn't exactly in it just for the money, I was no longer burning with ambition. One thing I knew for sure: I would never be a Joan Crawford, wearing a turquoise bird outfit and begging an empty theater not to abandon me.

"Esther Williams, the swimming movie star" was finished. The struggles with Ben and the IRS had used me up. It was time to give that Esther a rest, and the idea of taking care of this man, who was so handsome and had such panache, was much more interesting than the prospect of keeping up the public persona of Esther Williams, Mermaid without Portfolio.

It was time to ask for a dream. I'd found over time that prayer, although very good for quieting my nerves, was not particularly revealing when it came to providing guidance for life choices. My dreams, however, did that for me. Just as I had asked for dreams to tell me what to say to the judges in court when I divorced both Leonard and Ben, that night I asked for a dream to show me how the future would be with Fernando.

The dream was so powerful and so vivid that it woke me up. I wrote it down on the pad I kept by my bedside for exactly that purpose. In it I was riding on a merry-go-round that began to spin out of control. The carousel sped up, and soon it was whirling at a dizzying pace, too fast and very dangerous. You couldn't grab the brass ring, because you'd lose a finger if you tried. I was hanging on to my painted wooden horse for dear life, absolutely terrified, but I knew my hold was slipping and I couldn't hang on much longer.

All around there were huge klieg lights flashing in my eyes, blinding me. I spied a hand reaching up to me from beyond the carousel. It was just like the hand in *Dangerous When Wet*, when I was training for the Channel swim. It was Fernando's hand, and it wore a gold band on the fourth finger, a band that had been his father's ring. The music was too loud to hear if he was saying anything, but the hand was always there and stayed steady. Every time the merry-go-round completed a circle, the hand was there. He beckoned me to take hold, and I reached for it. He caught my hand even as I was falling and pulled me to safety.

In my dream, Fernando led me over to a bench. Suddenly I was away from the bright flashing lights, and as my eyes adjusted I could see the frightened people whizzing by who were still clinging to the carousel. Fernando was holding my hand, and I felt safe and out of danger. Then I looked down and saw that there was a leather strap around my ankle. I was tethered to the bench.

In the morning, there it was written down: what I called a prophecy dream. Marriage to Fernando offered shelter and security, but the shackle was the price I'd pay. Having been in so much danger in my marriage to Ben, the idea of being safe seemed worth the trade-off. And with that, Esther Williams, formerly of MGM and star Dressing Room B, stepped down from her pedestal. For the next twenty-two years, the very safe but very tethered Esther Lamas took her place.

I was to be Fernando's fourth wife. It is curious to consider that but for my old LAAC swimming coach, Aileen Allen, I might have been the first. Fernando was on the Argentine swim team when the Pan American Games took place in Buenos Aires in the spring of 1940, the meet she deliberately kept me from attending by withholding my telegram of invitation.

When I explained to Fernando what had happened with Mrs. Allen, he said, "Let me guess. She probably told you that you'd find a Latin lover and never leave Argentina."

"That's exactly what she said."

"Well, I was waiting. I had seen your picture in the paper. I was looking forward to meeting Esther Williams."

Fernando was older than I was, and in 1940 he was already twenty-five. At the Pan Am Games he would have exuded that same charisma and sex appeal—and that same little-boy neediness—that he still had as a man in his forties. He would have romanced me, and his sophisticated charm would have easily swept the impressionable seventeen-year-old that I was off her feet.

It was okay in 1961 to put Esther Williams aside after I'd been her for so long, but in 1940 I hadn't been her yet. I wouldn't have wanted to meet Fernando Lamas then, because chances are there wouldn't have been an Esther Williams if I had. I'd been livid at the time about not going to the meet, but with the benefit of twenty-one years of hindsight, I realized that Aileen Allen had kept me from almost certain disaster. Had it not been for that intercepted telegram, Fernando probably would have been the first love of my life, and I might have ended up tethered to a kitchen sink in Buenos Aires before I was eighteen.

As it turned out, Fernando's first wife was Perla Mux, "the Argentine Deanna Durbin." She was the mother of his oldest daughter, Cristina. Perla's father was an unrepentant Nazi, and he and Fernando got into such terrible fights that the marriage disintegrated.

Fernando told me he was convinced that his second wife, Lydia

Babacci, a beautiful Uruguayan heiress of Italian descent was a distinct liability in Hollywood. When Lydia had too many drinks she would regale the Beverly Hills dinner crowd with her incendiary political opinions ranging from pro-Communist remarks to an unwavering affection for Mussolini, whom she believed was simply right about everything. In 1950, with the Korean War heating up, Lydia was not a welcomed guest. Fernando, who was very ambitious at MGM, saw that he was saddled with a wife whose inappropriate mouthings could shatter his nascent career in a moment's notice.

It wasn't long before he moved out on Lydia and took up with Lana on the set of *The Merry Widow*. Fernando clearly had his eye on more than his career. That was about as much as Lydia could take. She packed her things and with their six-year-old daughter Alexandra, took the next plane back to South America.

The next wife, of course, was Arlene Dahl, who was the mother of Fernando's only son, Lorenzo. That first night together in Cypress Gardens, he told me that her beauty reminded him of the mother he had lost. He described Arlene as a chameleon, and like so many women of that era, during the dance of courtship she presented herself as everything that her fiancé wanted in a wife, and of course Fernando had quite a bill of particulars he wanted to fill. Once the ring was on her finger, however, the show closed and the curtain came down. Her world revolved around how she looked, her hair, her skin, her complexion, what people said about her—her image.

"You know," I said to Fernando, "I watched the two of you as presenters at the Academy Awards. You reminded me of an 8 x10 glossy photograph of yourselves."

"That was it!" exclaimed Fernando with a gasp of recognition. "For Arlene, being that glossy *was* real life!"

Arlene might as well have been the role model for the original Barbie doll. If Lydia had conflicting thoughts, Fernando felt that Arlene had no thoughts whatsoever. He insisted on giving her a nickname. He called her "paper-head," because, he said, "she has a mind like a paper hat." I never understood the name. It must have been a direct translation from a Spanish insult. When Fernando was through with somebody, he was through!

On June 18, 1961, while I was still shooting in Munich, the telephone rang in the early morning while we were still in bed and I heard Fernando saying, "That's impossible. Clark Gable died last year!" I knew immediately what was happening in the conversation. Someone was conveying news of the death of a famous American movie star, except it was not the already deceased Clark Gable. It was Jeff Chandler. I understood instantly, because Jeff had been compared so often to Gable. Fernando got the message straightened out from the confused messenger and relayed it to me: Jeff had undergone back surgery the day before, and during the operation, the surgeon had mistakenly cut a major artery. Despite fifty-four blood transfusions, they couldn't save him.

Fernando studied me carefully as I received the news. He knew, of course, that Jeff and I had been lovers. I never told Fernando why I broke up with Jeff. Fertnando would never tolerate the idea that I would show emotion about another man in his presence. I spent the morning alone in my dressing room grieving for that good, lovable man who almost had been my husband. I prayed that Jeff had found peace. I cried into towels so that Fernando would not hear.

After *The Big Show* wrapped in Germany, Fernando and I were off to Spain again with him newly installed on the pedestal and me in the "also starring" role, both in real life and in *The Magic Fountain*. Fernando, of course, not only played the lead in the film, but loved my insisting that he direct as well. Fernando had never directed before; however, he instinctively knew that with me in the movie, there had to be the mandatory swimming sequence. He learned quickly, but this was a stumbling first effort. Still, I could see that there might be a future for him in directing. Directing put his bossy personality to good use, and he always met the deadline. (He did eventually go from *The Magic Fountain* to TV. In TV they don't want it good; they want it Wednesday.) When released, *The Magic Fountain* played around Spain and then, mercifully, disappeared without ever being shown in the United States.

After *The Magic Fountain*, we stayed in Spain, where Fernando renewed old friendships and I escaped reality. As soon as we arrived in Madrid, he made a few phone calls and the word quickly got around that we were in town. In short order we were invited to a rash of parties and barbecues, some of which were given by our new "friends," the family of Spanish dictator Generalissimo Francisco Franco, who entertained lavishly and often.

At Spanish parties, the men sing and recite poetry, and there is always dancing. Fernando was a wonderful raconteur, and of course he still had his magnificent baritone voice. He told stories and sang—he knew all of the most haunting Carlos Gardel tango melodies. Gardel was the troubadour of Argentina and had been the top singing idol of his day, the Argentine equivalent of Elvis or Sinatra. Tragically, he died young in a plane crash at the height of his fame, and like James Dean and Princess Diana, his legend had grown exponentially after his death.

Soon Fernando became the troubadour of Madrid, and we were flooded with invitations. People not only loved him, they loved *whom* he had in tow—Esther Williams, the famous movie star from Hollywood. Within weeks of our arrival, we became astonishingly popular—Fernando and I were the Bogey and Bacall/Taylor and Burton of the smart set in Madrid. It was a new role for me. No one ever had ever known who Leonard or Ben were. I found it terrific to be half of a famous couple.

Since Spain had a fairly rigid social hierarchy, your position in it was determined by your family. Coming from "a good family" counted more than individual ethics or character. People tended to overlook the fact that you were a cretin or a shoplifter if you could rattle off a last name that traced five generations of the family tree (Diego María García de Ramirez de Gonzales de Arellano de Rodriguez y Colón). Movie stars, however, enjoyed an interesting status in that world. The most exclusive social circles opened their doors to us on the basis of fame alone. Our celebrity gave us the right to break the rules and leapfrog into high society. Just plain Esther Williams (de Bula y Lou de Orchard Avenue de Inglewood de MGM y Chlorine) found herself rubbing elbows with government leaders and hobnobbing with royals and bluebloods.

Franco surrounded himself with an exclusive coterie of displaced Spanish royalty. The last king of Spain, Alfonso XIII, had been deposed in 1931 in a prelude to the very nasty Spanish Civil War. Franco was now getting on in years and had made it known that he would designate a member of the royal family to be king when he died. The competition among the potential candidates was intense, as they all jockeyed for position and curried favor with the generalissimo.

I was again grateful for all my finishing school lessons at MGM U, which had taught me enough about manners to be comfortable at these gatherings. At a party given by Franco's daughter, Carmen, and her husband Cristobal, I met Prince Juan Carlos Alfonso Victor María de Borbón and his wife, Princess Sofía, late of Greece. Fernando finally made good on his ten-year-old promise to introduce me to the "crowned heads." Juan Carlos was most anxious to talk to me, having been a swimmer himself. Eventually he became the king of Spain, but at the time he was considered a long shot. He and Sofía were prosperous, but some of the other royals weren't so flush. Many were down to lesser titles, like countess and marquis; worse yet, others were reduced to working for a living. I shook the hand of Prince Simon, the heir apparent to the not-so-apparent throne of Bulgaria, who worked as a teller in a bank.

One afternoon we were guests at Franco's palace for a picnic. Even though my Spanish was virtually nonexistent, everyone wanted to chat with me. They had loved *Escuela de Sirenas* (*Bathing Beauty*) and the rest of my musicals and had seen them so often they could recite dialogue from memory and sing most of the songs. This made it hard not to be Esther Williams—Fernando had plunked me down in the middle of what turned out to be a royal fan club. I knew that being lionized like that was not going to sit well with him, so I withdrew from the group, stretched out on a blanket and pulled a book out of my purse that I'd been wanting to read. It was Ernest Hemingway's *For Whom the Bell Tolls*.

Fernando was all over me like a shot, with something resembling a flying tackle. He snatched the book out of my hand and hid it under the blanket.

"Are you crazy?" he asked with a wild look in his eyes.

"What the hell's the matter with you?" I was clueless.

"Esther, don't you know that this is the most banned book in Spain?"

"Banned? By whom?" I still didn't get it.

"By who do you think? By your host this afternoon!"

I had wanted to read the book because I loved Hemingway and I loved the movie, which had starred Gary Cooper and Ingrid Bergman, who had been so blindingly beautiful together, ignoring the fact that the characters they portrayed were Loyalists who were at war with Franco's *Falangistas*. Hemingway himself had ardently supported the Loyalist cause. He traveled with them and with other antifascist Americans in the Abraham Lincoln Brigade. Despite that, the Loyalists had lost in a bloody civil war. Madrid fell to Franco's forces in March of 1939, and for twenty-three years thereafter the generalissimo had ruled Spain as *el caudillo*.

So what I'd done was no mere faux pas. It was roughly equivalent to pulling out a copy of the Talmud at a Hitler Youth Rally. If anyone else besides Fernando had seen me, we'd have been instant pariahs, and all the movie star celebrity in the world wouldn't have saved us.

If you wanted to see someone who had lost the golden halo that came with Hollywood stardom, all you had to do was look at Ava Gardner, my old MGM friend, who left Hollywood and moved to Spain in the late fifties. She had gone from famous to infamous to notorious and was now regarded as something of a menace to polite society in Madrid. After her much-publicized affair with superstar matador Luis Miguel Dominguín, Ava bought a house in the high-rent district of the capital and busied herself trying to recreate her role as *The Barefoot Contessa* in real life. Ava loved flamenco dancing, and she took up with a hard-drinking group of flamenco entertainers who were a band of Gypsies.

Dominguín probably never got over being in love with her, even after he married a beautiful Italian actress named Lucia Bose. Fernando and I were invited to a party at their home. As always, there was flamenco music and dancing. Suddenly Ava arrived, trailing her entourage of wasted *gitanos*. Obviously they'd all been drinking sangria by the gallon. They also had not been invited. Nevertheless, Ava decided to get up on a table and dance flamenco.

In the early sixties, Spain was still a very conservative country, almost puritanical, in fact. People behaved in a way that was very chaste, reserved, and formal, until they danced flamenco and all that repressed sex burst into the open. Flamenco *is* all about sex. The tops the women wear while dancing accentuate their bosoms, and they throw out their chests to make sure everyone can see how well endowed they are. When a woman takes her scarf, throws it over the head of a man and pulls him to her, it's the signal of a woman in heat who has chosen not just a dancing partner, but a bed partner as well.

Ava was wearing a skirt that revealed everything as she twirled—she was not wearing panties. For our hostess, the sight of her husband's former mistress in her own home, dancing on an ornate antique walnut table, unabashedly exposing herself, was pretty much the last straw. Lucia found Dominguín and said, "Get her out of here."

Like all the other men (and perhaps a little more so), Dominguín was mesmerized by the sight of Ava clapping, rustling her skirt, whirling and stomping her feet to this intensely sensual music. "But she doesn't mean any harm," he protested.

Lucia wasn't having any of it. "Tell her to take that Gypsy army of hers and leave. Throw them out if you have to. But check the jewels before they leave."

My heart went out to Ava and what she had become. I remembered the young Ava who had sat with me at Donna Reed's house, when the three of us were all just starlets taking our classes at MGM. She was the most beautiful girl you ever saw in your life, with naturally curly hair and a perfect figure. She was also the sweetest person you could meet, but she had such low self-esteem for a woman who was considered one of the most beautiful of the MGM roster.

Ava had been one of six children in a loveless sharecropper family in backwoods North Carolina, and it was drummed into her from an early age that she was nothing but poor white trash. For the rest of her life, she tried to live down that condemnation. Despite her beauty, her talent, and a body of work in Hollywood that included *The Sun Also Rises, On the Beach,* and an Oscar nomination for *Mogambo* opposite Clark Gable, there was a kind of infinite sadness about her, as if everything good that came her way was undeserved. It made her easy prey for bad relationships. Donna and I each appeared in an *Andy Hardy* movie with Mickey Rooney, but Ava had actually married him—something I found absolutely unimaginable, at least from a physical viewpoint. Ava told me years later that he was a difficult and arrogant fellow.

That marriage was the first proof of Ava's hypothesis that she and Lana were "the worst pickers of men in Hollywood." I tried to chat with her at the parties at Louis B. Mayer's, but if she was a little tipsy she'd say, "You don't want to talk to me, Esther. I'm just trailer trash." Now here she was, desperately self-destructive and keeping company with a drunken band of Gypsies—the ne plus ultra of trailer trash. Sometimes she would just disappear with them for four or five days. You didn't need a Gypsy's crystal ball to predict that it would end badly.

By comparison, Fernando and I were pillars of the community, even if we were "living in sin." We presented ourselves as man and wife, but we hadn't had either a church or a civil ceremony to make our union official. We kept that to ourselves, of course, Spain being the very straitlaced Catholic country that it was.

Because Carmen and Cristobal had taken a shine to us, we were invited to a lot of grand events. They asked us to be the Guests of Honor at a black tie soiree at the generalissimo's summer palace, but shortly thereafter Cristobal called to inquire whether we would mind if there was a second set of Guests of Honor—the Duke and Duchess of Windsor. I was delighted, since as a teenager I'd followed the story of their romance and his abdication.

We were briefed on protocol before the party. It was imperative that all guests be there when the Windsors arrived, so that everyone could stand and applaud their entrance, and that no one leave before they did. The generalissimo had an ornate theater in the palace, all done in red plush, where we gathered to watch the evening's entertainment. Fernando and I were seated next to the Duke and Duchess of Windsor. Between acts the duchess turned to me and bellowed, "They tell me you're Esther Williams. Is that true?"

Nothing was happening onstage at the time; she didn't have to yell. I always thought she might be deaf, because her whiskey-cigarette voice was like a chainsaw, and now she had the attention of everyone in the theater.

"Yes, I am," I said.

"And you made all those movies in the water."

I nodded respectfully that I did.

"What are you doing now?"

I had anticipated this question. Unlike the royals, for whom being royal *was* what they did, I thought I ought to have some respectable line of work, since I was no longer acting in movies. It didn't seem appropriate to say I'd taken on Fernando as a full-time job. "I'm in the swimming pool business," I said. At this point, the Esther Williams Swimming Pool Company was very successful.

The Duchess nudged the Duke. "Did you hear that, Darling?" she roared.

"Wha? . . . Wha?" stammered the Duke. "What am I supposed to have heard?"

"She makes swimming pools."

You might have thought that there was no way for the Duke *not* to have heard it—all the other guests certainly did. But the Duke had had too much to drink, and the Duchess had only partially rousted him out of his stupor.

"Who does?" The Duke, at this point in the evening, didn't know who *he* was, much less who I was.

"My dear, this lady next to me is a swimmer. She's Esther Williams and she makes swimming pools."

A look of astonishment spread across the plastered face of the former king of England. "I say . . . with a pick and shovel?"

"Well, I don't know about that, but I'm very happy for her, aren't you?"

"I'm happy for all of us," he said, slurring his words. With that, his head dropped to his chest and he passed out cold.

This posed a social difficulty of some considerable proportion, because by protocol none of the other guests could leave until they got the Duke sobered up enough to stand up and walk out under his own power. That was obviously going to take some doing. He wanted to lie down somewhere, and we all figured it was going to be a long night. Finally, the Duchess took him into a bathroom upstairs and emerged with him on her arm. He wasn't steady by any means, but at least he was vertical. "I used your favorite thing," Wally shouted to me proudly, even though I was less than a foot away.

"I beg your pardon?"

"I threw water in his face!" she screamed.

The next day we were rehashing the evening with Franco's son-in-law, Cristobal. "They were working last night," he said of the Windsors, as if that would explain the bizarreness of it all.

"I don't understand."

"When you invite the Duke and Duchess of Windsor to a party, before they will come, you must send them a check for five thousand dollars."

That struck me as a pretty good fee for just showing up for an evening, and whatever their personal scene was, this entertaining royal duo certainly seemed worth the investment. They were the talk of any social event to which they were "invited."

Cristobal and his wife Carmen often invited us to their country house for long weekends. It was one of those places that was both rustic and elegant at the same time. Located near Guadalajara, the house was built overlooking the Pantano, which was a reservoir fed by snowmelt from the mountains. The water was incredibly clear. Fernando and I would swim side by side. No Busby, no cameras, no studio. Just the two of us. The house was one of several within a compound. Franco had declared that only family could build there. All of the guests had separate private cottages around the main house, and each couple had a personal staff of two—a maid for the woman and a valet for the man. They unpacked your suitcase, and even ironed everything. The pure cotton sheets on the regal bed were ironed as well. For the family of el caudillo and their friends, nothing was too good.

The food was extraordinary, both in quality and quantity. It seemed as if we ate all day long: whole fish from the mountain streams, grilled to perfection; huge paellas; salads and breads and flan. And, of course, there was endless pouring of wine with each course. After a meal like that, you could barely keep your eyes open. You weren't supposed to—finally I grasped the concept of the siesta. After stuffing ourselves, Fernando and I would retire to the cottage and make love, then emerge at 7 P.M. when the maid came to announce it was time to eat again.

I just let this Spanish lifestyle flow over me. This was the safety and security that my dream had promised me, together with a great deal of romance and self-indulgence that made it easy to ignore that tether. Besides, I wasn't the only one tethered; all the Spanish wives behaved according to a very strict code of behavior. The women waited on the men hand and foot and never disagreed with them or poked fun at them in public. In exchange for that, they were revered. Fernando was very adoring and loving toward me; there was no other woman in the world for him. He was keeping his part of the bargain, which was not to fool around, and I was keeping mine, which was to be the loyal sidekick and helpmate.

In fact, we were enjoying each other so much that I didn't object when Luis María Casaras suggested that we stage a fake wedding. He was Fernando's old friend from Madrid who had pretended to be the doctor when I was dodging the unit manager from *The Big Show*. We were visiting in Marbella, Spain, and Luis María had a devilish sense of humor. Fernando and I dressed up for a "Just Married" picture and Luis María sent out announcements to various of our friends. Naturally, news of our faux marriage leaked to the newspapers and was published as fact. I would not have married Fernando then, even if he had asked me, which he hadn't. I wanted him to accept my children first, and I wanted them to accept him.

This tension between Fernando and my children hung over our la dolce vita life in Europe. The same thing was wrong with it that was wrong when I thought about becoming a jet-setter with Giorgio in Rome. Despite the flamenco and the princes and the paella and a very happy love life, I missed my children desperately. The boys didn't want to come to Spain. As fledgling adolescents they were involved with Little League and their friends. They were no longer under Ben's care; Fernando had convinced me to enroll them in military school because he thought they lacked "discipline." Funny— that was exactly what I liked about them. At home they were free to be themselves, and if they had an argument with me they were free to speak their minds; that was certainly how I'd been raised. Kim didn't mind the uniforms and the regimentation, but Benjie hated it.

Susie, who was nine, continued living with my sister June and her family at the beach. Just as I made plans to bring her to Spain, Fernando got a call to come to Rome. They needed someone to replace

Edmund Purdom in an Italian period film called *Duella nella' Silla*. We had to leave immediately and the only reservation I could get for Susie on such short notice was to Paris, so Fernando and I packed his Alfa Romeo convertible and drove from Madrid to Le Bourget to pick her up. Fernando put the top down and sang *Rigoletto* at the top of his voice—all of it, even the women's parts. Then he moved on to *Tosca* and *La Traviata, Aida,* and *La Bohème.* He knew them all by heart. I was with someone who loved opera as much as I did.

With Fernando singing all the way, the three of us drove to Milan, where we met up with Fernando's daughter Alexandra, now a teenager, and who Fernando had sent for after I convinced him that she would be good company for my Susie. Fernando hadn't had much contact with her since Lydia had gone back to Argentina. Now she wanted to get to know him; she had been longing so much to have a father, but all she really knew of him was that he was this famous person who was in the movies. Once in Milan, Fernando flew off to make the film, and I drove with the two girls to Rome. (The fact that I wrecked the transmission of Fernando's brand new car when the cuff of my mink got caught in overdrive remained my little secret.) We weren't coddled, as we had been in Spain; I knew how to cook *la cucina italiana,* and we were happy. Coming back to Rome after the filming of *Raw Wind in Eden* was strange. I hoped the paparazzi would concentrate more on my relationship with Fernando than on my past with Jeff and Georgio.

Fernando rented the first floor of a small Italian villa in Montemario, just above the 1960 Rome Olympic stadium. Susie and Alex shared one bedroom and Fernando and I took the other. I was thrilled that Susie wanted to be with me, and especially for her birthday. I couldn't have been happier. Alex hadn't seen her father in years and had these wonderful fantasies of her father being the handsome, dashing actor who would squire her about the movie set.

What looked for all intents and purposes like the perfect family reunion, was simply a charade. Fernando really wanted no part of children, his own or mine. Alex to him was an interruption, and Susie, unnecessary. I took over the job of being not only mother and father, which was all right for me, but also their attorney constantly pleading with Fernando on Alex's behalf to spend more time with her. The result, of course, was that the children were constantly bickering with each other. Alex, who was now fifteen, felt neglected and took it out on little Susie, who had her ninth birthday with Alex and me. (Fernando gratefully had a work day at the studio). I wasn't working so I could celebrate with the two girls without him.

Because we were planning a lengthy stay, Susie attended an English-speaking elementary school. Alex would stay in her room just wishing she could be with her dad. When I explained this all to Fernando, he answered, "You like kids, you take care of them." As with Ben, I saw the warning signals, but chose to ignore them—or at least put off dealing with them until a later time. The truth was, of course, there would be no later time. That was the way it was, and that was the way it would stay.

In an odd way, Fernando was both proud that he had captured that person who had been Esther Williams the movie star and proud of me in my new wifely role. He liked giving dinner parties so that he could show off what a good cook I was. If I made a good dinner with no help, he would say to our guests (many of whom were actors and actresses themselves), "Just remember that Esther Williams cooked this dinner, so appreciate it." And then he would always give me a slap on the bottom, which was like a badge of ownership.

That tether was still there, and from time to time I was reminded of it when Fernando found it necessary to jerk my chain. French actress Corinne Calvet was married to an American actor named Jeff Stone, and that summer we were invited for cocktails at their penthouse. I loved the clothes I had in Italy. That night I was wearing a chiffon dress with little straps, and I carried with me a lovely fan that I'd bought in Madrid. It was hot, and when I saw that Jeff had perspiration running down his face, I started to fan him so he could cool off. Suddenly I felt a sharp something at the back of my neck. I turned and there was Fernando saying, "We don't fan other men."

Maybe Argentinean women grew up with this, I thought to myself, but I'm not trained for it. I was angry, and on the way back to our apartment I took him on about it. I was fighting back, which I learned not to do later in the relationship because it just wasn't worth it—he always made me pay somehow. Going into the garage under our building I said, "You know, that was really stupid."

"Esther," he said, tugging on one of the pretty little chiffon straps on my dress, "don't ever say that I am stupid or ridiculous." And with that, he pulled it so hard that it broke.

"Dammit! Look what you did!" I said.

"You like that dress?"

"It's my favorite."

He grabbed the bodice of the dress and wrenched it down, ripping both side seams down to the waistline. The dress was completely ruined, and I was sitting in the parking garage exposed and humiliated by what had now become a public display.

"You sonofabitch!" I screamed as I struggled to cover myself.

"Don't criticize me when I break a strap," he said calmly. "Don't *ever* criticize me, because I will always go further than you."

A few weeks later I was again getting ready for a cocktail party given in my honor by some old friends from *Raw Wind in Eden*. It was an evening I was very much looking forward to. My hair was done, my makeup was on, I was ready to leave when I caught sight of Fernando who was still in his robe, unshaved.

"Fernando, you're not dressed."

"Oh, do you really want to go?"

"Yes, very much," I said.

"Well, Esther, I don't think I do." I knew by now that Fernando would never attend an affair where I was to have center stage much less an event that might rekindle memories of Jeff and *Raw Wind*.

I ventured, "Do you mind if I go alone?"

"Of course I mind! That's out of the question."

"Is this how it's going to be?" I asked. "If I want something, you're going to *not* want it? The only way to deal with that and have any harmony is for me not to want anything anymore."

"That would probably be the best way."

The next day my friends called and asked why I didn't go to the party. "Fernando wasn't feeling well," I lied. It was the first of many times when I would make up an excuse for him, but for me that was easy. After all those years with Ben, I was a virtuoso at plausible excuses.

Years later, when the truth of all this came out, people asked me why I stayed. What I said was, "I didn't have another place to go," which was true, but there was more to it than that. The deeper answer was that I have always been a person of my word, and only death could set me free from the vows I took that first night in Cypress Gardens. Only when he died could I really walk away, even though the deal we made was often rather inequitable. He was keeping his part of the bargain; he didn't cheat on me, or so it seemed. He loved his home and, even more, he loved me there waiting for him. But it didn't work for my children, and that was the problem when we returned to Los Angeles in the fall of 1962. It was to be a heavy price to pay.

CHAPTER 24

TETHERED
1964–1982

*W*hen we flew home from Rome, I had no idea just how cruel Fernando would be about my children. The truth is that it was terrible beyond my worst fears. Fernando didn't like them, and they didn't like him. To him they were another man's children. As far as he was concerned, their existence was living proof that Esther Lamas must have slept with someone else, which was something he couldn't accept. He had no intention of sharing me with them. I belonged to him alone. He intended to shut them out, and he let them know it. When Fernando had a house built for us in Bel Air, he designed it with just one bedroom, our master suite. There was no way I could move even one child, much less three, into Fernando's life.

By this time Ben Gage was living in a modest house on Eighteenth Street in Santa Monica. The $75,000 good-bye payment I'd given him at the divorce was long gone. At first, he sold real estate; then he sold paper products. He made just enough money to scrape along. He was indebted to the IRS as I was. He still drank, but had gotten close to Benjie and Kim in his big overgrown kid kind of way, and they were living with him. There was no longer a choice for me. The unsuccessful experiment with military school was over, and the boys were attending Santa Monica High. After spending time with us in Italy, Susie was once again at my sister June's house. But if I couldn't have her with me, I really wanted her to be with her brothers. I devised a strategy to get through the years until they were all out of high school; I called it my seven-year plan.

At first, the boys were unhappily sharing a room when Susie came to live with Ben. I talked Ben into turning part of his garage into a room for Benjie. Then I fixed up Susie's room in Ben's house, which had been rather shabby. Because Ben was so unreliable, I also had to make sure on a regular basis that my children had food in the refrigerator. I didn't even consider asking Fernando for money to do this. I tapped what was left of my fifty-thousand-dollar Sam Katz nest egg from MGM, money I had kept hidden all this time from the IRS. I was still paying off my part of the $750,000 collateral agreement, and they would have seized it if they'd known about it. With the help of Jane, who stayed with me all these years, I began servicing the two houses.

I had the only station wagon in Bel Air that smelled of gravy. I slept every night in our one-bedroom house with Fernando, and in the morning in my own kitchen I made whatever the kids were going to eat that evening. Then I drove what I prepared to Ben's house in Santa Monica, so I was there when they came home from school. I stayed with them while they did their homework, and we talked while they had dinner. In Ben's kitchen I made the veal Milanese or whatever it was that Fernando and I were going to eat together that night. At 11:00 P.M., Jane came and stayed the night with the children. Most of the time I had no idea where Ben was, which was just as well. I'd rather have him passed out in his car someplace, than staggering around where the children could see him. When Jane arrived, I returned to Bel Air for a late supper with Fernando. The next morning it started all over again.

I was on this incredible treadmill, but the alternatives were to give up Fernando or allow him to wall me off from my children's lives completely. I chose the treadmill. One night as I left Eighteenth Street with Fernando's dinner, I was driving a bit erratically because

I was adjusting the foil on the roasting pan, which had slipped a little. A policeman pulled me over.

"May I see your license, lady? . . . Say, something smells delicious. What is that?"

The car was full of the aroma of garlic and rosemary. "It's veal Milanese. The foil was slipping and I didn't want the gravy to spill."

"Smells good. May I taste it?"

"Sure, you can taste; you can even have one. But then you can't give me a ticket. You can only give me a warning." I wondered whether this could be considered bribing a policeman.

"What's the story?" he asked between mouthfuls.

"Please don't ask. Too complicated. Do you mind if I go now?"

I kept my story to myself. The fact that my children were in another house when I went to bed at night was such a painful reality that I couldn't share it with anybody.

I drove away without even having to show him the driver's license that proved that I used to be Esther Williams. In fact, I didn't feel like Esther Williams anymore. I felt plain and unglamorous; I had accepted the tether. I cooked and cleaned and did the gardening and cleaned the pool. Fernando expected me to do it all without complaining, and so I did.

For years I settled into that tethered life, shuttling between houses and dividing my attentions. Benjie and Susie were remarkably good kids and grew up well despite these difficult conditions. But Kim had been difficult, beginning in the womb; he always was recalcitrant and stubborn. He would never open up to me, no matter how hard I tried, and as he grew into those teen years he found new ways to make me worry. He hung out with friends who were doing drugs, and I wasn't sure how much past marijuana the drug use went.

Part of my shuttle routine was to stop at the Fireside Market on Montana Avenue to buy food every day at 3 P.M., because whatever I had put in the refrigerator the previous day had been wiped out by Ben and three hungry kids. Kim knew my schedule, and as soon as he saw my car coming up to the house, he would duck out the back window and sneak over to a neighbor's house to smoke dope. Usually he stayed out until I left to have dinner with Fernando. After

Benjie and Susie had eaten the dinner I fixed for them, I would supervise the schoolwork. I brought my trusty Olivetti typewriter along and helped Benjie and Susie with their homework for most of the night; I wasn't sure if Kim ever did any homework. Despite his efforts to keep me out of his life and despite the things he did that upset me, I loved him and worried about him.

As he approached driving age, he had wanted me to get him a motorcycle; but I felt that it would be too dangerous, and I had refused. He got a job as a box boy at the local supermarket after school and the first thing he did was to buy a small used Honda motorcycle. I remembered saying to him in frustration, "That stubbornness of yours is going to get you someday."

And it did. On October 29, 1966, the day before his sixteenth birthday, I received a call at night from Santa Monica Hospital. Kim had been riding his Honda when he was struck by a car. He was alive, but badly injured. I was frantic; Fernando refused to drive me to the hospital. I jumped into the station wagon and raced to the hospital. Apparently, a USC professor driving through an intersection on Wilshire Boulevard, had turned away for a split second to look at his four-year-old daughter. He hadn't seen my son in time to avoid hitting him. Kim was thrown forty feet through the air. His left leg was badly broken from the impact, and when he came down, he hit the curb with his right leg and shattered it. The doctors told me they would have to amputate both legs.

Hysterical with fear for my son, I phoned Bula. I sobbed helplessly, telling her, "Mom, Kim's been hit by a car and both legs have been shattered. They're going to cut them off."

Bula reacted calmly. "Oh, dear," she said. "Life has stopped Kim in his tracks. He'll be in that hospital, lying on his back for a long time. Maybe you can reach him now." That's how Bula's mind worked.

Meanwhile, I wasn't going to allow them to cut off my son's legs. The trauma surgeon Dr. Ralph Beasom arrived, and before I could say a word to him, he told me, "We won't cut his legs off. I'm going to see if I can put him back together." He was comforting, but candid. Kim's X-rays looked as though someone had thrown a snowball and there was nothing left but the splatters. "Do you really think you can put all those splinters together again, doctor?" I asked. He drew me a picture of how he was going to insert stainless steel pins and add artificial bone, and I began to feel hope.

At some point, Kim's father wandered into the hospital. Ben had had a long night of celebrating his own birthday. "Ben, get out of here," I told him. "You are no help and you are in the way."

"Where shall I go?"

"I don't care. Go out and sit on the curb. Just get out of here."

So dear, sweet Susie went out and sat on the curb with her father while I talked with the doctors and discussed Kim's chances for recovery.

The initial painful weeks stretched into months and finally almost a year that Kim spent in and out of that hospital. He had a total of twenty-seven operations on his legs, and Dr. Beasom was as good as his word. Against the medical odds, he managed to rebuild Kim's legs. Although Kim was stoic, he was in constant pain. I stayed with him every night he was in the hospital and watched the slow healing progress of his terribly emaciated limbs. The pins in the right leg held the bone together and new bone was growing. But in the left leg, bones continued to separate, because there was so little skin or flesh to cover the shin bone. When Kim was finally allowed out of bed, he had to learn to walk again. That was a long process, too. To make matters worse, the escalating doses of morphine that they had to give him to combat the pain eventually led to addiction.

There is a long story to how Kim dealt with his new, more serious drug problem by transferring to alcoholism. The story has a positive ending. An Alcoholics Anonymous sponsor brought Kim to the Church of Religious Science, where he and I renewed our bonds of family love in a strong, joyous way. Kim's recoveries and his happy life today are a special satisfaction to me. But this is his story to tell, not mine, and I am pleased to be a part of it.

During that long, painful year of operations on his legs, my financial problems escalated rapidly. Dr. Beasom discounted his surgery bills and AFTRA was generously supportive; but there were tens of thousands of dollars in medical costs that were not covered. There was no way I could have asked Fernando for money. For him, my children were another man's offspring. In his usual desperation for money, Ben insisted upon handling the lawsuit for damages against the USC professor. He settled quickly with the professor's insurance company for twenty-three thousand dollars, a woefully inadequate amount. In an accounting sleight of hand, he took nine thousand dollars of that money to repay a lawyer who was suing him over the collapse of the marble quarry deal.

Then Ben did something that was so in character for him, I can hardly believe I didn't recognize it until too late. He deliberately would miss doctors' appointments for Kim, then falsify the insurance reports so that the forms indicated that medical services had been performed, and pocket the money. By the time I caught on to him, there was only six thousand dollars left of the settlement money. I went to the judge at Santa Monica Superior Court, but he kept setting my case aside, week after week. Finally, I cornered him in the parking lot as he was trying to leave. He actually said to me, "I don't want to get involved in a domestic quarrel."

I said, "This is hardly a 'domestic quarrel,' Your Honor. This is a case about a boy who is trying to save his legs from amputation and a father who is stealing the settlement money faster than we can spend it on doctors. Don't call this a domestic quarrel, and don't run away from me."

He looked at me blankly and said, "There's nothing I can do." He got in his car and drove away.

Throughout this ordeal, Fernando was of little help. Though we were living together, we were not married. He had no legal obligation to help me financially, and he didn't, and I was too proud to ask. Still, his behavior here, and elsewhere, seems, as I put it down now on the cold page, almost beyond comprehension. And still I stayed—and would stay, for twenty-two years.

Besides, though it may be hard to believe, I loved the sonofabitch. And he *knew* it.

Fernando was a strange animal. One day, I turned to him. "You know, you got a hell of a lot of nerve. You expect me to answer your every wish, your every expectation."

"That's true," he said. It was just a fact of life.

"I'm to clean the pool perfectly, plant the lawn perfectly, and make sure our garden is beautiful. I've even become a plumber!

Plumbers cost money." Because perfection was always his expectation, I always fell short. The moment his eyes fluttered open, I knew
that his first thought was not going to be, Good morning, darling.
It's so wonderful to wake up beside you, but rather, What are you
going to do today that I'm not going to like?

"Don't you understand that I'm doing you a favor?" he asked seriously. "How will you ever know your full potential if nobody ever demands it of you?"

He didn't raise a hand in his home. You brought him things—or
rather, *I* brought him things. He had a pair of velvet slippers with
crests on them that had been custom-made for him. I called them
his "full-of-shit" slippers. When he put them on his feet, that was the
end of all effort for him. "Esther," he would say, "please bring me a
glass of Coca-Cola with some ice."

He was sitting in a chair right next to the refrigerator. "Darling,
all you have to do is open the door. The Coke is right in front."

"If I have to get my own Coca-Cola," he said, "what's the use of
having a wife?"

But he supported the two of us through his own efforts, which
was a new experience for me. He had turned to directing, and with
the help of producer Roy Huggins and his friend Ben Gazzara, he
hooked up with Universal and did a lot of work on several successful series, beginning with *Run for Your Life, The Rookies,* and *Mannix,* and continuing with *Starsky and Hutch* and *Alias Smith and
Jones.* As a director, Fernando was competent, and he was fast. Frequently, producers would call him when somebody else had screwed
up and the production was behind schedule. We would work on the
script to make it shootable in the time they had left, and somehow
he always made the deadline. In TV, the clock was the master.

Our friends were the actors who were working on his shows.
Through *Run for Your Life,* we became part of a circle that included
Gazzara and his wife, Janice Rule, and their pals John Cassavetes
and Gena Rowlands. Fernando loved entertaining friends in our
home. We had frequent dinner parties for ten, which was as many
as we could seat at our dining room table. These were not catered
affairs. I was a one-woman band: shopped for the food, prepared it,
served it, and cleaned up afterward. As Fernando sat at the head of

the table, I had the pleasure of seeing how good he felt in his home. We were that kind of couple.

As he wished, I lived in Fernando's shadow. Whenever we went out together, I made very sure that I was on his arm when the photographers were at work. I was never photographed alone. That would be Esther Williams again. At one fund-raiser we attended, Don Rickles entertained, and it was like a game of hide and seek. I loved Rickles's insult humor, but I didn't want it aimed at me. I was too vulnerable. We were sitting at a table with a group of people, and every time he looked in our direction, I ducked, using the other members of our party to block his view. Finally he was too fast for me. "Who is that behind Fernando Lamas?" he cried out into the mike. "Aha! It's Esther Williams! How do you like getting to the nunnery, Esther?" Good old clairvoyant Rickles. Here I thought I'd done such a good job of covering it up, and he saw right through me.

In 1968 we went back to Spain. Fernando had a part in a western called *100 Rifles*, with Burt Reynolds, Raquel Welch, and former Cleveland Browns fullback Jim Brown. Brown arrived on location in Almeria with a cloud of scandal over his head, having just been accused of tossing his girlfriend from a third-floor balcony. Amazingly enough, she was still with him, her arm was in a sling and with two blackened eyes. I sat with her at dinner and said that it seemed to me that if she were going to hang out with Jim Brown, she should get a room on the ground floor or find one with a handy bush beneath it.

Brown was a large man, very handsome and muscular. Often decked out in velvet shirts and heavy gold chains, he had a big-time macho image and an ego to match. He was proud of his reputation as "the greatest football player of all time."

Brown swaggered up to Fernando one day and issued a challenge. "I hear you're a tough guy."

"What's it to you?" Fernando snapped. You could feel the tension crackle.

Jim Brown was twenty years younger and fifty pounds heavier than Fernando, so he continued. "They say you're a boxer."

It was true. Back in Argentina, Fernando had trained as a boxer because he didn't want anybody ever to be able to beat him in a fight. He was always ready to defend himself. Without another word, Fernando rose to a standing position, leaned back, and shot his Italian pointed shoe at Jim's chin, deliberately missing him by nothing more than an inch.

"What the hell was that?" asked the surprised fullback.

"That, my dear Mr. Brown, was savate." Savate is a form of kick-boxing in which the blows are delivered with either the hands or the feet. Fernando was an expert.

"You coulda knocked my teeth out!"

"I chose not to. Might I add that if you feel like fighting again, you should know that a well-placed kick to the balls is a great equal-izer against a man of any height."

That was classic Fernando, the man who liked to push the enve-lope as far as it would go. It always worked. The challenge was over. From then on, Brown had respect. The next time I saw them to-gether, Fernando was draped elegantly in an easy chair, and Brown was sitting humbly on the ottoman near him, learning basic Span-ish phrases.

Fernando's knowledge of the martial arts gave him an interesting take on the news, because he knew all the parts of the body that were most susceptible to attack. When there was a story involving personal violence, he would often give me a discourse on how it could—or could not—have happened. One evening there was one of those "On This Date in History" segments that discussed the 1958 murder of Lana Turner's lover, mafioso Johnny Stompanato. Lana's daughter, Cheryl Crane, had supposedly stabbed him to death after he threatened her mother.

"Impossible," said Fernando. "There's no way Cheryl could have stabbed Johnny Stompanato with that little knife. Stompanato was a boxer, but he was a lot more than that. He was a hit man, and there's no way you can come up on a hit man the way she was sup-posed to have done it. She was a teenage kid. He'd have taken that knife out of her hands and thrown her out the window—or slit her throat with it."

"Well, how in the world did he get stabbed then?"

"He must have been asleep," said Fernando, "not just asleep, but passed out. He had to remain in a prone position for anyone to get that knife between his ribs. Lana did it, so Cheryl had to take the rap. Jerry Geisler was their lawyer. He must have instructed her on how the scene would be played in court. Lana and Cheryl rehearsed before they told this version to the police."

That was Fernando's version. I didn't argue. He knew all of the participants. Cheryl was acquitted. Lana survived and went on to do those really successful movies with Ross Hunter at Universal Studios, all of them dramatizing the plight of a beautiful woman. They even included daughters caught up in the melodrama.

After *100 Rifles* was finished, we were invited to a party at Burt Reynolds's house. Fernando and I were talking at the bar with Burt and Robert Wagner, when suddenly Wagner's face brightened as he saw someone come through the door.

"Bette! How great to see you!" he said enthusiastically. "Do you know Esther Williams?"

Bette Davis narrowed her eyes and looked at me coldly. "Yes, I most certainly do know Esther Williams . . . and I wish I didn't!"

She certainly had a way of stopping conversation. In order to get things moving I said, "Fernando, have you met Miss Davis?"

Suddenly Bette turned on the charm. "Oh, Fernando!" she gushed, giving him this big Hollywood hug and managing to turn her back on me at the same time. "Fernando! I've seen you so often on the Carson show! You look even more wonderful in person!"

Fernando sort of puffed up in appreciation—with Bette Davis fawning over him like that, he couldn't help himself. "But, Fernando, you must tell me something . . ." He leaned forward. At this point he was so flattered that he would have told her anything. "What are you doing with . . ." She jerked her thumb over her shoulder in my direction. ". . . *her*?"

Bette and Gary Merrill were long since divorced, but she still held a grudge. As far as she was concerned, I'd been a willing accomplice that night when Ben passed out in her bathtub and Gary made a pass at me. She was sure I'd slept with him.

I let it go. Once Bette Davis's mind was made up, there was no way anyone was going to change it. "You'll have to excuse me," I said. "I'm going to the powder room."

When I returned, she was gone.

"What the hell was that about?" asked Burt.

"She convicted me in absentia a long time ago, Burt," I explained. "It doesn't matter that it never happened. Just chalk it up as another Bette Davis moment."

Toward the end of 1969, Fernando said to me casually, "We're getting married on Wednesday, New Year's Eve."

I was astonished, because after our faux wedding in Marbella he had never mentioned the subject again. In truth, neither had I.

"Why now, Fernando?"

"Because I've had a very good year and I need the write-off."

How romantic can you be? In one sense, our wedding was simply the formalization of a relationship that began in 1960 and clearly was not going to end until death did us part anyway. In another sense, I was bowing to his demands again and agreeing to a marriage that I had secretly vowed would never take place until Fernando accepted my children.

We were married on December 31, 1969, in the chapel of the Church of Religious Science in Los Angeles. Dr. Bill Hornaday presided. No family members were present. My children were not even welcome at my wedding. There was a reception in the church for a few friends. I wept helplessly through the entire ceremony. I must have known in my heart what lay ahead.

I missed my children terribly, and there were times when shuttling between houses almost killed me; but when Fernando and I were alone, things were often fine. Not always, but often. In his self-centered way, he loved me very much, and he was faithful. His sexy reputation was well deserved, and I was the sole beneficiary.

He loved not to wear any undershorts, which was a twofold conceit. The first motivation was to make sure people looked at his crotch. The reason they did, which he spelled out to me in great detail, was that he was "hung very high."

"Somehow, my genitalia have been placed high on my pubic bone," Fernando explained clinically, "so it looks like this thing of mine goes on forever. It's really quite normal, but of course it's very grand if it's erect." He talked about his penis as if it were a dear and talented friend with excellent posture, rather than a part of his body.

Late one afternoon I was preparing for a dinner party when I looked out the kitchen window and saw him getting ready to take a swim in the pool. (He was at leisure until our guests arrived. If he refused to get his own Coca-Cola, you can be sure that it never occurred to him to help me with party preparations.)

He kept the pool fairly cold. His Celtic ancestry made him a penny-pincher, particularly when it came to utility bills. Heating the pool was expensive. But the cold pool, instead of shrinking his genitalia like it did any other sensible, ordinary man, made him become erect. He came to me triumphantly in the kitchen, stark naked, arms raised, and proud as a peacock, and said, "Look at that!"

"Oh honey, your timing is terrible. I've got a soufflé in the oven!"

He reacted as if I'd been rude to an old school chum who'd just dropped in unexpectedly. "You should never turn down a glorious erection like this!" he chided. "You should applaud it and treat it with great respect, because you never know when it will come again."

I knew what was going to come next, which was probably Fernando, and I also knew that I would have to drop everything and head upstairs with him to the bedroom. I left the veal piccata that I'd been pounding to a faretheewell and turned off the oven.

So the soufflé would fall. So what. So dinner that night would be less than perfect, but things would be perfect upstairs. Fernando brandished his equipment with a particular kind of sexual joy which most American men do not have. My mother had noticed it the first time she met him. "Why doesn't he have any underwear on?" she asked me.

"Mother! Why are you looking at his crotch?"

"Because I think he wants me to!"

Bula by this time was almost eighty. She didn't see so well and may have become a little vague about some things, but she was absolutely right about that. Fernando had a way of thrusting his hips forward that made it very obvious what was in those pants, which was very substantial. It was his way of letting people know that he was a tremendous package.

The second reason that Fernando didn't wear any jockey shorts was that he was preoccupied with his appearance. He always wanted to be "camera ready." He had excellent taste. He was a regular at Dorso and Carroll & Co. and the other fine men's shops in Beverly Hills. He bought the finest clothes he could afford, and then had them tailored to his precise specifications. It was the one part of his life where he didn't try to economize. He didn't want any creases, lines, bumps, or bulges—except one. Because he wore his pants very tight, if he wore underwear there would always be what women would call a "panty line" at the junction of his ass and his legs. For someone hell-bent for sartorial elegance, this simply would not do. The exquisite line of the trousers had to be unbroken. He even had the pockets cut out and sewn up so there wouldn't be any telltale ridges.

He absolutely hated wrinkles. If we were driving to a party, he often would get behind the wheel nude from the waist down, with his perfectly pressed English gabardine pants on a hanger behind him. When we got within a couple of blocks of our destination, he'd find a secluded spot, leap out into the bushes, and put on his trousers, so that they would still be perfectly pressed when he made his entrance.

Entrances mattered to Fernando. That time in 1952 when he made the grand entrance at Marion Davies's blowout gala with Lana Turner on one arm and Ava Gardner on the other had been a supremely calculated moment. Now Fernando became almost as famous for his guest shots on *The Tonight Show* as he was for acting and directing, and a lot of it had to do with his entrances. It was with Johnny Carson, when he knew millions of people were watching, that Fernando's narcissism came to full flower, reaching delirious heights.

Watching him sit down when he was introduced by Johnny was a treat in itself. Fernando would saunter out on stage and go through a whole ritual, just to settle himself into the seat next to Johnny's desk. It was terribly important how he sat in that chair. When you're vain, you're vain; and people who are that self-absorbed are funny, because they do things that they think are perfectly normal, which everyone else finds unbelievable.

Did his watch sit exactly as it should on his wrist? He had changed from walking to sitting, and this demanded some adjustment. Was his tie properly square? He touched it to be sure. What about his coat and shirt? He crisply shot his cuffs to be certain that they displayed just the right amount of linen extending from his jacket. Finally he reached down to smooth out the front of his pants so that they did not wrinkle at the crotch. All this adjustment took some time, and through the whole routine Johnny never said a word.

Only when Fernando was satisfied with his appearance would he turn to Johnny and say, "So, how are you?"

Great host and deadpan comic that he was, Johnny let a one-beat pause elapse before he responded. "I'm fine, and you certainly look fine." This was, of course, the genesis of "You look mahvelous," which lived on long after Fernando was gone, thanks to Billy Crystal.

One night, Johnny asked, "Fernando, which would you rather do, look good or feel good?"

"Well, Johnny," he answered, "if you feel good but you look bad, nobody knows that you feel good. They only remember that you look bad. So I would rather look good and feel bad. Because if you look good, you can forget for the moment that you feel bad."

Carson was mesmerized. He sat there in bemused astonishment, glancing out at the audience every so often to share has amazement with the folks at home. "Can you go through that again, Fernando?"

"Johnny, if you can't listen to me the first time, I can't talk to you at all."

That brought the house down. Fernando often set Johnny up as his straight man. In the late night duel of witty repartee, Fernando frequently got the last word, and audiences loved him for it. He made something like over fifty appearances on the Carson show, and everyone thought they were great because Fernando had a certain kind of irreverence for Johnny that really worked.

One night Johnny asked Fernando about his temper. If you worked in Hollywood long enough, you knew Fernando had one.

"I learned to fight with this hysterical grandmother who raised me," he explained. "When she yelled, I was only six years old but I yelled back. Then there was a shouting match and everyone got laryngitis. When we couldn't yell anymore, we made up."

"What happens when you yell at Esther?"

"I yell and I yell, and all of a sudden the only voice I hear is my own."

"And then what happens?"

"A lot of the fun goes out of the argument if nobody will argue with you."

Esther Williams became sort of a running off-screen character for Fernando's appearances on the Carson show, and not surprisingly Johnny kept asking when I was going to join Fernando for a guest shot. Fernando and Johnny were friends; they played tennis together, but that friendship was not enough to make Fernando even begin to consider letting me appear on the show with him. This was his time in the limelight, and I was not to share it.

Still, whenever he appeared on *The Tonight Show*, he did the taping and headed straight for home. After he walked through the door, he slipped off his just-so jacket and his still-unwrinkled pants and his brocade vest and put on his full-of-shit slippers. He loved being with me at home, even though there was a lot more of me to love than there used to be.

One of the things I'd told Fernando early on was that if I stopped being Esther Williams, I'd get fat. He adored my cooking and bragged about it to everyone, but he always nagged me about every pound I put on. "So you got fat on my time!" he'd say. "Just remember, you can't go on camera looking like that." Although he mocked me about my size, I have no doubt that on a deeper level he was happy it was there. It was a great way to keep me tethered, as if he needed one.

Difficult people get riled easily over insignificant things. If you are easygoing and want to keep peace and harmony, you don't argue. It's almost always simpler to say, "It bothers him more for me *not* to do it than it does for me to solve the problem." Eventually, however, the line of least resistance becomes a drug. Fernando wanted more and more, and after a while I thought I was being eaten alive.

I asked my insightful sister Maurine why I decided to gain weight. "When somebody is feasting off your flesh," she explained, "you can't let them go hungry."

When Ben and I still owned The Trails restaurant, we had displays of monkeys, fish, and birds. After it went bankrupt, I brought the birds to an aviary at the house in Mandeville Canyon. The parakeets were very pretty, but what I didn't know was that the term "pecking order" was well named. The stronger birds would peck all the feathers off the heads of the weaker ones, and they kept pecking, even after the feathers were all gone. Some mornings I'd go out to the aviary to see my lovely birds and find one stone cold on the ground. The bird looked perfectly healthy, except that it was dead. The stronger birds had pecked a hole clear into its brain and killed it. After Fernando kept remarking about my weight, I didn't want to go anywhere because I felt as though I was as big as a house. He'd pecked that into my parakeet brain.

Once, however, I lost about fifty pounds and was back into my size-ten dresses again. "That's the way you should look on the arm of Fernando Lamas," some Fernando sycophant told me approvingly.

"He likes me fat; he likes me thin"; I answered, "but most of all he likes me home."

In truth, Fernando regarded my being slender as threatening. In 1971, I got a call from my old pal Joe Barbera, who had made Fernando sing like an octopus for the underwater Tom and Jerry cartoon sequence in *Dangerous When Wet*. Joe's friend Ronald Neame had been tapped to direct *The Poseidon Adventure*, a big-budget Irwin Allen disaster movie. Neame was a venerable English director who had made some highly regarded films, including *Tunes of Glory* and *The Prime of Miss Jean Brodie*, and for *Poseidon* he was looking for a star who could swim. Fernando didn't even give me a chance to say no. Instead, he blew up at both Neame and Barbera for what he called setting him up to ask. (Shelley Winters got the role.)

I became angry—I wanted to be able to say whether or not I wanted to do a film without him nearly punching somebody out. This was no longer about not sharing me with my children—the kids were all out of high school. This was about keeping me from doing anything at all. I was doing nothing more than taking care of Fernando, throwing dinner parties, and playing tennis—a lot of tennis. (You get very good if you do it a lot.) I just wanted to get out of the house, but now Fernando didn't want to share me with anyone. Increasingly, it felt like the walls were closing in. That tether was getting shorter all the time.

In 1974, Irwin Allen tried again. He wanted to know if I was interested in being in another of his disaster flicks, *The Towering Inferno.* "Forget it, Irwin," I said. "We went through too bad a time over *The Poseidon Adventure.*" A short time later, Jack Haley Jr. invited me to narrate on camera part of the hugely successful *That's Entertainment, Part I.* As usual, Fernando mentioned how much weight I had gained.

Fernando suffered from migraines. During one Bob Hope special that he worked on, Fernando got a migraine that was so bad Bob himself drove him home because he was so worried about him. Fernando was in a fetal position when they pulled up. Without a doubt, rage was the cause. He had been angry so much of his life about so many things and at so many people that his rage was like a steel band around his head.

He couldn't stand it if anyone came to the house and made the slightest noise while he was suffering. During one episode, his doctor, Omar Farid, came to see him and brought a friend with him who was a big fan of mine. The two of us were in the living room chatting while the doctor checked on Fernando. I guess Fernando could hear us, because he came out totally nude, stood in the doorway, and demanded, "Esther, come to the kitchen with me. Now!"

His face was white, his hair wild, and there was a little spittle at the corners of his mouth. He began yelling at me at the top of his lungs. I was never afraid of him when he lost control like that; it was just the little six-year-old boy lashing out at Carmen. As he was yelling I opened the drawer and took out a mirror. When he finally stopped screaming long enough to take a breath, I held it up to his face. "Take a look," I said. "Does this remind you of anyone? Gray face . . . spittle . . . wild hair . . . you look just how you described your crazy grandmother Carmen to me."

He was stunned, and I could see that he recognized *abuelita* Carmen staring back at him. "That was a very mean thing to do," he said after a moment, but he came out of his rage immediately and was quickly in total exhaustion.

I said, "Do you realize how funny it is when you yell at me in the nude? I can't look at anything except your genitalia. Were you aware that you get an erection when you yell?"

Fernando couldn't move his aching, splitting head, so he took the mirror from me, glanced again at his face, then slowly lowered it until it was in front of his crotch. A look of astonishment crept across his face. "Could it be that I enjoy yelling?" he asked.

"I don't know, but it sure turns you on," I said.

That was the way our marriage went for twenty years. A friend once told me, "Fernando gives the best facade of anyone I know." And it was true. The confidence he showed the world was his best act, because underneath was all that torment. One part of my job was to protect that facade, to keep making him look like Fernando Lamas to the world at large. Another part was to comfort the motherless little boy lurking within. And when that didn't suffice, the last part was to hold a mirror up to him to show him when he was behaving like an idiot.

Susie, by now out of high school, suffered a problem endemic to the children of Hollywood stars: She was constantly compared to the forty-foot-high screen image of her mother. Teenage candor borders on cruelty. "How come you don't look like your mother?" they would ask. However much I reassured Susie, I couldn't seem to convince her of her own beauty. "How could anyone look like Esther Williams, or Elizabeth Taylor, or Lana Turner," I would say, "without all that MGM help—the lights, the makeup, the costumes? Without them even *I* don't look like Esther Williams."

Susie was a natural swimmer. She was tall and powerful, and the best swimmer of my three children. She joined the swim team at the Santa Monica YMCA and competed in the junior olympics. But after a couple of seasons, she suddenly quit. I never asked why. I knew the reason. She wanted to be Susan Gage, not Esther Williams Jr.

So it was a bit of a surprise when she decided to study acting, first at the University of the Pacific, and then at the Shakespeare Conservatory in New York. I didn't discourage her, but I didn't encourage her either. Show business was tough enough, and, I thought, given the problem of being a celebrity offspring, would be doubly hard.

Susie graduated college and drove to New York in a U-Haul truck and settled in Brooklyn in a dingy little apartment that only starving acting students and out-of-work poets seem to find. One day I got a frantically excited call from Brooklyn. When I heard the tone of her voice, I said to myself, Incredible! She did it! She's got the lead in a Broadway show.

"Mom," she squealed, "I'm getting married! Can you come to the wedding in Vermont? His name is Tom."

In the spring of 1977, I got a call from Benjie, who told me his father had died during heart surgery. Ben had been living in Santa Monica with his new wife, Ann Arnold, a cocktail waitress he met in Hawaii.

I put the phone down and quietly began to cry. Although my life with Ben was long past, I felt the pain of a failed marriage and a broken family.

Fernando asked me what the call was about, and I told him that Benjie had told me that Ben had died. Fernando was quick to sneer. "You're not crying, are you?"

Without answering, I walked out into the garden beyond the kitchen. Nine-year-old Lorenzo, who had been visiting, followed me outdoors and put his arms around me. "Essie," he said, "you can cry if you want to." I released a flood of tears for a man I once loved.

CHAPTER 25

THE LAST JOURNEY
August–October 1982

"*N*othing is going to keep me from going to Vermont, Fernando."

Twenty years earlier, when we were in Italy, he'd warned me not to want anything too badly. He was so self-centered and controlling—me, me, me—that when I really wanted something, my desire was sufficient to make him automatically reject it. That first time it was just over a party, but he took the same approach with my children as well. Because I wanted so much to be with them when they were growing up, he made it impossible.

"I'm not going to change my mind," I said, "no matter how much you carry on, stamp your feet and throw tantrums. I'm going to my daughter's wedding, and I'm going to pay for Benjie and Kim to go, too." I was prepared to go to the mat with him over this one. "If you're a good boy, you can come along. I'll even buy you a new suit for the occasion—Armani, if you like—if you promise to behave."

"Okay."

I was amazed. That was it? "Just 'okay'?" There was no argument? Fernando went through life with a chip on his shoulder, ready to argue or fight with anyone who crossed him. He called our arguments "situations." Early in our years together, if I said something he thought was worth arguing about he would waggle his finger at me and say, "Do you want a situation with me?"

"Honey," I told him, "marriage *is* a situation. We've got a situation going, and whether it's pleasant or not depends on how often you're going to be a problem."

I'd been prepared for a major "situation" over Susie's wedding, and his simple "okay" was so out of character that I wondered what was behind it.

Maybe the Armani bribe was incredibly effective. Maybe I hadn't been strong enough over the years, or maybe this unusually difficult man had been just a paper tiger all along. Maybe I should have trusted more in the fact that he truly loved me. . . .

I didn't consider the possibility that maybe this was the first indication that there was something physically wrong with him.

I phoned Susie with what I knew would be an awkward request. "Susie, this will be like turning the other cheek, honey. Could you . . . would you let Fernando give you away?"

She had every reason to say no. Ben, her father, who had died five years earlier on the operating table, was not there to give her away and never knew how to be a father.

I could hear her sigh on the other end of the line. "I can do that for you, Mom." For Susie to let him walk her down the aisle meant extending an olive branch he had done nothing to earn.

Fernando picked out a double-breasted summer-weight suit in a lovely shade of dusty blue and hassled the tailor until the alterations were just so. Then we packed to leave for Vermont. We flew into Montpelier, the capital, where Susie and Tom were to meet us for the drive to Greensboro, a tiny community on Lake Caspian about thirty-five miles south of the Canadian border. Tom's family kept us company until they arrived, and Fernando bowled them over with his suave Argentine charm and his engaging stories.

I was glad he was on his best behavior, but for a moment it made me wish that I was merely a new acquaintance he was trying to impress, and not his wife. I saw this charming side of him all too infrequently. Sonofabitch, I said to myself. You can do this any time you want. You really can wave a wand and make this dashing, delightful human being appear.

Susie and Tom drove us to a century-old farmhouse that a neighbor had lent them for our visit. It was lovely, but the next morning Fernando complained of a pain in his back. He still had back trouble from the time he'd driven into the wall of the Bel Air Hotel, and it flared up now and then. He had never had the operation they said he needed (partly out of fear after Jeff Chandler had died on the operating table during spinal surgery), and I was afraid this was a recurrence.

I was so concerned that I called Susie. On the day before her wedding that valiant girl, who'd never received one moment of affection from him, drove the two and a half hours into Montpelier to find Fernando a chiropractor. The session didn't alleviate the pain, so we rented a back brace for him. Then we got into the car for the long ride back to Greensboro.

The next day there was a picture-perfect summer wedding in a classic New England white clapboard church with a tall steeple, and a radiant Susie came down the aisle on Fernando's arm. The ceremony was followed by a reception in the beautiful apple orchard that belonged to the groom's family. Fernando, of course, put on a gracious show. With his silver hair and his perfectly tailored clothes, he was utterly charming. But after it was over he went straight to bed. He took some painkillers, but they couldn't touch whatever was wrong. In order not to disturb him, I slept on the couch in the sitting room. When I heard him moaning in his sleep, I realized that whatever was wrong, it was serious.

The next morning it was time to head back to Los Angeles, and Fernando knew he was released from being a good boy. He sat impatiently in the truck for half an hour before it was time to go, like a dog does when he's been allowed to go on the family outing and wants to let everyone know he's ready to leave. He acted as if the knowledge that he was out there waiting should push us to start saying our good-byes.

Back in Los Angeles, we spent the last days of August seeing a series of chiropractors and osteopaths, but all we had to show for it was a huge pile of bills. No one could make the back pain go away. I tried to get Fernando to see an MD, but he refused. I made two ap-pointments for him, hoping I could talk him into going, but he can-celed them when he found out. "Stop doing this!" he shouted. "No more appointments! I don't want a doctor!"

The Labor Day weekend was interminable. By this time Fer-nando was zonked out on Empirin and codeine. He spent his time just sitting in a chair staring at the TV—lying down was much too painful. I tried again to get a doctor's appointment for him, but everyone was away for the holiday. I talked to a lot of answering ma-chines, but nobody called me back.

Before dawn the next morning Fernando woke me and showed me what looked like a nasty boil on his shoulder. "You can call the doctor now," he said quietly.

Then he stretched out beside me on the bed and said, "I love you so much. . . . If only I could make love to you one more time."

I understood—my father had spoken almost the same words to my mother when he was dying of emphysema. This is what a man says when he's dying, I thought.

Dr. Omar Farid came to the house, took one look at Fernando's shoulder, and said, "Don't bother to get dressed. You're going straight to the hospital." He took Fernando to the UCLA Medical Center Oncology Department—the shoulder abscess was one of the telltale signs of lymphoma, cancer of the lymph nodes.

I went with Fernando to UCLA, and I could tell he was scared. He used to say, "If I ever have to go to the hospital, I won't ever come out." The haunted look in his eyes when I kissed him good-bye told me he hadn't changed his mind.

When I got home that morning, it was still early. To fight off the too-quiet emptiness of the house, I turned on the TV. *Good Morning America* featured a man who was "surviving" lymphoma. He'd had it for ten years and was living a fairly normal life because he was tak-ing care of himself with a regimen of medical treatments and diet. "Ten years? All right," I said to myself. "This is something I can do. Fernando will be an outpatient and I'll be able to drive him for his treatments. I'll make him broccoli shakes in the morning to get rid of the toxins and make sure his nutrition is good. . . . We'll make every day count. Ten years from now Fernando will be seventy-seven. If we follow this program, we can make these next ten years good years." I told myself that I was making peace with the lymphoma, but I was wrong. I didn't realize it, but I was really trying to bargain with death.

Stars in hospitals make news in the media. Reporters kept a vigil at the entrances to local hospitals trying to catch a glimpse of whatever celebrity in his last months. I, of course, wanted to downplay Fernando's illness as much as possible. He had been cast in the new TV series *Gavilan*, opposite Robert Urich, and they'd already shot two segments. The series was something that he very much wanted to do; he also had a contract to direct many of the episodes. Because I still held out the hope that he would recover, I didn't want him to lose his role in the series if he was going to get well. We told NBC that Fernando had back trouble, a diagnosis that was also likely to arouse less curiosity in the press than lymphoma. When friends called about visiting, I fended them off, saying that he was in traction and that he didn't dare laugh or move because it was painful.

Medical institutions have become more humane since, but in 1982 hospitals really didn't want family members involved in patient care. They wanted you to come during visiting hours and then go home. Dr. Charles Adams, the reserved, clinical oncologist who was Fernando's doctor, more or less told me this when we had our first conversation about Fernando's condition, and I told him I wanted a second opinion. "I'm managing this illness," he stated firmly. From that point on I was not to meddle in caring for my husband. In the hospital I was on someone else's turf and I was supposed to behave like a guest—or a piece of furniture.

Fat chance. Fernando needed an advocate, and I didn't let the fact that the doctors didn't want me there keep me away. I came to the hospital every day, ready to do battle.

Years before, when we had Susie and Alex with us in Italy, there was often a lot of adolescent girl noise in the house. The clamor didn't bother me, but Fernando frequently put his hands to his head and said, "I just want some peace!"

Back then smart-mouth me had answered, "Look, when you're gone you'll have all the peace you need. In this messy, noisy business called living, you don't get peace until you're completely out of breath."

Now my own words came back to me and I thought, At least he's going to have peace while he's here at the hospital. I walked up and down the hall, patrolling to keep unwanted visitors at bay. It was a lot harder than it should have been.

I became the guardian at the gate. They'd put him in the ninth-floor celebrity suite, the John Wayne Room. When word spread that Fernando Lamas was there and Esther Williams was with him, total strangers would ask at the nurses' station for the room number, and they'd get it.

You might have thought that we were a stop on the tour for people who'd bought one of those maps to stars' homes. They'd knock on the door. "Hello. So this is the John Wayne Room! Very nice! Are you Esther Williams? And is that Fernando Lamas over there in bed? He doesn't look too good. He used to be so-o-o handsome."

The medical staff was no better. One day Dr. Adams arrived with six young med students. They paraded around Fernando's bed, took his pulse, and began poking and prodding everywhere. Meanwhile, Adams droned on professorially, as if Fernando were a Petri dish that had germinated an array of particularly intriguing microbes.

I know that patient observation is an important part of resident training, but this was done in such a crass, impersonal manner that I couldn't take it. I lost it. "Is this why they call what you doctors do 'practice'? I won't have my husband used as the lesson of the day. Get the hell out! Go practice on somebody else!" Dr. Adams pretty much stopped talking to me after that, but on Saturday, October 2, he phoned me and said, "I'd like to see you at two-thirty this afternoon."

By this time I'd seen Fernando become the picture of Dorian Gray before my eyes. Since Labor Day he'd been transformed from that dashing figure at Susie's wedding, who didn't show a sign of being ill, to his own father, then his grandfather, and finally his great-grandfather.

"The reason I asked you in today, Mrs. Lamas, is that I need you to give us some sort of word on 'extraordinary measures.' "

"I beg your pardon? What do you call 'extraordinary measures'?"

"Well, like restoring your husband's heart to beating when it stops."

"Dr. Adams, are you talking about jumping on his chest and pounding on him, or shocking him to resuscitate him?"

"That's not a clinical description, but that's more or less what I'm talking about, yes. We don't enjoy it and it's very hard on the patient."

"*Dying* is very hard on the patient, doctor."

I didn't understand why he was bringing up the subject, at least not so soon. From everything I read about lymphoma (and by that time it was considerable), I knew that even with severe lymphoma, patients often lived for two years or more after the diagnosis.

"I thought lymphoma took longer to progress."

"It does. But your husband has cancer of the pancreas in addition to the lymphoma."

"When did you discover that?"

Dr. Adams consulted his records. "On September 8 . . ."

That meant Dr. Adams had known about the second cancer all along. ". . . Pancreatic cancer caused his back pain, and it was already well advanced when he came in here. It is terminal."

"Are you saying that he could die at any moment?"

"Yes, that's correct." There was not an ounce of sympathy in his voice. Nothing but the truth, nothing to soften the blow.

All the pent-up anger in me exploded. "How come you know so much about medicine and nothing about people? Do you realize what you've done to me?" I was almost delirious. All I could think of was how I could get his daughters and grandchildren here from Argentina. What possible excuse could I have for not telling them sooner? "What possible excuse do *you* have for not telling *me* sooner?"

"I didn't want you to get upset."

"And you thought hiding the fact that my husband was dying wouldn't upset me?"

"You have business arrangements to take care of, Mrs. Lamas. You need to put his affairs in order," he said coldly.

"I don't have any more time to talk to you, doctor. You've given me too much work to do and no time to do it." I thought if I don't get his family here from Argentina to say good-bye they will be bitter and angry with me for the rest of their lives. "So, yes, I do want extraordinary measures. When Fernando's daughters and grandchildren arrive, I want him to be alive, with a beating heart and a warm hand. And one other thing . . ."

"What is it, Mrs. Lamas?"

"When this is over, don't ask me for a donation, like you people always do."

I had to make up for lost time. I called Susie, Benjie, and Kim, both for moral support and to help make all the arrangements I knew were ahead of me. The boys drove up from San Diego, and Susie and Tom were on the next plane from the East Coast. Then I began tackling the problem of bringing Cristina and Alex and the two grandchildren, Diana and Sergio, from Buenos Aires. Contacting anyone in government—any government—on a weekend was difficult, but finally we got them cleared to fly out on Monday. They'd arrive Tuesday morning, but nobody could say whether that was soon enough or not. We were in a race against time.

With Dr. Adams still "managing the illness," the nurses came more and more frequently to draw blood. I sent them away. "What are you getting, dust? There's no more blood to take," I protested, "so please leave." The hospital staff was preoccupied with Fernando's body, but I had other work to do—with his mind and spirit.

I had sat the deathwatch with my mother in 1975, at a nursing home in Laguna Beach, and I knew that someone who was dying needed a companion to see them through to the other side. "Esther, what are you doing here?" she'd say to me. "There's something I have to do and I can't seem to do it."

"You're trying to die, Mother," I said gently.

I could get real with Bula, because she was the kind of person who had to know what she was doing at all times; and she certainly didn't want anybody feeding her a line, least of all me.

"You do what you have to do, Mother, and I'll just sit here beside you."

And then she said something wonderful. "Well, Esther, I appreciate your understanding, because I'm going through the filing cabinet of my life." My sister Maurine had told me that this was a chore everyone had to do before they passed on. If they died before finishing it in this dimension, they'd have to complete it in the next.

I spent every night in Fernando's room. He loved the sound of my voice, and I would talk to him until he fell asleep. Sometimes I made up stories about little animals or an imaginary running soap opera with a host of characters and subplots. I had read the *Egyptian Book of the Dead* and attended lectures by Elizabeth Kubler-Ross. I knew about the tunnel and the rushing noise you hear as you go into the light. I needed to impart all of that to Fernando during those long nights when I would lie beside him, holding him in my arms. At last I was grateful for my weight. My flesh was a safe haven for him; by this time he was so thin that he could almost blow away. I'd cradle him up against me and he'd lapse into a semiconscious state, his painful bones cushioned by my softness. Then I would talk to him about what his experience was going to be, and who was going to be waiting for him when he got there . . . the father he never really knew . . . his beautiful mother . . . his grandmother Generosa by the river . . . that special aunt who had taken him to the opera when he was a boy.

By doing this I was seeing him through to the next dimension. I was also getting rid of what my mother had called the "if only's."

It was a phrase that stuck with me from the time I was a young girl, when my grandmother lived in Alhambra, about twenty miles east of Inglewood. She had a room in Uncle Charlie and Aunt Clara's house, and that worked well enough until she got sick and needed someone with her all the time. This was during the depression, and Uncle Charlie and Aunt Clara were both lucky enough to have jobs. Grandma had always been a cantankerous woman, even when she was healthy. Now she was bedridden, and she complained about everything. Nevertheless, we took care of her, because that's what families do.

We took turns; each of us did a two-week stint. We all lined up, like the batting order on a baseball team. When you got to the bottom of the order, it was time for the lead-off man to go again. I was twelve, the youngest in the line-up, and my turn came right after Aunt Elsie's daughter.

Even though we waited on her hand and foot, Grandma never

appreciated any of us. She didn't like her sons or their families. The only relatives she loved were her daughter, Ethel; Ethel's husband Pearl; and their two obnoxious daughters. Wouldn't you know it— they were the only members of the family who didn't step up to the plate to take their turns at bat, caring for Grandma. They never even came to visit her, which meant the rest of us had to listen to her whine, "Why doesn't anybody love me? Where are Ethel and the girls?"

This went on for two and a half years, until Grandma finally died. All of us caregivers went to the funeral, filed past her coffin, and said our farewells to that old lady with all the lines that life had given her because of her sour disposition—her face looked like a bad road map. Then we waited at the chapel to see if Aunt Ethel, Uncle Pearl, and the two cousins would show up. Finally they came in, and Aunt Ethel dramatically threw herself across the coffin. After the melodrama was over, my mother, being the lady that she was, graciously invited them back to our house for some lunch.

The Williams clan had scattered, and we didn't all get together often. Like any sort of wake, it was a celebration of living. There was laughter and a lot of catching up on family gossip. We were all enjoying each other's company until we saw the sour faces of Aunt Ethel and Uncle Pearl; they were very disapproving of our "irreverence" toward Grandma. They thought this should be a solemn, somber occasion, and of course it was nothing of the sort.

Finally my mother had had enough. "What you have to do in this life," she declared, looking squarely at the grim quartet, "is not have any 'if only's' when people die. . . . 'If only' I'd been there when she needed me . . . 'if only' I'd spent more time with her . . . *that's* why you threw yourself across the coffin, Ethel, when you saw your mother lying there dead. You missed your chance—there's no way now for you to make it up to her that you never went to see her while she was sick. The reason why we can eat and laugh together is that we don't have any 'if only's' about Grandma. We all did our part while she was still living, but the four of you have to look at yourselves in the mirror and live with your 'if only's' for the rest of your lives."

Now it was time for me to make sure that I didn't have any "if only's" when Fernando died, and I had to do what I could so that others who knew him didn't have any either. I phoned NBC and informed them that Fernando would have to withdraw from *Gavilan.* After that I began the sad task of calling old friends and telling them that Fernando didn't have back trouble, that he was dying. People started gathering on the ninth floor that Sunday. Friends came in to visit with him, but after everyone had left and I was alone with him he said, "Is it that bad?"

"What do you mean?"

"You got everybody in here to say good-bye to me, didn't you?"

"No," I lied. "It's Sunday and they're all off work. This was when they could get here."

If Cristina and Alexandra had already arrived from Argentina, I might have told him the truth, but since they weren't coming until Tuesday, it seemed better to fib. For them not to see him alive would be my biggest "if only," and I very much wanted to avoid those "extraordinary measures" if I could.

"This didn't happen on other Sundays. . . . If I'm going to have visitors, I need a haircut. It makes me look younger."

It was a sweet but heartbreaking request from a man who always wanted to look his best, even now that he was so gaunt I no longer let him look in the mirror. I had been cutting his hair myself ever since our time in Spain, when he came home with a terrible bob that looked like someone had put a bowl on his head. I'd always cut my sons' hair, and Fernando loved things that saved him money, so he let me correct the Beatle cut he'd been given. After that I had a steady customer. He always had his hair cut in the nude, and he was as finicky about that as he was about everything else. He took the salon drape and wrapped it meticulously around his neck, so he didn't get any little hairs on his sensitive skin. When I was done, he'd take two mirrors and examine each side and direct me in making minuscule improvements, and he always found something to fix.

Now, with the idea that a haircut would make him look younger, I knew he was in denial. I looked at his ravaged face and emaciated body and thought, He hasn't accepted any of this at all. He kept a book by his bedside, and in it he had written, "We will beat this thing with Science of Mind and positive thoughts."

When Benjie and Kim arrived, they were shocked to see how emaciated he'd become. He couldn't eat anymore; nothing would stay down. He was in constant pain, and they kept changing his pillows and fluffing them up to make him as comfortable as possible. Benjie had graduated law school, and he started helping me with the financial and business arrangements that had to be made. "Mother," he asked, "do you have access to Fernando's bank accounts?"

The answer was no. Fernando was very secretive about his business affairs, a paranoia he developed because his grandmother had constantly meddled through his things.

"Do you know which bank he uses?"

All I knew was that there was a note on his desk in tiny print, and it changed all the time. Back during the Carter Administration, when interest rates were sky high and you'd get a free toaster or a set of luggage for making a deposit, Fernando ran from bank to bank like Johnny Appleseed, opening accounts and switching funds around to get the best deal. It was almost a hobby with him.

Benjie tracked down Fernando's money. He had squirreled it everywhere, in something like twenty-five bank accounts, and even today I can't be certain that we found them all.

Then came the hard part. I had to get Fernando to give me power of attorney. "I've got to have it for business reasons," I told him, which was true, in a way. Otherwise, the moment a person dies, a lid is clamped on all business affairs. All assets, including checking accounts, savings accounts, and stocks and bonds, are frozen until the will is settled. Reluctantly and after a great deal of coaxing, he signed it.

The will, however, was a bigger problem. No one knew where it was. His attorney didn't have it. I didn't want to ask Fernando, since that would be the sure tipoff that he was dying. As people kept coming to see him, however, he started to get the picture anyway. "This is it, huh?" he asked. I hesitated for a moment, not sure what to say. "Don't bullshit a bullshitter," he said. Finally, I knew he knew.

Susie came and spent time with him on Monday. She took his hand and he looked at her and said, "Sue, I just want to tell you that I forgive you everything."

It was unbelievable, something only Fernando could say.

Afterward when Susie and I were talking together, I said, "Can you stand it that he said that to you, instead of making his own deathbed apology, like he should have?"

"It's all he could do, Mother. I take it as an apology."

Susie was pregnant, and the fact that she was going to bring a new life into the world may have made her magnanimous to someone who was leaving it. Nevertheless, I was proud of her. My God, I thought, I must have done something right with that one.

There was now quite a large group of us at the hospital. I had to see to it that everybody was fed. I went to the administration and said, "From now on there will be someone from the family with my husband at all times. I want you to give us the room next to the John Wayne Room, so we can stay there when we're not with him. No one will be going out for food, so I'll need daily menus for breakfast, lunch, and dinner. I'm going to select a variety of trays for all of us; just put it on the bill. You will be paid, but I don't want any nonsense."

Fernando was insured through the Directors Guild and had excellent coverage. In the kind of bizarre levity that comes over you in tragic moments like this, I thought, When the DGA gets the bill for all these meals, they're not going to believe that Fernando Lamas died of pancreatic cancer. They're going to think he died of a tapeworm.

On Tuesday, Cristina and Alexandra and the grandchildren arrived. They all spoke Spanish to him, and from that moment on Fernando never spoke English again. I guess you go out of this dimension in the same language you're born into. He spoke Spanish to them all day Tuesday. Wednesday he lapsed into a coma. The end of that "if only" was just in time.

When Lorenzo came to see Fernando, he was wearing a jaguar pendant. Tenderly he took it off and put it around his father's neck. He had fallen into deep grief over his father, who had been so strong and commanding, and now was so weak and failing.

"Lorenzo . . . honey," I said gently, "you're going to tell your mother sometime, but can you wait until . . ."

I had already asked Lorenzo not to talk to his mother, because I didn't want the media descending on what should have been a very private affair. Arlene was always very publicity minded, and I had no idea what she might do. It wasn't entirely selfish on my part. By this time Lorenzo himself was a star on *Falcon Crest* (his father had directed some of his episodes), and I didn't want the press hounding him for details.

Just then Lorenzo got a call at the nurses' station. It was Arlene in New York. Having just seen his father, he was still overcome with emotion. He started to cry and just couldn't help blurting out the truth. "Dad's dying," he said into the receiver.

Fernando died on Friday, October 8. He had family with him always; he was never alone. To the very end, I honored the commitment I'd made to him so long ago in Cypress Gardens to set aside Esther Williams and take care of him like the mother he'd lost when he was four. It wasn't always easy, but I kept my promise until his final breath.

CHAPTER 26

GODMOTHER TO A SPORT
1982–1984

I had no "if only's." I had been by Fernando's side all through his illness and had seen him through to the next dimension. Everyone had an opportunity to say good-bye. His daughters and grandchildren from Argentina had a day with him before he slipped into unconsciousness. Those who wanted a chance to forgive him had final conversations. My children forgave him as best they could for the past.

I had prepared a tasteful, dignified obituary that described all of his films in Argentina and the United States and his work in television, but as far as I know it was never used. Many of the accounts of his death drew their material from an interview Arlene Dahl gave to the *New York Post,* which made it sound as if she had been at his bedside when he died. It was mostly about her and not about him— how he was the love of her life and how perfect they were together. At the end she said, "His present wife is Esther Williams," as if I were just passing through. There was no mention of the fact that he and I had been married for twenty-two years.

I didn't find out about the *Post* interview until the day of his memorial service, when someone felt compelled to show it to me, but I wasn't surprised. I certainly knew Arlene was capable of something like that—she'd sent a floral arrangement for the funeral that was a valentine heart with little red roses on it saying, "Our Love Always." It was beautiful, but grotesquely inappropriate for the occasion.

Friends wrote me wonderful condolence letters. They were both comforting and funny in their remembrances, but I realized that many of them expressed a thinly veiled concern that I would take my own life. Friends feared that I'd been so caught up in taking care of Fernando that I'd have nothing to live for after he died. "Don't do anything foolish," they warned.

Shirley MacLaine called me a few days after the memorial service, and I was happy to hear from her. She was so bright. I knew that people made fun of her for her otherworldly ideas and all that "stuff" about other lifetimes, but she and I connected on a spiritual level. We shared metaphysical points of view. After telling me how sorry she was about Fernando she said, "You can be yourself again. Esther, finally, you're free to be you."

She was right about many other things that she told me, too. She knew that marriage to a difficult man means that when he dies, you are out of a job. It was time for the woman who had the organizational horsepower to produce *Esther Williams at Cypress Gardens* to get out of the house and stretch her wings.

The problem was where to start. I had been "Mrs. Fernando Lamas" for so long that at first I didn't know what other role to play. I also had to sort out the complex conflicting emotions that I felt. Along with my deep sense of loss, I wrestled with feelings of anger and frustration. Mixed with the many rich hues of love were profound dark streaks of resentment. Although I was ashamed of it at the time, most powerfully of all I felt relief. Relief that Fernando's terrible suffering was over . . . relief that his smothering domination had ended . . . relief that my children could be welcomed back . . . relief that in death, dear Fernando had given me back my life.

Shortly after Fernando's memorial service, Gloria Luckinbill, a good friend who was a publicist with Rogers and Cowan Public Relations, came to comfort me. She said, "I'm going to give you some advice that I've heard for people who have just lost somebody dear: Redo your kitchen and take a cruise."

My immediate reaction was that this sounded idiotic. However, Fernando and I had been invited to go on a cruise in the spring of 1983. We had wanted to do it, but we'd been waiting to find out when he would have a hiatus in his work on *Gavilan* before we accepted. The Greek cruise line graciously said I could take the cruise and bring my Susie, even though she was pregnant, and her husband, Tom and my sister, June. In November, we flew to Greece to board the Royal Odyssey for a cruise through the Mediterranean, along the coast of Africa, across the Atlantic to the Caribbean, and ending in Florida.

I decided to use that cruise to help me find closure and reenter the world as Esther Williams. I figured that if I could cope with the inquiring eyes of the nine hundred passengers, I could cope with the world. After dinner one of my films would be shown in the ship's main lounge, and then I would give a brief talk and answer questions afterward. Needless to say, I was anxious and wanted to get it over with early in the voyage. That was my first mistake. My second mistake was agreeing to screen *Dangerous When Wet*. As I sat there in the darkened lounge, surrounded by strangers, watching Fernando in his prime and reliving our love scenes together, I was overcome with emotion. I was transported back thirty years, as love and grief washed over me. The lights came up, the cruise social director introduced me, and I moved to the podium in a trance.

"Good evening, ladies and gentlemen. This is the only movie I ever made with . . ." I could not say his name. I broke down and wept uncontrollably. I stood there for a few minutes with tears streaming down my face, trying to compose myself. Finally, I managed to say, "I'm sorry, I just can't talk with you tonight. It's too soon. I hope you enjoyed the movie and I hope that by the end of the cruise I will be ready to answer your questions." Susie helped me to my stateroom, where I just let it go. I ate my meals there for a few days until I regained the strength to come out.

Maybe Gloria Luckinbill's advice had been wiser than I knew. I needed the time to rest, sit on the deck, and stare out across all that blue water. By the time the ship passed Africa, crossed the Atlantic, and came into the warm waters of the Caribbean, I was feeling better. I basked in the warmth of my family. Susie had become seasick going around Genoa, but she wanted to finish the cruise with me. I said, "If you're too sick to come to dinner, you have to lend me your husband, because I can't go to dinner alone." So Tom was my escort through those platters of food at the buffet. By the time we got to Saint Thomas in the Virgin Islands, I had rehearsed with Susie, June, and Tom the song from *Dangerous When Wet*, "I Got Out of Bed on the Right Side." We wore warm-up suits and sang the song with the orchestra and won first prize in the ship's talent show. I even joined in the jitterbug contest with the host and won a bottle of champagne, which we took right up on the deck and drank, and I was fine.

Eventually, I faced my question-and-answer session with the other passengers and felt comfortable. I'd had enough time to get back into the experience of being with people again. Someone asked, "I understand that when you lose someone, you always wish you had done things differently. Do you feel that way?"

Without a single tear, I said that because Fernando was taken so abruptly, I didn't have any "if only's." "My 'if only's' had been taken care of all those nights I sat beside him and talked him into the next dimension. I had met his every need for twenty years. You can let a person go without mourning if you have really been there for him in life." I was glad, as I summed it up for myself, that I had met the needs of that needy little boy in a handsome grown-up facade.

When we returned from the cruise, Susie and Tom agreed to move from Vermont and stay in the house in Beverly Hills with me for a while. What joy it was to know that I could have the freedom to have my family come and live with me! I redecorated Fernando's office as a guest room for them. Blue was Susie's favorite color, so blue it was. There was a lot of guilt in my heart, because I knew I had not prevailed with Fernando and there had been that awful wall between my children and me. Now I wanted to just turn myself inside out and be the best mother I could be. It took a while for Susie to forgive me. I hoped that when she had her baby, she would understand better what I went through. I looked forward with real excitement to being a grandmother.

That first Christmas in twenty-two years without Fernando—and with my family—held tremendous importance to me, and I wanted to make it perfect. For most of my childhood, our family had had a tradition of shopping for the Christmas tree on Christmas Eve. The tradition began in the depression, when my daddy couldn't really afford to buy a tree for us, so he went to the tree lot and picked up all of the branches they were sweeping up at the end of the day. He wired them together so we could have a tree. I drove around Beverly Hills that afternoon and had no luck, until I saw a florist shop on Doheny with a beautifully decorated tree in the window. I went in and asked if I could buy the tree, exactly as is. The owner explained he was very sorry, but that tree was not for sale. He had planned to take it home to put in his living room. I guess I was already close to tears, and the dam just burst. I blubbered that my husband had just died and my family was coming for Christmas dinner and I couldn't find a tree anywhere and it was Christmas Eve. . . .

The florist started crying and assured me he could decorate another tree for himself. He had the one in the window wrapped in a sheet and helped me put it in the back seat of my convertible, and then he followed me home to help me set it up. It was a beautiful tree, and I sat in the living room surrounded by Susie, Benjie, Kim, Lorenzo, and their families and I thanked God for how fortunate I was to have my children again. That year Lorenzo brought me Barbra Streisand's album with her haunting rendition of "Memories" from *Cats*, and I sat under the tree listening to that song and couldn't stop crying.

Susie said, "What is it, Mom?"

And I said, "I don't know. I don't know." That first year someone dies, you cry over everything. I made dinner, and I couldn't stop crying because I finally had my children all together. I thought, "Oh God, Fernando, you mercifully died so I could have my life back and be Esther Williams again."

There is a kind of guilt about running away from a problem that settles on you, and I had to make my confession to my children. That Christmas, I told them that I didn't know whether I could ever be able to make it up to them for not being there at a time in their lives when they needed me. Now, we had to make up for lost time. I was so sorry that my children were going to have to heal with me, that I hadn't done right by them, and that there had been this interruption in the natural relationship between a mother and her children.

I became the most enthusiastic mother and grandmother-to-be in the world. By the time my grandson Thomas was born on May 13, 1983, I think Susie was finding my maternal attentions a bit smothering. However, I did have the grandmother's advantage: I knew a lot about taking care of babies. Little Thomas was a delight, and I wasted no time getting him into that nice, warm pool in the California sunshine. Our friend Dick Arlett, who had been the producer of the *Dinah Shore Show,* saw me in the pool with Thomas one day and suggested that a video about how to teach your child to swim would be a natural. I located the same producer who had created Jane Fonda's successful workout tapes, Stewart Karl, and— businesswoman that I still was—combined my grandmotherly duties with a moneymaking enterprise.

I found the home movies of me swimming with my own children as babies. Even when I was busy making movies, I never allowed the nurse to give them their baths because bath time had to be exercise time. When they were in the bassinet, I would play with them and teach them to be water safe. There on those home movies was the living proof that my teaching techniques worked. All of my children loved the water and became wonderful swimmers. To prepare for the main portion of the videotape, I worked with Thomas and a group of other children for about three weeks before bringing in a video crew. Although we had worked out a script, I was more comfortable ad-libbing discussion with the children and commentary for the viewers.

Teaching a child to be water safe is relatively simple. You hold the child by the arms and shoulders and blow in his or her face. The child's reflex is to close the eyelids and take a breath. Then, briefly, you and the child go underwater together. Underwater you look at him and he looks at you. The kids will quickly learn to hold their breath. Then you turn her on her back in the water and shield her from the sun with the shadow of your body, and you let her float on your hands. Eventually, you turn him over on his stomach in your hands and he kicks and paddles. This makes their legs strong enough so that when they're ready to swim, they have developed enough muscles to keep themselves afloat. For the video, we taped my early lessons with the children at about age three months, and then taped them again at six months, when they were completely water safe.

Preparations for *Swim, Baby, Swim,* which is the title of the video, made me sorely aware that the last time the public had seen me, I was an athletic thirty-eight-year-old, size ten. I looked in the mirror and decided Mother Nature needed a little assistance.

A plastic surgeon said I needed some work on my eyelids. The surgery took a sheet away from my eyes and allowed me to open them wider than I had been able to for decades. I realized that I hadn't given any real thought to my appearance in more than twenty years. I looked for my "famous" smile in that mirror and saw a yellow grin. The trips to the dentist were tiresome and expensive, but those nice white caps made me feel good, and so did the comments about my smile. If I were going back into the public eye, I had one other problem to face. I had to lose weight. I asked Dick Arlett to arrange a visit to the spa at La Costa in Escondido. I got back in the pool, and in two weeks I lost twenty pounds. I threw away those caftans that I had been hiding in and began to be Esther Williams again.

Barbara Walters had called several times after Fernando's death to invite me on her prestigious interview show, but I hadn't been ready for prime time. Now that I had invested in my own video, *Swim, Baby, Swim,* I needed promotion, but even then I tried to duck when Barbara called once more. I told her that I still wasn't sure I wanted to emerge on national television, middle-aged, out of the public eye for twenty-five years, and competing with the memory of myself in a bathing suit in my thirties.

"Okay," said Barbara casually, "I just thought that you might want to come on my show to refute the rumors about you."

"Oh, Barbara, I heard you were tricky," I responded, but I couldn't resist. "*What* rumors?"

"You know the kinds of things they're saying, Esther." (Actually, I didn't, and I've always been curious about exactly who "they" are.) "They say that all those years of chlorine-water made you blind, that your hair is falling out. They say you're so fat that you can hardly waddle across your bedroom. Do you want to hear more?"

"No. Thank you, Barbara. I'll do the show."

I hung up with a chuckle. I remembered a comment that Katharine Hepburn, with her feisty Yankee nature, had once made when Dick Cavett asked her why she bothered to appear on talk shows: "The wonderful thing about television is that it allows you to rot in public." I considered that I had been rotting quietly in private for twenty-two years. However, with my recent cosmetic reclamation work and my reemerging figure, I was definitely in better shape than the "rumors" suggested. Barbara also promised me that my segment would run on the night that the Winter Olympics opened at Sarajevo, February 6 of 1984. My interview would be shown right after the Opening Ceremonies, which guaranteed a huge audience. Better yet, she assured me that I would be the only female guest on the show. She placed my interview right between Mr. T and Howard Cosell.

"You'll be fine, Esther. I'll protect you," assured Barbara. "Just be yourself."

Yeah, sure. But who was I, anyway? Despite Barbara's reassurances, I knew that this first interview in twenty-five years would be a major test. I was going to find out how much was left of Esther Williams. I studied tapes of Barbara's interviews with other celebrities and practiced my patter as though I were preparing for a debating match. My nephew, Ken Karpi, was a public relations adviser to Pete Wilson, who was then a senator from California, and Ken made it his business to know how to handle the media.

"Barbara Walters is well prepared and thorough in her research," he told me. "She's the one politicians fear the most because she, being a woman, feels she has the right to dig into your personal life. She knows things about people like Pete that he's never really ever talked to anyone about. We run when we see her coming."

I said, "Well, I'm not going to have that problem."

He said, "You better be prepared for the moment when she slips you the question you never want to answer. Because she will. It cuts like a knife. That's her trademark. You're going to look stupid when you have no answer."

When Barbara rang the doorbell at my home at 8:00 A.M. to film the interview, she was visibly surprised as I greeted her. I had been up since 5:00 and had carefully prepared my makeup and hair before dressing for the interview. Barbara was in her travel clothes and had arrived the night before from New York. She had Julius, her hairdresser, in tow, and looked as though she needed his help. I said, "Barbara, come upstairs, your dressing room is waiting for you and Julius." I had all the lights on, and a clean, fresh towel on the counter so that they could lay out all the makeup and the brushes and the hair products as they do in the makeup department. She was kind of embarrassed, because she doesn't like being seen without her makeup and hair done. But I wanted her on my side, and I had prepared coffee and fresh muffins to prove it to her.

Barbara emerged from the dressing room looking smashing, and we went downstairs. While she had been dressing, her crew had turned my backyard into a location set. Although flowers weren't blooming in my garden in November, the prop men had replanted the flower beds with lovely colors. You want spring? They'll give you spring. They had our chairs placed precisely to catch a bit of Los Angeles skyline in the background, with three cameras to follow all angles and monitors for us to watch ourselves.

Barbara's producer, Beth Polson, was pretty and quick and bright. (Holly Hunter in *Broadcast News* reminded me of Beth Polson). I had dressed in a striped blouse with jewel-toned colors, but Beth decided that it looked like I was cinched up too high; so I changed into a champagne-hued shirt and the same color pants with a colorful chiffon scarf. Barbara then changed into something from her wardrobe that was color-coordinated with my clothing.

She had four changes of clothing, so that she could dress to coordinate with her guest. If someone is wearing a low-cut blouse, then she'll wear a blouse, but not as low-cut as the star. God, I love women who understand the principles of femininity, even though they're businesswomen or hard-hitting interviewers. I looked at this woman with admiration and thought, She makes networks quake. She's earning millions of dollars a year interviewing celebrities, and she's changing her outfit so that we will both look good on television. Barbara was liberated long before anyone ever used the word.

As the cameras rolled, Barbara was charming and supportive. I was completely comfortable. She led me into the material we had agreed to discuss, and the answers I had rehearsed were smooth. I even managed to drop in a plug for my *Swim, Baby, Swim* video. For something I hadn't done in twenty-five years, this felt great. But eventually along came that question my nephew had warned me about. Barbara turned to me with that troubled look on her face. "There's something I don't understand. You seem to be so bright . . ." and I thought, Here it comes. "I don't understand how you got into such terrible financial trouble with your husband Ben Gage." She paused. "If that's too hard a question, you don't have to answer." She was very feminine and very sweet, but she was wielding the knife. Ben's financial fiasco was a can of worms I didn't want to open, because I was still living with it. I was ready for her.

"Oh, Barbara, you know, I look across at my view of the Los Angeles basin and I almost can see southwest Los Angeles, where I grew up. I lived through that depression, and I think of all the hard times my mom and dad had supporting five children in that time when there wasn't any money. I think of the fact that your father, Lou Walters, owned the Latin Quarter, one of the most popular nightclubs in New York, where the girls all danced topless. And there you were, this little girl standing in the wings, wondering why those women had taken off all their clothes. I just thought, here we are, two old broads in this lovely California sunshine, just sitting here talking. . . ."

About then I heard Beth Polson's voice on the loudspeaker saying, "Uh, Barbara, I think we'd better interrupt the taping for a moment. There's a shadow on your face and we have to take a break. Barbara, can you come into the van for a moment?"

"That's okay," I said. "I'll just wait here."

Beth must have had a little talk with Barbara about that money question, because when Barbara returned, she said "Now, let's see, where were we?"

"I don't remember," I said.

"Neither do I," she responded brightly. "Let's go on."

Score one for creative amnesia. The subject of my finances was not brought up again.

My daughter Susie and I were in the kitchen side by side during breaks, making sandwiches and coffee for the crew. I noticed that Barbara watched us with obvious interest. When the taping was over, she said, "I'd love to talk to you about being a celebrity and having a daughter. I have a daughter, and I feel that she doesn't appreciate that I'm trying to be her mother, even when I am busy with my television career. How do you deal with that?" I was amazed to hear myself offering advice to Barbara on how to combine celebrity with motherhood. It was advice I wished someone had given me. But celebrities rarely ask each other for meaningful advice.

"You must have the ability as a parent to put yourself—your image—on hold and pick it up later," I told her. "You need to give that child your total love and total attention, and there may be a time when that's inconvenient. You have to be there to say, 'Let's talk about it.' Most of all, you have to put in the time listening."

Barbara was listening at that moment with all her heart. She was supposed to leave at 5:00 for some function at the Beverly Wilshire, but it was well after 6:00 before she left. We sat there at my dining room table and talked. We became friends. I had learned how to communicate honestly with women through my relationships with my mother and my sister Maurine. There was a sweetness to my conversation with Barbara that day, and I felt free of the limitations that I'd had in my marriage with Fernando. I was back, communicating on my level, enjoying this wonderful woman who was so successful and had been so many places in her life. I felt good being a mature woman, and being in that place and realizing that I couldn't know the things I know if I hadn't lived through so much.

Billy Crystal had reinvigorated his career in February of 1982 with a new character. The "Fernando" caricature was one of several running spoofs on his short-lived *Billy Crystal Comedy Hour*. The show was canceled so quickly that my husband had basically ignored it. Fernando was a proud man, and he hated to appear ridiculous. After his death, I didn't think about the spoof again until Crystal resurfaced in the fall of 1984 on *Saturday Night Live* with a segment called "Fernando's Hideaway." By this time *SNL* had a huge audience, and Crystal's signature line, "You look mahvelous, daahling," was everywhere. Billy eventually parlayed this schtick into a hit song and LP "Mahvelous"; a Fernando video; even a line of T-shirts. He has always admitted that he developed the character from years of watching Fernando on *The Tonight Show* with Johnny Carson. In a recent appearance on *Inside the Actors Studio*, Billy expressed his admiration for Fernando's wit and recalled actually taking notes to use for his parody. He told *People* magazine, "I was a big fan. I liked that macho thing where he would sit and fix a crease in his pants before he says hello to Johnny. He used to make me giggle."

Late in 1983 my telephone rang and the voice on the other end was so melodious—so warm and intelligent—that it instantly caught my attention. "Miss Williams, my name is Edward Bell. I am coordinating special events for Atlantic Richfield, for the 1984 Olympics."

"Mr. Bell, you have a lovely voice," I said.

"Thank you, Miss Williams. I'm going to use every bit of that voice and all my persuasive powers to ask you to do something."

"I can hardly wait." I definitely meant it.

"We are planning a reunion of the athletes from the 1932 Olympics, and we would like you to be the hostess for the event."

"But I'm not an Olympic champion."

"You qualified. That's close enough for me."

By now, I was curious to see the face that went with the voice. "How about discussing this further—in person."

Edward strolled into my living room that afternoon—six feet two, wavey brown hair, winningly handsome, and well educated. He had been a professor at SUNY Stony Brook and had taught French literature at Villanova. We discussed the details of the Olympic hospitality event, but my mind was elsewhere. Impulsively, I interrupted his explanation of how the Olympic village was organized to say, "Do you mind if I ask a personal question?"

He looked at me quizzically. "No. Go ahead."

"How old are you?"

He was ten years younger than I was. . . .

"That's still in the ball park."

Edward looked confused. "It is?"

"Are you married?"

"I'm separated. My divorce will be final in the spring."

"That's good timing."

"Any other questions?"

"No. I can tell that's all your own hair."

We both laughed and I told him *he* had to ask the next question.

"Am I supposed to ask, 'Whatta ya doin' New Year's?' "

We laughed and made a date for lunch at Scandia on Sunset Strip. Scandia was old Hollywood—a quiet, traditional restaurant where we sat in a dark booth that offered a lot of privacy.

He said, "Esther, I read in the trades that you're going to do your life story as a movie." I was feeling very comfortable with him, which was saying something. Edward was the first new person— male person—I'd felt comfortable with in a long, long time. I didn't think that I would ever again have the feelings that were stirring within me. I wasn't attentive to the conversation. He prompted me: "So, are you looking forward to that?"

"Yes, I guess so," I said with a shrug.

"Why would you want to do your life story at this point in your life?"

"What do you mean?"

"Your life isn't over yet."

That was such a perceptive insight that I didn't know what to say. He was right: I had been thinking that my life was now over, and I was going to tell the story. "What should I do instead?"

"That depends. What do you want to do with the rest of your life?"

It came to me bright and clear: "I'd like to have a reason to get up in the morning. I'm idle. I was married to a really difficult person. When he died, I was out of a job."

"There's no reason for you to be out of a job. Has it occurred to you that your name should be on a swimsuit?" I smiled to myself— Cole of California—could I go through that again?

Within minutes, we were talking about a partnership, and that partnership with my husband, Edward Bell, which continues today, has expanded and opened my life in more ways than I knew were possible. This is a part of my life that has just begun.

Edward was my introduction to the 1984 Olympics in Los Ange- les. This soon led to much more for me. When *Bathing Beauty* came

out in 1944, moviegoers saw the possibilities of beautifully choreographed dancing in the water with a corps de ballet swimming in
unison. About a year later, the first synchronized swimming meet
was held in Chicago. Unwittingly, I was godmother to a sport!

NBC Sports asked me to join their team as synchronized swimming was recognized as an Olympic sport for the first time in 1984.
I began by working as color commentator at the synchronized
swimming pre-Olympic trials in Indianapolis. My partner was
Donna DeVarona, the Olympic 400-Meter Individual Medley gold
medalist in Tokyo in 1964. By this time, she was an experienced
television and radio broadcaster who had a great reporting style. We
were a good team, with a lot of banter back and forth. By the time
we finished covering the trials in Indianapolis, NBC confirmed that
we would be the pair to go to the Olympics in Los Angeles.

NBC's Olympic assignment was sweet vindication for me. For
decades I had worked for recognition of synchronized swimming as
an Olympic sport. In order to qualify as a sport for the Olympics,
stringent requirements must be met, including a history of international competition. This means that competitors had to travel to
Australia, France, Japan, Italy, and other countries, which put the
sport on the map. The creators of this international movement were
the coaches and parents who had been "my girls"—fans of my
movies. They called me from all over the country saying, "We want
to start a water ballet group. How do we do it?"

Over the years, Bula, my dear mother, helped me to research the
answers to their questions, and she created packets of information
for hundreds of synchronized swimming groups, with names like
the Aquamaids or the Walnut Creek Aqua Belles. She had watched
all my films and quizzed me on how to do a ballet leg in the water,
how to point your toe, and how to "scull" so that you stay in place. I
was able to provide these groups with instructions on all the techniques of water ballet that I had developed in water shows, from
Billy Rose's Aquacade to the underwater chases in *Jupiter's Darling*,
my last MGM movie. After tremendous effort at the neighborhood
and college level, synchronized swimming became a recognized
event at the 1955 Pan American Games in Mexico City and was
named a demonstration sport at the 1956 Olympics in Melbourne,
Australia.

Despite the growing interest in synchronized swimming, the International Olympic Committee refused to certify the sport because of the IOC's ill-tempered old chairman, Avery Brundage. Although I never spoke to him directly, I was told that time after time he would reject appeals for synchronized swimming. He complained that the swimmers wore sequins in their hair, makeup, and pretty bathing suits, as if that should be sufficient reason to dismiss it from consideration. "They're all just clones of Esther Williams! That's not a sport!" he was reported to have said. The athletic component of what I did was still unrecognized, at least by the head of the IOC. After all these years, I was still being condemned as "fluff."

Whenever I tried to help the appeal for synchronized swimming, there would be items in the media and my efforts backfired. As far as Avery Brundage was concerned, my name was a stigma, so I stayed out of sight. For all those years, I couldn't even attend a meet or give out a medal without attracting Brundage's ire. Perhaps I inherited his leftover grudge against Eleanor Holm, who had preceded me in Billy Rose's Aquacade. Eleanor had qualified to participate in the 1936 Olympics in Berlin, the infamous "Nazi Olympics." However, she had been so bold as to be seen quaffing champagne in public, and Brundage had sent her home without allowing her to compete. Fifty years later, he was still giving women athletes a hard time. Finally, the grouch died, and a new Olympic sport was born.

The producer of NBC's Olympic coverage, Kurt Gowdy Jr., invited me for a planning session at the network offices, and at the end of the meeting he spoke to me privately. "Esther, I know you have been a star in the movies. And stars can be late. But announcers cannot. Also, when I speak to you in your earpiece and tell you to do something, you have to do it. Is that clear?"

I smiled at him and replied, "Mr. Gowdy, even when you are a star in the motion picture business, you have directors, producers, and studio executives who tell you what to do. You have to do it because you are an employee. Now I'm your employee and I understand perfectly what you are telling me."

Naturally, the first day that I was scheduled to appear for NBC, I arrived late. We left the house right on time, but the driver NBC had sent for me couldn't find the Olympic Village. By the time I got to the control booth, Kurt Gowdy Jr. had steam coming out of his ears. I rushed up to the stands and arrived in plenty of time to join Donna for the prebroadcast briefing. I was dazzled by the skill of all the athletes and by the underwater technology of NBC's coverage. Some of those girls were underwater for more than half of their five-minute programs and you could see every balletic move. The underwater photography made these events even more exciting for the television audience than for the judges, who were watching from the stands. Tracie Ruiz-Conforto and Candy Costie took the gold in the duet with some strong, graceful lifts. Tracie won another gold medal for her performance in the solo category, in which she made thirty different moves underwater on her first dive. I was never quite in her league.

Despite Avery Brundage's sexist notions, synchronized swimmers are superb athletes. They have to learn ballet and first do their routines on dry land as exercises. They have to hold their breath for long periods of strenuous activity. They exercise with weights and pulleys to strengthen their arms for underwater work. When they come out of the water, they look just as I looked in the movies: sparkling and beautiful in their sequined swimsuits, with bright lipstick and pretty hair. They even improved on my old trick of setting my hair with Vaseline and baby oil. Now they set their hair in gelatin, which holds it tight in the cold water and looks shiny.

Donna asked me some questions about my swimming movies and how this all started. I was touched to realize how these girls had seen those movies and gotten together in their little groups and wanted to swim pretty and not fast. They created a sport and went all over the world to teach it and sell it. I was proud to be there when it came into the Olympics. I was proud to be an inspiration, a godmother to a sport. It was a very emotional moment for me. Tears came to my eyes on camera, and I thought, I love every one of those girls in the water.

CHAPTER 27

REFLECTIONS AND COMPENSATIONS

"*D*idn't you used to be Esther Williams?" asked the fiftysomething butcher behind the meat counter, a faint glimmer of recognition in his eye.

"Yes," I said, "I used to be." It was a truthful answer. A year after Fernando's funeral, I still didn't really feel like Esther Williams. I was in a strange sort of limbo—over the immediate impact of his death, but not yet fully recovered.

"What the hell happened to you?" I could tell that seeing me in person had deeply disillusioned the butcher.

I struggled to find a diplomatic response. "Are you asking about what I did after I stopped making movies?" He shook his head no. "Or are you referring to how I look?"

His eyes swept over the lines in my face. "You've gotten . . . older." It was an accusation.

"Have you looked in the mirror lately? You've gotten older, too." Widowhood had done nothing to curb my smart mouth. So much for diplomacy.

"Yeah, I know," he shot back, "but you weren't supposed to."

I knew what he meant. When you're out of sight for as long as I was, there's a funny feeling of betrayal that comes over people when they see you again.

If John Kennedy were still alive, he'd now be in his eighties. All of us have trouble envisioning him as an octogenarian, because our mind's eye sees him as a youthful, energetic leader in his thirties and forties. He can never get any older.

For someone who has been in the movies, it's almost the same phenomenon. Once I married Fernando, I became invisible. After twenty-two years, my absence was far more than hibernation, and my reappearance was almost as if I'd died and been resurrected. My films, bolstered by the powerful machinery of the MGM publicity department, fixed my persona as a perfect size ten, age twenty-five or so, wearing a gold lamé swimsuit and a tiara. Because I hadn't been seen "rotting in public," in Katharine Hepburn's perfect description, it was somehow incumbent on me to remain that way forever. My image was set in concrete; for better or worse, I was frozen in time as the *Million Dollar Mermaid*.

But what the public expects and what is healthy for an individual are two very different things. Joan Crawford, feeding off the adoration of sycophants and decked out in her turquoise bird outfit, begging an imaginary public not to abandon her, is just one of many stars who became almost pathologically unable to deal with growing older.

Not me, I hoped. I always took it for granted that there would be life after Hollywood. Thanks to Bula, I also understood that this new life would be very different from what had gone before. As I was growing up, she often repeated a line that I always thought should be done on a pillow as a needlepoint sampler:

"Every age has its compensations."

I internalized that message so early in my life that I swore I would never become an aquatic version of *Sunset Boulevard*'s Norma Desmond, harboring unrealistic expectations of a Hollywood comeback. After all, it was just common sense, and Bula was nothing if not commonsensical. In Hollywood you peak in your thirties, and it's the rare actress who is still a leading lady at forty, rarer still at fifty. After that, it's strictly "character parts." But as a person, you still have the next forty years of your life to fill. You've got to invent something to occupy your time. For two decades, I'd let Fernando do that. Now it was time for something else, hopefully something more fulfilling.

After he died, my first compensation was my family, and I rejoiced at being able to welcome my children back into my home. I also had the satisfaction of being able to start working on the "if only's" I had piled up about having allowed Fernando to keep me apart from them when they were teenagers.

Benji Gage, my eldest, and Patty Bongo were married in Syracuse, New York, Patty's hometown. They moved back to San Diego where Ben (I no longer call him "Benji") is a partner in his law firm. Since then they've had two beautiful children, Austin and Erin. Kim is also in San Diego, and by now has rediscovered his life and is working in computer programming. Susie moved up to the Bay Area where she lives with Thomas who will soon be on his way to college. Susie works in a nonprofit counseling agency.

Latin lovers may have ceased to be the rage, but Lorenzo Lamas, who has four children of his own, has successfully followed in his father's footsteps, this time as a television action hero. Alex Lamas visits from Argentina from time to time and is a successful artist in her own right.

I'm still called "Mom," also "Mammaw," sometimes "Es." My grandson Thomas was staying at the house one evening when Edward and I were going out to a gala black-tie event. I cooked dinner, finished up, took off my apron, and went upstairs to get dressed for the evening. I put on my makeup, set my hair, and grabbed a sparkly outfit out of the closet along with a pair of heels. As I came downstairs, young Thomas called to his mother, "Mom, look—Mammaw went upstairs and Esther Williams came down!"

"You don't have to be the same from one decade to another," Bula often told me. "You get to evolve—as your body changes, everything changes. So you've got a few wrinkles . . . but you're not only smarter, you're *wiser.*"

But the wisdom acquired with the passage of time is a useless gift unless you share it. I wanted to share my wisdom, not just with my family, but with a broader segment of the community, young women in particular. My interview with Barbara Walters, coupled with my television commentary on synchronized swimming at the 1984 Olympics, launched a comeback of a different kind. These two successes reassured me that I had a message to deliver, that I had a point of view to share.

It was time for Esther Williams to get back into circulation. My first speaking engagement was set in Dayton, Ohio. I was to address members of the local chapter of the Junior League—three thousand of them—and I was petrified. The day before I was to leave, I called Edward in a panic. "I don't have any idea of what I'm going to talk about," I said nervously, "and I'm getting a handsome speaker's fee. I don't want to take money under false pretenses, but my mind is a complete blank."

"I'll be right over."

Edward and I had launched our business partnership, but we were not yet married. Immediately he calmed me down with his wonderful common sense and his reassuring words of advice about public speaking. "It's so simple, Esther," he said soothingly. "All you do is pick out somebody in the front row. Pretend she's an old friend you haven't seen in twenty years and play catch up on what you've been doing for all that time."

"I can do that," I said, taking heart from his words. "It's just like having lunch with somebody." In fact, I'd been spending a great deal of time lately doing exactly that, having lunch with old pals I hadn't seen in years, renewing friendships that had atrophied during my years of enforced exile as Esther Lamas.

I left for Dayton with a new enthusiasm for my mission, but still nervous about what these women would think of me. After all, I'd "betrayed" them by getting older, just as I had "betrayed" the butcher. I wasn't sure what they would think now of the new, older Esther in her sixties.

I was waiting in the wings when I heard the Mistress of Ceremonies launch into her introduction. She gave me the perfect entrance when she said, "Ladies, our speaker today is somebody you have known and loved for years . . . and didn't we all want to look like Esther Williams in a swimsuit?"

Before she could continue, I walked out onstage quickly, took the microphone from her, faced those three thousand ladies, and said, "*I'd* like to look like Esther Williams in a swimsuit!"

It brought the house down. From that moment on, I was at ease. I picked out someone down front and talked to her about my life after the movies—Edward's advice had been perfect. It was a great success.

Oddly enough, when I make an appearance now, I'm told, "That smile . . . I'd know your smile anywhere. You look exactly the same." The sweet myth that I haven't changed is something I don't argue with. I love the fact that I'm in a place in people's hearts that keeps me forever the same.

In part, I have Ted Turner to thank for my "immortality." When he bought the MGM film library and began running our old films on his cable channel, Turner Classic Movies, he introduced the MGM stars to a whole new generation of viewers, and reestablished us in the minds of people, now middle-aged, who had seen our movies when they were growing up. We were a happy part of their childhoods, and we get the benefit of those rose-colored glasses they put on to look past their own gray hairs in the mirror and think back to their own youths.

Initially, I was annoyed that I didn't get any residuals when Turner acquired the broadcast rights to my films, but I've come to look at the situation in a different light. It would seem that I got the fountain of youth in return, which in itself is quite a compensation. "All things work together for good," Bula used to tell me. So here I am, kept at age twenty-five in perpetuity by the magic of television.

The autumn following my stint as Olympic color commentator for synchronized swimming, I was invited to take part in an awards ceremony sponsored by the Women Sports Foundation, honoring U.S. female Olympic medalists from the Los Angeles games. I arrived in New York a day ahead of the event. Most of the athletes were already there, and we were all staying in the grand old Waldorf-Astoria. The buzz among the Olympians waiting at the elevator bank was all about how they could capitalize financially on their athletic success. Talk of agents, speaking tours, and endorsement contracts swirled around me. I heard Mary Lou Retton's name all over the lobby, because she had gone straight from her gymnastic triumph to the front of the Wheaties box.

My part in the awards ceremony was to have been a small one. I was there to accept an award on behalf of swimmer Ann Curtis, the 1948 gold medalist in the 400-meter freestyle, who had been made an honorary member of the Women Sports Foundation. Because the awards ceremony was being televised, every segment of the program had been precisely scripted. My time allotment onstage was but a few seconds, just a simple acceptance and thank you. Nevertheless, there was something I felt I had to say. As I stood before the microphone, I felt as if I were talking to each winner face-to-face.

Gold medalists, there was a drama and a struggle to prepare yourself for your Olympic triumph and glory. Now that you have attained it, enjoy it with all your heart. No matter what else happens to you the rest of your life, no matter how much you have to endure, you will always have that certain knowledge that you are winners. What's more, you have a gold medal to prove it. When you run into life's disappointments and problems, always remember your physical, mental, and psychological strength were there for you under the most trying circumstances, and you were not only equal to the stress, but able to best it.

There is wisdom to the phrase "Personal Best." You know the meaning of the phrase—you were there, and you accomplished it. Stay with this moment. You have just won, and the prospect of fleeting worldly gain can never match the way you felt the moment you heard your name announced as the winner. It's what all the training was about, from the moment you said, "I'm going to try," until the moment they handed you the gold medal.

Here you are, in this rarefied air with your sister colleagues, winners all. The applause has not yet died down. When it does, stay with the truth, which you have a right to know for the rest of your life. Remember: You are a winner. It will be with you when you are called upon to be a daughter, a wife, a mother, even a grandmother. I will know you anywhere, because you carry yourselves with pride and self-assurance, just as you did when you stood high on that winners' platform with the American flag unfurled behind you.

If the phone doesn't ring with an offer to endorse a pair of running shoes, or to put your face on a cereal box, don't despair. You have many things to do now. You are no longer competing with other qualified girls, but you're in the game still. It's the game of life, and knowing how to work hard has given you an edge. You know what you are capable of. You know how to be first. You will always carry with you the values that brought you to the medal platform. Remember that there are no former Olympians—once a champion, always a champion. My congratulations to you. Let's hear that welcome applause. Believe me, you deserve it.

When I finished, the audience rose as one in a standing ovation, and I felt relieved that my words had resonated with these women in the audience. My Olympic coanchor Donna DeVarona, who was hosting the program, was looking daggers at me for taking so much time, but the response reinforced my belief that what I had said was more important than a network schedule.

It wasn't until the next day, however, that I received the real compensation for my words of the night before. I was keeping an interview appointment for brunch with a journalist, and as we sat there in the coffee shop, a crowd began to form. To my surprise, the women who were waiting to talk to me were gold medalists from all different sports, not just the swimmers. They didn't want my autograph; they wanted to thank me for what I'd said to them.

The group continued to grow, and at a certain point it became apparent that my interview could not continue. It turned into a wonderful rap session on how fleeting fame and fortune can turn out to be, and on the values you carry with you from athletic competition into the rest of your life. The journalist was happy, because the story of all of us talking together was far more interesting than what he'd originally planned.

After it was over, I boarded the plane home with a happy and contented heart, realizing once again how fortunate I had been to become a swimming champion, even just for two years, and what a privilege I'd been given when MGM decided that there was a place in the movies for swimming musicals and for me.

But my life—as a child, woman, lover, wife, mother—has been

more than just these public events. Some of it has been lived on the heights of personal happiness and passion. Some of it has been filled with terrible conflict and anguish. Yet somehow I kept my head above water. I relied on the discipline, character, and strength that I had started to develop as that little girl in her first swimming pool in southwest Los Angeles. I guess that's what I was trying to tell those Olympic champions when I told them that when they ran into life's problems, they should never despair, even after temporary discouragement or defeat. I told them they should call upon their inner spirit to see them through.

We can't all win Olympic gold medals. Even I never won one. But the message applies to all of us because each of us in our own way has races to run or swim. And with sufficient endurance and courage, we all can achieve some kind of victory in our lives.

As I took my seat on the plane back to Los Angeles, I looked forward to planning my life together with Edward, both personally and professionally. I was secure in the knowledge and wisdom of my years. But I wasn't looking back. I was looking forward to the new challenges and compensations that lay ahead.

Before the plane began to move toward takeoff, the flight attendant said, "Are you *really* Esther Williams?"

"Yes," I said. "I really am. Thank you for asking."

INDEX